UNDERSTANDING

STRUCTURES

UNDERSTANDING

STRUCTURES

Fuller Moore
Illustrated by Fuller Moore

Boston   Burr Ridge, IL   Dubuque, IA   Madison, WI   New York   San Francisco   St. Louis
Bangkok   Bogatá   Caracas   Lisbon   London   Madrid
Mexico City   Milan   New Delhi   Seoul   Singapore   Sydney   Taipei   Toronto

WCB/McGraw-Hill
A Division of the McGraw-Hill Companies

UNDERSTANDING STRUCTURES

This book is printed on acid-free paper.

2 3 4 5 6 7 8 9 0 QPD/QPD 9 3 2 1 0 9

ISBN 0-07-043253-8

Vice president and editorial director: Kevin T. Kane
Publisher: Tom Casson
Executive editor: Eric M. Munson
Editorial assistant: George Haag
Marketing manager: John T. Wannemacher
Project manager: Kari Geltemeyer
Production supervisor: Heather D. Burbridge
Freelance design coordinator: JoAnne Schopler
Compositor: Fuller Moore
Typeface: 10/12 Bookman Light
Printer: Quebecor Printing Book Group/Dubuque

Library of Congress Cataloging-in-Publication Data

Moore, Fuller
    Understanding structures / Fuller Moore ; illustrated by
Fuller Moore
        p.   cm.
    Includes index.
    ISBN 0-07-043253-8
    1. Structural design.   I. Title
TA658.M66   1999
690'.21--dc21   98-4749

http://www.mhhe.com

—to Jane

for everything

TABLE OF CONTENTS

FOREWORD

The path to structural wisdom begins with understanding how structures work. Armed with this understanding, the student of architecture may begin to make decisions about what type of structure to use in a particular building that he or she is designing, and may make a preliminary determination of spans and member proportions by means of approximate rules of thumb. With this knowledge, he or she is also prepared to explore the ways in which mathematical expressions have been developed to describe how structures work.

The role of mathematics in structural design is often misunderstood. Every great structural designer of our time has written that mathematical analysis can play a role only after the important decisions have been made regarding the form and proportions of the structure, at which time it becomes useful in confirming and fine-tuning those decisions. Yet most beginning books in structures make no attempt to develop an understanding of structural function, and push the student blindly into structural mathematics from the first page.

In this book, using little by way of mathematics, Fuller Moore imparts a marvelous understanding of how structures work. Avoiding distractions and sticking to essentials, he takes the reader inside the material of cables, arches, trusses, beams, columns, and slabs to discover how tension and compression act and interact to support the loads imposed on buildings by gravity, wind, and earthquakes. The basic modes of action of various types of structural devices become tactile experiences on these pages, understandable not just in one's mind, but also in the muscle and bone of one's body. These modes of action are further explained in relation to the common elements of steel, concrete, masonry, and wood from which we assemble structures. Together with an admirable emphasis on the paths that loads follow in being conducted through a building to its foundations, these explanations bring the reader swiftly to the point of being able to visit a building or a construction site and understand immediately how the building is supported. More importantly, they enable the reader to begin to function effectively as a designer of structures, an ability that is greatly facilitated by the numerous examples of well-known buildings that are offered to illustrate each structural principle.

Prof. Moore brings unique qualifications to this task. As an architect who is accustomed to designing and detailing not just the form and space of his buildings, but also their systems of thermal control, illumination, enclosure, and structure, he has a comprehensive understanding of the roles and interactions of every aspect of architecture. As a lifelong teacher of architecture, he has become famous for the patient, thorough, lucid explanations that have found their way out of his classrooms and studios, into a splendid series of books that he has written, illustrated, and designed in their entirety.

The study of structures is a lifelong pursuit, one that will bring the reader many insights and satisfactions along the way. There is no better place to begin it than on these pages.

— Edward Allen

PREFACE

The goals of this book are to introduce the concepts of structural support in buildings and to emphasize the importance of integrating structure and architectural design. I've always felt that basic physical concepts must be thoroughly understood and internalized in order to intelligently integrate structure and design. To this end, I've relied extensively on conceptual diagrams and illustrative case studies to help the reader develop an intuitive understanding of how structure affects the design of buildings.

But I recognize the limitations of such a qualitative approach. It should be the prerequisite to quantitative study involving mathematics. As the late Mario Salvadori once said, "No thorough knowledge of structures may be acquired without the use of . . . mathematical tools." Hopefully the present volume will arouse the reader's interest and provide the basic understanding and design context for more advanced study.

The case studies, some recent and others classic examples, were selected on the basis of their suitability for clearly demonstrating specific structural principles. Because of this criteria, these selections represent a bias toward very visible structural expression and emphasize an aesthetic of structural efficiency and least means. This is not to suggest this is a prescription for good architecture, only that it offers the best built examples for demonstrating structural principles.

ACKNOWLEDGMENTS

In looking back over the manuscript, I'm struck by how little original material I have contributed . . . and how indebted I am to others on whose work I have so heavily drawn. I've tried to be thorough in my citations, but somehow their brevity and formality fail to adequately represent the importance of others' contributions and my appreciation for the opportunity to include them.

Perhaps even more important are my teachers, students, and colleagues who have helped me form the values and priorities that underlie my own teaching and practice and, inevitably, this book: Cris Benton, Tom Briner, Day Ding, Chris Lubkeman, Michele Melaragno, Charlie Mitchell, Don Peting, Guntis Plesums, Jack Poulton, John Reynolds, Sergio Sanabria, Wolfgang Schueller, Mike Utzinger, John Weigand, and Charles Worley, to name a few.

I am grateful to several people who have contributed parts of the text, Phillip Corkill (for his preliminary structural design charts which were redrawn to include metric sizes), Richard Kellogg (for his demonstration models), and Craig Hinrich (for many of the quotations used throughout).

Tom Bible, Mark Cruvellier, and Robert Benson reviewed the manuscript, and I am particularly grateful for their thoroughness, candor, and numerous thoughtful comments and suggestions.

I am especially indebted to Edward Allen who also reviewed the manuscript in detail and has been a continuing source of encouragement, humor, support, and infectious enthusiasm thoughout this project.

— Fuller Moore

INTRODUCTION

The process of visualizing or conceiving a structure is an art. Basically it is motivated by an inner experience, by an intuition. It is never the result of mere deductive reasoning.

—*Eduardo Torroja*

Building technology is a science, but the practice of it is an art.

—*A. Roderick Males*

Structure and architectural design are inseparable. Whether a simple shelter or a grand enclosed space for worship or commerce, a building is shaped from materials so as to withstand natural forces such as gravity, wind, or fire.

As Vitruvius decreed in ancient Rome, architecture should have *firmness* (structural permanence), *commodity* (functionality), and *delight* (beauty). Of the three, firmness is the most basic quality, and it is structure and the method of construction that satisfy this need for firmness.

It is tempting to assert that structural correctness is essential to great architecture. But there are many examples where designers have ignored structural principles in favor of aesthetic or functional considerations to create useful and beautiful buildings—works of sculpture where the supporting and constructional systems are hidden or camouflaged. In general, this is easiest in small buildings where structural requirements are modest and can be satisfied in any of several ways, many of them structurally inefficient and inappropriate.

But in larger buildings, it is impossible to ignore structural principles, and the structural systems have a major influence on the function and the aesthetics of the design. The largest buildings inevitably become quite expressive of the structural system.

Traditionally, the architect served as the *master builder* designing the structure as an integral part of the building itself. This was possible because traditional structural systems evolved slowly and could be sized and built based on accumulated experience from previous projects.

The Industrial Revolution led to larger and increasingly complex buildings. Buildings could be taller (due to the development of the structural frame, elevators, and pressurized plumbing) and wider (due to the development of the steel and concrete beam, electric lighting, and mechanical ventilation). This increased complexity meant that the entire assembly of structure, materials, and mechanical systems could no longer be designed and understood by a single individual. Instead the role of the architect evolved into that of a design team leader assisted by specialized technical consultants.

But, in order to sustain the role of design team leader and maintain control of the overall design, it is essential that the architect have a conceptual understanding of these technical disciplines. There are three reasons for this. At the most elementary level, this conceptual understanding allows the architect to better communicate with the consultants. Secondly, it allows the architect to place each of the consultants' technical recommendations within the broader context of the overall design, preserving design and budgetary control. Finally, and most importantly, it allows the designer to begin considering technical issues during the very earliest stages of design—in those soft pencil sketches when the form and order of the building are determined.

Part I

STRUCTURAL THEORY

It is not enough to study all theories of resistance and all calculation methods. One must absorb all details and experiments until he becomes completely familiar in a natural and intuitive way with all phenomena of stress and deformation.

—Eduardo Torroja

1

MECHANICS

*Precise computation is no more certain than a belief or a dream,
but we must try by means of more exact analyses to prevent
the harmful effects of human error.*

—Louis I. Kahn

Mechanics is that branch of physical science which deals with forces and their effect on bodies. It includes *statics* and *dynamics*. Statics deals with forces that produce equilibrium among bodies, while dynamics deals with forces that produce acceleration among bodies. Because building structures generally do not move, they are usually understood and analyzed using principles of statics. However, analysis of certain types of movement in buildings (due to earthquakes and wind, for example) requires the application of the principles of dynamics.

FORCES

The concept of *forces* is fundamental to architectural structures. A *force* is that which tends to exert motion, tension, or compression on an object.

While, technically, the unit of force is the *pound force* [equal to the force required to accelerate 1 pound (lb) of mass at the rate of 32.17 feet per square second (ft/s^2)], the mass equivalent *pound* and *kip* (1000 lb) are used conventionally in engineering practice and throughout this book.

The basic unit of force in the International System of Units (SI) is the newton [the force to required to accelerate 1 kilogram (kg) of mass at a rate of 1 meter per square second (m/s^2)]. One pound = 4.448 newtons (N).

VECTOR REPRESENTATION

Because a force has both magnitude and direction, it is a *vector* quantity (as distinct from a *scalar* quantity which has magnitude but no direction). Such a force can be represented graphically as an arrow where the direction of the force is represented as the direction of the arrow and the magnitude of the force is represented by the length of the arrow (Figure 1.1).

The *line of action* of a force is a line of infinite length that coincides with the force itself. A force applied to a rigid body can be regarded as acting anywhere along the line of action. This principle of the transmissibility of a force is demonstrated in Figure 1.2.

When two or more forces meet at the same point, they are *concurrent*. Because of the principle of force transmissibility, separated, nonparallel forces are equivalent to concurrent forces (Figure 1.3). Parallel forces are a special condition that will be considered later.

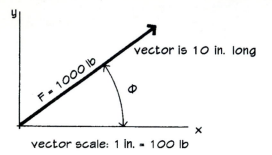

Figure 1.1: Vector representation of a force.

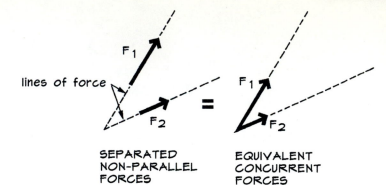

Figure 1.3: Separated, nonparallel forces and equivalent concurrent forces.

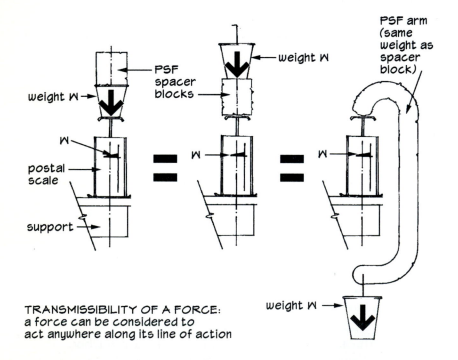

Figure 1.2: Model demonstrating the transmissibility of a force.

with other types of vectors, the resultant of two nonparallel forces can be determined by translating the forces along their respective lines of action to the point of intersection and "boxing them in" to create a parallelogram. The resultant extends from the intersection diagonally across the parallelogram. The effect of adding multiple additional forces is determined in the same way (Figure 1.4). A resultant is the simplest representation of the effect of several forces acting on a body.

Force components

Conversely, a single force can be *resolved* (broken down) into two or more force *components* that have a combined effect equal to the original force. In analyzing the effects of forces on structures, it is useful to use this principle to resolve forces acting in various directions into rectilinear components parallel to the cartesian coordinate system. This is accomplished by creating a rectangle around the original force. The sides of the rectangle represent the components, and the diagonal hypotenuse is the original force (Figure 1.5). While it is possible to scale the magnitude of the components, trigonometry is typically used to calculate the components of a force. For example, force F can be resolved into x and y components: $F_x = F(\cos \emptyset)$ and $F_y = F(\sin \emptyset)$.

Once the forces acting on a body are resolved into their respective rectangular components, these components can be added alge-

Resultant forces

When the lines of action of two forces intersect, there is a single force or *resultant* that is the exact equivalent of the two forces. As

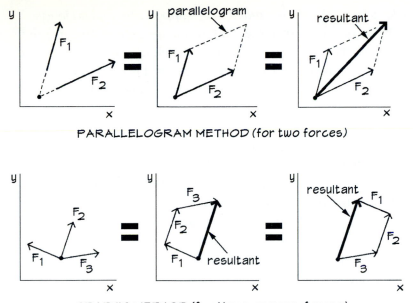

PARALLELOGRAM METHOD (for two forces)

GRAPHIC METHOD (for three or more forces)

Figure 1.4: Methods for determining the resultant of multiple forces.

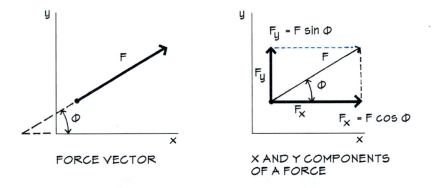

FORCE VECTOR

X AND Y COMPONENTS OF A FORCE

$F_y = F \sin \varnothing$

$F_x = F \cos \varnothing$

Figure 1.5: Resolving a force into its rectilinear components.

braically to obtain the resultant force's rectilinear components. Finally, these components can be used to determine the single resultant force. This can be done graphically (Figure 1.6), or the direction of the resultant force F can be calculated as $\varnothing = \tan^{-1}(F_y / F_x)$, and the magnitude of force as $F = F_y / \sin \varnothing$ (or $F = F_x / \cos \varnothing$).

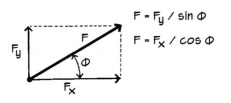

$F = F_y / \sin \varnothing$

$F = F_x / \cos \varnothing$

Figure 1.6: Combining rectilinear components into a resultant force.

Distributed forces
The forces discussed above were assumed to be *concentrated* and to act through a single point. Forces may also be *distributed*, acting over a distance or even an area. The units of a distributed force over a distance are pounds per linear foot (lb/ft) [newtons per meter (N/m)] and over an area are pounds per square foot (lb/ft^2) [newtons per square meter (N/m^2)].

The force distribution may be uniform or may vary. These are typically represented graphically by a polygon. For example, a rectangle is typically used to represent a uniformly distributed load, while a triangle represents a load that varies linearly along its distributed length (Figure 1.7). For the purpose of determining the effect of a distributed force on a rigid body, an *equivalent* force has the same total magnitude with its line of action through the centroid of the area of the polygon.

Force reactions and translational equilibrium
Newton's third law requires that for each action there is an equal and opposite reaction. Therefore, when a force (or the resultant of several forces) is *applied* to a body, there must be—and always is—an equal and opposite *reaction* force in order for the body to remain at rest. If a force is not counteracted by an opposite reaction, the body will translate (move from one location to another)—an undesirable event in most architectural structures. Figure 1.8 shows the relation between two applied forces acting on a body, their resultant, and the reaction force necessary for the body to be in *translational equilibrium* (in other words, to not move from one location to another). The equivalency of reactions and forces is shown in Figure 1.9.

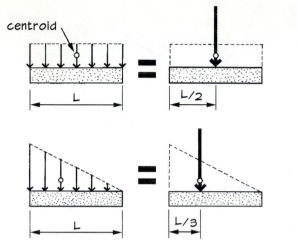

Figure 1.7: Distributed forces and equivalent concentrated forces acting on a rigid body.

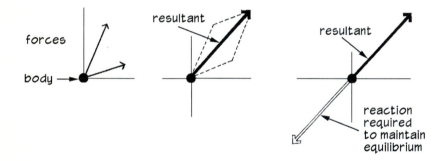

Figure 1.8: Two applied forces acting on a rigid body, their resultant, and the reaction force required to maintain equilibrium.

Figure 1.9: An applied force has the same effect as a reaction.

Hooke's law—the elastic reaction of supports to applied loads
Weight is one type of force that must be considered in analyzing structures. For example, if an object such as a book is dropped, the only force acting on it is its own weight and it will fall because there is no opposing reaction force. (Eventually, as the book's speed increases, the friction caused by air resistance will increase until this reaction force equals the downward force caused by the book's weight and acceleration becomes zero.)

If, instead, the book is placed on a *support* (such as a table), it remains stationary. This is because the table responds to the object by creating the reaction force required to counteract the object weight, thus holding it in translational equilibrium. The creation of this reaction to the weight is not obvious because the table top is stiff and it doesn't appear to be affected by the object. But actually the table-top is *elastic* and compresses very slightly, like a spring, under the load of the book. When the book is placed on the table, the table top (like a spring) presses up with a force equal to the weight of the book creating the resultant necessary to maintain the book's equilibrium (Figure 1.10).

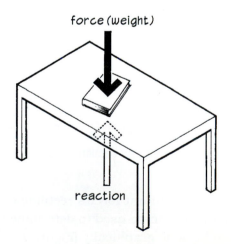

Figure 1.10: The table supports the book as a result of an elastic spring-like reaction of the tabletop surface to the force of the weight.

This principle was discovered in the seventeenth century by Robert Hooke and is the basis for the science of elasticity which is concerned with the interactions between forces and deflections in materials and structures.

Analyzing translational equilibrium

The concept of stationary objects being in translational equilibrium is fundamental to structural analysis. It was noted above that an analysis of forces typically requires resolving forces and reactions into cartesian *(x, y, z)* component forces. It follows that the algebraic sum of forces (and reactions) in each of the three cartesian dimensions must equal zero: $\Sigma F_x = 0$, $\Sigma F_y = 0$, and $\Sigma F_z = 0$ (Figure 1.11). Conversely, if the components of one or more forces is given, then the components of the resultant force can be calculated algebraically to be equal with the opposite sign (Figure 1.12).

the line of action of the force (Figure 1.13). Furthermore, the effects of an applied moment remain constant regardless of where it is applied to a rigid body (Figure 1.14).

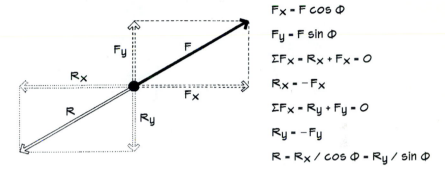

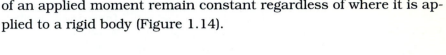

$$F_x = F \cos \varPhi$$
$$F_y = F \sin \varPhi$$
$$\Sigma F_x = R_x + F_x = 0$$
$$R_x = -F_x$$
$$\Sigma F_x = R_y + F_y = 0$$
$$R_y = -F_y$$
$$R = R_x / \cos \varPhi = R_y / \sin \varPhi$$

Figure 1.12: Calculating reaction components.

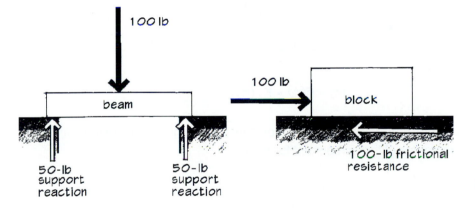

Figure 1.11: For translational equilibrium, the sum of forces in each dimension must equal zero.

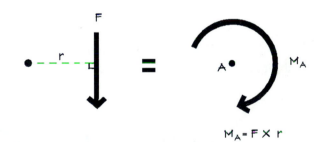

$$M_A = F \times r$$

Figure 1.13: The moment of a force about a point is equal to force × distance *r*.

MOMENTS

A *moment* of a force is the tendency of a force to cause an object to rotate. The moment of a force (usually referred to as simply *moment*) with respect to a given point in a structure is equal to the force multiplied by the distance to the point measured perpendicular to

The units of moment are foot-pound (ft•lb) and foot-kip (ft•kp); the SI equivalent is newton-meter (N•m). By convention, moments which tend to cause counterclockwise rotation are defined as positive, and those producing clockwise rotation as negative (Figure 1.15). This can be remembered by using the *right-hand* rule: If you turn your right hand so that the fingers point to the direction of the rotational tendency, the extended thumb indicates the sign of the moment (up for positive; down for negative). While widely used, this convention is arbitrary, and if the opposite convention were used

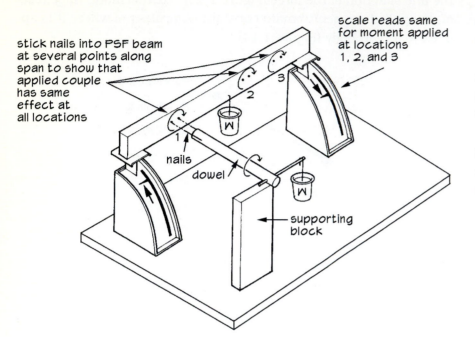

stick nails into PSF beam at several points along span to show that applied couple has same effect at all locations

scale reads same for moment applied at locations 1, 2, and 3

nails

dowel

supporting block

Figure 1.14: Model demonstrating that the effects of an applied moment remains constant regardless of where it is applied to a rigid body.

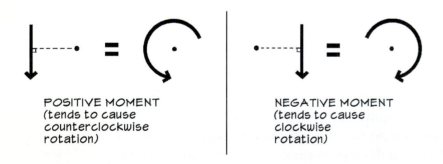

POSITIVE MOMENT (tends to cause counterclockwise rotation)

NEGATIVE MOMENT (tends to cause clockwise rotation)

Figure 1.15: Moment sign convention.

consistantly, it would produce the same end result. Moments around a certain point are represented graphically as a circular arrow around that point.

Moments are designated by the point or axis around which they are calculated. For example, the moment about a point A would be designated as M_A, and the moment about coordinate axis x as M_x.

Moments of forces are usually analyzed by determining the moments of their component forces around axes in the x, y, and z directions. The moment of a force about a point is equal to the sum of the moments of the component forces (Figure 1.16).

Just as a distributed force has an equivalent concentrated force acting through its centroid, a moment of a distributed force is the same as the moment of the equivalent concentrated force (Figure 1.17).

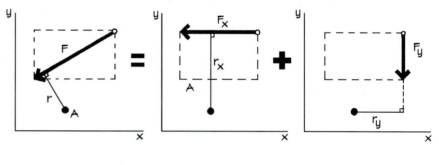

$$M_A = F(r) = F_x (r_x) + F_y (r_y)$$

Figure 1.16: The moment of a force about a point is equal to the sum of the moments of the component forces.

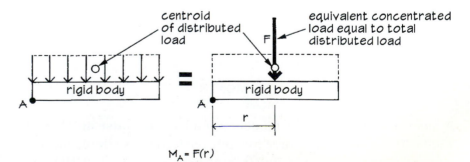

centroid of distributed load

equivalent concentrated load equal to total distributed load

rigid body

rigid body

$$M_A = F(r)$$

Figure 1.17: Moment of a distributed load.

Moment reactions and rotational equilibrium

A moment without an opposing *moment reaction* would cause a body to rotate. Again Newton's third law applies. For a body to remain at rest (be in *rotational equilibrium*), each applied moment must have an equal and opposite moment reaction (Figures 1.18 and 1.19).

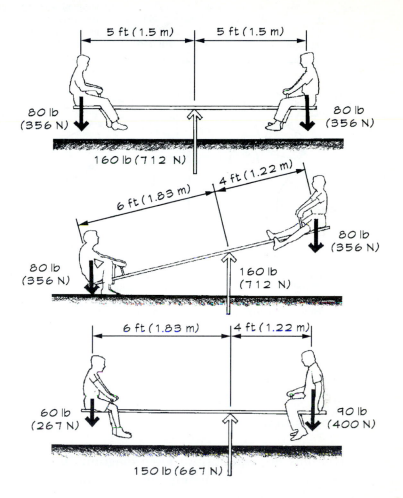

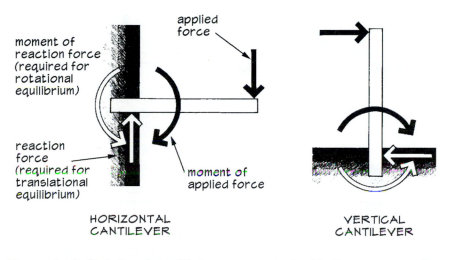

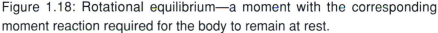

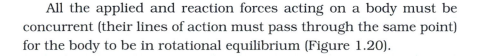

Figure 1.18: Rotational equilibrium—a moment with the corresponding moment reaction required for the body to remain at rest.

Figure 1.19: The seesaw demonstrates how combinations of weights (forces) and pivot location (distances) can produce equilibrium.

All the applied and reaction forces acting on a body must be concurrent (their lines of action must pass through the same point) for the body to be in rotational equilibrium (Figure 1.20).

Analyzing rotational equilibrium

Like its translational equivalent, the concept of rotational equilibrium is also fundamental to structural analysis. An analysis of moments typically requires determining the moments of components of all applied and reaction forces. For rotational equilibrium to occur, the algebraic sum of all moments around each of the three cartesian axes must equal zero: $\sum M_x = 0$, $\sum M_y = 0$, and $\sum M_z = 0$.

Total equilibrium

A body with forces applied will remain at rest only when both translational and rotational equilibrium exist. In all, six conditions must be met: the sum of the forces in each of the three directions must be equal to zero, and the sum of the moments of these forces around each of the three directional axes must be zero.

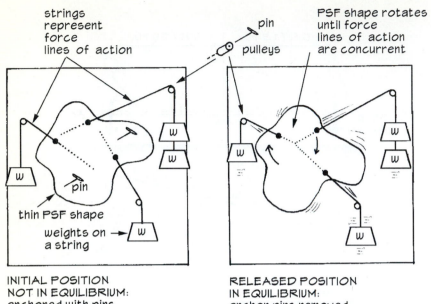

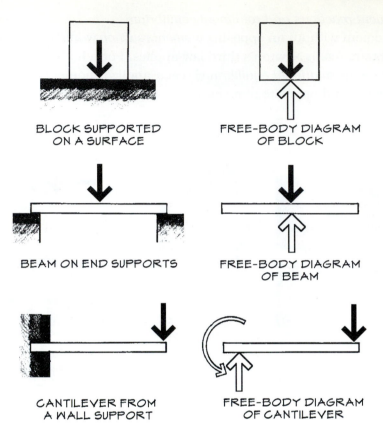

Figure 1.20: Model demonstrating the concurrence of forces as a condition of equilibrium.

Figure 1.21: Free-body diagrams.

FREE-BODY DIAGRAMS

Free-body diagrams are equilibrium force diagrams that show all the applied and reactive forces acting on a body or a portion of a body. They are useful in understanding (as well as quantitatively analyzing) structural behavior (Figure 1.21).

STATIC LOADS

Static loads are applied slowly to the structure and result in gradual deformations in the structure that are greatest when the loads are greatest. Static loads typically include dead loads, live loads, and forces due to foundation settlement or thermal expansion.

LOADS

> *The work itself is never born from the calculation.*
>
> —Eduardo Torroja

Dead loads

Dead loads are those forces resulting from gravity which are relatively permanent in character such as the building structure itself and other permanently attached building elements.

Loads are forces applied to a structure either as gravity or from external sources. Loads can be either static or dynamic.

While dead loads can be calculated directly from the volume and density of building components, they are more typically determined from tables approximating the loads per unit of roof and floor areas for different types of construction (masonry, concrete, steel, wood frame, etc.)

Live loads

Live loads are those forces which are applied to or removed from the building such as wind, snow, seismic, occupant, or furnishings. Although movable, live loads are applied so slowly that they are still considered as static loads. Live loads include people, furnishings, stored materials, and snow. Most building codes specify the minimum design live load (usually in lb/ft² or kg/m²) for roofs, floors, and decks. In general, gravity loads accumulate and increase as they are directed downward through columns and bearing walls to the foundation (Figure 1.22).

Some wind loads are static in behavior. These result from the relatively constant aerodynamic flow of wind over and around the building. Because these flows are a function of building shape and

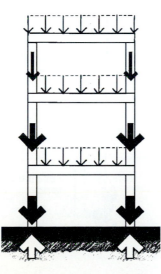

Figure 1.22: Accumulation of static loads down the height of a building.

wind direction and speed, it is very difficult to predict wind loading as accurately as gravity loads. For this reason, wind loads are approximated for structural design purposes as a constant, uniformly distributed live load acting perpendicular to the surface. The amount of the wind load to be included as a live load depends on local weather conditions and is typically determined by building code applicable to that region.

DYNAMIC LOADS

Dynamic loads are those which change rapidly. The rapidly changing nature of these loads can cause some unusual behavior in buildings, which can result in structural failure if unanticipated. Dynamic loads can be dangerous either because they are suddenly applied (impact loads) or because they are rhythmic (resonant loads) in nature.

Impact loads

Impact loads are those which are applied suddenly. The dynamic effects of an impact load are at least twice as large as the static effects of the same load applied slowly. If a 1-lb weight is placed slowly on a spring scale, the scale hand will stop at the 1-lb mark. If the weight is held just touching the scale and released suddenly, the hand will jump to 2 lb, oscillate, and eventually stop at the 1-lb mark.

If the weight is held about 3 inches (in) above the scale and dropped, the hand will reach the 4-lb mark before coming to rest at the 1-lb mark. The higher the drop height, the greater the impact velocity, and the greater the impact load (Figure 1.23). This is why a pile driver which drops a heavy weight from a height is able to drive the pile into the soil while resting the same weight on the top of the pile has no effect.

The sudden sideways movement of the ground under a building caused by an earthquake is an impact load of particular importance in building structures. The effect is the same as that created when a truck traveling at a constant speed is suddenly stopped by applying the brakes. The wheels of the truck stop immediately, but the inertia (momentum) of the higher and more massive truck body tends to continue. Cargo in the truck will slide unless securely tied down. Similarly, when the ground shifts suddenly in an earthquake, the building foundation shifts immediately, but the mass of the building above tends to remain stationary and tries to slide (shear) off of the foundation.

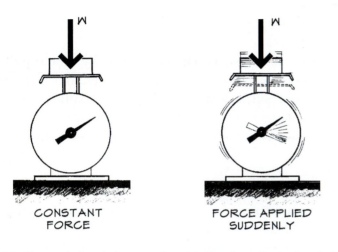

CONSTANT
FORCE

FORCE APPLIED
SUDDENLY

Figure 1.23: Dynamic loads have at least twice the effect of a static load.

Resonant loads

Resonant loads are those loads which vary in a rhythmical manner that matches the natural frequency of the structure. In order to ring a heavy church bell, a sexton pulls its rope rhythmically and the bell swings progressively further with each pull until eventually it rings. The sexton could not achieve this result with a single hard pull or even several pulls at irregular intervals. The pull match the natural frequency of the bell.

To understand why this is necessary, let's consider what happens on a typical swing of the bell. The bell behaves as a pendulum. When the bell reaches one side of its swing, it slows to a stop on its circular path and begins to accelerate on its downward swing until it passes the bottom of the arc. Rather than stopping there, the inertia of the bell causes the swing to continue up the arc on the opposite side decelerating (again because of gravity) until it stops and

then the sequence reverses. The distance between the center of gravity of the bell and its pivot point (the length of the pendulum) determines the bell's natural frequency. This frequency remains constant regardless of the amount of swing. It would even remain constant if the weight of the bell were to change. To ring the bell, the sexton must pull on the downswing of the bell and release on the upswing and do this in time with the natural frequency of the bell (Figure 1.24).

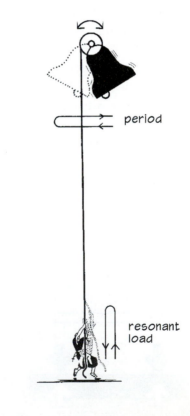

period

resonant
load

Figure 1.24: To ring the bell, the sexton must pull on the downswing of the bell in time with the natural frequency of the bell.

All structures are *elastic* in that they deflect under loads and return to their initial position once the loads are removed. As a result of this elasticity, structures have a tendency to oscillate. If the radio antenna on a car is pulled to the side and released, it will oscillate back and forth. A skyscraper sways from side to side after the passing of a gust of wind. A bridge oscillates up and down after the passage of a heavy truck. The time required for a structure to go freely through a complete oscillation depends on both its size and stiffness; this is its natural frequency.

Short, stiff buildings have short natural frequencies, while taller, more flexible buildings have a longer period of oscillation. A steel skyscraper may have a natural frequency greater than 8 s. If an external load is applied repeatedly at intervals that coincide with the building's natural frequency, like the sexton ringing the bell, then the effect will increase with each oscillation.

For this reason, the dynamic effects of an earthquake are greatly multiplied (compared with the static effects) when the ground vibrations match the natural frequency of the building (Figure 1.25). In a similar manner, machinery vibration in buildings may resonate with the building's natural frequency causing increasing oscillations. Floors, walls, columns, foundations, and even entire buildings may be damaged by rather modest loads with a resonant period (Figure 1.26).

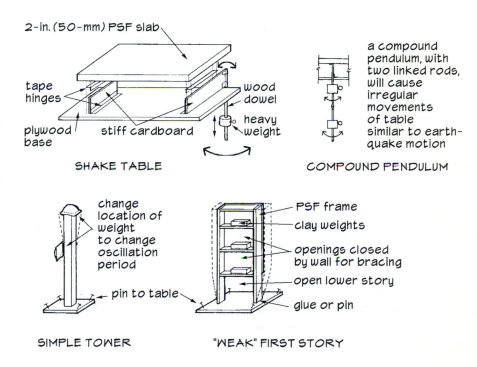

SHAKE TABLE

COMPOUND PENDULUM

SIMPLE TOWER

"WEAK" FIRST STORY

Figure 1.26: The effects of an earthquake on building models can be studied by using a shake table.

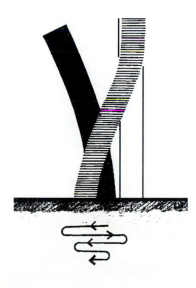

Figure 1.25: The effect of an earthquake on a tall building increases with each oscillation if the earth's vibrations resonate with the natural frequency of the building.

Wind can also produce oscillations due to aerodynamic effects. This may be demonstrated by blowing against the edge of a sheet of paper causing it to flutter up and down. If these fluttering oscillations resonate with the natural frequency of the structure, their effect may cause motion discomfort to building occupants or may increase to the point of structural failure.

Such resonant vibrations may be reduced by tuned dynamic dampers which are large masses attached by springs to the upper part of the building. The relative motion of these masses is damped by friction. These masses vibrate in resonance with the dynamic loads applied to the building, while the building itself remains at rest.

A most dramatic example of structural failure due to aerodynamic oscillations was the collapse of the Tacoma Narrows suspension bridge. It failed because of wind-induced flutter when exposed to a modest and constant wind flowing over its relatively thin deck structure. The bridge began to oscillate in a rhythmic twisting motion. These oscillations increased for 6 hours until a 600-ft section collapsed, falling into the water below (see Chapter 10).

SUPPORTS

A *support* is a connection between a structural member and the rigid body providing the support (the ground, for example).

SUPPORT CONDITIONS

Supports and other structural connections vary in the way they restrain or permit translational or rotational movement (Figure 1.27).

A *fixed* connection is the most restrictive; translation and rotation are both restrained. The base of a flagpole is an example of a fixed support.

A *pinned* connection has unrestrained rotation, but translation is restricted in all directions. A hinge is an example of a pinned support where rotation is permitted around one axis; a trailer hitch (socket and ball) is a pinned support with rotation permitted around all three axes.

A *roller* connection has unrestrained rotation, free translation in one direction and restricted translation in the remaining directions. A unicycle is a roller support, providing freedom to rotate in any direction and to translate in one horizontal direction but restricting translation in the other direction and vertically; its frictional resis-

tance to side skidding makes it behave as a pinned connection in that direction. A swiveling roller caster on a chair leg is a less restricted roller connection; it is free to rotate in any direction, free to translate in two directions, and restrained in the third.

A *free* support condition isn't really a connection at all; the end of the member is free to translate and to rotate in any direction. It is the least restrictive of all joint and support conditions.

A *cantilever* is a member with one end fixed and the other end free. The flagpole is a vertical cantilever. A wall bracket supporting a shelf is a horizontal cantilever.

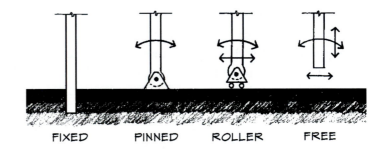

FIXED   PINNED   ROLLER   FREE

Figure 1.27: Types of support conditions.

SUPPORT REACTIONS

A force may be held in equilibrium by one or more parallel reactions. For example, a bridge may be supported at each end. The weight of the bridge constitutes the downward force, with each support providing an upward reaction; the sum of these support reactions will be equal to the weight of the bridge. Because the weight of the bridge is uniform along its length, the equivalent force occurs at the center of the span, and each support reaction is equal to half the weight of the bridge (Figure 1.28).

A slightly more complicated situation occurs when a heavy locomotive engine crosses the bridge. When the engine first begins the crossing, most of the added weight is carried by the support on that side. As the engine reaches the center, the support reactions equalize, and as the end of the bridge is reached, the support on that end carries most of the weight. In each case, the total of the support reactions equals the sum of the weights of the bridge and engine, and the proportioning of the support reaction depends on the position of the engine (Figure 1.29).

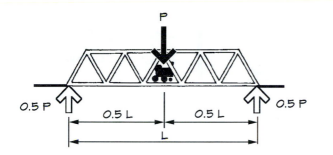

Figure 1.28: Bridge reactions.

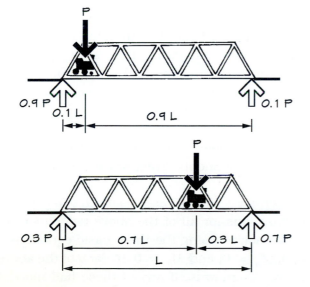

Figure 1.29: The bridge reactions change with the location of the engine.

Effect of support condition on reactions

It is important to recognize that the reactions that can occur at supports depend on the type of support condition. Recall that a *roller* connection has unrestrained rotation, free translation in one direction, and restricted translation in the remaining directions. This means that a roller support can have reaction forces only in the direction perpendicular to the face of the supporting body (if the supporting body is the ground, then the only support reaction possible would be upward). A *pinned* connection has unrestrained rotation, but translation is restricted in all directions. This means that a pinned support can have both vertical and horizontal reaction forces (but, because rotation is free, no reaction moments).

If both supports were rollers, then the structure would remain in equilibrium only if the applied forces were exclusively vertical. Any applied side force would cause movement (because the roller supports allow free sideways translation). If, on the other hand, both supports were pinned, the structure would be restrained laterally against side forces. This could cause internal stresses to develop resulting from thermal expansion of the structure. For these reasons, supports often have a pinned connection at one end and a roller connection at the other, providing the required lateral support while allowing thermal expansion and contraction to occur freely.

Fixed supports provide vertical and horizontal translation restraint while preventing rotation in any direction. For this reason, a fixed support may be used in isolation; no other support is needed to provide equilibrium.

Vertical reaction forces

To calculate the support reactions for any structure:

1. Determine (or assume) the restraint condition of each support.

2   Select one of the two support locations and rewrite the rotational equilibrium equation for summing the moments about that point equal to zero ($\sum M_A = 0$) to find the reaction at the other end. Use the right-hand rule to determine the sign of each moment. It doesn't matter which support point you begin with — either will

work. In fact, the moments can be summed around any arbitrary point; however, any point other than the supports requires the solution of simultaneous equations. It's much easier to begin with the support points.

3. Finally, use the translational equilibrium equation ($\Sigma F_y = 0$) to find the other reaction.

The above bridge support reactions can be calculated for any given location of the locomotive using the equilibrium equations (Figure 1.30).

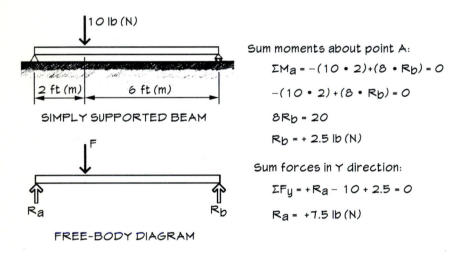

Sum moments about point A:

$$\Sigma M_a = -(10 \cdot 2) + (8 \cdot R_b) = 0$$

$$-(10 \cdot 2) + (8 \cdot R_b) = 0$$

$$8R_b = 20$$

$$R_b = +2.5 \text{ lb (N)}$$

Sum forces in Y direction:

$$\Sigma F_y = +R_a - 10 + 2.5 = 0$$

$$R_a = +7.5 \text{ lb (N)}$$

Figure 1.30: Calculating the support reactions for vertical loading only.

Because cantilevered members (fixed support) are not free to rotate, no other support is required for them to be in equilibrium. For example, consider a horizontal cantilever beam with a vertical distributed load applied to the outer half (Figure 1.31).

Horizontal and vertical reaction forces
Consider another example problem involving a person standing on a weightless ladder leaning against a wall (Figure 1.32). Don't be confused by the angle of the ladder; it isn't relevant to our calculations.

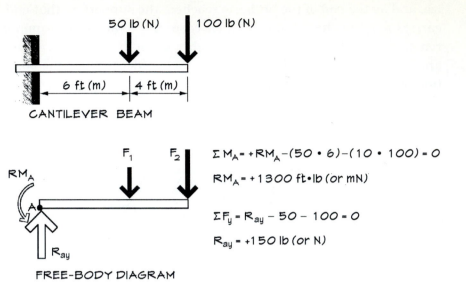

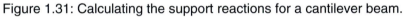

$$\Sigma M_A = +RM_A - (50 \cdot 6) - (10 \cdot 100) = 0$$

$$RM_A = +1300 \text{ ft} \cdot \text{lb (or mN)}$$

$$\Sigma F_y = R_{ay} - 50 - 100 = 0$$

$$R_{ay} = +150 \text{ lb (or N)}$$

FREE-BODY DIAGRAM

Figure 1.31: Calculating the support reactions for a cantilever beam.

There is sufficient friction at the base of the ladder to assume it is pinned there; assume a roller connection at the top. Since the top allows unrestrained vertical movement, no vertical reaction force is possible at this support. Begin by summing the moments around the base support point and setting their sum equal to zero. Next, sum the forces in the y direction and set it equal to zero. Finally, sum the forces in the x direction and set it equal to zero.

Reactions to diagonal forces
If any of the applied forces are diagonal, begin by resolving them into their x and y components. Then proceed as above.

Statically indeterminate structures—too much of a good thing
The support reactions for all of the above two-dimensional structures can all be solved using the three basic equations of equilibrium: $\Sigma F_x = 0, \Sigma F_y = 0,$ and $\Sigma M_A = 0$. In each of the above problems, there were three unknowns. If any of these had more than three unknowns, it would not be solvable by these simple static equilibrium equations.

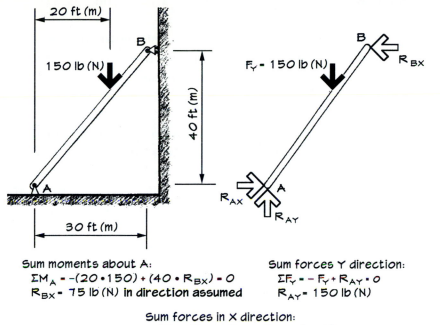

Sum moments about A:
$\Sigma M_A = -(20 \cdot 150) + (40 \cdot R_{BX}) = 0$
$R_{BX} = 75$ lb (N) in direction assumed

Sum forces Y direction:
$\Sigma F_Y = -F_Y + R_{AY} = 0$
$R_{AY} = 150$ lb (N)

Sum forces in X direction:
$\Sigma F_X = R_{AX} + R_{BX} = R_{AX} + (-75) = 0$
$R_{AX} = +75$ lb (N)

Figure 1.32: Calculating the vertical and horizontal support reactions for a person on a ladder.

For example, if the cantilever beam also had a roller vertical support added to the free end, there would be no way to tell how much of the end load was being carried by the moment resistance of the fixed end and how much was being carried by the added roller support. To determine this, it becomes necessary to determine the deformation of the beam. Such a condition is called statically indeterminate and requires a more complex solution (Figure 1.33).

Mechanisms—too little of a good thing
Conversely, having too few support reactions (less than three) means that the structure is not stable and is prone to distortion or movement. Such systems are called *mechanisms* and offer no structural resistance.

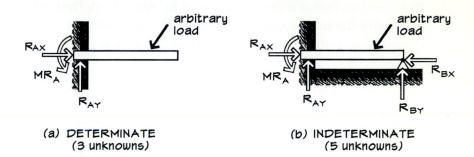

Figure 1.33: (a) Statically determinate cantilever beam has three unknown load reactions which correspond to the three equations of equilibrium. (b) Statically indeterminate beam has five unknowns and three equations of equilibrium (statically indeterminate to second degree).

SUMMARY

1. *Mechanics* is that branch of physical science which deals with forces and their effect on bodies.

2. *Statics* is that branch of mechanics that deals with forces that produce equilibrium among bodies.

3. *Dynamics* is that branch of mechanics that deals with forces that produce acceleration among bodies.

4. A *scalar* quantity has magnitude but no direction.

5. A *vector quantity* has both magnitude and direction.

6. A *force* is that which tends to exert motion, tension, or compression on an object. It is a vector quantity that may be represented graphically as an arrow with the head of the arrow representing the direction of the force and the length of the arrow representing the magnitude of the force based on some scale (for example, 1 in equals 100 lb of force).

7. The *line of action* of a force is a line of infinite length that coincides with the force itself. A force applied to a rigid body can be regarded as acting anywhere along the line of action.

8. *Concurrent* forces are those which meet at the same point

9. A *resultant* force is the exact equivalent of two nonparallel forces.

10. A single force can be *resolved* (broken down) into two or more force *components* that have an effect equal to the original force.

11. A *concentrated* force acts through a single point; a *distributed* force acts over a distance or area. The effect of a distributed force acting on a rigid body may be represented by a single *equivalent* force.

12. A body is in *equilibrium* when it is at rest (neither moving nor rotating).

13. A *reaction* force equal and opposite to an *applied* force is required to maintain equilibrium.

14. *Translational* equilibrium means no translation from one location to another. The equations for translational equilibrium are $\sum F_x = 0$, $\sum F_y = 0$, and $\sum F_z = 0$.

15. *Elasticity* allows a support to *react* when a force is applied. For example, when a book is placed on a table, it applies a force to the table equal to the weight of the book; because the table is elastic, it compresses slightly and "pushes back" with an equal reaction force. This effect is known as Hooke's law.

16. A *moment* of a force is the tendency of a force to cause an object to rotate. By convention, moments which tend to cause counter-clockwise rotation are defined as positive.

17. For a body in *rotational equilibrium*, each applied moment must have an equal and opposite moment reaction. The equations of rotational equilibrium are $\sum M_x = 0$, $\sum M_y = 0$, and $\sum M_z = 0$.

18. *Static loads* are applied slowly to the structure and result in gradual deformations in the structure that are greatest when the loads are greatest. *Dynamic loads* are those which change rapidly.

19. *Dead loads* are those forces resulting from gravity which are relatively permanent in character. *Live loads* are those forces which are applied to or removed from the building such as wind, snow, seismic, occupant, or furnishings. *Resonant loads* are those loads which vary in a rhythmical manner that matches the natural frequency of the structure.

20. A *support* is a connection between a structural member and the rigid body providing the support (the ground, for example).

21. A *fixed* connection is the most restrictive; translation and rotation are both restrained. A *pinned* connection has unrestrained rotation, but translation is restricted in all directions. A *roller* connection has unrestrained rotation, free translation in one direction, and restricted translation in the remaining directions. A *free* support condition isn't really a connection at all; the end of the member is free to translate and to rotate in any direction.

22. A *cantilever* is a member with one end fixed and the other end free.

23. A *statically indeterminate structure* is one in which the number of unknowns exceeds the equilibrium equations available to solve them.

24. A *mechanism* is a system which has fewer than three support reactions, is prone to move as the result of applied forces, and offers no structural resistance.

2

STRENGTH OF MATERIALS

A structure is nothing but a system of reactions and internal stresses capable of balancing a system of external forces; and therefore, it must be conceived as a material organism directed to that precise end.
—*Pier Luigi Nervi*

Structural members are able to withstand the effects of forces acting on them because of the molecular composition of the materials that comprise them. If a cable is pulled at one end and anchored at the other, it does not simply separate. Because of its internal strength, the cable resists being pulled apart, instead it stretches slightly. It is this elastic action that creates the reaction opposing the pulling force while transmitting the forces internally along the cable's length. If the cable's capacity is exceeded by the load, the cable will break.

Obviously, a thicker cable can carry a greater load than a thin one, because the internal forces are being distributed over a larger cross-sectional area. In other words, the concentration of internal force in the thicker cable is less.

STRESS

Stress is the term for this concentration of internal force within a structural member (Figure 2.1). It is a concept fundamental to analyzing the strength of a structural member. More specifically, stress is force per unit area (expressed as stress $f = P/A$). The units of stress are pounds per square inch and pascals (Pa) (1 Pa equals 1 N/m^2).

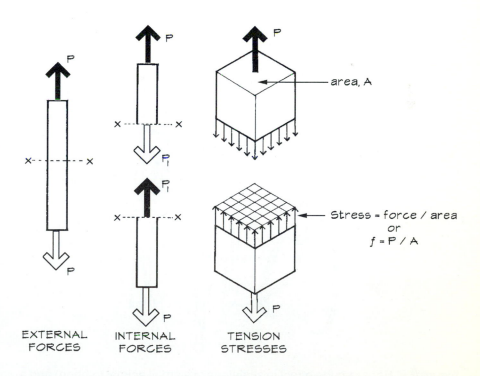

Figure 2.1: External forces, internal forces, and stress in a tension member.

SCALE AND THE SQUARE-CUBE EFFECT

A structure that is adequate at one scale is not necessarily adequate when all parts are made proportionally larger. The problem is that building loads are primarily determined by the weight of the building components and weight is determined by volume, but the strength of the building is determined by the cross-sectional *area* of the members. As the structure is scaled up, the volume (and gravity load) increases at the rate of the *cube* of the scale, while its members' strengths increase at the slower rate of the *square* of the scale.

Galileo first noted this effect in 1638 when he described how the bone of a small animal would look if it were to fulfill the same function in an animal three times as large. Simply making the bone three times larger would not carry the increased weight of the animal; the bone would have to be enlarged disproportionately to carry the new weight. This effect can be noted by comparing the skeletons of large and small animals. For small animals, the bones are relatively thin; larger animals have bones of very massive proportions (Figure 2.2).

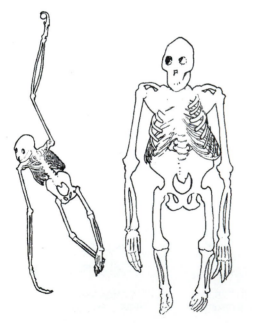

Figure 2.2: Square-cube effect in skeletons of a small animal (gibbon) and a large animal (gorilla) drawn at the same scale.

Consider, for example, an umbrella-shaped shelter (Figure 2.3) that is 10 ft (3.05 m) high and 10 ft deep with a flat concrete roof slab 1 ft (0.305 m) thick and a single center column having an area of 1.0 ft² (0.093 m²). Assuming the density of the concrete is 150 lb/ft³ (2400 kg/m³), the total load on the top of the column is 15,000 lb (6818 N) and the compressive stress is 15,000 lb/ft² (73,312 N/m²).

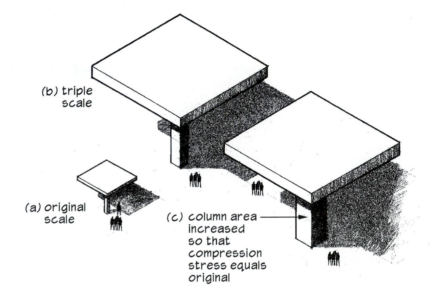

Figure 2.3: Square-cube effect in building structure: (a) small structure; (b) larger structure with all dimensions tripled; and (c) larger structure with column area increased so that compression stress is the same as for the smaller structure.

If the same structure were increased in scale threefold, the overall size would triple to 30 ft (9.15 m) in each dimension; the thickness of the roof slab would also triple, resulting in a slab volume of 2700 ft³ (76.45 m³) and a weight of 405,000 lb (183,480 kg). The area of the center column would increase to 9 ft² (0.82 m²). The stress in the column would be 45,000 lb/ft² (219,936 N/m²), which is three times that of the smaller structure. In order to effect the same compressive stress, the column area would have to triple to 27 ft² (2.46 m²) with column dimensions increasing to 5.2 ft (1.58 m) on each side.

STRAIN

When any material is stressed, it deforms slightly. This springlike deformation isn't inherently a bad characteristic. In fact, deformation is what gives members their ability to resist applied forces and generate reaction forces. This deformation is called *strain*. More specifically, strain is the amount of distortion per unit of length of the member, and the units of strain are inches per inch (in/in) and meters per meter (m/m).

Up to a point, material under stress behaves in an *elastic* manner—that is, the strain is proportional to stress (Figure 2.4a). Eventually, however, if the stress continues to increase, the strain becomes disproportionate to the stress—in other words, a small amount of additional stress results in much larger increases in strain. Furthermore when the stress is removed, the strain does not completely disappear and the member is permanently distorted. This is *plastic* behavior. If stress continues to increase, eventually the material fails completely.

The relationship between stress and strain may be diagrammed (Figure 2.5). Notice that in the elastic region of the diagram, where strain is proportional to stress, the line is straight. The slope of this portion of the line is the *modulus of elasticity* which is a primary indicator of the strength of the material. Moduli of elasticity of some common materials are shown in Table 2.1.

TABLE 2.1: MODULI OF ELASTICITY
FOR SOME COMMON STRUCTURAL MATERIALS

material	lb/in.	(GPa)	type of stress
STEEL	29,000,000	(200)	tension, compression
ALUMINUM	10,000,000	(70)	tension, compression
TIMBER (softwood)	2,000,000	(14)	tension (parallel to grain)
CONCRETE	4,000,000	(27)	compression

STATES OF STRESS

Order is sought by the discipline of measures.
—*Louis I. Kahn*

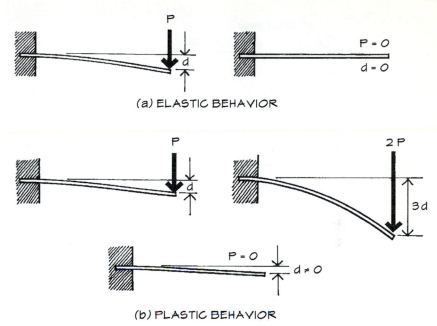

(a) ELASTIC BEHAVIOR

(b) PLASTIC BEHAVIOR

Figure 2.4: (a) Elastic behavior: Strain is proportional to stress, and the member returns to its original length when the load is removed. (b) Plastic behavior: Strain is disproportionate to stress, and the member does not return to its original length when the load is removed.

There are three basic states of structural stress: tension, compression, and shear. These terms are also often used to describe applied and reaction forces in terms of the way that they affect a member (Figure 2.6). For example, a tensile force is one that results in tensile stress in a member.

TENSION

Tension is the tendency of the particles of a material to be pulled apart. When forces are applied to each end of a structural member pulling in opposite directions, the structural member elongates (stretches) slightly. The amount of elongation per unit of length is *tensile strain*. The units of tensile strain are inches per inch or milli-

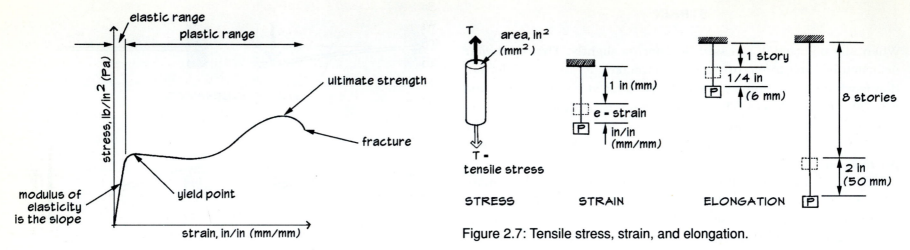

STRESS / STRAIN DIAGRAM

Figure 2.5: Example of a stress-strain diagram for a material.

Figure 2.7: Tensile stress, strain, and elongation.

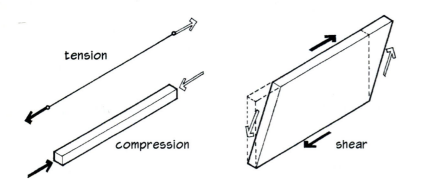

Figure 2.6: Forces which produce tensile, compressive, and shearing stress.

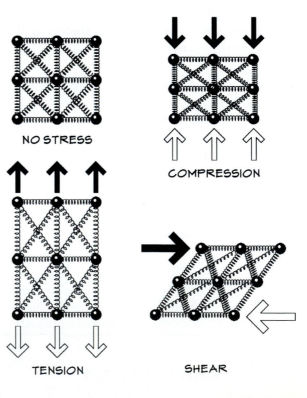

meters per millimeter, which cancel out and become dimensionless.

The total elongation of a member depends on stress (load per unit of cross-sectional area), length (longer members will stretch more), and material (stronger materials will stretch less)(Figure 2.7).

Steel is a material with exceptional strength in tension; steel chains, cables, and solid rods are commonly used as tension members in a structure.

Figure 2.8: Conceptual molecular model showing the particles of a material when subjected to various stresses.

COMPRESSION

Conversely, *compression* is the tendency for the particles of a material to be pressed together (Figure 2.8). When forces press against each end of a structural member, it shortens slightly. The amount of shortening per unit of length is *compression strain;* the unit of compressive strain e (like tensile strain) is inches per inch which cancels out and becomes dimensionless.

The total shortening of a member depends on compressive stress (load per unit of cross-sectional area), length (longer members will shorten more), and material (stronger materials will shorten less).

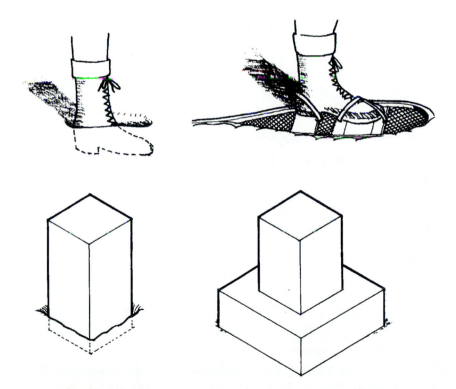

Figure 2.9: Snowshoes and foundation footings as ways of reducing compressive stresses.

Snowshoes and foundations

Walking in the snow in regular boots is difficult because you sink. This is because the stress (pressure) of the boots exceeds the allowable stress (bearing capacity) of the snow. The stress due to walking can be reduced by wearing snowshoes which increase the area, thus reducing the stress (Figure 2.9).

Columns and bearing walls are commonly used in buildings to transfer the building loads (roof and floor loads, for example) down to the supporting foundation. While these vertical loads can be quite large, the compressive strength of commonly used wall and column materials (wood, steel, and concrete, for example) is great enough to withstand the high compressive stress created by these concentrated loads. However, it is ultimately the soil under the building that must withstand these loads, and usually the allowable compressive stress of the soil is considerably below that present in the columns and bearing walls. Like the snowshoe, foundation footings are used to distribute the load over a larger area so that the resulting stress is below that allowed by the soil. Typically the foundation wall or pier rests on a wide concrete footing. The area of the footing required is equal to the load divided by the allowable bearing stress for that particular soil type.

The middle-third rule

When a member is loaded in compression, the load must be applied near the center in order for the entire body to remain in compression. Placing the load near the edge of a short column will result in the opposite side of the column actually going into compression. The middle-third rule requires that the load be applied in the middle third for the entire member to remain in compression.

SHEAR

Shear is the tendency of the particles of a material to slide past one another. Scissors cutting paper is an example of shear.

Another example of shear is the deformation that occurs when a short post anchored in the ground (fixed) and free on top is pressed to the side. If the side force is applied near the ground, there is a scissorlike shearing action caused by the applied force, and the resultant force from the ground producing a tendency for the post material particles to slide past one another in the plane of the ground. If the force is applied at the top, the same shearing action occurs throughout the length of the post, and it will tend to distort like a parallelogram.

Equivalency of shear to tension and compression

One characteristic of shear is that it produces sliding in not one, but two directions at right angles to one another. If a square element of the post located near the ground line is isolated and examined, the top would experience a stress caused by the applied force, while the bottom would experience the opposing stress caused by the resultant force (the resistance of the ground). While the opposition of these two equal stresses would not cause translation movement, it would cause the element to tend to rotate. In order for the element to remain in equilibrium, the adjacent faces must experience an opposing set of shear stresses which counteract the rotational tendency.

The combination of the applied horizontal shearing stresses and the resultant vertical shearing stresses makes the square element tend to distort into a parallelogram. This results in tension stresses forming along the long diagonal of the parallelogram and compression stresses forming along the shorter diagonal in the opposite direction. This is why any shearing stresses that occur in a member generate tension and compression at a 45° angle to the direction of the originally applied and resultant forces (Figure 2.10 and Figure 2.11).

This tendency of shearing stress to translate into tension and compression at a 45° angle can be observed when a concrete column supporting a concrete slab fails in shear. The top of the column will tend to punch through the slab in the shape of a 45° cone (Figure 2.12). Similarly, a short column made of a brittle material like concrete will tend to fail in shear when it is loaded in compression until crushing failure. The top and bottom of the cylinder will fail in shear forming 45° cones; the cones act like wedges to split the remainder of the material in the middle (Figure 2.13).

Shearing stress is calculated in a manner similar to tensile and compressive stresses: shear stress is equal to the shearing load di-

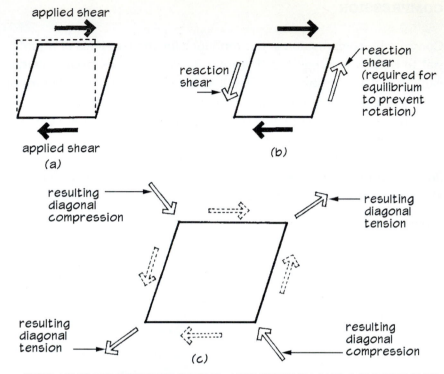

EQUIVALENCE BETWEEN SHEAR, AND TENSION AND COMPRESSION

Figure 2.10: Small square element showing equivalency of shear to tension and compression: (a) vertical shears, (b) vertical shears with horizontal reactions required to maintain rotational equilibrium, and (c) 45° resultant tension and compression.

vided by the area being sheared ($N = P/A$). The units are pounds per square inch and newtons per square meter (Figure 2.14).

Shear strain is the angle that the square element is distorted into a parallelogram as a result of shear stress. This angle g is usually measured in radians (which are dimensionless). For any given material, if shear strain is plotted against shear stress, a stress-strain curve is generated. For small and moderate amounts of shear, Hooke's law applies, and strain is proportional to stress resulting in a straight line in the elastic region. As with tension and compression, the slope of the straightline portion of the curve is the shear modulus $G = N/g$ (Figure 2.15).

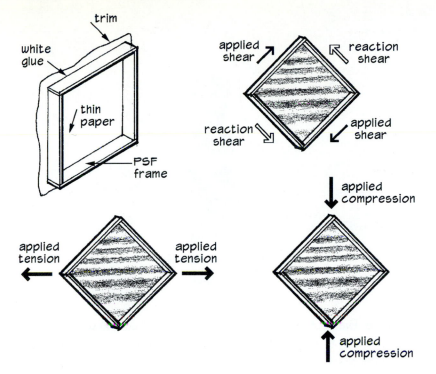

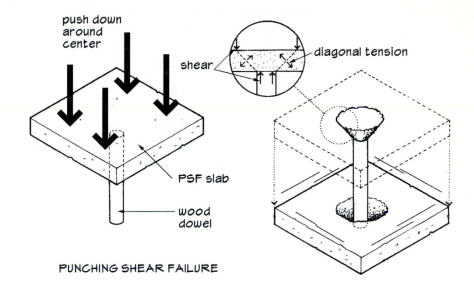

PUNCHING SHEAR FAILURE

Figure 2.12: Model demonstration of shear failure of column punching through a slab.

Figure 2.11: Model demonstration of the equivalency of shear and tension and compression.

Bias stretch

Woven cloth is a material that has a relatively high tensile strength in the directions of the warp or weft of the weave. (*Warp* threads are those running parallel to the length of a roll of cloth; *weft* threads run perpendicular to the warp threads.) When a load is applied in the direction of either the warp or weft, the cloth will stretch very little; in addition, there is very little contraction in the perpendicular direction.

However, cloth is comparatively weak in shear. If the cloth is pulled at a 45° angle to the directions of the threads—*on the bias*—there is a much greater stretch. In addition, there is a proportionally greater contraction perpendicular to the pull. Loosely woven cloth is more stretchy on the bias; a fishing net is the

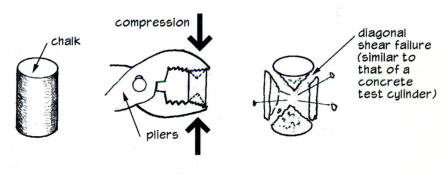

COMPRESSION FAILURE OF A BRITTLE MATERIAL

Figure 2.13: Compression failure of a brittle material.

most extreme example. This principle of bias stretch is used in dressmaking to create garments which easily conform to the shape of the wearer (Figure 2.16).

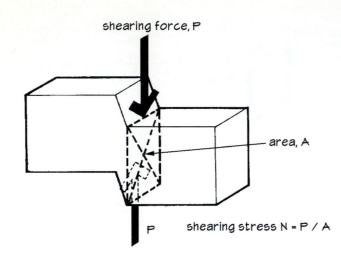

Figure 2.14: Shearing stress N = shearing force P divided by area being sheared A.

Figure 2.16: Bias cut in dressmaking uses the weakness of loosely woven fabrics in shear to create clothes which drape easily and conform to the shape of the body.

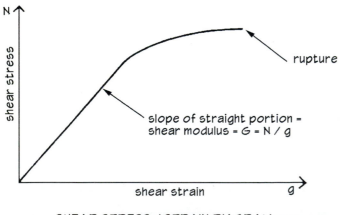

SHEAR STRESS / STRAIN DIAGRAM

Figure 2.15: Stress-strain diagram for shear is similar to that for tension and compression. The slope of the straightline portion in the elastic region is the shear modulus.

Torsion

Torsion is rotational shear that occurs when a member is twisted around its axis. Consider a round bar that is held stationary at one end and twisted around its center axis at the other end. If the surface of the bar were gridded with squares, these would tend to distort into parallelograms (sound familiar?). These square sections behave exactly like those in pure shear discussed above. Tension develops along the long diagonal of the parallelogram and compression along the short diagonal. Because the outer surface of the bar is distorted more than the material on the inside, the shearing stress is greatest there. Because of this, the most efficient shape to resist torsion is a round tube (Figure 2.17).

A spandrel beam being twisted by a floor beam intersecting at midspan is one example of torsion that is often found in building structures. Not only does the unbalanced load cause torsion, it also produces bending (Figure 2.18).

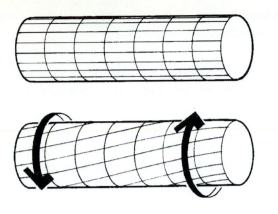

TORSION SHEAR

Figure 2.17: Torsion is shear around an axis caused by twisting. For a given amount of material, a hollow tube is the most efficient shape to resist torsion.

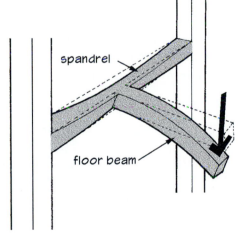

Figure 2.18: A spandrel beam in torsion and bending.

Couples

The steering wheel of a car being turned with the driver's hands at opposite points of the wheel is an example of pure torsion without bending. The torsion is applied to the steering shaft tending to twist it. No bending occurs because each hand is causing a pair of balanced, equal, and opposite forces.

A *couple* is just such a balanced pair of forces causing rotation. More specifically, a couple is a special moment condition, consisting of a set of two equal, parallel, nonconcurrent forces which tend to cause rotation but—because the forces are equal and opposite—no lateral translation. The moment a couple produces is equal to one of the forces multiplied by the perpendicular distance separating the forces $(M = F \times d)$. Couples are frequently found as *applied loads* in machinery but seldom in building structures. However, the concept of a couple will be helpful in understanding the *internal bending forces* that occur in a simple beam (Figure 2.19).

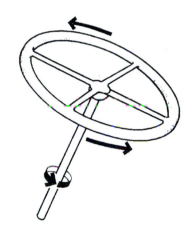

Figure 2.19: A couple produces torsion without bending.

SUMMARY

1. *Stress* is the concentration of internal forces within a structural member and is measured as the force per unit of cross-sectional area.

2. The *square-cube effect* reflects the fact that structural capacity varies as the square of the size of a structure, while gravity load varies as the cube of the size. Thus the cross-sectional areas of structural members have to increase disproportionately when the scale of a structure is increased.

3. *Strain* is the relative change in size and shape of a material resulting from the application of stress.

4. *Elastic* behavior means that strain is proportional to stress, and the member will return to its original size when the stress is removed.

5. *Modulus of elasticity* is the ratio of stress to strain (in the elastic region).

6. *Plastic* behavior means that strain is disproportionate to the stress, and the member will never return to its original size when the stress is removed.

7. The three basic states of stress are *tension, compression,* and *shear.*

8. *Tension* is the tendency of the particles of a material to be pulled apart.

9. *Compression* is the tendency for the particles of a material to be pressed together.

10. The *middle-third rule* requires that a compression member must be loaded in the middle third if no tension stresses are to occur.

11. *Shear* is the tendency of the particles of a material to slide past one another. Shearing stresses translate into tensile and compressive stresses acting at 45° to the shearing stresses.

12. *Shear strain* is the angle (in radians) that the square element is distorted into a parallelogram as a result of shear stress.

13. *Torsion* is rotational shear that occurs when a member is twisted around its axis.

14. A *couple* is a special moment condition consisting of a set of two equal, parallel, nonconcurrent forces which tend to cause rotation but no lateral translation.

Part II

TRUSSED SYSTEMS

Technical correctness constitutes a sort of grammar of architectural speech, and, just as in spoken or written language, it is impossible without it to advance to a higher form of literary expression.
—*Pier Luigi Nervi*

Trussed structures are assemblies of *ties* (acting in tension) and *struts* (acting in compression) arranged in pin-connected triangles so that all internal forces are axial (in direct compression or tension with no bending or shear). This general category of triangular structures includes *cables, trusses, space frames,* and *geodesic frames.*

This triangular geometry is fundamental to truss behavior because the triangle is the only polygon that has an inherently stable geometry. The shape of a triangle can only be changed by changing the length of its sides. This means that, with hinged joints, the sides of a triangle need only resist tension or compression (not bending) in order to preserve the shape. Other polygons require one or more rigid joints (which, in turn, introduce bending in the sides) to maintain their shape (Figure II.1).

In practice, secondary bending occurs in truss members whenever the joints are not frictionless pin connections or when loads are applied directly to the members perpendicular to their axes. These bending forces are typically ignored in trusses because they are minor compared with the axial forces.

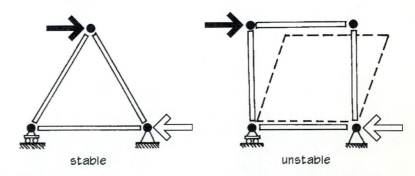

stable   unstable

Figure II.1: The triangle is the only hinged polygon that has an inherently stable shape.

3

CABLE STAYS

*The beauty of tensile constructions is that they are
functional as well as aesthetic.*
—*Maggie Toy*

Wire rope, string, and thin rod are examples of tensile members that behave as *cables*. The simplest example of a tied structure is a weight suspended from a single cable. The weight will come to rest directly below the support point with the tie stretched between in a straight line.

A more useful structural configuration is a cable suspended from two supports, suspending a single load at midspan. Under such a load, the cable *sags* and half the load is transmitted to each support. Assuming that the weight of the cable is insignificant compared with the load, the cable assumes a V-shape. The tensile force in the cable is determined by the load and the slope of the cable.

If the supports are close together and the slope of the cable is very steep, then the tensile force in the cable is approximately half the load (each side of the cable is supporting half of the load). Conversely, if the supports are wide and the cable slope is shallow, then the tensile force in the cable is much greater.

To understand why, consider the reactions at each support. Recall (from Chapter 1) that a force can be represented by force components acting in the vertical and horizontal directions. The vertical components of the reactions at each support must total the vertical load. In this case, because the load P is in the center, each reaction vertical component equals $P/2$. Because the cable is sloped (not vertical) there is a horizontal thrust exerted on each support tending to pull them together. This is the horizontal force component of the reaction. While the vertical reaction component at each support remains the same regardless of the cable slope (it will always be equal to the vertical load), the horizontal reaction component will vary with the slope of the cable; as the slope changes from vertical to nearly horizontal, the horizontal reaction component will change from zero to approaching infinity. The tensile force in the cable will always equal the resultant of the vertical and horizontal reaction components (Figure 3.1).

If the load in the above example is shifted off center, the supports develop different vertical reaction components but equal horizontal components (which must be equal to achieve static equilibrium). The tensile force in the cable is different on each side and will equal the resultant of the vertical and horizontal reaction on each side.

Cables which are loaded continuously along their lengths are *cantenaries*; they are considered separately in Chapter 10.

CABLE-STAYED STRUCTURES

Cable-stayed building structures support horizontal spans by means of diagonal cables suspended from a higher support. The use of the term *cable* in this designation typically includes both flexible (cable) and rigid (rod) ties. (They are distinguished from *catenary* structures which hang from a draped cable like a suspension bridge; these will be considered in a later chapter.) Most cable-stayed structures are designed so that the supporting mast is rigidly fixed at the base. To provide additional lateral resistance against thrust, additional cables are usually extended to the opposite direction. In larger structures, this is usually achieved economically by making the stays symmetrical about the supporting mast. This symmetry equalizes the horizontal loads on the mast and minimizes bending.

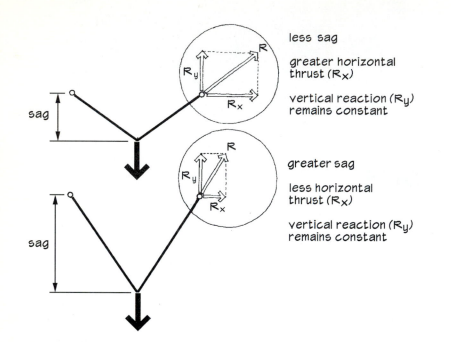

less sag

greater horizontal
thrust (R_x)

vertical reaction (R_y)
remains constant

greater sag

less horizontal
thrust (R_x)

vertical reaction (R_y)
remains constant

Figure 3.1: Cables with steep, medium, and shallow slopes. Notice that while the vertical reaction components remain the same regardless of slope (total of these equals the vertical load), the horizontal reaction component (thrust) increases dramatically as the slope approaches horizontal. The tensile force in the cable will always equal the resultant of the vertical and horizontal reaction components.

Cables can also be center-supported and used to carry overhanging loads at each end of the strut. Typically, additional ties are used to pull down each end for stability. This configuration is similar to the standing rigging used to support a sailboat mast. On sailboats, the objective is to support the mast to keep it from tipping over and provide intermediate support (from the *struts*—called *spreaders*) to prevent buckling. On buildings, the objective is to hang the roof (which acts as a strut) from the top of the mast.

CABLE-STAYED CASE STUDIES

> *A joint is visible, it is something expressed and becomes the mark of the person who made it.*
> —*Renzo Piano*

Patcenter
Patcenter (1986; Princeton, NJ; Richard Rogers Partnership, architects; Ove Arup and Partners, structural engineers) is a research facility for P.A. Technology. It was designed for circulation flexibility and maximum flexibility in the arrangement of offices, laboratories, and services. This was achieved by a wide structural grid of column-free space. The exposed structure is consistent with the client's desire for a strong visual presence that would emphasize the company's innovative technical orientation. The architect responded by dramatically expressing the structure on the exterior of the building in stark contrast to the "bland boxes" that characterize the research "think belt" around Princeton (Brookes and Grech, 1990) (Figures 3.2 through 3.5).

The basic design concept featured a center spine 29.5 ft (9 m) wide. This forms an enclosed glazed arcade, with the building's services prominently located directly above on the exterior supported

Figure 3.2: Patcenter, exterior.

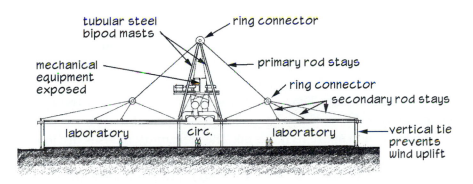

Figure 3.3: Patcenter, section.

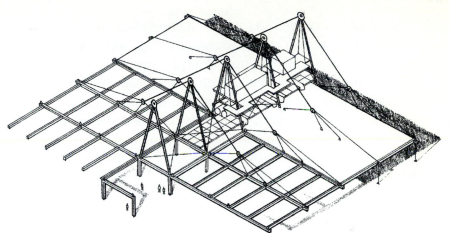

Figure 3.4: Patcenter, cutaway axonometric drawing.

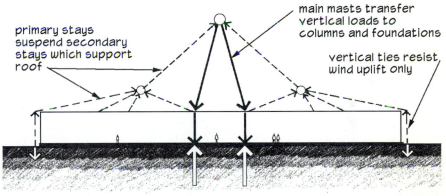

Figure 3.5: Patcenter, load path diagram.

on frames suspended from the roof structure masts. On either side of the center circulation spine are two large single-story enclosures, each 236 ft × 74 ft (72 m × 22.5 m), used for research. To provide the necessary spatial flexibility in these research areas, a visually dramatic cable-stayed (actually thin solid steel ties) roof spans the width of the space leaving the interior column free. The main structure consists of a 24.6-ft (7.5-m)-wide rectangular steel frame which acts as the base for the 49-ft (15-m)-tall tubular steel A-frame masts. These provide the primary vertical support for the entire building. From the top of the masts a single steel tie on each side hangs diagonally to a joint from which four smaller steel ties branch out (much like an inverted tree) to support the roof span at each end and at two points near the center. The connections at the top of the masts and between the primary and secondary roof ties are articulated in the form of a doughnut-shaped steel plate drilled to receive the forked terminals of the ties.

Vertical ties to the foundation at the end of the roof span resist wind uplift; the function of these slender ties is emphasized by their separation from the wall cladding. This plane arrangement of masts is repeated nine times at 29.5-ft (9-m) intervals. To preserve the visual clarity of the system, longitudinal stability is achieved, not with cross-bracing, but with rigid connections between the beams supporting the services and the masts. As a result, the masts appear to behave independently, emphasizing the separate flexibility of each bay.

Darling Harbor Exhibition Center

This exhibition center structure (1986; Sydney, Australia; Philip Cox and Partners, architects; Ove Arup and Partners, structural engineers) is a series of five staggered bays the arrangement of which was determined by the location of adjacent elevated highway structures. Each bay is independently structured by four supporting masts forming the large exhibition spaces with a clear height of 44 ft (13.5 m) and a clear span of 302 ft (92 m) (Brookes and Grech, 1990) (Figures 3.6 through 3.9).

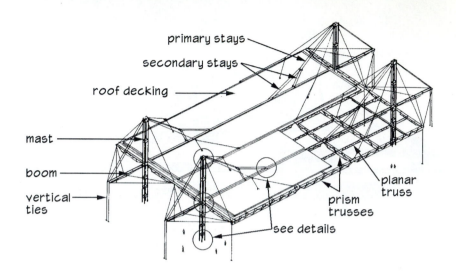

Figure 3.7: Darling Harbor Exhibition Center, structural axonometric drawing.

A typical structural bay consists of four masts (which provide the primary vertical support), each being a group of four tubular steel masts arranged in a square. Each mast was bolted at its base to the concrete slab. Diagonal rod stays from the top of the masts suspend the ends of primary space trusses (triangular in cross section) which each span 49 ft (15 m). These primary trusses are joined with a hinged connection to allow movement due to thermal expansion. Secondary space trusses span 86 ft (26.3 m) perpendicular to the main trusses and are slightly curved to allow for roof drainage. These then support plane truss purlins which, in turn, support the steel roof deck.

The masts, which occur at the sides of the building, have diagonal backstays from the top to counterbalance the tension thrust of the roof-supporting stays. The backstays connect to the outer end of space-trussed outrigger struts; these counterbalance the compression thrust of the roof plan against the side of the masts, minimizing bending in the mast. Finally, the outrigger struts are guyed to the ground by vertical rod ties.

Figure 3.6: Darling Harbor Exhibition Center, exterior.

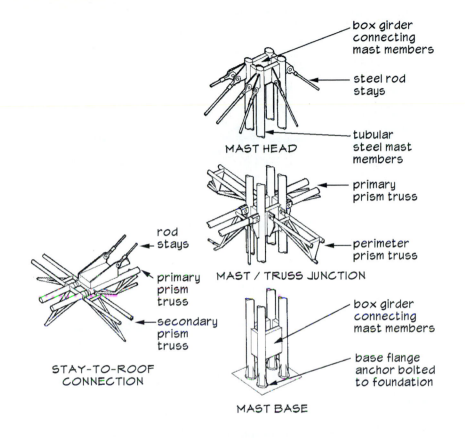

Figure 3.8: Darling Harbor Exhibition Center mast detail.

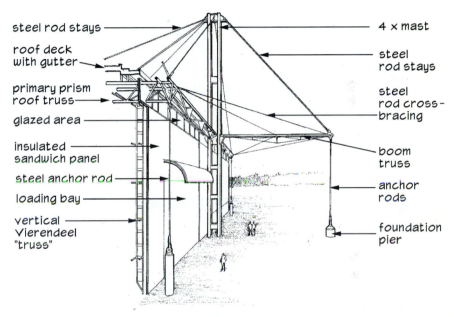

Figure 3.9: Darling Harbor Exhibition Center, section perspective.

Alamillo Bridge

This remarkable bridge (1992; Seville, Spain; Santiago Calatrava, structural engineer), designed in conjunction with Expo '92, is representative of the beauty and innovative structural design this Spanish architect-engineer has introduced, first into bridge structures and more recently into architecture. The roadway has a span of 656 ft (200 m) and is supported by diagonal parallel cable stays all suspended from one side of a 466-ft (142-m)-tall mast. Most large-span, cable-stayed structures have a symmetrical arrangement of stays hanging from a mast with a hinged base to eliminate bending. This design is unusual because the stay configuration is unilateral and the mast is cantilevered at the base. The thrust from the stays is counterbalanced by the weight of the concrete-filled steel mast which is inclined 58° in the opposite direction, eliminating the necessity for backstays (Figures 3.10 through 3.12).

The center spine of the bridge deck is a hexagonal steel box beam to which the stay cables are attached. The bridge deck (three-lanes wide on each side) cantilevers laterally from each side of this spine (Frampton, et al., 1993).

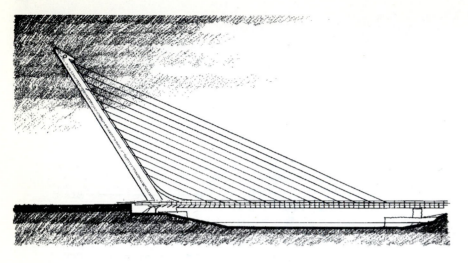

Figure 3.10: Alamillo bridge, elevation.

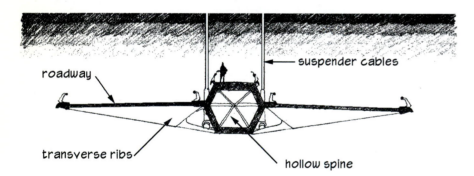

Figure 3.11: Alamillo bridge, section through roadway.

roadway

suspender cables

transverse ribs

hollow spine

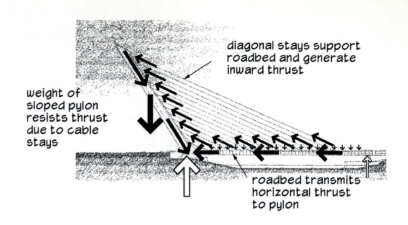

diagonal stays support roadbed and generate inward thrust

weight of sloped pylon resists thrust due to cable stays

roadbed transmits horizontal thrust to pylon

Figure 3.12: Alamillo bridge, load path diagram.

SUMMARY

1. A *cable* is a thin tensile member that is unable to resist compression. Wire rope, string, and thin rod behave as cables.

2. *Catenaries* are cables which are loaded continuously along their length.

3. A *strut* is a compression member.

4. *Cable-stayed* building structures support horizontal spans by means of diagonal cables suspended from a higher support.

TRUSSES

A *truss* is a triangulated assembly that distributes loads to supports through a combination of pin-connected members arranged in triangles so that ideally all are in either pure compression or tension (no bending or shear) and all thrust forces are resolved internally. In practice, some bending stresses may occur as a result of joint friction and distributed loads applied to members between the joints; these are usually minor compared with the axial forces and are typically ignored for analytical purposes.

The triangle is the basic geometric unit of the truss. The triangle is a unique form in that its shape cannot be changed without changing the length of its sides even when the joints are hinged. All other hinged polygons (the rectangle for example) are unstable.

If a cable is suspended between two anchor points, the horizontal thrust is resisted by supports (which are fixed; Figure 4.1a). If the configuration is changed so that one support is hinged and the other is a roller support, it becomes unstable. Both supports can resist vertical reactions and the hinged support can resist horizontal reactions, but the roller support will be pulled toward the center by the horizontal thrust of the cable (Figure 4.1b).

To resist this thrust (and make the system stable), a horizontal strut can be added. This assembly behaves as a simple truss due to its triangular geometry, pinned connections, and internal resistance of thrust (Figure 4.1c).

If the truss assembly shown in Figure 4.1c was inverted, compression and tension forces would reverse. Figure 4.2 shows the evolution of more complex trusses from this basic configuration. In each case, note that the basic geometric unit remains the triangle.

The top and bottom truss members are termed the *top* and *bottom chords*, respectively. All members between the top and bottom chords are *web* members. *Plane* trusses have all members in a single plane, while *space* trusses have members in a three-dimensional configuration. Both plane and space trusses span in one direction only. (This unidirectional spanning characteristic distinguishes trusses from *space frames* which span in two directions and are considered as a separate system in Chapter 5.)

TRUSS TYPES

The perimeter shapes of most plane trusses are triangular, rectangular, bowed (curved top or bottom side), or lenticular (curved top and bottom). These perimeter shapes are invariably broken up into smaller triangular units. All members (ties and struts) are discontinuous at the joints, and all joints behave as though pinned (see Figures 4.3 through 4.10).

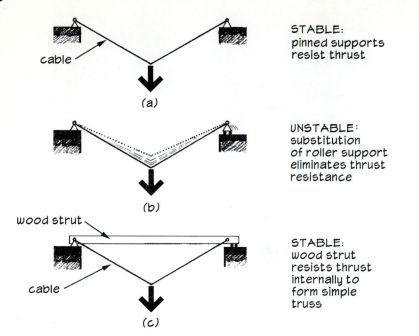

STABLE:
pinned supports
resist thrust

(a)

UNSTABLE:
substitution
of roller support
eliminates thrust
resistance

(b)

STABLE:
wood strut
resists thrust
internally to
form simple
truss

(c)

Figure 4.1: Center-loaded cable with (a) pinned supports (stable), (b) pinned roller supports (unstable as roller moves with nothing to resist horizontal thrust), and (c) pinned roller supports, with horizontal strut to resist thrust (stable).

TRUSS CASE STUDIES

Centre Georges Pompidou

> *We tend to put structure on the outside because we're looking for maximum flexibility of loft spaces. We believe that uses tend to have a much shorter life than buildings.*
> —*Richard Rogers (on the Centre Pompidou)*

Because of its role as the national center for the arts, the Centre Georges Pompidou (1977; Paris; Piano and Rogers, architects; Ove Arup and Partners, structural engineers) was controversial even be-

fore its completion due to its uncompromising machine aesthetic. This dramatically contrasts to the siting of the structure within an historic area. Intended by the architects to be a "nonbuilding," the building is a neutral backdrop against which various activities and exhibitions could take on their own character. The building is original in its particular type of construction and detail. The rectangular volume is 551 ft (168 m) long and designed to accommodate future expansion at the ends. Vertical ducts and other mechanical services are placed on the east street facade and treated as brightly colored ornamentation. Because the wall cladding is set behind the exposed

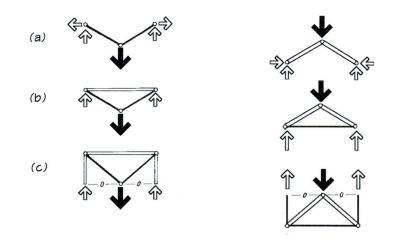

Figure 4.2: Trusses derived from ties and struts. All joints are hinged. Struts are in compression only and cables are in tension only. The trusses on the right are the inverted equivalents of those on the left; notice that the struts become ties and vice versa as the forces in members reverse. (a) Basic cable unit; (right) inverted equivalent is a basic three-hinged arch. (b) Simple truss formed by adding horizontal strut to withstand inward thrust; (right) equivalent truss formed by adding horizontal tie to withstand outward thrust. (c) The same configuration can be raised vertically by end posts (the new bottom chord members are not stressed directly but are needed to provide lateral stability) (continued).

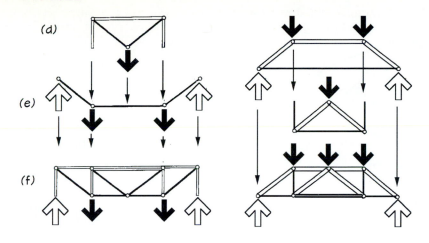

Figure 4.4: Metacarpal bone of a vulture's wing, stiffened in the manner of a Warren truss.

Figure 4.2 (continued): (d) A more complex truss can be created by imagining the entire assembly shown in (c) to be carried by another tie. Another horizontal strut is needed to resist the new tie thrusts. (e) The same process can be repeated to form even more complex trusses. Note that the forces in the web members (verticals and diagonals) increase away from the middle of the truss since the applied loads accumulate from the center to the ends. (f) On the other hand, the greatest forces in the upper and lower chords occur at midspan where the individual chords (and the forces they carry) combine into one.

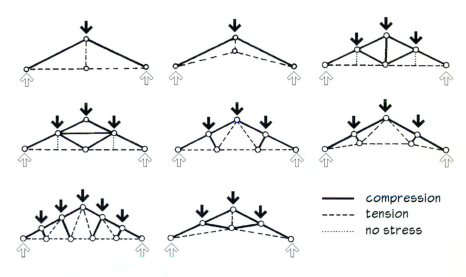

Figure 4.5: Tension and compression in triangular trusses.

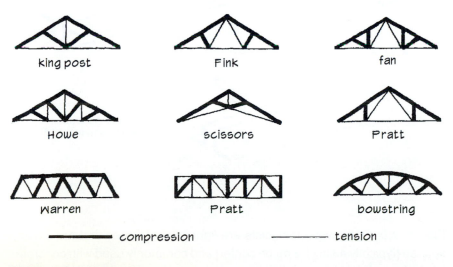

Figure 4.3: Truss types.

structure, circulation elements, and mechanical equipment, it has only a minor contribution to the building's final appearance (Orton, 1988; Sandaker and Eggen, 1992) (Figures 4.11 and 4.12).

It is the trussed structural frame that is emphasized on the other three sides which organizes the building visually, providing the facade texture, scale, and visual detail. Pinned connections are extensively used and visually emphasized in response to its vast scale, considerable loadings, and temperature movement. The building utilizes an entire structural vocabulary of members and connections—including massive cast steel overhanging beam brackets—that gives

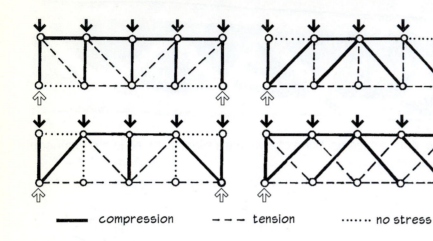

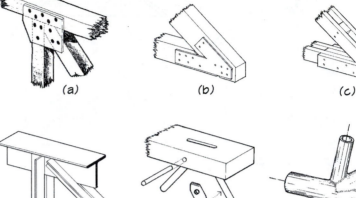

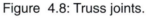

Figure 4.6: Tension and compression in rectangular trusses.

Figure 4.8: Truss joints.

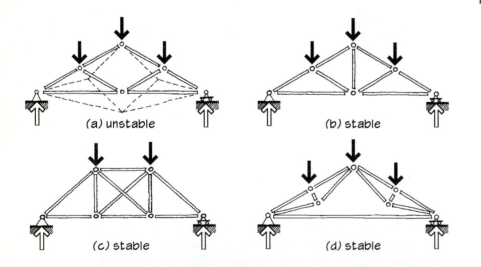

Figure 4.7: Stability in trusses: (a) unstable truss—the nontriangulated central area of the truss will greatly distort under an applied loading, leading to the collapse of the entire truss; (b) and (c) stable truss—the member pattern is fully triangulated; and (d) stable truss with a nontriangular member pattern—each of the two simple trusses behave as the top chord struts of a larger simple triangle.

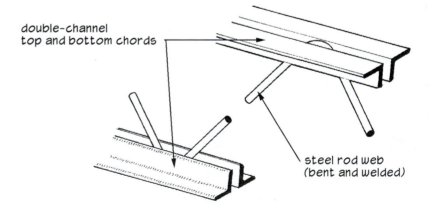

Figure 4.9: Open-web steel joists are lightweight trusses that are closely spaced [typically 48 in (1.2 m) on center] and commonly used with concrete-topped metal decking for roof or floor construction.

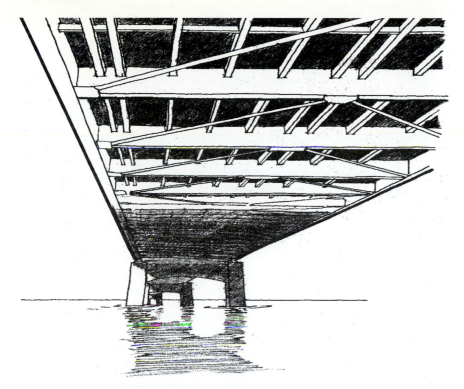

Figure 4.10: Truss as a horizontal wind bracing system in a bridge.

refinement and vitality to the structure and thus to the entire building.

The aboveground portion of the structure consists of 14 two-dimensional frames spanning 157 ft (48 m) with an additional 25-ft (7.6-m) zone on each side (for the movement of people on the west side and for housing mechanical services on the east side). These frames are six stories high with a typical floor height of 23 ft (7 m) and are joined by floor slabs and laterally braced by cross ties of steel rods.

The primary columns are 34-in (850-mm)-diameter thick-walled tubular steel filled with water for fire protection. These columns support cast steel brackets at a pinned connection. The outer end of the

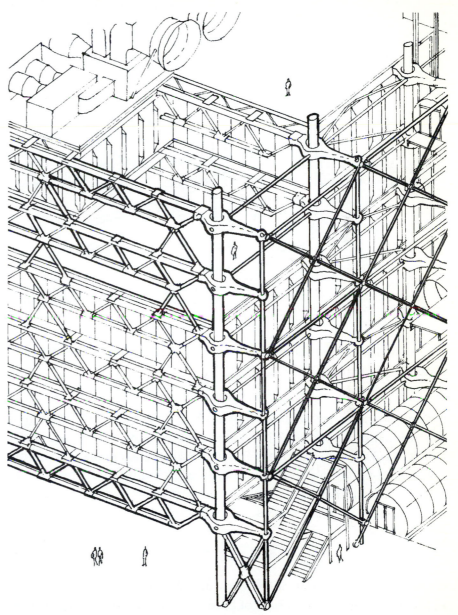

Figure 4.11: Centre Georges Pompidou, cutaway axonometric drawing from southwest.

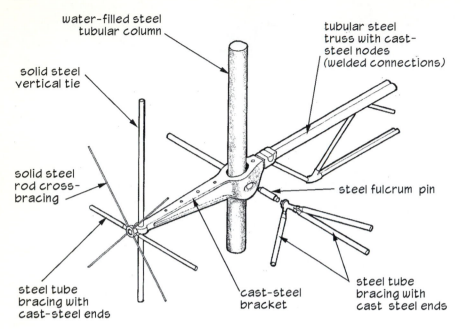

water-filled steel tubular column

tubular steel truss with cast-steel nodes (welded connections)

solid steel vertical tie

solid steel rod cross-bracing

steel fulcrum pin

steel tube bracing with cast-steel ends

cast-steel bracket

steel tube bracing with cast steel ends

Figure 4.12: Centre Georges Pompidou, detail view of column and surrounding members.

pivoted brackets are held down by an 8-in (200-mm) vertical tie-rod; the inner end supports the ends of the main truss. Each truss spans 147 ft (44.8 m), has a depth of 9.3 ft (2.82 m), and consists of double 16-in (419-mm) top chords, double 9-in (225-mm)-diameter bottom chords, alternative single tubular (compression) or solid (tension) round compression members, all joined by welding at the cast-steel joint members.

Gund Hall

Gund Hall (1972; Cambridge, MA; John Andrews, architect) houses the Harvard Graduate School of Design which includes programs in architecture, landscape architecture, and urban design. The design concept utilized a large single studio space to encourage greater communication between students of the various disciplines of the school. Andrews describes it as "a large factory-loft space with smaller spaces attached for specialized activities. To provide the necessary amount

of space, the studios are tiered like overlapping trays and covered by the single sloping plane of the roof" (Taylor and Andrews, 1982). The architect wanted the structure and mechanical systems of the roof exposed, partly as a teaching tool (Figures 4.13 through 4.15).

The nine planar trusses are spaced 24 ft (7.3 m) on center, have a span 134 ft (41 m), are 11 ft (3.4 m) deep, and have a 12-in (300-mm)-diameter tubular steel top chord and smaller tubular bottom chord and web members. The truss is supported on a pinned connection at the top and by a sliding joint at the bottom (to allow for thermal expansion and other incidental movement). Tubular members were selected to allow cleaner fabrication (compared with wide-flange members) and facilitate application of the 0.125-in (3-mm)-thick intumescent paint fireproofing. Lateral resistance is provided by cross ties at both end bays.

Figure 4.13: Gund Hall, exterior showing the west-facing stepped roof over the large studio space.

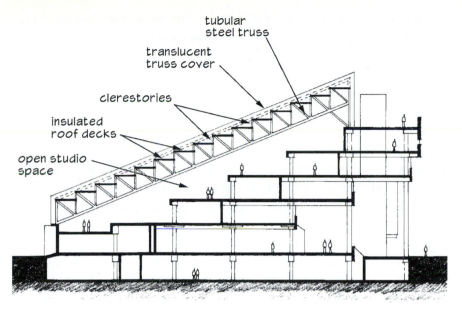

Figure 4.14: Gund Hall, section.

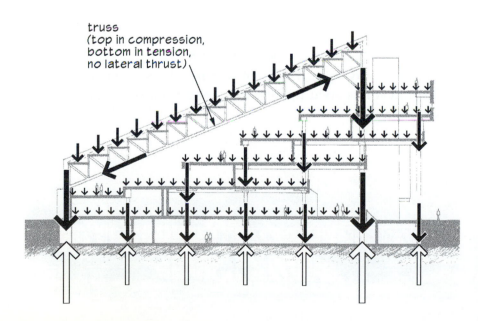

Figure 4.15: Gund Hall, load path diagram.

The top chord projects through the roof which is stepped to accommodate west-facing clerestory windows intended for daylighting. These top chords are enclosed by translucent glass-reinforced plastic; below the roof line the truss members are exposed. [The choice of the west-facing stepped roof by the architect was apparently based on formal, rather than technical, considerations. Solar heat gain through the unshaded glazing is excessive and the heating, ventilating, and air conditioning (HVAC) system as originally designed is reportedly inadequate to provide comfort.]

Sainsbury Center

The principal function of this building (1978; Norwich, England; Foster Associates, architects; A. Hunt Associates, structural engineers) is to house an art gallery, but one-third of the building is used for an art school, a multipurpose room, and a restaurant (Figures 4.16 through 4.18). The building form is a simple rectangular shape, with the two ends fully glazed. It is detailed with great care in order to preserve the simplicity of form and surface. Daylight is controlled and diffused by venetian blinds. The design is important for the extent to which it treats the building as an object of high quality constructed primarily of shop-fabricated components with great attention to the final appearance of the components—especially the space trusses and matching trussed columns (Orton, 1988).

Figure 4.16: Sainsbury Center, exterior from the south.

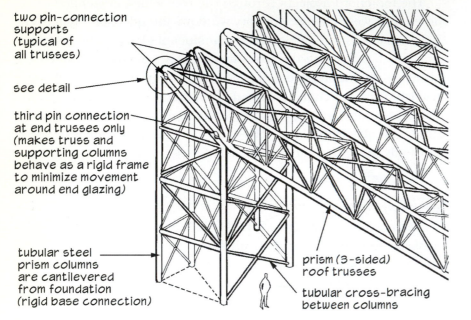

two pin-connection supports (typical of all trusses)

see detail

third pin connection at end trusses only (makes truss and supporting columns behave as a rigid frame to minimize movement around end glazing)

tubular steel prism columns are cantilevered from foundation (rigid base connection)

prism (3-sided) roof trusses

tubular cross-bracing between columns

Figure 4.17: Sainsbury Center, cutaway axonometric drawing of trusses.

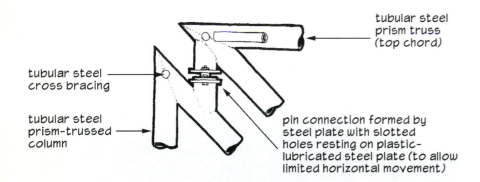

tubular steel prism truss (top chord)

tubular steel cross bracing

tubular steel prism-trussed column

pin connection formed by steel plate with slotted holes resting on plastic-lubricated steel plate (to allow limited horizontal movement)

Figure 4.18: Sainsbury Center, detail showing the connection between the top of a truss and a column; at the end trusses which surround glazing, an additional connection was added to increase rigidity around the glazing.

The structure consists of 37 trusses (triangular in cross section) arranged along the 430-ft (131.4-m) length of the building spanning 113 ft (34.4 m). Each truss is 8.2 ft (2.5 m) deep and 5.9 ft (1.8 m) wide at the top. Each is pin-connected at the top on each end to the trussed columns which cantilever from the ground. (The trusses at the glazed end walls require additional stiffness to prevent distortion of the glazing mullions, and pinned connections are added at the bottom of the truss, making the columns and the truss combine to behave as a rigid frame.) The cladding is a combination of solid insulated aluminum, grilled, or glazing panels fitting into a 5.9 ft × 3.9 ft (1.8 m × 1.2 m) modular grid of neoprene gaskets.

Crosby Kemper Arena

This multipurpose facility (1974; Kansas City, MO; C. F Murphy Associates, architects and structural engineers) locates its huge space trusses above the roof to minimize the interior volume and the apparent bulk on the exterior while emphasizing the structure (Figures 4.19 and 4.20). The three huge space trusses are triangular in section, span 324 ft (99 m) and combine with a space column to form a rigid frame with two pinned connections at each foundation. Each truss is 27 ft (8.23 m) deep and fabricated of round steel tubes: 4 ft (1.22 m)- diameter top chord, two 3-ft (914-mm)-diameter bottom chords, and 30-in (762-mm) web members. This space truss configuration has great rigidity and resistance to vertical, horizontal, and twisting forces.

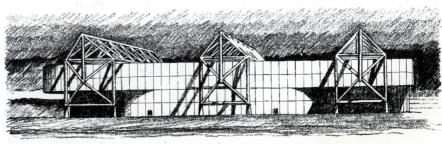

Figure 4.19: Crosby Kemper Arena, view from the west.

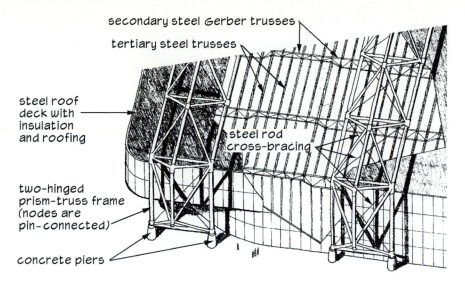

Figure 4.20: Crosby Kemper Arena, cutaway axonometric drawing.

Suspended below the primary space trusses are secondary plane steel trusses in a Gerber-beam configuration on 54-ft (16.5-m) centers at each space truss joint. Tertiary lightweight steel trusses on 9-ft (2.74-m) centers span between the secondary trusses. Metal roof decking spans between the tertiary trusses.

The joints of the primary truss are noteworthy because they allowed the very large members to be completely assembled at the site. In addition, they allow for movement due to thermal expansion without causing damage.

STADIUM CANOPIES

Because of the need to preserve a clear field of view, cantilevers are an attractive configuration for providing shelter from sun and rain for large stadiums. There is evidence that the ancient Romans incorporated *vela* (shade structures) on several arenas. Using the sailing ship technology of the times, retractable fabric panels were suspended from horizontal "booms" which were supported by rope stays from the top of vertical "masts" which rose from stone buttresses behind the seating (Figure 4.21).

Sydney Football Stadium

The Sydney Football Stadium (1988; Sydney, Australia; Philip Cox, architect; Ove Arup & Partners, structural engineers) was designed as a soccer and rugby facility with seating for 38,000 spectators with 65 percent under cover. The round stadium seating consists of lower-level stepped concrete slab-on-grade and an upper-level grandstand made of precast concrete planks spanning 27 ft (8.5 m) between sloped steel beams which rest on concrete columns (Brookes and Grech, 1992; Jahn, 1991) (Figures 4.22 through 4.25).

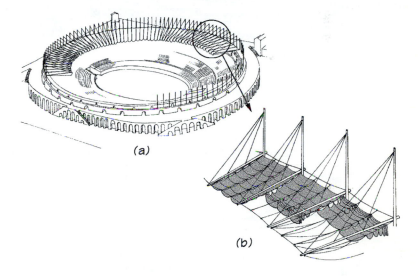

Figure 4.21: Roman amphitheater in Pompeii: (a) installation of *vela*, and (b) detail of retractable vela system.

The metal roof canopy utilizes steel space trusses to cantilever up to 96 ft (30 m). All the truss members are rigid and able to withstand tensile or compressive forces allowing the trusses to resist wind-induced uplift as well as gravity loads. The trusses transfer loads to a ring of concrete columns and walls that connect the raking beams of the grandstand. The structural system was analyzed by testing a 1:200-scale model. The stiffness of the members was deduced from computer modeling.

Figure 4.22: Sydney Football Stadium, exterior.

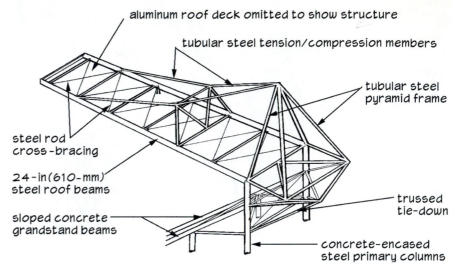

aluminum roof deck omitted to show structure

tubular steel tension/compression members

tubular steel pyramid frame

steel rod cross-bracing

24-in(610-mm) steel roof beams

sloped concrete grandstand beams

trussed tie-down

concrete-encased steel primary columns

Figure 4.24: Sydney Football Stadium, axonometric drawing showing canopy structural bay.

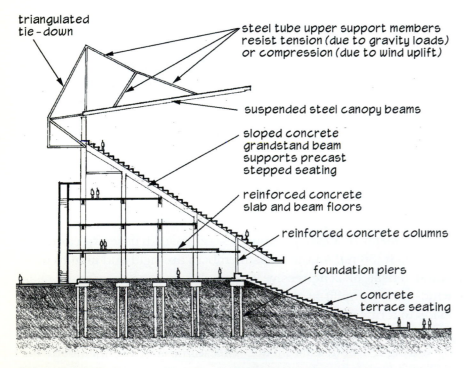

triangulated tie-down

steel tube upper support members resist tension (due to gravity loads) or compression (due to wind uplift)

suspended steel canopy beams

sloped concrete grandstand beam supports precast stepped seating

reinforced concrete slab and beam floors

reinforced concrete columns

foundation piers

concrete terrace seating

Figure 4.23: Sydney Football Stadium, section through stands.

SUMMARY

1. A *truss* is a triangulated assembly that distributes loads to supports through a combination of pin-connected members arranged in triangles so that ideally all are in either pure compression or tension (no bending or shear) and all thrust forces are resolved internally.

2. The top and bottom truss members are termed the *top* and *bottom chords*, respectively.

3. All members between the top and bottom chords of a truss are *web* members.

4. *Plane* trusses have all members in a single plane.

5. *Space* trusses have members in a three-dimensional configuration. The most common space truss is triangular in cross section.

5

SPACE FRAMES

I often see a building as a struggle between heaviness and lightness: one part is a solid mass joined to the ground, whereas the other soars upward.
—*Renzo Piano*

A *space frame* is a three-dimensional trussed system spanning in two directions where members are in tension or compression only. While the term *frame* correctly refers to structures with rigid connections, the term *space frame* as it is commonly used includes both pinned and rigid connections. Most space frames consist of identical, repetitive modules, with parallel upper and lower *layers* (which correspond to the chords of trusses).

While the geometry of space frames can be quite diverse (Pearce, 1978; Borrego, 1968), the half-octahedron (four-sided pyramid) and the tetrahedron (three-sided pyramid) are widely used polyhedral modules for buildings (Figure 5.1). While frequently used to cover large spaces with horizontal flat roofs, space frames are adaptable to a variety of configurations, including walls and sloped and curved roofs.

Space frame depths as low as 3 percent of span are possible; however, the most economical depth is about 5 per cent of the clear span or 11 percent of the cantilever span. The most economical module size is between 7 and 14 percent of the span, taking into account that the number of members (and labor costs) goes up dramatically as module size decreases (Gugliotta, 1980). The depth of a

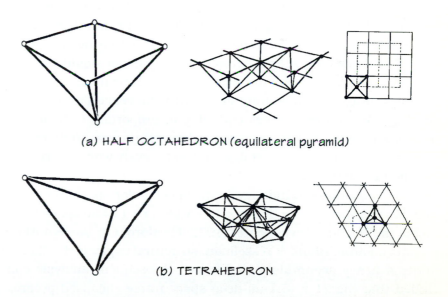

(a) HALF OCTAHEDRON (equilateral pyramid)

(b) TETRAHEDRON

Figure 5.1: Commonly used space frame geometric modules: (a) half octahedron (equilateral pyramid), and (b) tetrahedron. Of the two, the half-octahedron module is square in plan and more suitable for rectilinear buildings.

space frame is less than a comparable system of trusses (spanning the primary direction) and purlins (beams or smaller trusses spanning in the opposite direction) (Figure 5.2).

(a) SPACE FRAME   (b) TRUSS - PURLIN SYSTEM

Figure 5.2: Comparison of space frame and truss-purlin systems. (a) Space frames are three-dimensional and span in two (or more) directions. (b) In contrast, truss-purlin combinations are essentially two-dimensional and span in only one direction at a time.

Space frames are efficient and safe structures in which loads are supported in part by each chord and web member in proportion to the strength of each. The applied load will travel by the stiffest routes to the various supports, with most of the load detouring around the more flexible members. Space frame stability is not significantly affected by the removal of a few members, which results in rerouting of forces around the resulting gaps, with the remaining members sharing the additional forces equitably in proportion to their stiffness or strength. This inherent redundancy is the reason that space frames are comparatively stable and safe, even when overloaded (Gugliotta, 1980).

Even with this redundancy, some spectacular space frame failures have occurred. The 300 ft × 360 ft (90 m × 110 m) space frame roof of the Hartford Civic Center (1972; Hartford, CT; Vincent Kling, architect; Faroli, Blum, & Yesselman, structural engineers) collapsed under a heavy accumulation of snow. Subsequent analysis concluded that the 21 ft (6.4 m)-deep space frame collapsed progressively, beginning with buckling of the perimeter members which were not adequately cross-braced (Levy and Salvadori, 1992).

Historically, multilayer space frames evolved directly out of the plane trusses of the nineteenth century. In 1881, August Föppl published his treatise on space frames, which formed the basis for Gustave Eiffel's analysis for his Paris tower (although the Eiffel Tower actually consists of an assembly of plane trusses). Alexander Graham Bell is widely credited as the inventor of the space frame and was preoccupied with tetrahedral forms to obtain strength with a minimum of material weight as part of studies to develop structures suitable for flight. His early space frame structures included kites, a windbreak, and a tower (Schueller, 1996).

Two important developments in space frames occurred in the early 1940s. In 1942, Charles Attwood developed and patented the Unistrut system, consisting of stamped steel nodes (connectors) and members (Wilson, 1987). In 1943, the Mero system was invented and first manufactured by Dr. Ing. Max Mengeringhausen, consisting of tapered tubular steel members that screw into spherical steel nodes (Borrego, 1968). Notably, both systems continue to be manufactured today.

CONNECTIONS

Because of the three-dimensional arrangement of members in a space frame, the nodes that join these are inherently complex. For small spans, the node may be stamped out of steel plate and bolted to the ends of members. These members are typically rectangular in cross section facilitating the simple attachment of decking, skylights, glazing, and other components.

For larger spans, the Mero-type system with tubular members screwed into solid spherical nodes is more common. In addition to being capable of spans up to 650 ft (200 m), the solid spherical node allows tube diameters and wall thicknesses to be varied depending on the forces present in each member. Other companies (Unistrut, for example) now manufacture similar systems based on Mengeringhausen's original design.

Because of the complex geometry of space frame connections and the relatively large forces present there, steel and aluminum are the materials most commonly used. However, space frames have been constructed of wood (for example, the roof over the mall at Simon Frazier University), and plastic space frames are used for nonstructural interior applications (Figure 5.3).

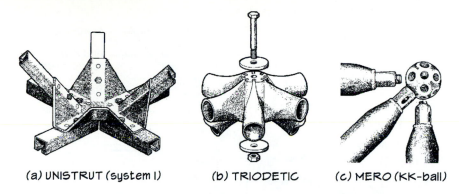

(a) UNISTRUT (system I) (b) TRIODETIC (c) MERO (KK-ball)

Figure 5.3: Space frame connections: (a) Unistrut system I is fabricated from pressed steel components which are bolted together and is suitable for short spans; (b) Triodetic system consists of an extruded aluminum node with serrated keyways and galvanized steel tubes with ends formed into a keyed edge that fits into the node keyway; and (c) Mero KK-ball node system consists of tubular members that screw into solid spherical nodes and is suitable for longer spans.

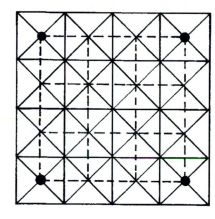 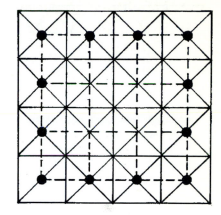

(a) CORNER SUPPORTS (b) PERIMETER SUPPORTS

Figure 5.4: Space frame supports: (a) corner, and (b) perimeter. Perimeter supports greatly reduce the maximum forces in members at the cost of additional columns and foundations.

SUPPORTS

If a space frame is supported by columns (cantilevered from the ground for lateral stability) at a series of points, the forces in the members surrounding the support are considerably greater than in other members. These greater forces can be accommodated by increasing the cross section of the members near the support.

Space frames need a minimum of three supports to be stable, although most have at least four supports. Generally, the more supports a space frame has, the more efficient the spanning structure will be. For example, the maximum member force in a square space frame with continuous perimeter supports is only 11 percent of that of a comparable design with only four corner supports. Furthermore, the range between maximum and minimum forces will be correspondingly less. And the narrower the range between the maximum and minimum member forces, the more standardized and uniform the members can be and, therefore, the more economical the member sizes and connections (Gugliotta, 1980). However, these savings may be offset by additional column and foundation costs (Figure 5.4).

For systems which utilize only identical members with a limited number of columns, stress at the supports may be reduced by distributing the support reactions over a larger number of members. This can be achieved by using treelike *lattice* columns to support the frame at several joints (Figure 5.5).

SPACE FRAME CASE STUDIES

Expo 70 Festival Plaza

At the center of Expo 70 in Osaka, Japan, was erected the world's largest space frame structure creating the roof over the center Festival Plaza (Kenzo Tange and Koji Kamiya, architects; Sadao Hirata, structural engineer). Designed to organize and harmonize the entire festival site, while providing an area for the development of the main theme—progress and harmony. The plaza connected with the theme exhibit space and was designed for various seating accommodations ranging from 1500 to 30,000 people depending on the type of event. Both the plaza and the exhibition spaces were unified by the great space frame roof that covered them (Tange, 1969) (Figures 5.6 and 5.7).

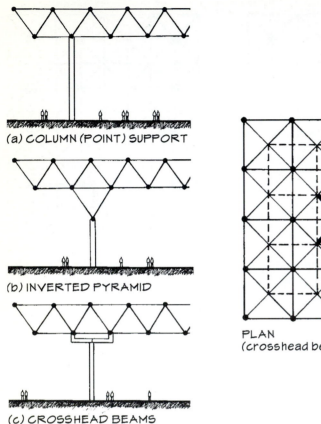

(a) COLUMN (POINT) SUPPORT

(b) INVERTED PYRAMID

(c) CROSSHEAD BEAMS

PLAN
(crosshead beam support)

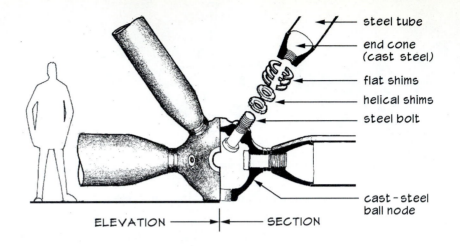

steel tube

end cone
(cast steel)

flat shims

helical shims

steel bolt

cast-steel
ball node

ELEVATION ————→|←—— SECTION

Figure 5.7: Expo 70 Festival Plaza: detail of space frame node connection.

Figure 5.5: Space frame supports: (a) column (point) support, (b) inverted pyramid support, and (c) crosshead beams. Point supports result in very large forces in members near the support. These forces may be either *reduced* by distributing them over a large area by using branched supports, or *accommodated* by increasing the size of members nearest the supports.

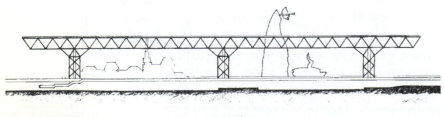

Figure 5.6: Expo 70 Festival Plaza, section.

The space frame itself consisted of half-octahedron (equilateral pyramid) modules 33.5 ft (10.2 m) square in plan and 29.3 ft (8.9 m) deep to cover an area 1082 ft × 394 ft (330 m × 120 m) (Kenzo Tange Associates, 1987). The Mero-type system used a spherical hollow steel node with tubular members with tapered ends bolted to the nodes. The entire roof was covered with a transparent, pillow-shaped, plastic inflated covering anchored to the top chord members around each module. The approximate dimensions of the components were 3.6-ft (1.1-m)-diameter spherical steel nodes, 2.2-ft (67-cm)-diameter upper and lower chord tubular steel members, and 1.4ft (46cm) diameter diagonal web tubular steel members. The structure was assembled on the ground and raised by pneumatic jacks 100 ft (30 m) into place. This entire assembly weighed 4700 tons (4260 metric tons) and was supported by six columns. It was disassembled at the end of the event.

In order to achieve this unprecedented scale, the engineers had to overcome difficulties that had restricted the size of space frames in the past: angular and dimensional accuracy, and the limits imposed by on-site construction. Since it is difficult to achieve accuracy during initial assembly, the resulting error accumulation as subsequent modules are added requires massive readjustments later.

This problem was solved by the provision of an access hole in the ball node to allow bolts to be inserted. This detail permitted small angular adjustments of the connecting members. In addition, special shimming washers between the ball node and the members permitted minor length adjustments to be made simply. The combination of these adjustments made it possible to limit assembly error to the point where large space frames, for the first time, became practical and economical (Editor, 1970).

Jacob K. Javits Convention Center

Five blocks long and even larger than Tange's Festival Plaza roof, the Javits Center (1980; New York; I.M. Pei & Partners, architects; Weidlinger Associates, structural engineers) stretches 1200 ft (315 m) along Manhattan's 11th and 12th Avenues and 600 ft (157 m) along 34th and 39th streets. In all, the building's floor area totals 1.6 million ft² (148,000 m²). The architects and client felt strongly that the public (which paid for the building) should have easy and festive access to it. The space given over to the public opens with a 270-ft (82 m)-square great hall, marked by a monumental entrance on 11th Avenue. It continues with a 360-ft (110-m)-long bridge overlooking the major exhibition hall and culminates at 12th Avenue with a restaurant that commands a view of the Hudson River (Editor, 1980) (Figures 5.8 through 5.10).

Because the exposition center is essentially what James Freed, partner in charge of design, calls "a warehouse," the designers could not rely on internal functions to modulate the long facade. The key to resolving the five-block facade lay in the space frame that supports the walls and roofs. Faceted chamfers mark the placement of columns on the upper exhibition floor at 90-ft (28-m) intervals. Sheathed in semireflective glass, the building appears opaque during the day, gaining an apparent lightness by mirroring the sky. At night, interior lighting makes the glass transparent, revealing the tracery of the space frame walls and roofs. Clear glass is used at the entrances and for the skylights, while matching opaque spandrel glass is used for the walls of the exhibition spaces.

The structure's 90-ft (27-m) bay spacing was derived as a multiple of the trade-show standard 30-ft (9-m) module determined by

Figure 5.8: Jacob K. Javits Convention Center, exterior.

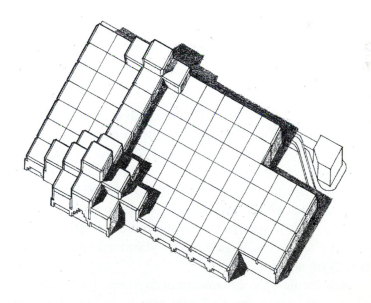

Figure 5.9: Javits Center, roof axonometric showing chamfered edges, bay grid, and expansion joint locations.

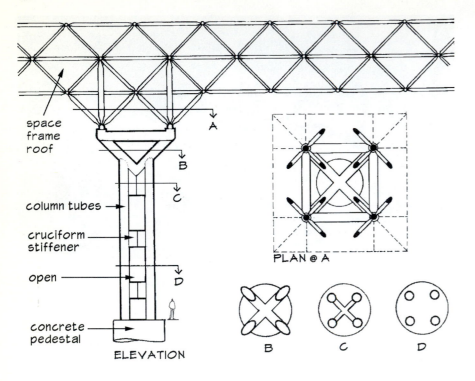

Figure 5.10: Javits Center, column details: (a) elevation, and (b through d) plan sections.

two 10-ft (3-m)-deep rows of booths separated by a 10-ft aisle. The quad columns supporting the space frame in the great hall and the main exhibition space are light and transparent. The space frame seems a natural outgrowth of these treelike columns. The columns consist of four 1.8-ft (55-cm)-diameter tubular steel columns in a 5-ft (1.5-m) cruciform which are connected by metal webs. The 10-ft (3-m)-square capital supports diagonals that diminish in size as they merge with the space frame above. The standard space frame module is 10 ft (3 m) square.

The space frame system was manufactured by PG Structures, Inc., and chosen, according to Freed, not based on the science of Buckminster Fuller nor the art of British high tech, but because it could be treated "as a flexible system that provided texture and trans-

parency." The use of this space frame construction is restricted to the building's primary structure, while the interior is divided by the concrete elements which are the hallmark of much of Pei's work (Editor, 1986).

The glass skin is chamfered at the vertical and horizontal edges and produces a "graphic description" of the structure behind it by following exactly its bends and folds. The curtain wall hangs 15 in (38 cm) outside the space frame. The 10-ft (3-m)-square glazing modules were subdivided into 5-ft (1.5-m) lights.

Addition to the Louvre Museum

While its size is modest compared with the two previous projects, the addition to the Louvre Museum (1989; Paris; I.M. Pei and Partners, architects) is one of the most famous—and controversial—examples of a space frame. While the addition consists of over 650,000 ft² (60,000 m²) of floor area—mostly underground—the main pyramid has received the most attention. "Its breathtaking clarity and elegant web-like support system — so daring, so *conspicuously* inconspicuous — make the structure a veritable emblem of the modernist ambition to dematerialize the wall and render the boundary between the inside and outside fluid. Its exquisite delicacy betokens the technological progress that has allowed the fulfillment of the architectural dreams of the teens and early '20s in the 1980s." (Kimball, 1989) (Figures 5.11 through 5.13).

The pyramid is 71 ft (21.6 m) high, 115 ft (35 m) on each side, with a slope of 51°. The space frame consists of tubular compression members (top chords and web struts) and tension cables (bottom chord). The depth of the frame tapers from 5.6 ft (1.7 m) at the center to nothing at the edges, resulting in a curvature in the bottom chord while the top chords are straight (and the glazing planar). In addition, cables are used for cross bracing between nodes to increase lateral stability. The space frame consists of 6000 tubular struts, ranging from 0.4 to 3.2 in (10 to 800 mm) in diameter, and over 21,000 nodes. The resulting connection details resemble sailboat mast rigging (Editor, 1988). The special water-clear insulating glass panes are diamond-shaped and weigh a total of 95 tons (86 metric tons).

Figure 5.11: Addition to the Louvre Museum, exterior.

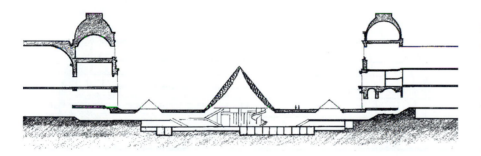

Figure 5.12: Addition to the Louvre Museum: site section through pyramid. Note the variation in the depth of the pyramid space frame.

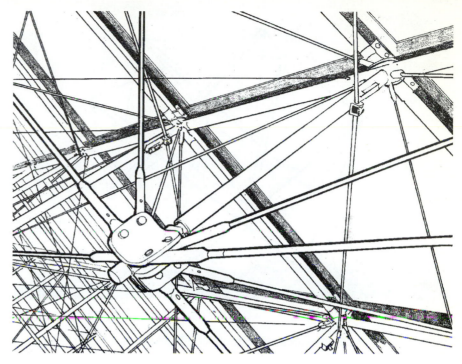

Figure 5.13: Addition to the Louvre Museum: pyramid space frame connection detail.

TENSEGRITIES

A *tensegrity* is a stable three-dimensional space frame assembly of cables and struts where the cables are continuous but the struts are discontinuous and do not touch one another. Invented by sculptor Kenneth Snelson in 1948 (Fox, 1981) and developed and pat-ented by Buckminster Fuller (Marks, 1960), these structures gain their stability by supporting compression struts between opposing sets of cables. Snelson, a student colleague of Fuller's, has completed several pieces based on tensegrity geometry (Figures 5.14 through 5.19).

In 1961, Fuller patented an *aspension* roof structure that used tensegrities to create a lightweight structure that was resistant to wind-induced flutter. Until recently, however, no practical building applications of Snelson's and Fuller's tensegrity theory had been built. This theory was translated into practice when David Geiger reduced the redundancies inherent in Fuller's triangulated configuration. In Geiger's approach, continuous tension cables and discontinuous compression struts are arranged radially, simplifying the flow of forces and making the cable dome statically determinate.

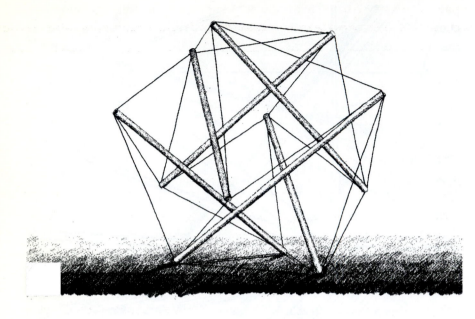

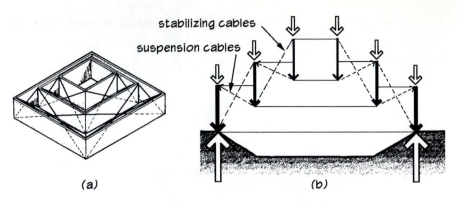

Figure 5.16: Square version of Buckminster Fuller's patented aspension roof structure: (a) isometric, and (b) load path diagram.

Figure 5.14: Tensegrity icosahedron, built by Buckminster Fuller, 1949.

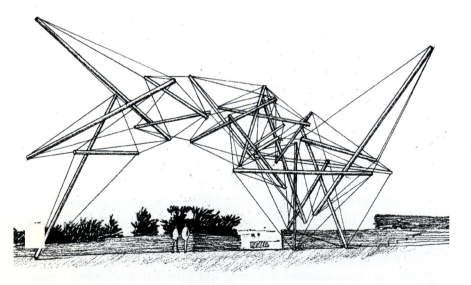

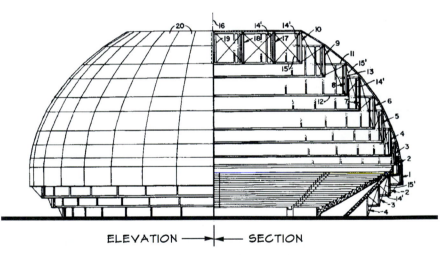

Figure 5.17: Patent drawing of Fuller's aspension dome.

Figure 5.15: *Free Ride Home* (1974, aluminum and stainless steel) is one of many Kenneth Snelson tensegrity sculptures.

With this configuration, shallow curves are feasible, with the resultant benefits of lower wind uplift, less drifting snow (and thus lower snow loads), and reduced surface area (which reduces fabric costs) (Rastorfer, 1988).

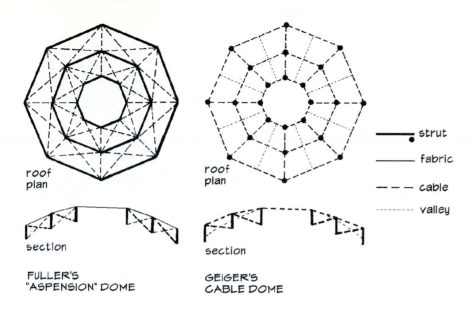

roof plan

roof plan

— strut
— fabric
--- cable
...... valley

section

section

FULLER'S "ASPENSION" DOME

GEIGER'S CABLE DOME

Figure 5.18: Tensegrity domes compared.

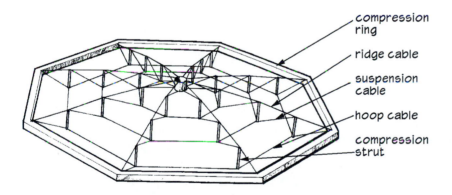

compression ring

ridge cable

suspension cable

hoop cable

compression strut

Figure 5.19: Perspective of a simplified eight-segment version of Geiger's cable dome; this version has three tension hoops.

TENSEGRITY CASE STUDIES

Olympic Gymnastics Stadium

Geiger designed two tensegrity domes for the 1988 Seoul Olympics. The larger of the two, the gymnastics stadium, was developed as

part of Geiger's search for a stadium roof enclosure that would be as economical as an air-supported structure while accommodating an insulated fabric membrane (Rastorfer, 1988).

Geiger's patented system achieved a span of 383 ft (120 m) by means of continuous tension cables and discontinuous compression struts. Loads are transferred from a center tension ring through a series of radial ridge cables, tension hoops, and intermediate diagonals until they are transferred in a perimeter compression ring. The gymnastics facility dome required three circular tension cables (hoops) set 47.5 ft (14.5 m) apart. A similar smaller dome for the fencing stadium is a two-hoop configuration. One of the system's advantages is that, as the span is increased, the unit weight [2 lb/ft² (9.8 kg/m²)] remains virtually constant and the cost per unit area changes very little (Figure 5.20).

The membrane that covers the dome consists of four layers: (1) a high-strength, silicone-coated fiberglass fabric; (2) an 8-in (200-mm)-thick layer of fiberglass insulation; (3) a 6-in (160-mm) airspace with a Mylar vapor barrier below and a 2ft (60cm) airspace below that; and (4) an open-weave fiberglass fabric acoustical liner. The overall light transmittance is 6 percent allowing daylighting to meet most daytime lighting needs.

Florida Suncoast Dome

The largest of Geiger's patented cable domes (1989; St. Petersburg, FL; HOK Sports Facilities Group, architects; Geiger Gossen Hamilton Liao, structural engineers), this multipurpose facility can be configured as a baseball stadium (43,000 seats), an exhibition facility [150,000 ft² (13,940 m²) of column-free exhibit space], a basketball or tennis arena (seating 20,000), or a concert hall (seating 50,000). The 690-ft (210-m)-diameter dome is a four-hoop configuration, tilted 6° to minimize the air-conditioned volume while providing the necessary clearance for baseball (Robison, 1989; Rosenbaum, 1989) (Figures 5.21 and 5.22).

Georgia Dome

The largest cable dome structure built to date (1992; Atlanta, GA; Heery International, Rosser Fabrap International, Thompson

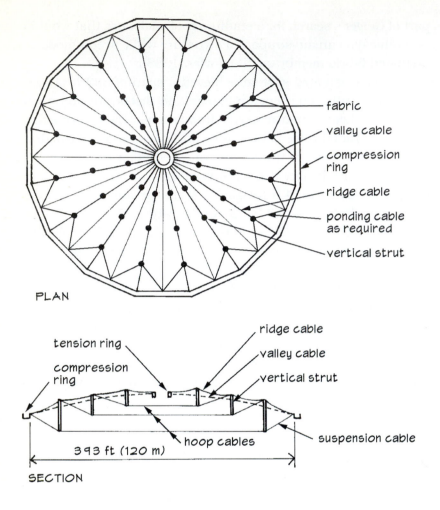

PLAN

fabric

valley cable

compression ring

ridge cable

ponding cable as required

vertical strut

tension ring

compression ring

ridge cable

valley cable

vertical strut

hoop cables

suspension cable

393 ft (120 m)

SECTION

Figure 5.20: Seoul Olympic Gymnastics Stadium cable roof plan and section diagrams.

Ventulett Stainback, architects; Weidlinger Associates, dome structural engineers), this immense structure differs from Geiger's designs in its return to Buckminster Fuller's original triangulated geometry. This permitted a non-circular configuration better suited for a football stadium, while providing greater redundancy and greater adaptability to nonsymmetrical loading conditions. Despite these

Figure 5.21: Florida Suncoast Dome, exterior.

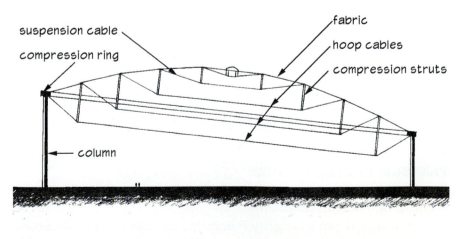

suspension cable

compression ring

fabric

hoop cables

compression struts

column

Figure 5.22: Florida Suncoast Dome, section.

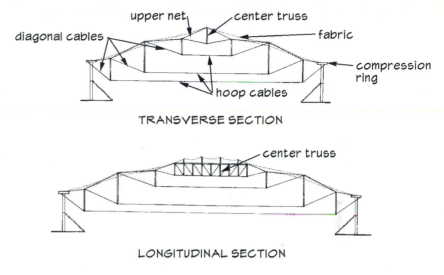

Figure 5.25: Georgia Dome, sections.

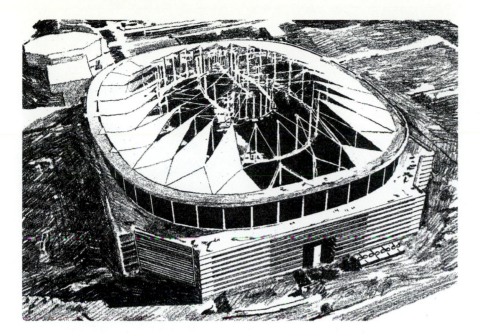

Figure 5.23: Georgia Dome under construction, exterior.

advantages, the triangulated design is more complex and results in some nodes having as many as six cables converging to the end of one strut (Levy, 1991; Levy, et al., 1994) (Figures 5.23 through 5.25).

The *hypar-tensegrity* dome (so named because it combines hyperbolic paraboloid fabric surfaces with tensegrity), in plan, consists of two semicircular segment ends separated in the center by butterfly-shaped sections. The "spokes" of the two semicircular segments are tied together by a plane truss that is 184 ft (56 m) long. The oval compression ring was designed to withstand both compression and bending forces due to the noncircular configuration. The 400,000-ft^2 (37,175-m^2) free-span roof spans 748 ft (228 m) across the shortest axis.

SUMMARY

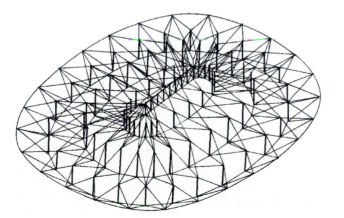

Figure 5.24: Georgia Dome, isometric drawing of cable and strut configuration.

1. A *space frame* is a three-dimensional trussed system spanning in two directions where members are in tension or compression only.

2. Space frames consist of identical, repetitive modules, with parallel upper and lower *layers* (which correspond to the chords of trusses).

3. The *half-octahedron* (four-sided pyramid) and the *tetrahedron* (three-sided pyramid) are widely used polyhedral modules for building space frames.

4. In a space frame, the applied load will travel by the stiffest routes to the various supports, with most of the load detouring around the more flexible members.

5. Space frame stability is not significantly affected by the removal of a few members, which results in rerouting of forces around the resulting gaps, with the remaining members sharing the additional forces equitably in proportion to their stiffness or strength.

6. A *tensegrity* is a stable three-dimensional space frame assembly of cables and struts where the cables are continuous but the struts are discontinuous and do not touch one another.

7. A *cable dome* is a tensegrity roof consisting of continuous tension cables and discontinuous compression struts arranged radially.

GEODESIC DOMES

The sophistication of a building varies inversely as its weight.
—*Buckminster Fuller*

A *geodesic dome* is a spherical space frame which distributes loads to supports through a system of linear members arranged in a spherical dome where all members are in direct stress (tension or compression). Typically, a thin infill material (of metal or plastic) is used to make the dome into a shelter.

The geometry of geodesic domes is based on the five platonic polyhedrons: *tetrahedron, cube, octahedron, dodecahedron,* and *icosahedron* (Figure 6.1). It is these five (and only these) in which all faces are regular polygons, all edges are equal, and the same number of faces meet at every *vertex* (point). In each case, the vertices touch a circumscribed sphere.

GEOMETRY

Geodesic domes are developed by subdividing one or more of the platonic solids. Because the octahedron and the icosahedron consist of triangles, they are inherently more stable forms and are the basis for most geodesic domes used for buildings. The greater the *frequency* of the divisions, the smoother the resulting dome (Figure 6.2). The familiar soccer ball is a three-frequency subdivision of the icosahedron (Figures 6.3 and 6.4). For further discussion of the geometry of geodesic domes, see Pearce, 1978 (also Kappraff, 1991; Van Loon, 1994). The geometry of geodesic domes is remarkably similar to that of microscopic radiolarian skeletons (Figure 6.5).

True geodesic domes were preceded by the development of braced, ribbed domes. The Schwedler dome (invented by a German engineer of that name in the late nineteenth century) consists of hoops and meridinal members with diagonal struts added for stability. The Zeiss-Dywidag dome system was first built in 1922 to test a planetarium projector at the Zeiss optical works; it consisted of a trian-

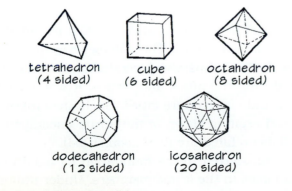

tetrahedron
(4 sided)

cube
(6 sided)

octahedron
(8 sided)

dodecahedron
(12 sided)

icosahedron
(20 sided)

Figure 6.1: The five platonic solids.

gulated framework of steel reinforcing rods onto which a thin shell of concrete was formed (Figure 6.6).

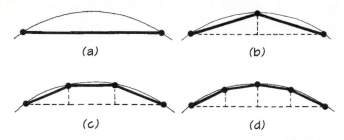

Figure 6.2: Subdivision of a geometric shape. The roundness of a platonic solid can be improved by dividing the edges into shorter lengths and raising more points to the surface of the enclosing sphere. Sections through part of a sphere showing (a) original face of platonic solid, with (b) two-frequency, (c) three-frequency, and (d) four-frequency subdivisions.

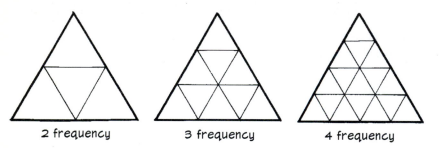

Figure 6.3: Subdivision of a triangular geodesic face.

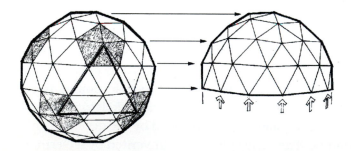

Figure 6.4: The soccer ball is a three-frequency subdivision of the icosahedron that results in regular pentagons surrounded by regular hexagons having the same *chord* (edge) lengths. This geodesic geometry is typical of that used for building domes.

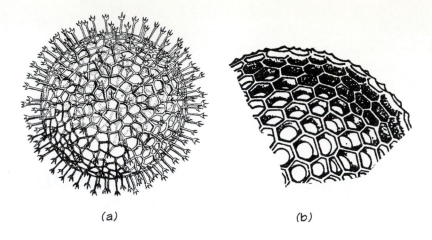

Figure 6.5: Geodesic geometry can be found in radiolarian skeletons: (a) *Aulastrum triceros,* and (b) portion of *Cenosphaera*.

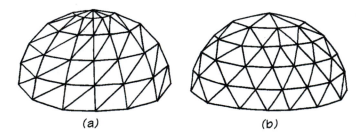

Figure 6.6: Braced, ribbed domes that preceded the development of the geodesic dome: (a) Schwedler dome, circa 1890, and (b) Zeiss-Dywidag dome, 1922.

Buckminster Fuller invented and, in 1954, patented the geodesic dome as it is known today. These domes can theoretically be of enormous size. In the enthusiasm generated by the evangelistic teaching of Fuller during the fifties and sixties, it was envisioned that giant domes could cover entire cities. Such structures seemed to offer a new and exciting vision of the future encompassing urban design as well as architecture (Van Loon, 1994).

Loads are transferred to the foundation by axial (tension and compression) forces in the frame members. Under uniform loading in a hemisphere dome, all upper members (those above approximately 45°) will be in compression; lower near-horizontal members will be in tension, while near-vertical members will be in compression. The shape of domes determines the direction of thrust reactions at the foundation. Hemisphere domes are nearly vertical at the base, have a near-horizontal base line, and generate a small amount of outward thrust. Quarter-sphere domes (approximately half the height of a hemisphere) provide five points of support and generate considerable outward thrust that must be resisted by buttresses or a tension ring. Three-quarter–sphere domes also provide five points of support but develop inward thrust (Corkill, et al., 1993) (Figure 6.7).

Concentrated loads are resisted by the relative truss depth of two adjacent chords. Where the frequency is low and chord lengths are great, the truss depth (and resistance to concentrated loads) is great. As the frequency is increased, the truss depth decreases along with resistance to concentrated loads. This problem of resistance to concentrated loads on large domes may be solved by creating a double layer to add truss depth, effectively wrapping a space frame which follows the geodesic divisions over the dome (Figure 6.8). Single-layer domes (with no surface depth) are limited to spans of approximately 100 ft (30 m). Domes greater than this employ a double-layer, space frame configuration (Figure 6.9).

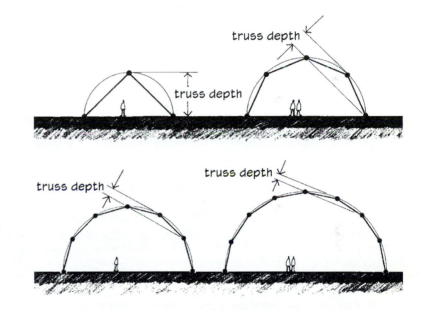

Figure 6.8: Resistance to concentrated loads depends on truss depth. For single-layer domes, as frequency increases, truss depth decreases.

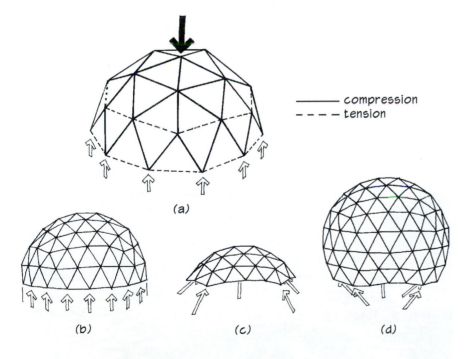

Figure 6.7: Load distribution in geodesic domes: (a) tension and compression stresses, (b) support reactions in hemisphere, (c) quarter-sphere, and (d) three-quarter–sphere domes.

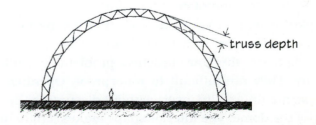

Figure 6.9: Truss depth in larger domes can be increased by adding a second layer to create a space frame.

In the late 1950s, Kaiser Aluminum, Inc., began manufacturing geodesic domes under Fuller's patents. Fabricated as diamond-shaped panels with stiffened edges and a cross strut, these modules combined the skin with the geodesic frame. The standard dome was less than a hemisphere (resting on five points), was 145 ft (44 m) in diameter, and consisted of 575 panels in 10 different sizes. The first was erected in Honolulu in 20 hours (588 worker hours) using a center mast for temporary support so that assembly, beginning at the top, could continue at ground level as the dome was gradually lifted to its full height to be permanently supported on a previously constructed foundation. Within a few months, three other domes of the same design were erected (Editor, 1958a) (Figure 6.10). But the commercial market envisioned by Fuller and Kaiser never developed and production ceased soon after.

Figure 6.10: Kaiser dome used as a convention center in Virginia Beach, VA.

In the late 1960s, the structural efficiency of geodesic domes captured the imagination of counterculture enthusiasts, and there was an explosion of do-it-yourself dome building, particularly in the United States. However, as attractive and structurally efficient as geodesic domes are, there are practical problems in building them satisfactorily. They are difficult to waterproof. Openings for doors and windows are difficult to insert without disrupting the structural continuity of the dome. The interior shape makes it difficult to adapt standard building components and furnishings. While this may be overcome in large structures, it is more difficult in small residences

where the disadvantages tend to outweigh the structural advantages (Van Loon, 1994).

GEODESIC CASE STUDIES

Missouri Botanical Gardens Climaton

The Climaton (1961, St. Louis, MO; Murphy and Mackey, architects; Synergetics, Inc., structural engineers) is a quarter-sphere greenhouse spanning 175 ft (53 m) and housing the plant collection of the Missouri Botanical Gardens. The structure is a double-layer space frame consisting of a hexagonal pattern of aluminum tubes stabilized by steel cables in a triangular arrangement. The dome is supported at five points on concrete buttresses and rises to 70 ft (21 m) at the center. The original clear acrylic glazing was suspended below the dome frame in a nonstructural triangular pattern of aluminum mullions (Editor, 1961c). The 3,625 acrylic panels deteriorated with age and were replaced with a freestanding glass enclosure consisting of larger hexagonal glass panels matching the pattern of the structural frame (Freeman, 1989) (Figures 6.11 through 6.13).

Figure 6.11: Missouri Botanical Gardens Climaton, exterior.

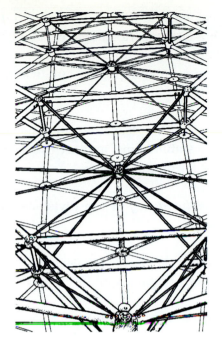

Figure 6.12: Missouri Botanical Gardens Climaton, exterior detail of original typical hexagonal panel.

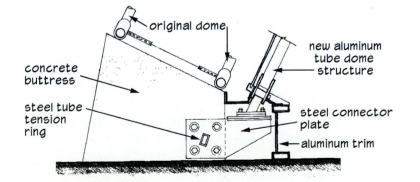

Figure 6.13: Missouri Botanical Gardens Climaton, section detail showing new glazing and old structure at support.

United States Pavilion, Expo 67

This pavilion (1967; Montreal; B. Fuller and S. Sadao, dome architects; Simpson, Gumpertz, and Heger, structural engineers) was designed to fill visitors with awe at United States technical virtuosity. The three-quarter sphere was Fuller's largest dome and housed a freestanding interior exhibit (Cambridge Seven Associates, architects) consisting of a series of platforms on different levels connected by escalators and bridges and containing exhibits of American arts, sciences, and technology (Editor, 1966; 1967) (Figure 6.14).

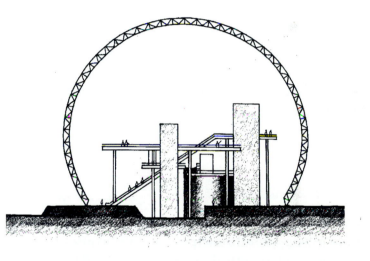

Figure 6.14: United States Pavilion, Expo 67, section.

The double-layer dome structure consisted of three systems: the outer layer which utilized a triangular arrangement of members; the inner layer which used a hexagonal arrangement; and web members which connected the inner and outer layers. The resulting dome was 250 ft (76 m) in diameter and 200 ft (60.8 m) tall. Its enclosed volume was 6.7 million cubic feet (190,000 m³), approximately the same as the Seagram's Building in New York. The members were tubular steel connected with star-shaped steel nodes. The covering skin was made of hexagon-base transparent acrylic domes attached to the inner layer and projecting toward the outer layer.

To control the inevitable solar heat gain, each hexagonal dome was fitted with six triangular metallized plastic roller shades around its perimeter. A photocell-activated motor pulled the shades to the center when sun protection was required. Each motor controlled 18 triangular shades covering three adjacent hexagons. The shading configuration was dynamic, changing in response to the movement of the sun across the sky.

Whatever the sophistication of the structural frame and sun control system, the fire resistance of the structure's skin is open to question; a major fire in 1977 reduced it to a skeleton. The surviving structural frame was renovated in 1994 into an interpretative center with a theme emphasizing water and the adjacent St. Lawrence River. The damaged glazing was removed leaving the geodesic skeleton as a vestige of the original exposition. The interior was replaced with a freestanding building (Blouin Faucher Aubertin Brodeur Gauther, architects) housing exhibitions, offices, a restaurant, and other facilities within the exposed frame (Ledger, 1994).

SUMMARY

1. A *geodesic dome* is a spherical space frame which distributes loads to supports through an arrangement of linear members arranged in a spherical dome where all members are in direct stress (tension or compression).

2. The geometry of geodesic domes is based on the five platonic polyhedrons: *tetrahedron, cube, octahedron, dodecahedron,* and *icosahedron.*

3. These platonic polyhedrons share the following characteristics: all faces are regular polygons, all edges are equal, and the same number of faces meet at every *vertex* (point). In each case, the vertices touch a circumscribed sphere.

4. Geodesic domes are developed by subdividing one or more of the platonic solids.

5. The octahedron and the icosahedron consist of triangles, are inherently more stable forms, and are the basis for most geodesic domes used for buildings.

6. The greater the *frequency* of the divisions, the smoother the resulting dome.

7. In a geodesic dome, loads are transferred to the foundation by axial (tension and compression) forces in the frame members.

8. Under uniform loading in a hemisphere geodesic dome, all upper members (those above approximately 45°) will be in compression; lower near-horizontal members will be in tension, while near-vertical members will be in compression.

9. Hemisphere domes are nearly vertical at the base, have a near-horizontal baseline, and generate a small amount of outward thrust.

10. Quarter-sphere domes (approximately half the height of a hemisphere) provide five points of support and generate considerable outward thrust that must be resisted by buttresses or a tension ring.

11. Three-quarter–sphere domes also provide five points of support but develop inward thrust which must be resisted by the floor slab or a compression ring.

Part III

FRAMED SYSTEMS

Framed systems transfer loads to the ground by horizontal members (such as *beams* and *slabs*) and vertical members (such as *columns* and *bearing walls*) which are resistant to bending and buckling as a result of their internal moment reactions.

7

COLUMNS AND WALLS

Vertical structural members include *columns* and *bearing walls*.

COLUMNS

The column is a certain strengthened part of a wall, carried up perpendicularly from the foundation to the top . . . a row of columns is indeed nothing but a wall, open and discontinued in several places.

— Alberti

If the column were not a monument in itself, humanity would have to erect a special one in its honor.

—Eduardo Torroja

A *column* is a linear (typically vertical) structural member that is loaded with compressive forces along its axis. Columns behave differently depending on their relative length.

COLUMN LENGTH

A *short* column, such as a single brick subjected to excessive compressive loading, fails by *crushing*. A *long* column subjected to increasing compressive loading will suddenly *buckle* (bend sideways). This critical compressive load value is the *buckling load* of the member and is the limiting load for compression members where the material is strong enough in compression (steel, for example) to require only a small cross-sectional area leading to a slender member (Figure 7.1).

This buckling action will occur even if the column is carefully loaded exactly along its center axis and the member is perfectly homogenous. And once the column buckles out of vertical alignment and begins to bend at the center, the misalignment between the ends and the center results in an increasing lever arm which further accelerates the bending. For this reason, once a column begins to buckle, it fails suddenly and without warning (unlike many other structural failures which are more gradual).

The buckling load of a column depends on its length, cross-sectional area and shape, and the type of connections at the ends. The lengthening of a column reduces its buckling load. For the same cross section, doubling the length of a column will reduce the buck-

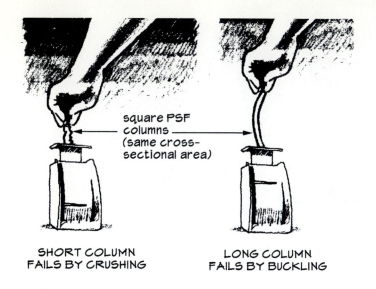

Figure 7.1: Model demonstration of crushing and buckling failure in columns.

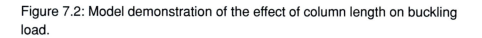

Figure 7.2: Model demonstration of the effect of column length on buckling load.

ling load to 25 percent. In other words, the buckling load varies inversely as the square of the length of the column. The effective length of the column can be halved by providing lateral support at midheight (Figure 7.2).

The mast on a sailboat behaves like a column; spreaders are struts often added to brace the mast against the shrouds (cables that support the top of the mast). While transferring the side load of the mast (caused by the tendency to buckle) to the shrouds adds to the compressive load on the top of the mast, this is more than offset by halving the column length which increases the buckling load by 400 percent (Figure 7.3).

COLUMN SHAPE

Columns will buckle along the path of least resistance. If the cross section is not equally wide in both directions, buckling will occur in the axis of the most slender dimension. For the same amount of material, columns with most of the material positioned as far from the center of the cross section as possible have higher buckling loads (Figure 7.4). *Moment of inertia* is the measure of the distribution of

Figure 7.3: Use of spreaders to provide lateral support to the midheight of a sailboat mast.

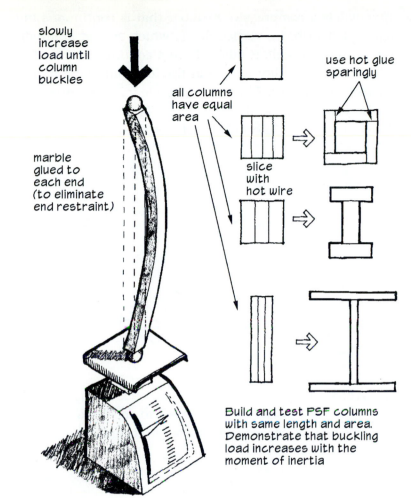

slowly
increase
load until
column
buckles

marble
glued to
each end
(to eliminate
end restraint)

all columns
have equal
area

use hot glue
sparingly

slice
with
hot wire

Build and test PSF columns
with same length and area.
Demonstrate that buckling
load increases with the
moment of inertia

Figure 7.4: Model demonstration of the effect of column shape on buckling load.

material around the center of an object. The moment of inertia is lowest when all the material is concentrated at the center (a solid round rod, for example). It is highest when the material is distributed furthest from the center (a hollow tube, for example). Buckling load is directly proportional to the moment of inertia (Figure 7.5).

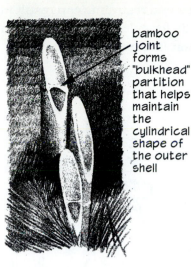

bamboo
joint
forms
"bulkhead"
partition
that helps
maintain
the
cylindrical
shape of
the outer
shell

Figure 7.5: The geometry of bamboo makes it an efficient shape for a column. The round cylindrical shape distributes the material away from the center resulting in a large moment of inertia. This shape is preserved by the solid partitions that occur naturally at the joints, preventing the cylinder from flattening and buckling.

END RESTRAINTS

The amount of restraint on the lateral movement and rotation of the ends of a slender column has a considerable effect on its buckling load. A column that is *hinged* (free to rotate but with lateral translation prevented) at each end will buckle in a smooth continuous curve. A column that is *fixed* at the base (rotation and lateral translation are both prevented) and *free* (free to rotate and translate) at the top will behave like the top half of a hinged column and will have an effective length twice the actual length; its buckling load will be 25 percent that of the hinged column (remember that buckling load is proportional to the inverse of the square of the effective length). Fixing one end and pinning the other has the effect of reducing the effective length to about 70 percent of a hinged column, increasing its buckling load to 200 percent. Fixing both ends further reduces the effective length (to half) and increases the buckling load to 400 percent. Thus various end restraints can result in an eight-fold variation in buckling loads for columns of the same actual length, material, and cross section (Figure 7.6).

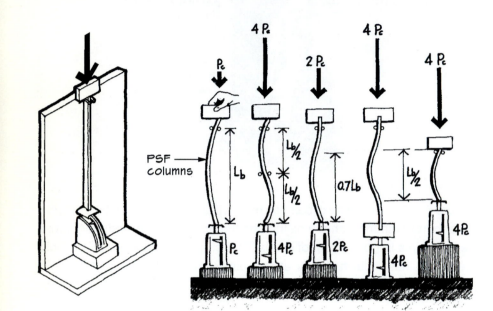

Figure 7.6: Model demonstration of the effect of end restraints on column buckling load.

BEARING WALLS

There is Jackson, standing like a stone wall!
     —Bernard Elliott Bee
     (of General T. J. Jackson
     at the Battle of Bull Run)

Before I built a wall I'd ask to know what I was walling in or out.

     —Robert Frost

A *bearing wall* is a compressive member that is continuous in one direction that distributes vertical loads which spread gradually to the support (usually soil). It differs from a continuous row of adjacent columns in its ability to spread the load out along its length (acting as a beam; Figure 7.7) and to provide inherent lateral resistance in the plane of the wall (diaphragm; Figure 7.8). Both of these actions result from the internal shearing stresses that can develop within the wall.

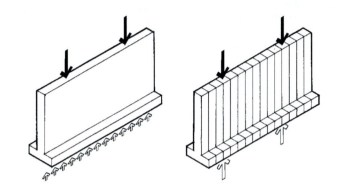

Figure 7.7: A bearing wall spreads concentrated loads along its length as a result of vertical shear resistance; the same load applied to a continuous row of columns remains concentrated in a single column.

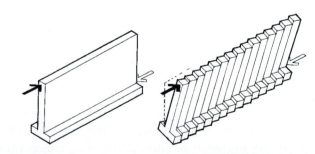

Figure 7.8: A bearing wall provides lateral stability along its length as a result of horizontal shear resistance (diaphragm action); this is lacking in a continuous row of columns.

Often traditional masonry walls were battered (thicker at the bottom). This provided greater lateral stability (a triangular shape is inherently more stable than a rectangle). In addition, this provided a larger bearing area at the bottom to distribute the load to the supporting soil. These same effects are achieved in contemporary masonry construction by the use of a spread footing that is anchored to the wall using steel reinforcing (Figure 7.9).

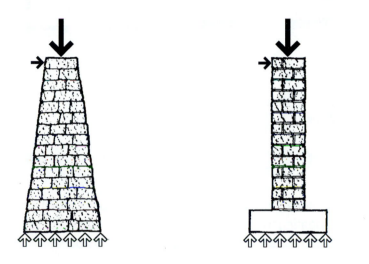

Figure 7.9: Battered walls and walls with spread footings resist overturning while distributing vertical loads over a larger area at the base.

In multistory buildings, bearing walls must carry not only the weight of the floor above (and their own weight) but also the accumulated weight of all floors and walls above. Because these loads are cumulative, they increase near the bottom, and the wall thickness must be increased to carry the increased load while maintaining an acceptable stress. In addition, the construction sequence is complicated when multistory bearing walls are used because typically wall construction must be halted at each level while the floor structure is installed. For these reasons, contemporary buildings usually use structural frames (columns and beams) to support the loads for walls and floors above in preference to bearing walls.

One exception to this is the combination of masonry bearing walls with precast concrete planks. In this system, the masons both build the walls and set the planks, making this method an economical, rapid choice for multistory apartments and hotels.

The last tall bearing wall: Monadnock Building
The Monadnock Building (1891; Chicago; Burnham and Root, architects) is one of the tallest masonry bearing-wall buildings ever built (Figures 7.10 and 7.11). It was also one of the last, being built at a time when the recently developed structural frame was emerging to replace the bearing wall as the preferred system for high-rise buildings. The 16-story structure consists of two exterior bearing walls running the length of the building.

These walls taper in thickness from 2 ft (60 cm) on upper floors to 6 ft (180 cm) on the ground floor. Perpendicular masonry bearing walls pierced by arched openings provide lateral resistance against wind loads, while cast-iron columns provide interior support. The Monadnock pushed the limits of tall masonry construction; the weight of the bearing walls themselves became the limiting design factor. Increasing building height further would result in disproportionate increases in the required wall thickness. So great is its construction weight resulting from the massive walls, the building has settled 20 in (50 cm) since its construction; 8 in (20 cm) was anticipated by the designers.

STRUCTURAL CONCEPTS

Bearing walls are best suited where the load is distributed relatively uniformly (such as by joists or closely spaced beams). Where loads are concentrated, they can produce areas of high local compressive stress; this concentration can be reduced by the use of bearing plates to distribute the concentrated loads over a larger area. Even here, a large area between the concentrated loads is nonbearing.

Pilasters are thickened portions of a bearing wall under concentrated loads that increase the area and reduce the compressive stress. They are in effect a column integrated into the bearing wall. Openings in a bearing wall produce local areas of high compressive stress on either side of the opening (Figure 7.12).

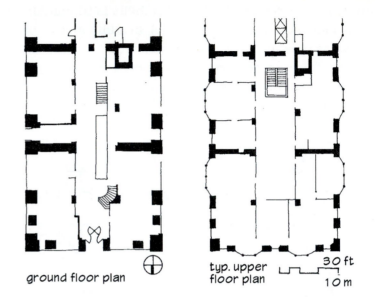

ground floor plan ⊕   typ. upper   ⌐_⌐ 30 ft
                          floor plan   ⌐_⌐ 10 m

Figure 7.11: Monadnock Building, partial plans. Notice how the thickness of the exterior bearing walls increases from 2 to 6 ft (60 to 180 cm) in order to carry the accumulated loads of the floors and walls above.

Figure 7.10: The Monadnock Building, located in Chicago, is one of the last tall masonry bearing-wall buildings ever built.

Since bearing walls carry vertical compression loads and are relatively slender compared with their height, they may tend to buckle laterally (like columns). Thin masonry walls which buckle actually fail in bending because of the inherent weakness of masonry in tension. Pilasters may be used to stiffen bearing walls against buckling without thickening the entire wall. Alternatively, the wall may be stiffened by building it in two separate wythes (layers) connected by internal pilasters forming the wall equivalent of an H-column. The internal rib is essential to resist the shearing forces that develop since each thin layer tends to buckle independently (Figure 7.13).

Parallel bearing walls

Parallel bearing walls are commonly used for multifamily housing. They provide not only the primary support for the floors and roofs of each unit but also serve to isolate the units for acoustical and fire control. The pattern of parallel bearing walls is particularly attractive for row-house and town-house plans where each unit has access to two sides for entry, view, and cross-ventilation (Ching, 1979) (Figure 7.14).

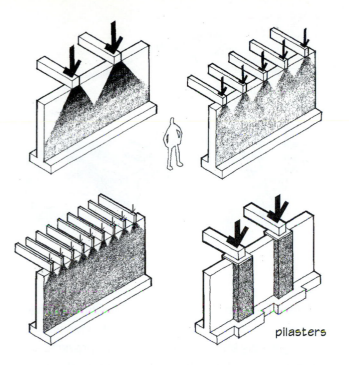

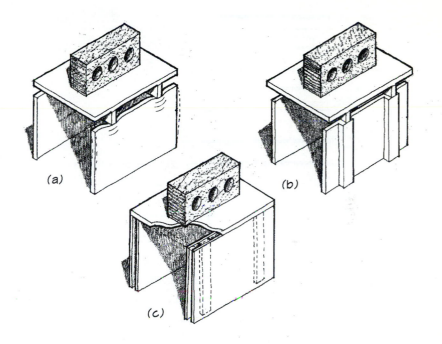

Figure 7.12: Effects of load distribution and openings on stress concentration in bearing walls. The pilaster is effectively a column integrated into a wall to accommodate a concentrated load.

Figure 7.13: Model demonstration showing effects of load concentration in a bearing wall: (a) local failure due to concentrated load under beams, (b) pilasters reduce stress by increasing area, and (c) cavity wall with internal stiffener to prevent buckling.

Because roof and floor structural members typically span perpendicular to the parallel bearing walls they rest upon, exterior walls in the opposite direction (parallel to the span) are typically non-bearing. These may accommodate large openings without compromising the structural integrity of the bearing wall (Figure 7.15).

Lateral stability
In order for a bearing wall to fall over, the resultant of all the lateral and vertical forces must fall outside of the base of the wall. If the development of tensile forces is to be avoided (if a masonry wall is not reinforced), then the resultant of all the lateral and vertical forces must be further restricted to the middle third of the wall at any height.

While increased wall thickness adds lateral stability (Figure 7.16), a more efficient alternative is manipulating the plan geometry of the wall. The addition of a perpendicular fin to a wall braces it and greatly increases its lateral resistance. The same bracing effect is achieved by intersecting and curved walls (Figure 7.17). Thomas Jefferson employed this principle to achieve a single-wythe thickness in the serpentine walls he designed for the University of Virginia (Figure 7.18). Louis Kahn used U-shaped walls to achieve a similar effect in the Trenton Bath House (Figures 7.19 and 7.20) and Hurva Synagogue (Ronner, et al., 1977).

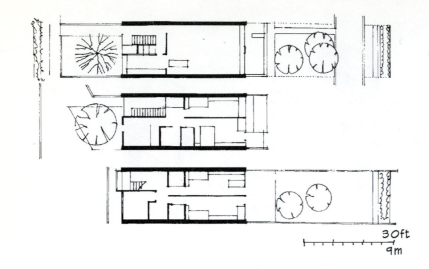

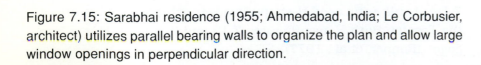

Figure 7.14: Siedlung Halen (1961; Bern, Switzerland; Atelier 5, architects) plan. This multifamily development utilizes parallel masonry bearing walls to provide support for floors and roofs, acoustical and fire separation between units, and access and ventilation across each end.

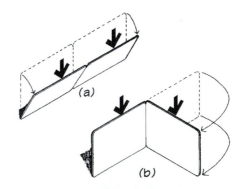

Figure 7.16: Adobe masonry used in Pueblo structures of the southwest is relatively weak in compression (and even weaker in tension) requiring thick walls for even single-story buildings. This thickness provides sufficient lateral resistance to wind loads without any additional bracing.

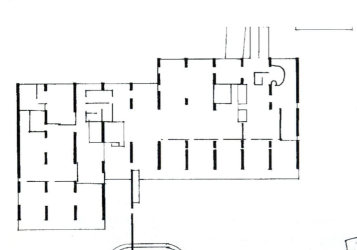

Figure 7.15: Sarabhai residence (1955; Ahmedabad, India; Le Corbusier, architect) utilizes parallel bearing walls to organize the plan and allow large window openings in perpendicular direction.

Figure 7.17: Demonstration of the use of plan geometry to increase lateral stability of bearing walls: (a) a card representing a wall is not laterally stable, but (b) folding the card to form a perpendicular corner makes it stable.

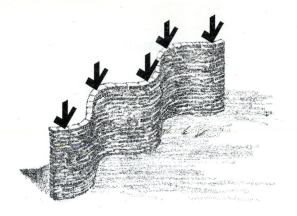

Figure 7.18: A serpentine brick wall (such as those designed by Thomas Jefferson at the University of Virginia) uses plan geometry to achieve lateral stability allowing the use of a single wythe of brick.

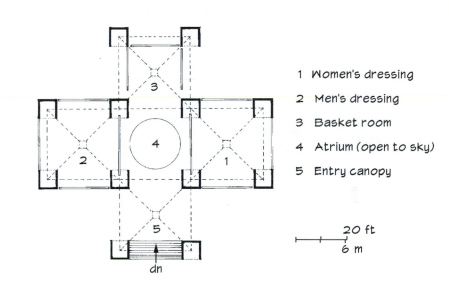

1 Women's dressing

2 Men's dressing

3 Basket room

4 Atrium (open to sky)

5 Entry canopy

20 ft

6 m

dn

Figure 7.19: Jewish Community Center Bath House (1953; Trenton, NJ; L. Kahn, architect), courtyard.

Figure 7.20: Jewish Community Center Bath House, plan. The U-shaped bearing wall geometry provided lateral stability while enclosing service and circulation functions—an example of Kahn's design distinction between *servant* and *served* spaces.

Habitat 67

Habitat 67 (1967; Montreal; Moshe Safdie, architect) is a manufactured housing demonstration project constructed for Expo 67. It consists of 354 prefabricated concrete modular bearing-wall construction units assembled like toy building blocks to create 158 dwelling units. In all, there are 18 different housing types, based on a single box with exterior dimensions of 17.5 ft × 38.5 ft × 10.5 ft (5.3 m × 11.7 m × 3.2 m) high. Since each box unit is capable of bearing loads, they could be stacked in a variety of configurations connected by posttensioning cables. As a result, each unit has an open garden (usually on the roof of an adjacent unit) and views in several directions (Safdie, 1974) (Figures 7.21 and 7.22).

Figure 7.21: Habitat 67 uses stacked bearing-wall boxes to assemble a variety of dwelling units, each with a garden and several views.

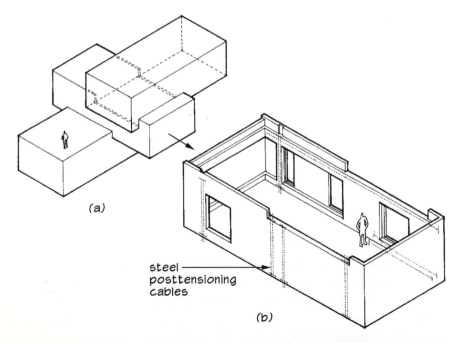

Figure 7.22: Habitat 67: (a) typical unit grouping, and (b) typical precast concrete house unit showing location of posttensioning cables.

SUMMARY

1. A *column* is a linear (typically vertical) structural member that is loaded with compressive forces along its axis.

2. A *short* column, such as a single brick, subjected to excessive compressive loading fails by *crushing*. A *long* column subjected to increasing compressive loading will suddenly buckle (bend sideways).

3. The lengthening of a column reduces its *buckling load*.

4. *Moment of inertia* is the measure of the distribution of material around the center of an object. Buckling load is directly proportional to the moment of inertia.

5. Possible column end conditions are *hinged* (free to rotate but lateral translation prevented), *fixed* at the base (rotation and lateral translation are both prevented), and *free* (free to rotate and translate).

6. A *bearing wall* is a compressive member that is continuous in one direction that distributes vertical loads which spread gradually to the support (usually soil). They are best suited where the load is distributed relatively uniformly (such as joists or closely spaced beams).

7. Geometry is more efficient than mass when developing lateral stability in bearing walls.

8. *Pilasters* are thickened areas of a bearing wall used under concentrated loads to reduce compressive stress.

BEAMS AND SLABS

Horizontal structural members include *beams* and *slabs*.

BEAMS

The moment this lintel (this latent thing) is laid upon the two piers and connects their activities—presto! By the subtlest of conceivable magic, the Science of Architecture comes into being, as surely, as inevitably as when two chemical elements unite, a new force or product at once appears.

—*Louis H. Sullivan*

A *beam* is a linear structural member with loading applied perpendicular to its long axis; such a load is a bending load.

Bending is the tendency of a member to bow as a result of loads applied perpendicular to its longest axis. Bending causes one face of the member to stretch (be in tension) and the opposite face to shorten (be in compression). And because these tension and compression stresses are occurring in parallel, shearing stresses are also present.

A beam is the most common example of a structural member in bending. It is the most direct solution to the common structural problem of transferring gravity loads horizontally to bearing members (Figure 8.1).

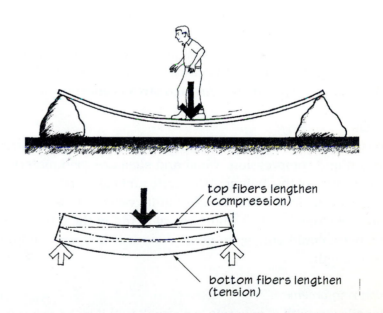

Figure 8.1: A simply supported beam bending under load. The top of the beam compresses and the bottom stretches, while the center remains the same length.

BEAM STRESSES

Consider, for example, a simple beam supported at each end and loaded in the center. The applied center load (and the dead load of the beam itself) causes the straight beam to deflect into a curve. As the beam curves, all the fibers within it curve also. The fibers nearest the convex face of the beam (bottom in this case) tend to stretch, causing tensile stress parallel to the face. The fibers near the concave face of the beam (top) tend to shorten, causing compression stress (again parallel to the face). The fibers in the center of the beam do not change in length and remain in a neutral state (neither tension nor compression). The greatest stresses occur at the outer faces and gradually decrease to zero at the *neutral* (center) axis (Figures 8.2 and 8.3).

Stress contours

It is an oversimplification that tension occurs in the top and compression in the bottom of a simple beam. Actually, the stress paths curve and intersect (Figure 8.4). Where tension and compression stress lines cross, they are always perpendicular. The spacing between stress path contours indicates the concentration of stress in that region (close spacing means high stress concentration).

Materials

The best materials for beams are those which have similar strength in tension and compression. Wood and steel are good materials for beams because of this balance. Concrete and masonry materials are relatively strong in compression but quite weak in tension. For this reason, the stone *lintels* (a short beam) found in the temples of ancient Greece could only span short distances and were quite deep for their length.

Tension reinforcement

The tensile strength of concrete is so weak that it is not even considered in structural design. Concrete beams must be reinforced with steel to prevent tensile cracking. Because the purpose of the steel reinforcing bars is to resist tension stress, they are always located on the convex side of the beam (Figure 8.5).

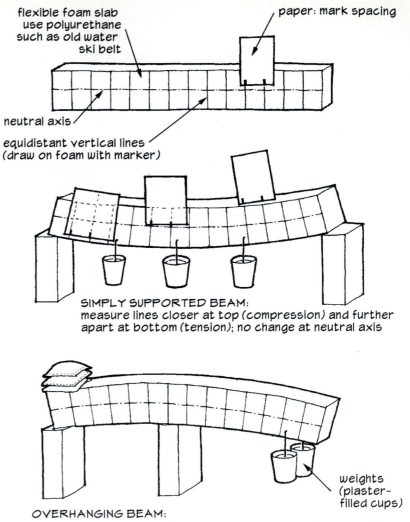

SIMPLY SUPPORTED BEAM:
measure lines closer at top (compression) and further apart at bottom (tension); no change at neutral axis

OVERHANGING BEAM:
behavior reversed, tension on top and compression on bottom

Figure 8.2: Model demonstration of tensile and compressive stresses and strains in a beam.

These opposing internal forces create the resisting internal moment. If the distance between the internal compression and tension forces is small (as in a shallow beam) then these forces must be large in order to create the required moment necessary to resist bend-

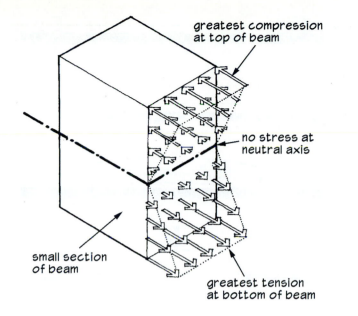

Figure 8.3: Tensile and compressive stresses in a simply supported beam.

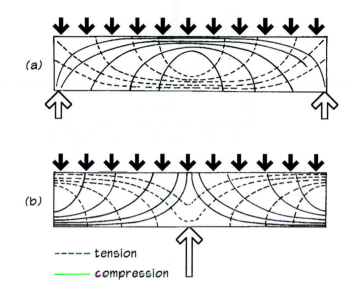

Figure 8.4: Stress contours in beams: (a) end-supported, and (b) center-supported. Notice the following: Where contours cross, they are always perpendicular; compression and tension contours are symmetrical to each other; and the closeness of the spacing between contours indicates the relative concentration of stress.

ing. If the distance between the internal forces is large (as in a deep beam) then these forces can be small and still create the required resisting moment.

Prestressed and posttensioned concrete beams
Even with steel reinforcement bars added to the beam, small tension cracks occur on the convex face. This is because the steel must begin to stretch before it can offer any bending resistance — in essence, a small amount of bending (and deflection) must occur in order for the tension resistance of the steel to take effect. This can be prevented by stretching (*prestressing*)the steel when it is installed in the beam formwork prior to pouring the concrete and maintaining that tension while the concrete hardens. When the tension forces applied to the ends of the steel are released, the steel contracts pulling the surrounding concrete into compression (Figure 8.6).

Alternatively, reinforcing steel can be *posttensioned* — installed in the concrete in hollow sheathes so that there is no bond between

the steel and concrete. After the concrete has hardened, the steel is tensioned, creating posttensioning (an effect similar to prestressing) (Figures 8.7 and 8.8).

SHEARING STRESSES IN A BEAM

Because the tensile and compressive stresses that occur on the upper and lower faces of a beam are parallel but in opposing directions, they create shearing forces along the length of the beam. As discussed previously, this horizontal shearing action must be balanced by corresponding vertical shearing forces in order for a square element within the beam to remain in equilibrium (Figure 8.9).

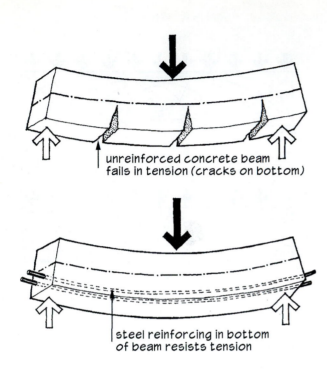

Figure 8.5: Bending in a concrete beam without and with steel reinforcing.

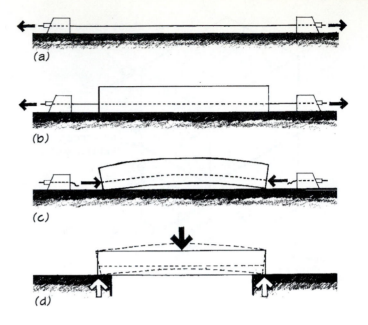

Figure 8.6: Prestressed concrete beam: (a) high-strength steel cables are pretensioned between abutments using hydraulic jacks; (b) concrete is cast around the pretensioned cables and allowed to cure; and (c) after the concrete has cured, the cables are cut. If the cables are in the lower part of the beam, cutting the cables has the effect of applying a compressive force to the ends of the beam at this level. This causes the beam to bow up, producing a camber that offsets the deflection (d) that will result once the beam is loaded vertically.

This resistance to shear is essential to a beam's resistance to bending. Compare a solid beam with a composite beam of similar size consisting of a stack of thinly sliced layers of the same material. When comparably loaded, the thin layers tend to slide and result in much greater deflection than the solid beam. This is the reason that a laminated wood beam consisting of several layers of wood glued together is much stronger than the same layers of wood unbonded (Figure 8.10). Prior to the development of modern adhesives, a similar effect was achieved by the use of *keys* to prevent shear slippage between multilayer composite timber beams (Figure 8.11).

These shearing forces tend to distort the square section into a parallelogram with equivalent tension and compression forces developing along the diagonals of the parallelogram. This causes the beam to behave in a trusslike manner (Figures 8.12 through 8.14).

BEAM DEFLECTION

Factors that affect the deflection of a simply supported beam include *span, depth and width, material, load location, cross-sectional shape, and longitudinal shape.*

Span
The deflection of a beam increases rapidly as the *cube* of its span. If the span is doubled, the deflection increases by a factor of 8 (Figure 8.15).

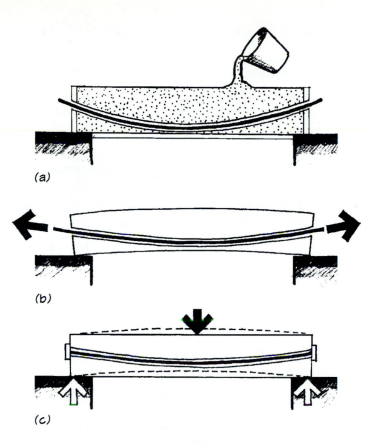

(a)

(b)

(c)

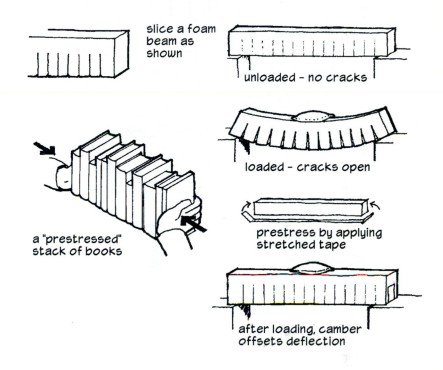

slice a foam beam as shown

unloaded – no cracks

loaded – cracks open

a "prestressed" stack of books

prestress by applying stretched tape

after loading, camber offsets deflection

Figure 8.8: Model demonstration comparing unreinforced, reinforced, and prestressed concrete beams.

Figure 8.7: Posttensioned concrete beam: (a) formwork is positioned, hollow sheaths containing unstressed cables are draped into place, and concrete is cast around the sheaths; (b) after the concrete has cured, the cables are tensioned by jacks at each end of the beam; and (c) after the formwork and jacks are removed, the cable force is maintained by permanent anchors at each end.

Width and depth

The deflection of a rectangular beam varies with its cross-sectional dimensions. Deflection is inversely proportional to the horizontal dimension. Doubling the horizontal width reduces the deflection to half; tripling the width reduces deflection to one-third. Changes in the vertical depth have an even greater effect on deflection which is inversely proportional to the cube of the depth. Doubling the depth reduces the deflection by a factor of 8. Thus a beam is more efficiently stiffened by adding material to the depth than to the width (Figure 8.16).

Material strength

For identically sized beams, deflection is inversely proportional to the modulus of elasticity of the material (Figure 8.17). An aluminum beam will deflect three times as much as a comparable steel beam (which has a modulus of elasticity three times that of aluminum).

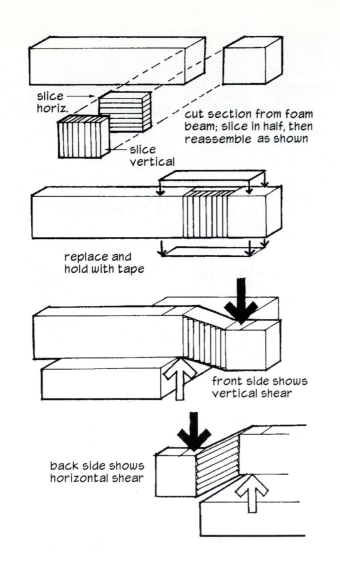

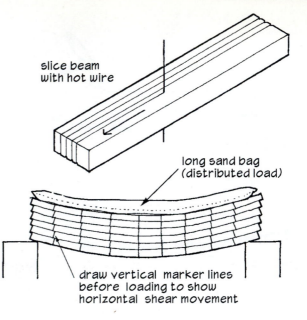

Figure 8.10: Model demonstration of how resistance to horizontal shear in a beam prevents it from acting as independent layers.

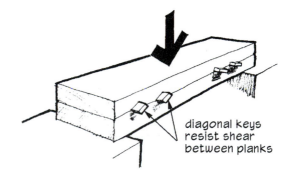

Figure 8.9: Model demonstration of local vertical and horizontal shear in a beam.

Figure 8.11: Traditional layered wood beam. Shear slippage between layers is prevented by wood keys.

Load location

Deflection at midspan is effected by the location of the load, increasing as the load moves from the support to the center of the span (Figure 8.18).

Cross-sectional shape

A problem with beams is the inherent understressing of material near the center of the cross section. As noted previously, the greatest internal tension and compression forces of a beam in bending

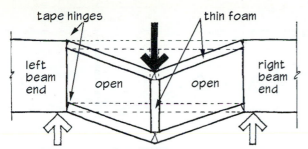

RECTANGULAR OPENINGS (no bending resistance)

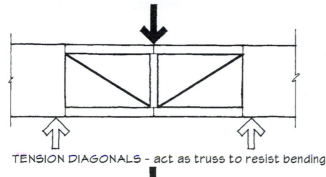

TENSION DIAGONALS - act as truss to resist bending

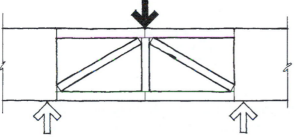

COMPRESSION DIAGONALS - resist bending also

Figure 8.12: Model demonstration of truss behavior in resisting bending in the center portion of a beam.

occur at the outermost fibers and decrease to zero at the center (neutral axis). If the beam is of uniform cross section (for example, a rectangle), this means that these outer fibers are under the greatest stress while the center of the beam is understressed. Because the strength of this center portion is underutilized, this rectangular shape

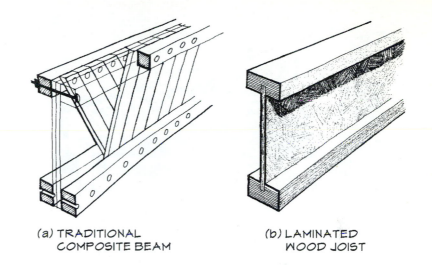

(a) TRADITIONAL COMPOSITE BEAM

(b) LAMINATED WOOD JOIST

Figure 8.13: (a) Composite timber beam behaves like a truss to resist horizontal shear between the upper and lower chords. This type beam has been superseded by (b) laminated wood joists.

is relatively inefficient in bending resistance. Much of the material near the center neutral axis could be removed without affecting the beams overall bending resistance. In other words, distributing most of a beam's material as far away from the neutral axis as practical increases bending resistance. Thus beam cross sections that place most material as far from the neutral axis as possible (box and I-shapes) are the most efficient. Because an I-shape is more easily fabricated than a box section, the wide-flange has emerged as the shape of choice for contemporary steel beam construction (Figures 8.19 and 8.20).

Longitudinal beam shape

Just as the cross section of beams can be optimized by maximizing the material in the upper and lower chords, the longitudinal shape can be optimized by maximizing the depth of the beam where the maximum bending moment occurs along its length. (As depth increases, the same internal resisting moment can be generated with smaller internal tension and compression forces.) For a simply sup-

Figure 8.14: Precast concrete lattice beam produced by Franz Visintini (Switzerland, 1904). The thicknesses of the top and bottom chords of this mass-produced trussed beam could be varied depending on the intended loading.

ported beam loaded uniformly along its length, this maximum depth optimally occurs at the center of the span tapering gradually to the ends. The moment at the end supports is zero (assuming a pin or roller connection) so that no depth is needed to resist the moment; at this point, the need for shear resistance controls the depth (Figures 8.21 and 8.22).

Vierendeel beams

One way of reducing the material in the center of a beam is to make the web thinner (Figure 8.19). Another way is to cut openings in the

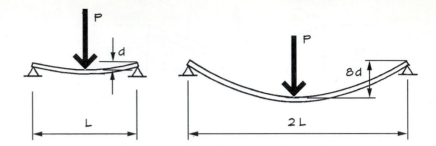

Figure 8.15: The effect of span on deflection. Deflection increases as the cube of the span.

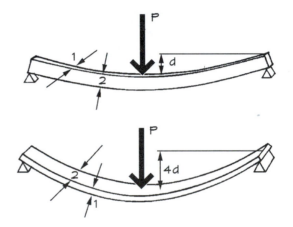

Figure 8.16: The effect of depth and width on beam deflection. Deflection varies inversely as the width and as the cube of the depth.

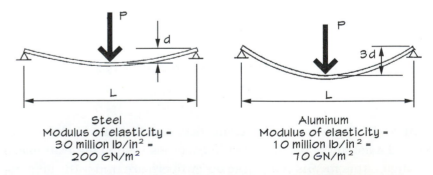

Steel
Modulus of elasticity =
30 million lb/in² =
200 GN/m²

Aluminum
Modulus of elasticity =
10 million lb/in² =
70 GN/m²

Figure 8.17: The effect of material strength on beam deflection. Deflection varies inversely as the modulus of elasticity.

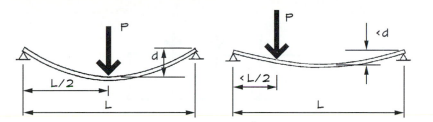

Figure 8.18: The effect of load location on beam deflection. Deflection increases as the load nears the midspan.

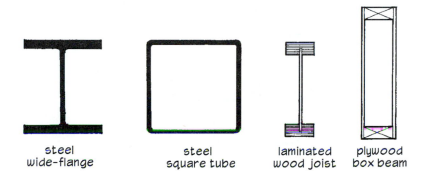

steel wide-flange   steel square tube   laminated wood joist   plywood box beam

Figure 8.19: Efficient cross-sectional shapes for wood and steel beams (and other materials which have comparable strength in both tension and compression). Bending resistance increases as the material is distributed as far as possible from the neutral axis while still being connected so as to act as a single beam. For example, the purpose of a web member of a wide-flange steel beam is to separate the top and bottom flanges (which provide most of the internal resistance to tension and compression) and provide the horizontal shear resistance necessary to prevent the flanges from sliding relative to each other.

web, leaving connecting struts between the top and bottom flanges. If these openings are triangular, the beam behaves as a truss using the triangular geometry to not only separate the chords but provide shear resistance. Vertical-only web members may also be used to provide the required chord separation, but in order to resist the horizontal shear between the chords the joints between the vertical web members and the chords must be fixed to prevent the rectangles

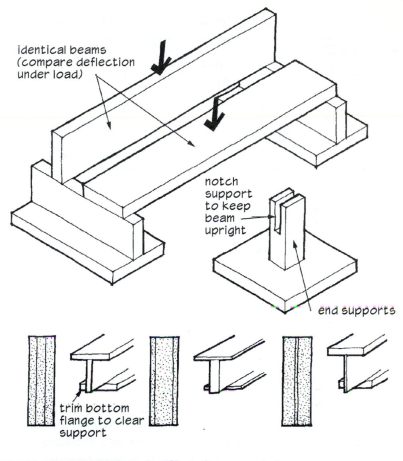

identical beams (compare deflection under load)

notch support to keep beam upright

end supports

trim bottom flange to clear support

Slice identical PSF beams in different ways and glue slices together as shown (so that cross-sectional areas are equal). Compare deflections under identical loading.

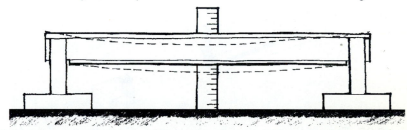

Figure 8.20: Model demonstration of the relative bending resistance of various beam cross sections.

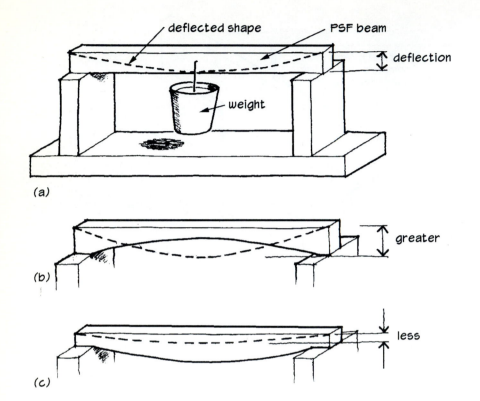

Figure 8.21: Model demonstration comparing the bending resistance of various longitudinal beam shapes. The total material in all beams is identical as is the applied uniform load. Beam (b) deflects least because material is concentrated at midspan where the bending moment is greatest.

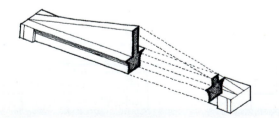

Figure 8.22: Tapered stone roof beam, Hieron, Samothrace (late fourth century BC). The maximum depth occurs at midspan where the bending moment is greatest. The bottom is thicker to compensate for the comparative weakness of stone in tension.

Figure 8.23: Model demonstration comparing a triangulated truss (stable with pin joints) with Vierendeel beams (unstable with pin joints, stable with fixed joints).

from shearing into parallelograms. (Because of the geometric stability of the triangle, truss joints may be pinned.) Known as a Vierendeel beam (sometimes incorrectly known as a Vierendeel truss), this is a relatively inefficient structural configuration (compared with the triangulated truss). The resulting rectilinear openings may be preferable for other purposes such as duct space or access (Figures 8.23 and 8.24).

Vierendeel beam case study: Salk Institute
In the Salk Institute (1965; La Jolla, CA; Louis I. Kahn, architect; A. Kommendant, structural engineer), Kahn used deep Vierendeel beams for the floor structure in the laboratories to accommodate the large

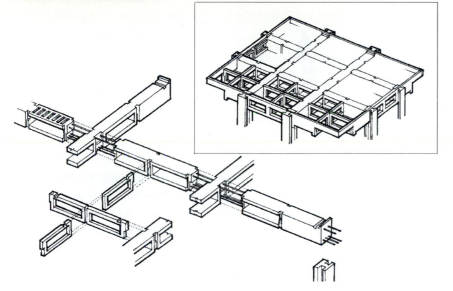

Figure 8.24: Precast, posttensioned concrete Vierendeel beams used in the Richards Medical Laboratory to provide accessible space for ducts and other service equipment (1964; Philadelphia; Louis I. Kahn, architect).

amount of services necessary to support a research laboratory without disrupting adjacent floors when extensive services reconfiguration, which inevitably occurs throughout the life of such a building, is needed (Figure 8.25). Describing the design evolution of this structural approach, Kahn noted, "The laboratories are conceived as work levels and service levels. Each of the three work levels is related to a garden or to a view of a garden. The space below each laboratory is, in reality, a pipe laboratory, where service men can install equipment relative to experiments and make changes to ducts and piping. This dismisses the apprehension of needing the room to satisfy the mechanical means for experimentation. The distinction of the construction of the laboratories from the spaces for the pipes has become greatly clarified to the point where a far more interesting construction, intended in the beginning to serve the distinction, has given way to a system of construction far less exciting but one that serves more characteristically the intended use." (Ronner, et al., 1977).

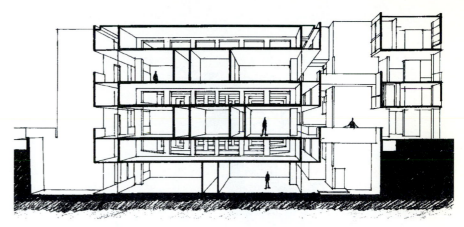

Figure 8.25: Salk Institute, section showing large Vierendeel frames used to provide a column-free span in the laboratories while providing an accessible "pipe space".

CANTILEVERS

The pier, lintel and arch are in their simplest forms primary propositions. The cantilever belongs in the province of morphology.

—*Louis H. Sullivan*

A *cantilever* is a member with a fixed support at one end only and loaded perpendicular to its axis so as to cause bending. A beam is a one-dimensional cantilever; a slab is a two-dimensional cantilever. A column fixed in the ground and side-loaded (by the wind, for example) behaves as a vertical cantilevered beam.

Stress distribution
Early understanding of beam behavior was furthered by Galileo in 1638 when he proposed a theory for understanding the bending in a cantilever beam. He mistakenly assumed that all fibers were equally stressed in tension and that compression contributed nothing to the bending (Figure 8.26). It was around 50 years later that Edme Mariotte, a French physicist, correctly concluded

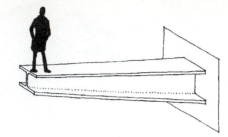

Figure 8.26: Galileo's study of bending in a cantilever beam.

Figure 8.27: Because the bending moment in an end-loaded cantilever beam increases with the distance from the load, the greatest depth is needed at the support and the least at the free end. This tapered shape is the most efficient for a cantilever because the bending stresses remain relatively constant along the length.

Figure 8.28: A palm tree, a flagpole, and the unstayed mast of a sailboat are examples of vertical cantilevers with rigid connections at the base. Notice that all share the tapered shape that is most efficient for a cantilever.

that the upper half of a cantilevered beam would be in tension and the lower half in compression (Elliott, 1992). Thus the stresses in a cantilever are similar to a simply supported beam, only they are inverted.

The greatest moment occurs near the support (root) because the moment arm (distance to the end load) is greatest there. And, if the member has a constant cross section throughout its length, it is here that the greatest bending stress occurs. The rest of the length is under progressively less stress as the distance to the load decreases. Because most of the cantilever is understressed, this constant cross-sectional shape is not efficient. For maximum efficiency, the depth of the member should decrease in order that the bending stresses remain constant (Figures 8.27 through 8.29).

CANTILEVER DEFLECTION

Cantilever deflection is affected by *length, depth and width, material, load location,* and *cross-sectional shape* in the same manner

CANTILEVERS VERSUS OVERHANGING BEAMS

The term cantilever is sometimes incorrectly applied to *overhanging beams*. An overhanging beam has multiple supports and extends beyond the last *simple* (hinged) support. It differs from a cantilever beam in that the last support is not fixed; thus the beam is free to pivot as it passes across the column (Figure 8.30). On the other hand, if the last support of the overhanging beam is fixed, then the overhanging portion behaves as a true cantilever. Thus, the condition (simple or pinned, or fixed) of the last support determines whether the overhang qualifies as a cantilever.

The Chinese bracket system, called *tou-kung*, used multiple layers of overhanging beams to distribute loads, allowing effective beam spans to be reduced and resulting in a visually rich system of structural ornamentation (Figures 8.31 and 8.32).

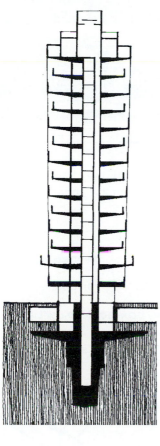

Figure 8.29: Research tower, Johnson's Wax Building. The sole vertical structure is the reinforced concrete central core cantilevered from the unique "taproot" foundation which was designed to resist the overturning moment caused by lateral wind loading.

and to the same degree as a simply supported beam. The cantilever beam behaves identically to half of an inverted simply supported beam (see Figures 8.15 through 8.18).

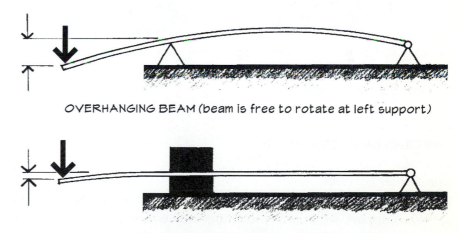

OVERHANGING BEAM (beam is free to rotate at left support)

CANTILEVER BEAM (beam is fixed at left support)

Figure 8.30: Comparison of cantilever and overhanging beams. The deflection of the overhanging beam is greater than the cantilever because of rotation of the overhanging beam at the simple support. If the overhanging beam support is rigid, then deflection is the same as for the cantilever.

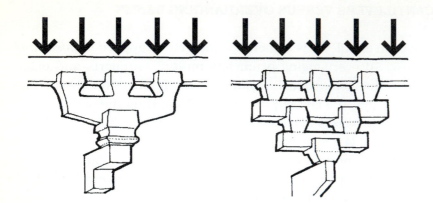

Figure 8.31: The Chinese bracket system (tou-kung) used to distribute reaction forces along a beam is a progressive set of overhanging beams.

Figure 8.32: Cantilevered wood bridge (Dudh Khosi, Nepal). One end of the cantilevering wood beams is anchored under stone; the cantilevering end supports the center span.

CANTILEVER CASE STUDIES

Bari Soccer Stadium

One of the structural advantages of the cantilever is its ability to provide support while still providing a view unobstructed by columns at one end. The structure of Bari Soccer Stadium (1989; Bari, Italy; Renzo Piano Building Workshop, architects; Ove Arup and Partners, structural engineers) utilizes cantilevers as major design elements (Figures 8.33 through 8.36). Built to host the 1990 World Cup Championship, a major factor in the design was the geometry dictated by adequate sight lines and viewing distances. Splitting the seating into two tiers with the upper overhanging the lower allowed

Figure 8.33: Bari Soccer Stadium (Renzo Piano Building Workshop, architects). The space between the upper seating tiers accommodates the access stairs.

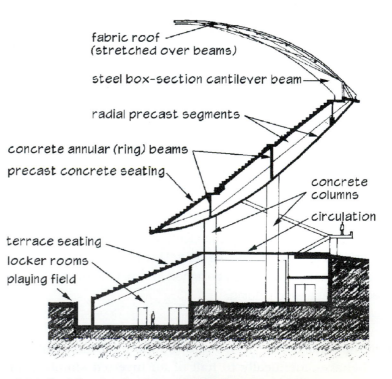

Figure 8.34: Bari Soccer Stadium, section through stands.

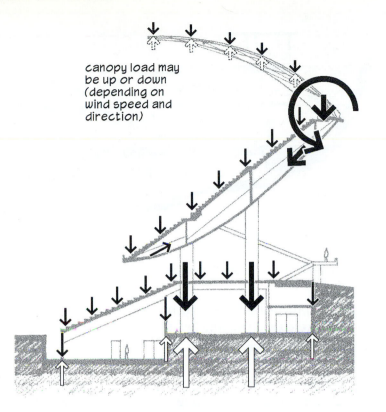

Figure 8.35: Bari Soccer Stadium, load path diagram.

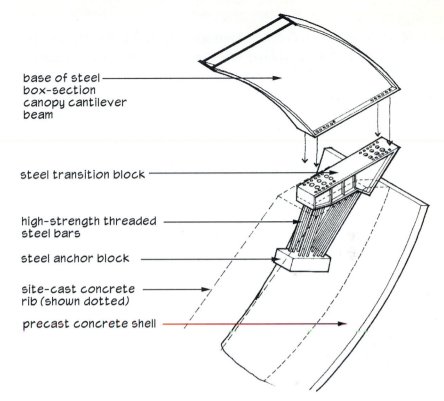

Figure 8.36: Bari Soccer Stadium, detail of fixed connection at base of cantilever canopy beam.

for an increase in the number of seats while still preserving recommended viewing distances. In addition, the project required the protection of a high percentage of the seats with a canopy. Substantial cantilevers were used to achieve both the overhanging upper tiers and the canopy without any supporting columns in the seating areas which would have obstructed the sight lines (Brookes and Grech, 1992).

The upper tier of seating and the overhead canopy are cantilevered from pairs of massive concrete columns located behind the lower seating tier. The dimensions of each column are 3.3 ft × 6 ft (1 m × 1.8 m). The upper seating tier is supported by two sets of curved reinforced concrete beams. These curved beams, in turn, support concrete T-section beams (a combination of precast and in situ con-

struction) which cantilever beyond each end of the supports. Each T-section beam was fabricated from three precast parts joined at the supporting curved beams. This connection was formed by making the steel reinforcing of both the supporting beams and T-sections continuous through the joint, resulting in a fixed connection.

The canopy is a lightweight steel and fabric structure. The supporting steel beams are tapered box sections cantilevering from a rigid bolted connection at the top. The curved beams taper in response to the decreasing bending moment as the distance from the support increases. This steel structure is covered with a stretched fabric membrane [glass-fiber woven fabric treated with an ultraviolet (UV)-resistant coating].

Falling Water

One of the most famous cantilevered structures is Falling Water (1936; Connellsville, PA; FrankLloyd Wright, architect) (Figures 8.37 and 8.38). The site is a dramatic rock outcropping over a mountain stream in a remote wooded location. Described by Wright as "an extension of the cliff beside a mountain stream making living space over and above the stream on several terraces upon which a man who loved the place sincerely, one who loved and liked to listen to the waterfall, might well live" (Sandaker and Eggen, 1992) (Figures 8.37 and 8.38).

> *Buildings with cantilevered terraces that seem to float in the air have the effect of "demolishing the box."*
> —*Frank Lloyd Wright*

The main reinforced concrete terrace cantilevers over 16 ft (5 m). Both the floor beams and the solid concrete railing contribute to the bending resistance of the structure. More significant than the technical achievement of the structure is the way that Wright used the

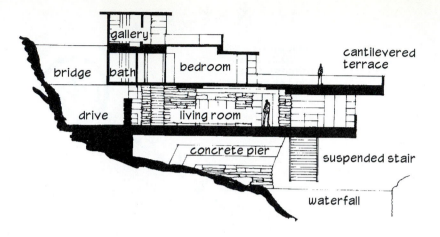

Figure 8.38: Falling Water, section showing cantilevered terraces.

cantilever, emphasizing the strong horizontal lines together with the unique site to create a visually dramatic form that appears to hover above the cascading water below.

Hongkong Bank Headquarters

The Hongkong Bank (1986; Hong Kong; Foster Associates, architects; Ove Arup and Partners, structural engineers) is 43 stories (plus 4 basement levels) with an overall height of 587 ft (179 m). The type of occupancy changes at different levels, with a public plaza on the ground level and a banking hall on level 3. Next are local offices, then executive offices, then headquarters offices, with boardrooms and the chairperson's apartment at the top. The main feature at the plaza level is a 12-story central atrium space daylighted by end windows and a curved reflector at the top. The design required a maximum clear space in the center of the floor areas with the services and vertical circulation at each end (Orton, 1988) (Figures 8.39 through 8.42).

To achieve this, a vertical structure of eight "masts" was used. Each mast consisted of four round tubular columns arranged in a square and connected with box sections at each floor level, resulting in a three-dimensional Vierendeel frame. From these masts, trusses cantilever at five heights, effectively dividing the building into five

Figure 8.37: Falling Water, exterior.

Figure 8.39: Hongkong Bank Headquarters clearly expresses its structure on the facade. "Masts" support the cantilevered trusses from which the intermediate floors are hung.

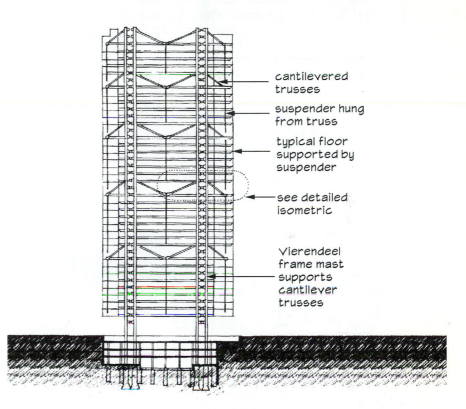

cantilevered trusses

suspender hung from truss

typical floor supported by suspender

see detailed isometric

Vierendeel frame mast supports cantilever trusses

Figure 8.40: Hongkong Bank Headquarters, section.

independent structures. The floors in each of the five zones are suspended from the cantilevered truss above. This structural organization is clearly expressed on the exterior facade. This combination is repeated four times and clearly articulated on the facade. According to Foster "the path of gravity loads—hung floors, sloping tension arms, and load bearing towers—is clearly expressed in this facade. Interrupting the hangers emphasizes their function" (Thornton, et al., 1993).

CONTINUOUS BEAMS

A *continuous beam* is a single beam that spans over several supports. It differs from a comparable series of simply supported beams

between each pair of supports (Figure 8.43). As the continuous beam passes over a support, it develops tension in the top, compression in the bottom, and a negative deflection curvature (concave down). In the midspan region, the opposite is true: tension develops in the top, compression in the bottom, and the deflection curvature is positive. The greatest bending moments occur over the support and at midspan; however, the moment at either of these locations is less than the maximum moment (at midspan) of a simply supported beam. For that reason, continuous beams can have a smaller cross section than comparable simply supported beams and are often employed in order to save construction costs.

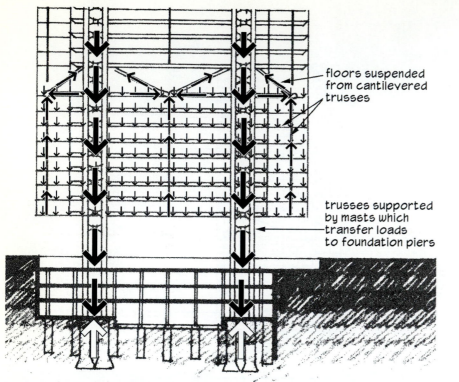

Figure 8.41: Hongkong Bank Headquarters, load paths.

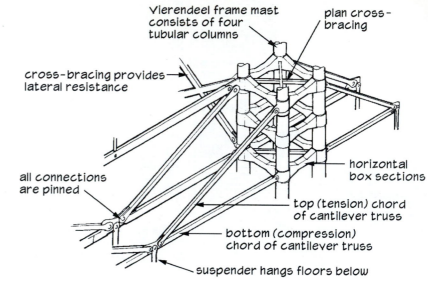

Figure 8.42: Hongkong Bank Headquarters, isometric drawing of external mast and suspension trusses.

Gerber beams

In a continuous beam (Figure 8.43), the deflection curvature changes from negative (concave down over the support) to positive (concave up at midspan). At the curvature *inflection* (changeover) point, the moment reduces to zero and no bending occurs. Because of this, a hinged joint could be inserted in the beam at this inflection point with no change in the structural effect. The continuous beam then becomes a combination of a short-span simple beam supported by the ends of overhanging beams. Because the effective span is less, the center beam can be of much smaller cross section than a simple beam spanning between the supports. Such beams are named for the German engineer Heinrich Gerber who first developed them. The Firth of Forth railway bridge is a trussed example using Gerber's principle (Figures 8.44 and 8.45).

JOISTS

Up until now, beams have been considered in isolation—as a one-way bearing component. To provide support over an area (such as a floor), beams are typically arranged parallel to one another. *Joists* are closely spaced beams spanning in a single direction. Because the bearing capacity of beams is inversely proportional to the square of the span, it is efficient (and usually most economical) to arrange joists so that they span the shortest direction of a rectilinear bay (Figure 8.46).

BEAM GRIDS

A *beam grid* is a system of beams that span in two directions with the beams in each direction joined to each other. Grids are typically

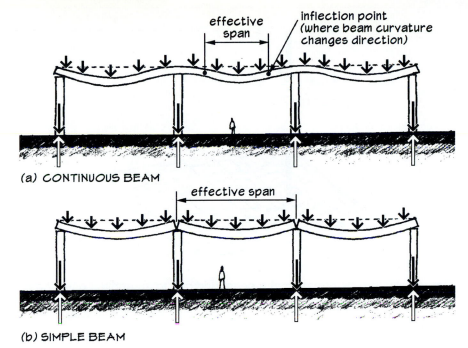

(a) CONTINUOUS BEAM

(b) SIMPLE BEAM

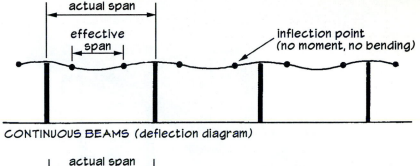

CONTINUOUS BEAMS (deflection diagram)

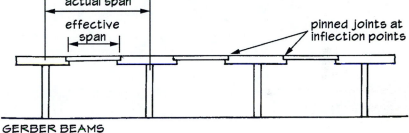

GERBER BEAMS

Figure 8.43: Comparison of (a) continuous and (b) simply supported beams of comparable size. The bending moment is greatest where the greatest curvature occurs. In the continuous beam, no moment occurs at the inflection point where positive curvature (concave up) changes to negative curvature (concave down).

Figure 8.44: A Gerber beam is hinged at the inflection point, effectively creating a shorter span between the ends of two overhanging beams; the cross section of this center beam can be reduced substantially. (a) Deflection diagram of continuous beam showing inflection points, and (b) Gerber beam with joints at inflection points.

supported on the four sides of an approximately square bay, and the total depth of the beams can be less than that of a comparable one-way beam system. In a beam grid, individual beams are partially supported by intersecting perpendicular beams, which are in turn partially supported by other intersecting beams. When a point load is applied at the intersection of two beams in a grid, both beams are deflected as well as other nearby beams. In addition to bending, this interaction results in twisting of adjacent beams. This results from the fixed connection at the beam intersections (Figure 8.47).

The beams in grids necessarily intersect, and their continuity through one another is essential to this characteristic two-dimensional bending behavior. This continuity is more easily achieved in

some materials than others. Concrete is easily formed into grids provided the steel reinforcing extends continuously through the intersections. Steel box-section beams can be welded at the intersections to provide the necessary continuity. Wood beams, on the other hand, would necessarily be discontinuous (in at least one direction) at the intersections and thus are inherently unsuited for use in beam grids.

The New National Gallery
The New National Gallery (1968; Berlin; Mies van der Rohe, architect) utilizes a steel beam grid to achieve the large clear span that culminated Mies's search for a "universal envelope to enclose a universal space" (Figures 8.48 and 8.49). The clear span allows for nonstructural partitions to be configured as required for varying

Figure 8.45: The huge cantilevered trusses of the Firth of Forth railway bridge behave as Gerber beams. Built in 1890, the center span is 1708 ft (521 m).

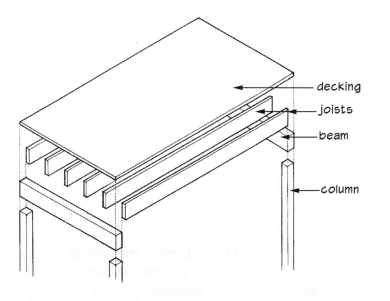

Figure 8.46: Joists are closely spaced beams spanning in a single direction. They are most efficient when spanning the shorter dimension.

decking

joists

beam

column

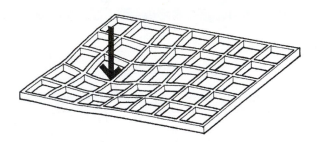

SECTION

Figure 8.47: The deformation of a beam grid due to an applied point load.

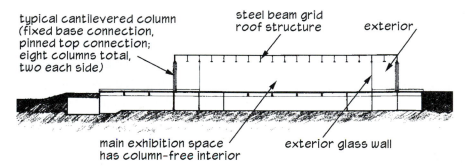

typical cantilevered column
(fixed base connection,
pinned top connection;
eight columns total,
two each side)

steel beam grid
roof structure

exterior

main exhibition space
has column-free interior

exterior glass wall

Figure 8.48: The New National Gallery, section.

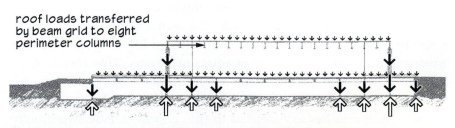

roof loads transferred
by beam grid to eight
perimeter columns

Figure 8.49: The New National Gallery, load path diagram.

exhibit needs. A glass wall set back under the roof on all four sides encloses the 26-ft (8.4-m)-high hall while emphasizing absence of any supporting members except the eight perimeter columns. The roof structure is a large steel beam grid 213 ft (64.8 m) square supported by two columns per side. The I-section beams are 6 ft (1.8 m) deep and spaced 12 ft (3.6 m) on center in each direction. The steel columns cantilever from the podium base to support the roof structure with hinged connections. The small size of these joints dramatizes the achievement of this large clear span (Futagawa, 1972).

SLABS

A *slab* is a bending component which distributes loads horizontally in one or more directions within a single plane. While the bending resistance of a slab is beamlike, it differs from a comparable series of independent beams in its continuity in both directions. If such a series of independent parallel beams is subjected to a single concentrated load, only the beam under the load will deflect.

But because the beams that form a slab are joined and act integrally, when a load is applied at a point, the adjacent portions of the slab are activated to contribute their resistance to bending. The load is distributed laterally within the slab as a result of the shear resistance between the loaded portion and adjacent areas. Thus concentrated loading results in a localized bending perpendicular to the primary span direction causing torsion in the slab (Figure 8.50).

Slabs are most commonly associated with reinforced concrete construction. However, slab behavior can be achieved in a variety of other materials, especially wood.

SLAB TYPES

Slabs are typically classified by the support configuration which determines the bending behavior of the slab (Figure 8.51).

One- and two-way slabs
One-way slabs are supported continuously by two parallel supports

(beams or walls) and resist bending primarily in one direction. *Two-way slabs* are supported continuously on all four sides (by beams or walls) and resist bending in both directions. Two-way slabs are stronger (and may be made thinner) than comparable one-way slabs. Two-way slabs are most efficient when the support spacing is relatively square; as the structural bay shape becomes more elongated, the two-way slab behaves increasingly like a one-way slab.

Flat plates
Slabs which are supported only at points by columns are termed *flat plates*. While simple in appearance, flat-plate systems experience a high concentration of shearing stress around the columns as the columns tend to punch through the slab. As a result, concrete flat plates must be heavily reinforced. However, the low formwork costs and low floor-to-floor heights more than offset the higher reinforcing costs and make this a preferred system for relatively short-span applications. In some building types (hotels and apartments, for ex-

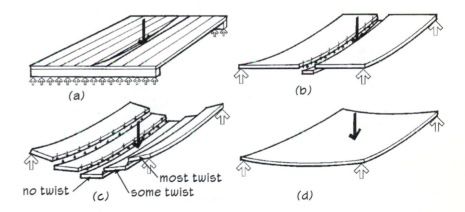

Figure 8.50: Comparison of a slab with a series of independent beams. (a) A series of beams under point load—notice how only the loaded beam deflects as it slips by adjacent beams. (b) In a slab, adjacent areas are joined to the loaded portion and contribute their bending resistance. (c) Adjacent portions are twisted as a result of this shearing action. (d) As a result, slab bending occurs in two directions and results in greater stiffness (for a given thickness) than a comparable series of independent beams.

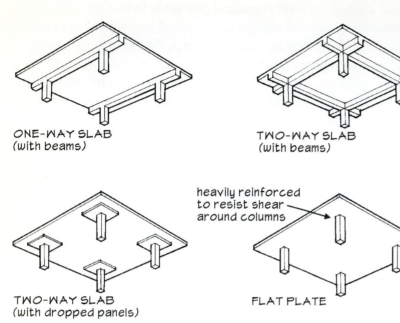

ONE-WAY SLAB
(with beams)

TWO-WAY SLAB
(with beams)

TWO-WAY SLAB
(with dropped panels)

FLAT PLATE

heavily reinforced
to resist shear
around columns

Figure 8.51: Slab types.

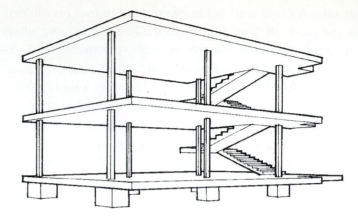

Figure 8.52: In Le Corbusier's "Dom-in-o" project (1914), concrete flat-plate floors rested directly on the columns and formed the structural concept for rational building of housing. This concept sketch had a major influence on the development of concrete as a bearing material in housing and office buildings.

ample), the underside is simply painted to form a ceiling at very low cost. An additional advantage is the suitability of flat plates for architectural situations requiring irregular column placement.

For larger spans or heavier loads, it is typically preferable to resist the shearing stresses around columns by increasing the area of the top of the column rather than by adding reinforcement. This is done by widening the top of the column to form a capital or by thickening the slab ("dropped panel"), or by a combination of both (Figure 8.52). (Such a configuration is still considered to be a slab; the term flat plate is reserved for column-supported slabs with no thickening in either the slab or column.)

Ribbed slabs

Slabs can be ribbed to reduce material, weight, and cost. In reinforced concrete slabs, such a ribbed configuration places most of the concrete in the top (*flange*, where this compressive material is

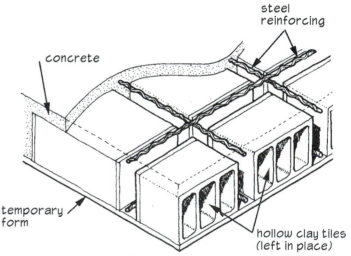

steel
reinforcing

concrete

temporary
form

hollow clay tiles
(left in place)

Figure 8.53: Ribbed slab formed using by hollow tiles.

most effective) and most of the reinforcing steel in the bottom of the *webs* (*ribs*) where it is most advantageous. Ribbed slabs are classified by whether their span is one-way (joists) or two-way (waffle slabs).

Joists

Concrete joists act integrally with the slab on top. The joists are typically used to span between heavier beams; typically the beams span the short distance of a rectangular bay, and the joists are used for the longer span.

Traditionally, concrete joists were formed by placing spaced rows of hollow clay tiles on a flat form (Figure 8.53). Reinforcing rods were placed in the bottom of the spaces between the tiles; concrete was poured filling the space between the tiles (to form the reinforced ribs) and over the top of the tiles to form the slab above. After the supporting formwork was removed, the lightweight tiles were left in place. This process resulted in an economical lightweight alternative (to solid slab construction) with an unfinished bottom surface that was typically covered with a ceiling finish material (often suspended to allow for mechanical and electrical distribution space).

Contemporary concrete joists are more economically made using reusable steel forms. The U-shaped "pan" forms are arranged in spaced rows over a supporting flat form. Tapered forms are used next to the supporting beams in order to thicken the joists as necessary to resist the local shear stresses. As with the tile forms, steel reinforcing is placed between the pans, and the concrete is poured between and over the forms. After the concrete cures, the bottom and pan forms are removed leaving the concrete exposed. Because of gaps between forms, cosmetic imperfections are common to this system, and it is seldom left exposed in finished construction (Figure 8.54a). Prestressed concrete *double-tees* are the precast equivalent of poured-in-place joists and are widely used in construction (Figure 8.54b).

Wood joist construction is common in residential floor construction. Plywood subfloor is nailed (and preferably glued) to the top of the closely spaced joists so that it contributes to the bending resistance of the assembly (Figure 8.54c).

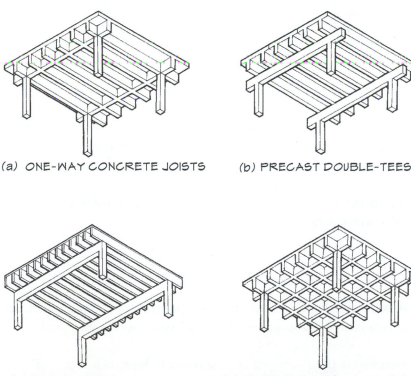

(a) ONE-WAY CONCRETE JOISTS   (b) PRECAST DOUBLE-TEES

(c) WOOD JOISTS   (d) WAFFLE SLAB (two-way joists)

Figure 8.54: Ribbed slabs: (a) one-way concrete joists, (b) precast double-tee joists, (c) wood joists, and (d) waffle slab (two-way joists).

Waffle slabs

Two-way ribbed concrete slabs are appropriately termed waffle slabs (Figures 8.54d and 8.55). These behave similarly to beam grids with the exception that the continuous top slab is an integral and continuous part of the system. Waffle slabs span in both directions, and the most economical bay proportion is square. Domed voids are formed using square fiberglass or metal pans; the resulting concrete finish can be very good and allows this visually interesting structure to be left exposed. Domes are typically omitted next to columns to increase shear resistance.

Isostatic joists

An alternative to the square pattern of the waffle slab is the gracefully curved pattern of ribs first suggested by the Italian engineer Arcangeli that follows the isostatic lines (lines of principle stress) of the slab (Figure 8.56). PierLuigi Nervi used such designs in several

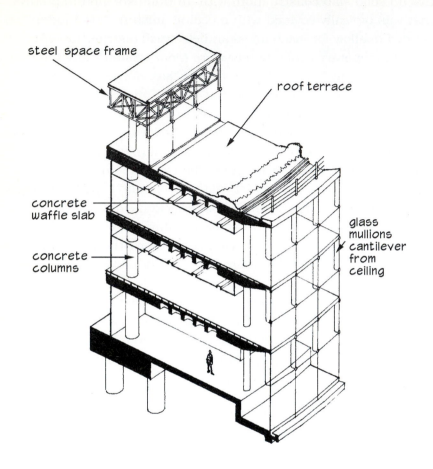

Figure 8.55: Waffle slab construction in an office building (1974; Ipswich, UK; Foster Associates, architects), section.

buildings (Nervi, 1963; Huxtable, 1960). Because a greater variety of forms are required than for waffle slabs (and because reinforcing must be curved), such construction is expensive and is only economical when the special forms can be reused numerous times.

Figure 8.56: Slab ribs following isostatic lines in floor slab which trace the principle lines of bending stresses (1953; Rome; Gatti Wool Factory; P. L. Nervi, structural engineer). Since no shear is developed along the isostatic lines, the slab becomes a grid of curved beams which meet at right angles but do not transmit loads to the adjoining beams by shearing action. Because of this, such an isostatic rib configuration is more efficient than a comparable waffle slab, but the formwork is considerably more expensive than the more repetitive waffle slab.

SUMMARY

1. A *beam* is a linear structural member with loading applied perpendicular to its long axis; such a load is a bending load.

2. *Bending* is the tendency of a member to bow as a result of loads applied perpendicular to its longest axis.

3. Bending in a beam results in tension stresses on the convex face and compression on the concave face.

4. Concrete beams must be *reinforced* with steel to prevent tensile cracking.

5. Reinforcing steel can be made even more effective by stretching it—*prestressing*—when it is installed in the beam formwork prior to pouring the concrete and maintaining that tension while the concrete hardens.

6. Alternatively, reinforcing steel can be *posttensioned*—installed in the concrete in such a way that there is no bond between the steel and concrete.

7. Bending resistance in a beam is increased by distributing most of a beam's material as far away from the neutral axis as practical. Because of this, an I-shape is an efficient beam shape.

8. A *Vierendeel* beam has rectangular openings in the web. While it is a relatively inefficient structural configuration (compared with the triangulated truss), the resulting rectilinear openings may be preferable for other purposes (such as duct space or access).

9. The longitudinal shape of a beam can be optimized by maximizing the depth of the beam where the maximum bending moment occurs along its length.

10. A *cantilever* is a member with a fixed support at one end only and loaded perpendicular to its axis so as to cause bending.

11. Factors which affect the deflection of a cantilever include length, depth and width, material, and load location.

12. A *continuous beam* is a beam that spans over several supports.

13. A *Gerber beam* consists of overhanging beams alternating with short spans simply supported from the ends of the cantilevers.

14. *Joists* are closely spaced beams spanning in a single direction.

15. A *beam grid* is a system of beams that span in two directions with the beams in each direction joined to each other.

16. A *slab* is a bending component which distributes loads horizontally in one or more directions within a single plane.

17. *One-way slabs* are supported continuously by two parallel supports (beams or walls) and resist bending primarily in one direction.

18. *Two-way slabs* are supported continuously on all four sides (by beams or walls) and resist bending in both directions.

19. *Flat plates* are slabs supported only at points by columns where there is no thickening in either the slab or column.

20. Slabs can be *ribbed* to reduce material, weight, and cost.

21. Ribbed slabs are classified by whether their span is *one-way* (joists) or *two-way* (waffle slabs).

22. *Isostatic joists* are slab ribs curved to follow the lines of principal stress.

FRAMES

When the lintel is placed upon two piers, architecture springs into being.

— *Louis H. Sullivan*

Beams, slabs, columns, and bearing walls combine to form orthogonal (rectilinear) *frames*, the most common support system used in buildings. Frames distribute loads horizontally (by means of beams) to columns which transmit forces vertically (to the supporting foundation). This is commonly refered to as *post-and-beam* construction. Slabs may be substituted for beams and bearing walls for columns, but the behavior remains similar. In addition to these vertical and horizontal components, the system must incorporate lateral support to resist horizontal loads such as wind and seismic forces (Figure 9.1).

Orthogonal framing systems may be classified by the number of layers (levels) of horizontal members in the system. One-level systems typically combine a one-way slab spanning between two parallel bearing walls. Two-level systems typically consist of a slab supported by parallel beams which bear on either two parallel walls or a row of columns (one under each beam). Three-level systems typically include a slab supported by closely spaced joists, supported by beams (perpendicular to the joists), and finally supported by columns (Figures 9.2 and 9.3).

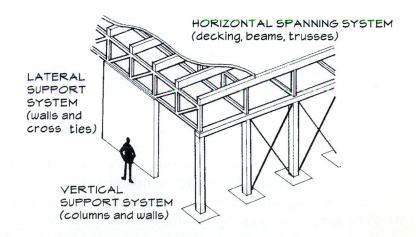

Figure 9.1: A typical framing system includes a horizontal spanning system (slabs or beams), a vertical support system (columns or walls), and a lateral support system.

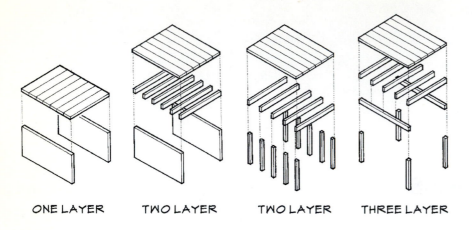

ONE LAYER   TWO LAYER   TWO LAYER   THREE LAYER

Figure 9.2: Framing systems classified by the number of layers of horizontal members.

LATERAL STABILITY

Resistance to wind and other horizontal forces is required for the stability of orthogonal frames. In general, this is achieved by using one or more of the following principles: *triangulation* (breaking the frame down into triangles which are inherently stable geometric forms), *joint rigidity* (creating a rigid connection where members intersect), and *shear walls* (utilizing the inherent shear resistance of a planar surface—such as a wall— to changing its shape) (Figures 9.4 through 9.14).

BAYS

A *bay* is an internal division of a repeating structural frame defined by the column (or bearing wall) spacing. Simple structural bays consist of columns along all four sides of the structural bays (Figure 9.15). While simple in appearance, this layout results in the columns in the center having the greatest load (that of a full bay), side columns having loads half that of those in the center (half bays), and corner columns having loads only one-fourth of the center (quarter bays). To equalize the loading on all columns, half-bays can be created on the perimeter by using overhanging beams. This equal-

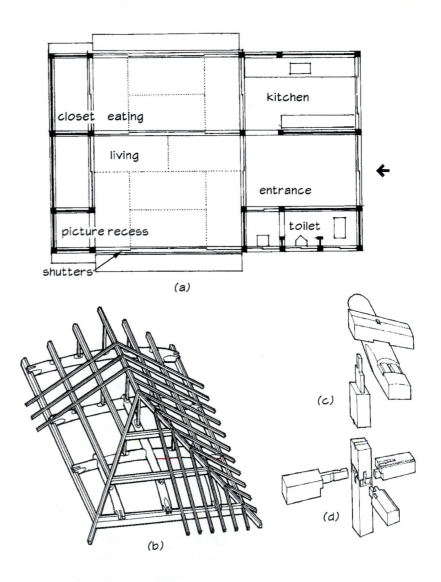

Figure 9.3: Post-and-beam timber construction in a traditional Japanese house: (a) typical floor plan of a house for three people, (b) hipped roof construction, (c) *orioki-gake* joint at roof beam, and (d) *ashi-gatane* column-floor beam mortised joint.

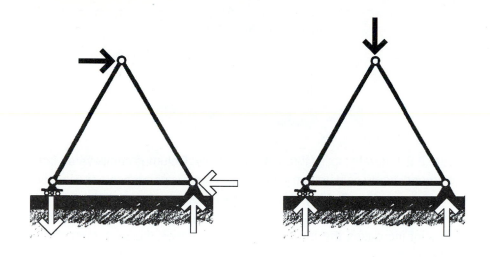

Figure 9.4: Lateral stability through triangulation: Triangular frame is inherently stable with hinged joints. Recall that a triangle cannot change shape without the length of one or more of its sides being changed.

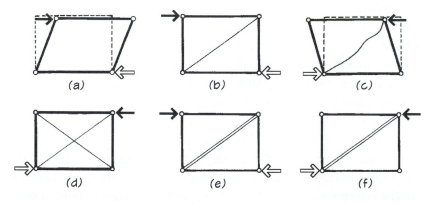

Figure 9.5: Lateral stability through triangulation: (a) a rectangular frame is inherently unstable with hinged joints; (b) adding a diagonal cable tie provides stability in one direction (when the cable is put in tension), (c) but not in the other direction (the cable cannot resist compression); (d) adding a second diagonal cable provides stability in both directions; (e) one diagonal strut provides stability in both directions because it can resist both tension and (f) compression.

Figure 9.6: Lateral stability is provided by cross-bracing expressed on the building exterior, John Hancock Center (1966; Chicago; Skidmore, Owings, and Merrill, architects and engineers). The structure was conceived to allow the slender building to resist the lateral wind loading. The architectural expression of the system was based on structural necessity.

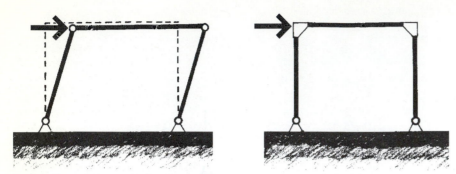

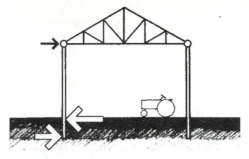

Figure 9.7: Lateral stability through joint rigidity: Rigid top joints form a table. Stability is achieved with one top rigid joint (which makes the frame behave as a stable triangle). More than one rigid joint increases the frame's rigidity but makes the system statically indeterminate.

Figure 9.9: Lateral stability through joint rigidity: Columns cantilevered from the ground create rigid bottom joints. This system is commonly used in "pole barn" construction. Stability is achieved with one bottom rigid joint (which makes the frame behave as a stable triangle). As above, more than one rigid joint increases the frame's rigidity but makes the system statically indeterminate.

izes the load on all columns and reduces the number of columns (and foundations) required.

RIGID FRAMES

The behavior of a simple post-and-beam frame (hinged joints at top) changes substantially when the column-to-beam joints are made rigid. Consider the model demonstration in Figure 9.16. If the columns are rigidly fixed to the beam, the assembly is a rigid frame. If supported at the beam ends (columns free to rotate) and loaded uniformly across the length of the beam, the beam will deflect and the columns will spread; a rigid frame with roller joints at the column bases would behave similarly. If the legs are prevented from spreading (if the column bases are hinged connections), they deflect in bending and thus contribute their strength to the bending resistance of the entire frame resulting in less deflection of the top beam.

The dotted parabola in Figure 9.17 shows the optimum arch shape for such a uniform load. If the frame followed this shape, there would be no bending. The amount of bending (moment) is directly related to the displacement of the frame from this ideal shape. Where this displacement is greatest (at the center span and at the column-beam

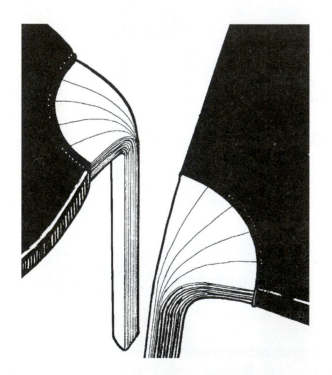

Figure 9.8: Lateral stability through joint rigidity: Laminated wood furniture detail designed by the Finnish architect Alvar Aalto.

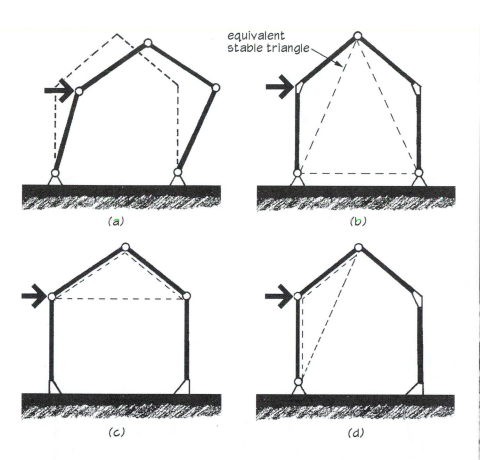

Figure 9.10: Lateral stability through joint rigidity: Three-hinged frame. (a) Pentagonal frame is unstable with four or more hinged joints. (b) Fixing the two "knee joints" makes the frame stable, behaving as a triangle (shown dotted). (c) Similarly, fixing the two bottom joints would also achieve stability. (d) As a general rule, to be stable, open frames can have no more than three of the joints hinged. In other words, such frames must be effectively reduced to triangles for stability.

Figure 9.11: Lateral stability through joint rigidity: three-hinged frame timber construction, Patoka Nature Center (1980; Birdseye, IN; Fuller Moore, architect), interior. The laminated timber frames form rigid joints at the thickened "haunches," resulting in an inherently stable triangular geometry.

Figure 9.12: Lateral stability through joint rigidity: rigid frame concrete construction, Riola Church (1975; Riola, Italy; Alvar Aalto, architect).

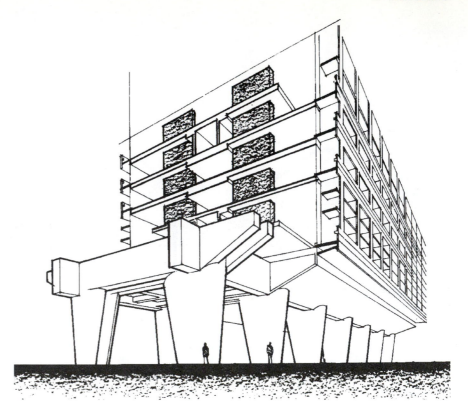

Figure 9.13: Cutaway revealing hidden rigid frame, l'Unité d'Habitation (1952; Marseilles, France; Le Corbusier, architect).

rigid connections), the bending moment is greatest and the frame depth needs to be greatest. Where the displacement is least (at column bases and at about the quarter-span points of the beam), the bending moment is zero and the frame can be hinged. But because this would result in an unstable, four-hinged frame, the upper joints are typically given some rigid thickness.

Multibay rigid frames

When rigid orthogonal frames are repeated, the fixed joints transmit the bending moment, and the deflection that occurs in any single bay (as a result of an applied load) is shared with surrounding bays. This interaction between adjacent bays means that the bending resistances of several bays combine to create a stiffer structure. It also

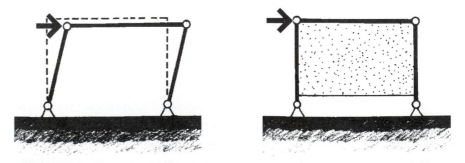

Figure 9.14: Lateral stability using shear walls. Adding an infill wall has the same effect as adding cross-bracing because the shape of the wall cannot be distorted without stretching or compressing the infill material.

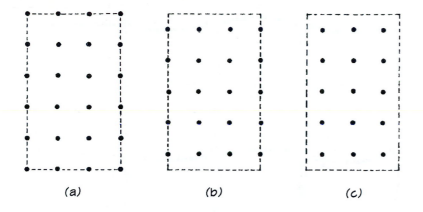

Figure 9.15: Structural bays: (a) simple bays, 24 columns required; (b) overhanging bays on two sides, 20 columns required; and (c) overhanging bays on four sides, 15 columns required.

means that deflection in one frame is transmitted throughout the entire structure. The model demonstration in Figure 9.18 reveals how the joint conditions of the frame (whether rigid or hinged) determine how bending loads are shared in multiframe structures. While a rigid frame is more efficient in its use of material, the additional labor required to ensure joint rigidity offsets some of this efficiency. The decision as to whether to make frames rigid is complex and requires much analysis and experience (Figure 9.19).

LIGHT-FRAME CONSTRUCTION

While the walls of *light-frame timber construction* consist of individual studs (acting as columns), the close spacing of these studs coupled with continuous plates that form the top and bottom and the attached sheathing of the wall makes this construction behave as a continuous bearing wall instead of discrete columns. (Similarly, the closely spaced joists covered with plywood behaves as a slab rather than discrete beams.) A *lintel* (short, heavily loaded beam) is used to span above an opening, transferring continuous wall loads to each side of the opening where multiple studs carry the increased load to the foundation below. Lateral stability is usually provided by the shear resistance (diaphragm action) of rigid sheathing (Figure 9.20).

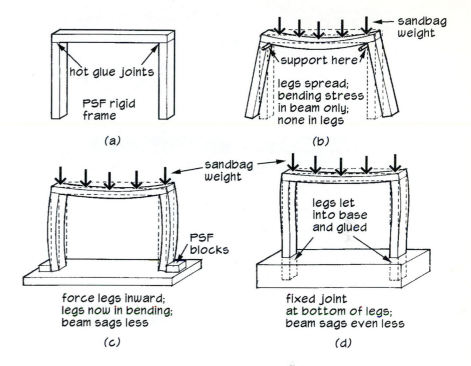

Figure 9.16: Model demonstration of rigid frame behavior: (a) unloaded rigid frame, (b) uniformly loaded, simply supported at top of columns (columns spread), (c) uniformly load rigid frame, hinged base (columns in bending, beam deflects less), and (d) uniformly loaded rigid frame, fixed base (columns bend in two directions, beam deflects even less).

History
Light-frame construction was made possible as a result of two developments of the Industrial Revolution: the mass-produced wire nail and *dimension lumber* [2 to 4 in (50 to 100 mm) thick and 2 in or more wide]. Prior to these developments, timber construction consisted of heavy timber columns and beams assembled using wood pegs and handmade nails.

The earliest light-frame system was the *balloon frame* (Figure 9.21) in which wall studs ran continuously from foundation to roof; intermediate floor joists were framed onto the side of the wall studs. This system required very long, straight studs and made construc-

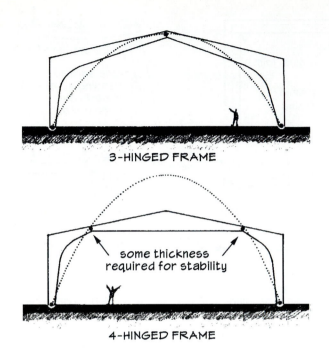

3-HINGED FRAME

4-HINGED FRAME

some thickness
required for stability

Figure 9.17: The bending moment at any point in a rigid frame is determined by the amount that the frame shape differs from an optimum arch shape that would result in no bending (a parabola in this case). The further a part of the frame is from the parabola, the greater the moment and the greater the necessary depth of the member. Where the parabola intersects the frame, the bending moment is zero, and a hinged joint could be inserted. In a four-hinged frame, some joint thickness is necessary for stability.

tion inconvenient in two-story buildings because the tall walls had to be constructed without the use of an intermediate floor to serve as a work platform. Finally, the tall voids between the studs created a chase that accelerated the spread of flames in the event of a fire.

The balloon frame has been virtually replaced by the *platform frame* (Figure 9.22) in which construction proceeds in a layered fashion: the floor construction rests on the foundation forming a platform for the construction of tilt-up stud walls. Next, these walls are

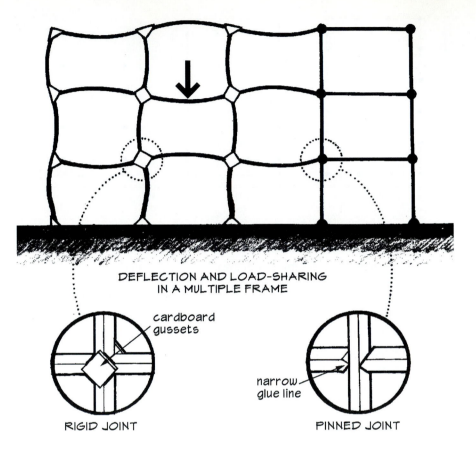

DEFLECTION AND LOAD-SHARING
IN A MULTIPLE FRAME

cardboard
gussets

narrow
glue line

RIGID JOINT

PINNED JOINT

Figure 9.18: Model demonstration of load sharing in a multiple frame. The left half of the frame has rigid joints; note how the bending moment is transmitted across joints deflecting adjacent members allowing them to contribute their bending resistance to the effects of the load. The right half of the frame has hinged joints; note how the bending moment remains localized with minimum effect on adjacent members. As a result the loaded member is the sole contributor to bending resistance.

tilted into place and temporarily braced. If a second (or third) floor is required, the floor-wall sequence is repeated. Finally, roof and ceiling joists (or, more commonly today, trussed rafters) are installed on top of the last wall.

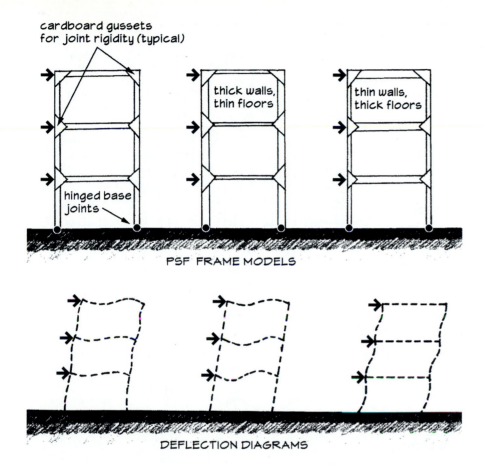

PSF FRAME MODELS

DEFLECTION DIAGRAMS

Figure 9.19: Model demonstration of the effects of varying the stiffness of beams and columns when a building frame is subjected to lateral loads.

The ease of wood frame construction, coupled with the abundant availability of construction-grade softwood dimensional timber and plywood, has made it the system of choice for single-family residential construction in the United States and Canada. It offers great design flexibility and is adaptable to a variety of styles (Figures 9.23 and 9.24). Finally, the voids between the studs afford a convenient space for thermal insulation resulting in high energy efficiency.

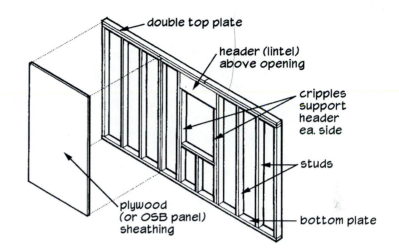

Figure 9.20: The stud wall commonly used in light-frame wood construction consists of closely spaced studs with continuous top and bottom plates and behaves structurally like a bearing wall. The addition of plywood sheathing (or equivalent) increases both bearing capacity and shear resistance.

POST-AND-BEAM CASE STUDIES

Keldy Castle Forest Cabins
These cabins (1979; Cropton, England; Hird and Brooks, architects; Chapman and Smart, structural engineers) were part of a forested development of 58 units. They are noteworthy as an example of post-and-beam construction due to their simple exposed structure with elegant joint details reminiscent of traditional Japanese house construction. Each cabin has a floor area of 100 ft² (30 m²) accommodating living space and beds for five people. The cabins are made of timber elements and panels which were prefabricated in order to permit rapid erection on the site. After foundation was complete, the building fabric of each cabin was completed in a single day by four men. It is an excellent example of the use of wood as a material for industrialized building (Orton, 1988) (Figures 9.25 and 9.26).

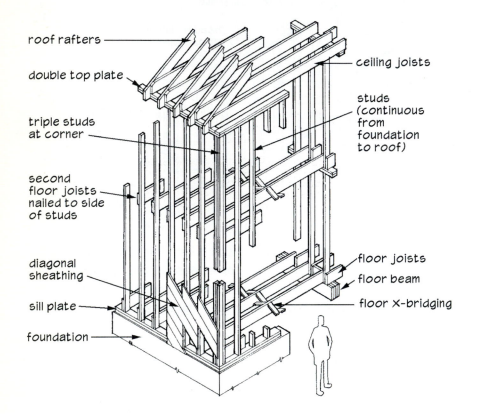

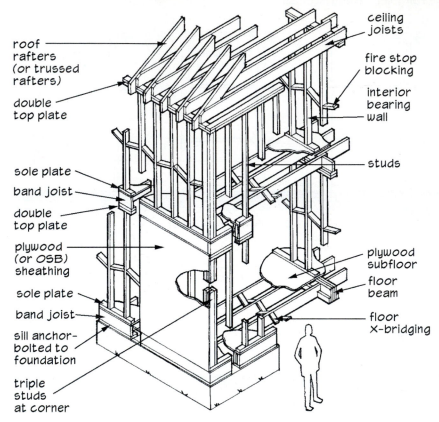

Figure 9.21: The balloon frame was the first light-frame timber construction. It is characterized by tall studs that run continuously from foundation to roof with floors framed onto the sides of the wall studs.

Figure 9.22: The platform frame is the modern evolution of light-frame timber construction. It is characterized by the alternating layers of floor and wall. Each floor provides a platform for the construction of tilt-up stud walls for that level.

The cabins are supported by 4 in × 12 in (100 mm × 300 mm) timber beams which rest on concrete grade beams or timber posts on concrete pier foundations, allowing the cabins to be positioned on slopes while providing lateral stability. All the connections behave as pinned joints. Lateral resistance to wind loads is provided by the roof, floor, and walls acting as shear panels.

Schulitz residence

The Schulitz residence (1978; Beverly Hills, CA; H.C. Schulitz, ar - chitect) is an excellent example of the use of manufactured steel components for residential construction. Like the pioneering 1949 Charles Eames house in nearby Pacific Palisades that preceded it, this design uses lightweight steel trusses arranged in a post-and-

Figure 9.23: The Cooper residence (1968; Orleans, MA; Charles Gwathmey, architect) demonstrates the flexibility of bearing-wall light-frame timber construction.

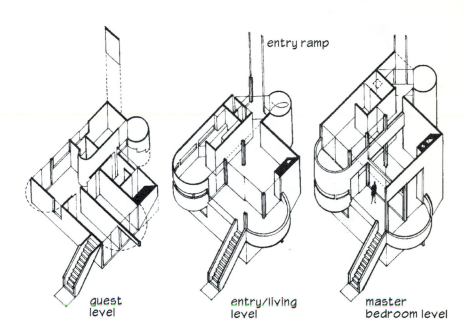

Figure 9.24: Cooper residence, axonometric plans.

beam configuration to provide a setting for the different infill textures provided by wood trellis slats, shades, venetian blinds, and other materials (Orton, 1988) (Figures 9.27 through 9.29).

Because of its location in an earthquake region, the structure must resist not only gravity and wind loads, but the very substantial ground accelerations resulting from seismic activity. The inherent light weight of the structure minimizes these inertial forces. Steel

diagonal cross ties provide the required lateral resistance and allow the joints between beams, trusses, and columns to behave as pinned connections. This results in economical construction and allows generous erection tolerances.

Located on a steep hillside, there are three stories to the house, the top being at street level. The steel frame structure consists of 6 in × 6 in (150 mm × 150 mm) tubular columns that support two main channel beams on each side. The ends of these are extended past the columns on the facade to visually emphasize the connection. The channel beams in turn support the lightweight steel trusses (open-web joists) spaced 4 ft (1.2 m) on center; these support the metal decking with lightweight concrete topping. The four rows of steel columns are supported by three rows of short concrete columns and the concrete retaining wall at the upper street level. These concrete supports are tied together by a reinforced concrete grade beam cast on the sloping surface of the ground.

Figure 9.25: Keldy Castle Forest Cabins, exterior.

West Beach Bathhouse

This single-story precast concrete building (1977; Chesterton, IN; Howard, Needles, Tammem, and Bergendoff, architects) provides changing facilities for bathers at the nearby beach. It is designed to blend into its sand dune setting and minimize the disturbance of the dune during construction. The featured construction element is a precast concrete column capital that connects the beams and columns. Located at both floor and roof levels, this capital provides a generous allowance for the connection between the cast-in-place round columns and the precast beams. The beams, in turn, support precast hollow-core planks. The floor planks are covered with a 2-in (50-mm) concrete topping; the roof planks are covered with rigid insulation and built-up roofing (Orton, 1988) (Figures 9.30 and 9.31).

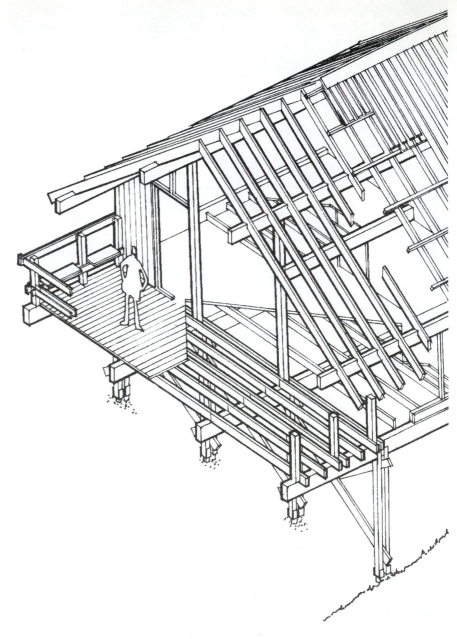

Figure 9.26: Keldy Castle Forest Cabins, cutaway axonometric drawing.

Figure 9.27: Schulitz residence, exterior.

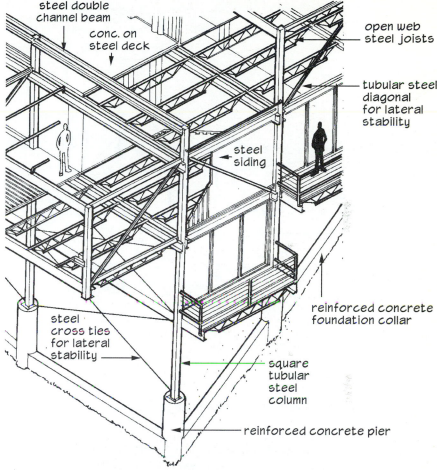

steel double channel beam

conc. on steel deck

open web steel joists

tubular steel diagonal for lateral stability

steel siding

steel cross ties for lateral stability

reinforced concrete foundation collar

square tubular steel column

reinforced concrete pier

Figure 9.28: Schulitz residence, cutaway axonometric detail.

The exterior nonbearing masonry walls turn the corners with a 45° bevel separating themselves from the columns, visually emphasizing their importance. The precast capitals are especially expressive at the corners because they are notched on all four sides to receive beams; the exposed slots at the corner columns articulate how the rest of the structure is joined.

Because the columns cantilever from the ground, the beam connections at the floor and roof level behave as pinned joints. An anchor bolt cast into the capital fits into a sleeved hole in each beam end; a nut secures the beam in place but allows movement due to shrinkage and thermal expansion. If the structure were higher, additional lateral support would be required (by cross-bracing or shear walls, for example).

Boston City Hall

Winner of a design competition that attracted entries from renowned architects across the world, Boston City Hall (1969; Boston; Kallmann, McKinnell, and Knowles, architects; Le Messurier Associates, structural engineers), this building helped reverse the trend of moving major urban resources to the suburbs. Because of its importance as the seat of government of this major city, it

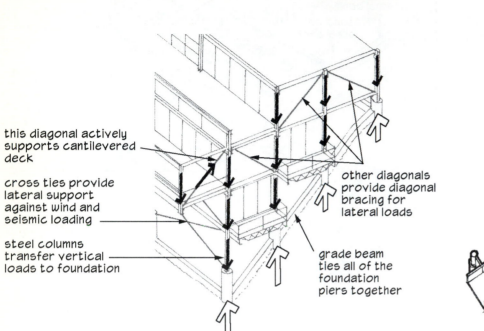

this diagonal actively
supports cantilevered
deck

cross ties provide
lateral support
against wind and
seismic loading

steel columns
transfer vertical
loads to foundation

other diagonals
provide diagonal
bracing for
lateral loads

grade beam
ties all of the
foundation
piers together

Figure 9.29: Schulitz residence, load path diagram.

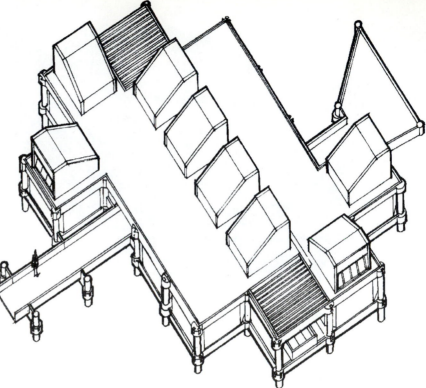

Figure 9.30: West Beach Bathhouse, axonometric detail.

is appropriate that this winning entry is such a serious and complete piece of architecture and not merely a skillful exercise in function, technology, or elevational effect. The most fundamental purpose of the building as a civic monument and symbol of the vitality of the city is clear (Orton, 1988; Editor, 1969b) (Figures 9.32 through 9.34).

It is advantageously sited in a large, brick-paved plaza sufficiently far from adjacent buildings to allow the building to be seen from some distance as well as giving generous pedestrian space at the main north and west entrances. On the inside the two entries flow into generous lobbies which are connected by monumental stairs and escalators. In addition, an open space on level 4 is reached from the plaza by outside steps on the west

side, making the building even more accessible to the public. This space also serves to separate the upper offices from the lower, more public spaces. Level 5 houses the city council chamber, offices, mayor's department, and exhibition and library spaces; each of these rooms is expressed individually on the exterior facades. Offices on the upper three floors are sheathed on the facade by three stepped tiers of closely spaced precast concrete fins combining into a cornice at the top of the building.

The floor system is a unifying element of the design, consisting of large cast-in-place concrete columns, 32 in (810 mm) square. These are arranged in a tartan grid (narrow bays alter-

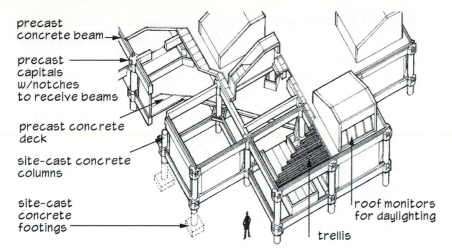

precast concrete beam

precast capitals w/notches to receive beams

precast concrete deck

site-cast concrete columns

site-cast concrete footings

roof monitors for daylighting

trellis

Figure 9.31: West Beach Bathhouse, cutaway axonometric detail.

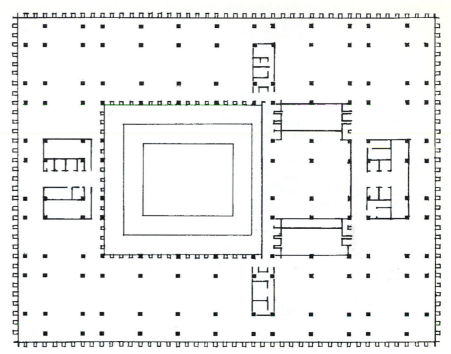

Figure 9.33: Boston City Hall, ninth-floor plan showing tartan column grid.

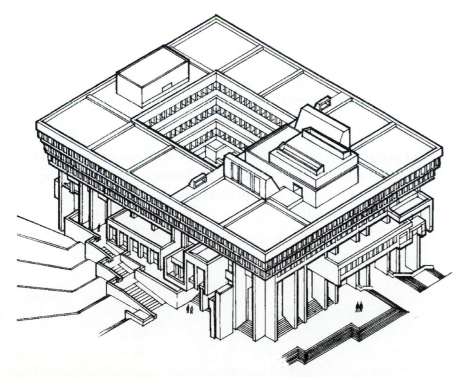

Figure 9.32: Boston City Hall, axonometric view from southwest.

nating with wide bays) with spacing of either 14 ft 4 in (4.37 m) or double that distance. This spacing serves to organize the plan functions; typically, activities and rooms are located in the large bays while service and circulation usually occurs in the narrow bays.

Pairs of precast-concrete Vierendeel beams, 5 ft (1.5 m) deep and 11 ft 8 in (3.5 m) long in both directions on 14-ft 4-in. (4.37-m) centers, align with the column face and join over the column. (Where there is no column, they are joined by a cast-in-place joint of the same plan area.) The open bays are further subdivided by intermediate cross-shaped precast concrete beams at the ceiling level. The 5-in (125-mm) floor slabs are cast-in-place. The air-conditioning ducts and other service conduits run within the precast Vierendeel beam openings. Gravity loads are transferred horizontally by the grid of beams which span in both directions.

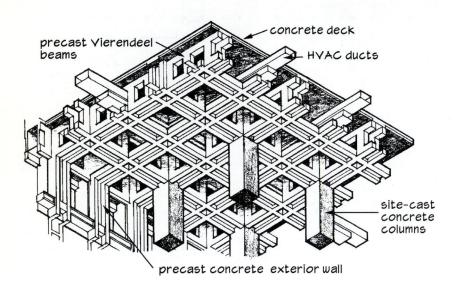

precast Vierendeel beams

concrete deck

HVAC ducts

site-cast concrete columns

precast concrete exterior wall

Figure 9.34: Boston City Hall, isometric detail showing interior floor construction.

SUMMARY

1. *Frames* distribute loads horizontally (by means of beams or slabs) to columns (or bearing walls) which transmit the forces vertically to the supporting foundation.

2. *One-level* framing systems typically combine a slab (or joists) spanning between two parallel bearing walls. *Two-level* systems typically consist of a slab supported by parallel beams which bear on either two parallel walls or a row of columns (one under each beam). *Three-level* systems typically include a slab supported by closely spaced joists, supported by beams (perpendicular to the joists), and finally supported by columns.

3. Lateral stability in frames may be provided by *triangulation, joint rigidity,* or *shear walls.*

4. A *bay* is an internal division of a repeating structural frame defined by the column (or bearing wall) spacing.

5. A *rigid frame* transfers moment from a beam to supporting columns, resulting in the columns sharing the bending resistance (and deflection) with the beam. This interaction between adjacent bays means that bending resistance (and deflection) resulting from an applied load is shared between several bays.

6. The *balloon frame* is an early light-frame timber construction system in which wall studs run continuously from foundation to roof.

7. The *platform frame* is the contemporary successor to the balloon frame in which each story is constructed as a separate layer, with the floor serving as a platform for constructing the walls which are tilted into place.

Part IV

FUNICULAR SYSTEMS

Funicular (also known as *form-active*) structures are shaped in response to applied loads so that the resulting internal stresses are direct tension or compression. As an example, consider a cable spanning between two supporting points and carrying a load. The cable assumes a V-shape with the load at the bottom and is in pure tension. If a second load is added, the shape of the cable changes into three straight segments in response to the location and magnitude of each load. Adding additional loads increases the number of segments approaching the sagging curved shape characteristic of a distributed load. In each case, the cable is in pure tension (Figure VI. 1).

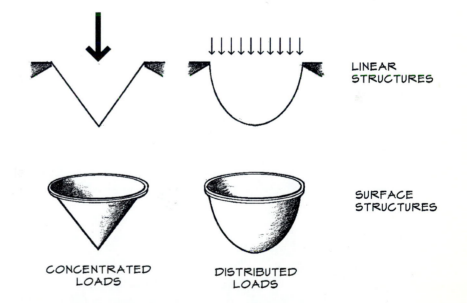

Figure IV.1: Funicular suspension structures.

CATENARY CABLES

The finest engineer in the animal world is the spider.
Her net, gentle like the water, flexible like the tree, is
a marvel of construction in its sophistication.
—Horst Berger

FUNICULAR CURVES

The catenary is the funicular shape for an unloaded cable and is determined solely by the self-weight of the cable (which is uniform along the length of the cable). A parabola is the funicular shape of a suspension cable loaded uniformly across its horizontal span, ignoring the weight of the cable. Where the span-to-sag ratio is greater than 5, the two shapes are nearly identical, and the mathematically simpler parabola is typically used for analysis (Figure 10.1).

In practice (and in this book), the term catenary is also used more broadly to refer to any curved suspension member which is loaded along its length, regardless of the exact loading distribution. For example, the main cables of a suspension bridge are the catenary cables, even though the curvature more closely approximates a parabola.

CATENARY THRUST

For a given loading condition, the depth of the sag of a catenary structure determines the horizontal (inward) thrust that is generated; the less the sag, the greater the thrust (Figure 10.2).

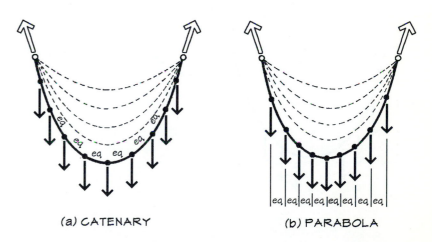

Figure 10.1: Funicular curves for distributed loads on suspension cables: (a) catenary for loading that is uniform across the curved length of the cable, and (b) parabola for loading that is uniform across a horizontal span. For span-to-sag ratios greater than 5, the shapes are approximately the same.

mast height and compressive forces as well as means of resisting inward thrust induced by the cable.

In general, cable forces are inversely proportional to sag; in other words, as the cable length decreases its required diameter increases. This relationship translates into an optimization problem of minimizing the total steel in the cable. A cable with a very small sag is short but requires a very large diameter because of the very large tensile forces; conversely, a cable with a very deep sag can have a small diameter due to the low tensile forces but becomes quite long. For a single load applied at midspan, the optimum sag is 50 percent of the span; for a uniformly loaded parabolic cable, the optimum sag is approximately 33 percent of the span. In practice, however, other considerations (depth available for sag and the design of the vertical support) reduce this ratio considerably; most cables used for building roof structures have sag-to-span ratios of 1:8 to 1:10.

Funicular suspension structures may be divided into three categories: single-curvature, double-cable, and double-curvature (Figure 10.3).

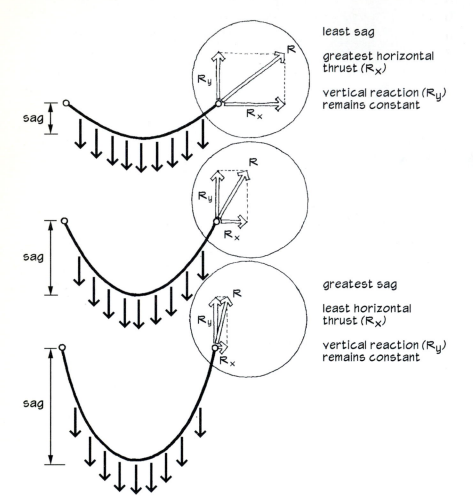

least sag

greatest horizontal thrust (R_x)

vertical reaction (R_y) remains constant

greatest sag

least horizontal thrust (R_x)

vertical reaction (R_y) remains constant

Figure 10.2: Thrust reactions vary inversely with the depth of the cable sag.

single curvature

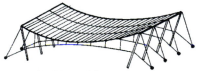
double cable

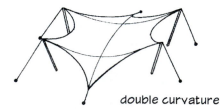
double curvature

Figure 10.3: Suspension structure types.

Catenary cable structures are capable of enormous spans. For particular spans and loading conditions, the sag-to-span ratio is a primary structural design consideration. Cable forces, length, and diameter all depend on this proportion. This also determines the

SINGLE-CURVATURE STRUCTURES

Single-curvature structures consist of two or more parallel catenary cables spanning between primary supports. They may support a deck *directly* (resulting in a curved roof, for example) or *indirectly* (using secondary vertical cables to support a flat roof or bridge deck, for example).

BRIDGES

The ancient rope suspension bridge (early examples have been identified in China, India, and South America) is the precedent for single-curvature structures. One existing example in a remote part of India consists of a single twisted bamboo rope spanning 660 ft (200 m). Travelers slide down it hanging from a loop and pull themselves up the opposite side. Other examples have two higher ropes that can be used as handrails. A further development includes a bottom and sides consisting of many ropes woven together forming a U-shape like a long hammock (Figure 10.4).

Findley's stiffened deck

A problem inherent with a bridge of such flexibility is that as travelers move across, its shape changes in response to the moving load. The stiffened bridge deck, developed in 1801 by James Findley, was a key development in the evolution of the suspension bridge. Findley's first bridge spanned 200 ft (61 m) over Jacobs Creek in Uniontown, Pennsylvania. The stiffened deck prevented the supporting wrought iron chain from changing shape under moving loads by distributing the loads over a large portion of the span (Brown, 1993) (Figure 10.5).

Figure 10.5: The Chain Bridge (1801; Uniontown, PA; J. Findley, designer) was the first to incorporate a stiffened deck to distribute loads over a large length of the supporting cable and greatly reduce movement.

Findley's bridge used the same basic geometry that has been used on all subsequent suspension bridges: two or more towers support a pair of main suspension cables from which vertical secondary cables suspend the deck which carries the roadway. To balance the lateral reactions at the top of the towers, the main cables continue to anchor in massive concrete buttresses ("dead men") at each end. In addition to requiring stiffness vertically (so as to distribute the load), the deck must be stiff laterally to resist wind deflection (Figure 10.6).

After the publication of Findley's innovation in 1823, suspension bridges were built in rapid succession, including Thomas Telford's Menai Striates Bridge [1826, Wales, spanning 327 ft (99 m)], James Roebling's Cincinnati Bridge [1866, spanning 1057 ft

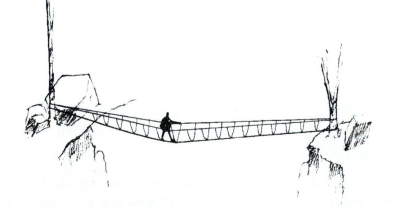

Figure 10.4: Primitive rope bridge.

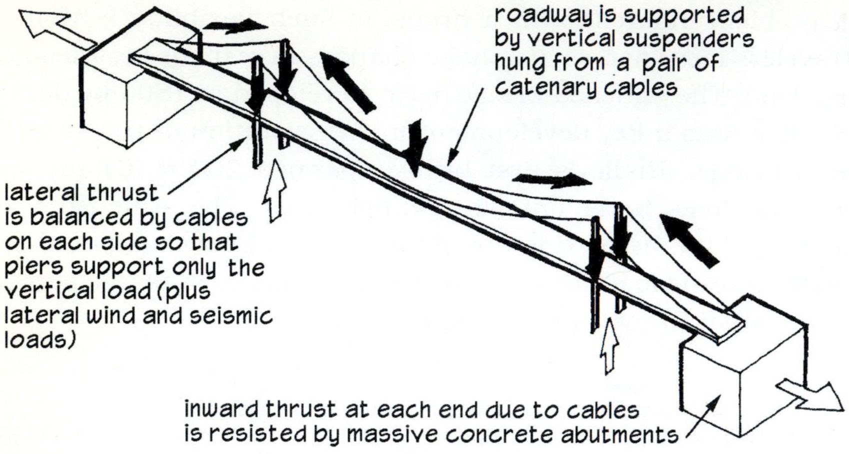

roadway is supported
by vertical suspenders
hung from a pair of
catenary cables

lateral thrust
is balanced by cables
on each side so that
piers support only the
vertical load (plus
lateral wind and seismic
loads)

inward thrust at each end due to cables
is resisted by massive concrete abutments

Figure 10.6: Suspension bridge load paths.

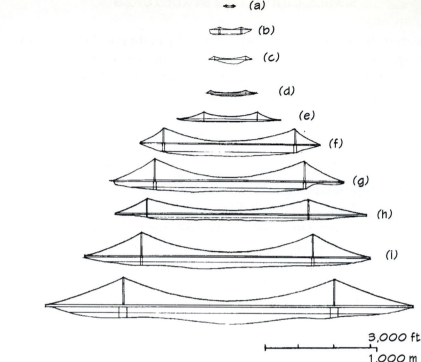

3,000 ft
1,000 m

Figure 10.7: Clear-span evolution in suspension bridges: (a) James Finley's Chain Bridge [1911; 210 ft (61 m)], (b) Menai Straits Bridge [1826; Wales, 579 ft (176 m)], (c) Grand Pont Suspendu [1834; Fribourg, Switzerland; 896 ft (273 m)], (d) Wheeling Bridge [1849; Wheeling, WV; 1010 ft (308 m)], (e) Brooklyn Bridge [1883; Brooklyn; 1268 ft (386 m)], (f) George Washington Bridge [1931; New York City; 3500 ft (1067 m)], (g) Golden Gate Bridge [1937; San Francisco; 4200 ft (1,280 m)], (h) Humber Bridge [1981; Humber Estuary, England; 4624 ft (1,410 m)], (i) East Bridge [1997; Sprogo, Denmark; 5328 ft (1624 m)], and (j) Akashi Kaikyo Bridge [1998 est.; Awaji, Japan; 6529 ft (1,990 m)].

(322 m)], and Roebling's Brooklyn Bridge [1883, spanning 1268 ft (386 m)]. As impressive as these nineteenth century examples were, their spans were modest compared with those that were to follow in the twentieth century (Figure 10.7).

As designers became more confident, spans increased, and both the supporting towers and the bridge decks became relatively lighter. When originally constructed in 1937, the Golden Gate Bridge incorporated a trussed deck for stiffness; however, the depth-to-span ratio of 1:168 was still much shallower than any previous bridge. An unanticipated lateral rippling effect (even in moderate winds) necessitated adding an additional 4700 tons (4262 metric tons) of lateral bracing underneath along its entire length. Still, designers attempted to make subsequent bridges thinner. In the pursuit of slenderness and grace, the Bronx-Whitestone Bridge (1939; New York City; O. Amman, structural engineer) reduced the depth-to-span ratio to 1:209.

"Galloping Gertie"
But the ill-fated Tacoma Narrows Bridge (1940; Tacoma, WA; L. Moisseiff, structural engineer) achieved the slenderest deck. While the 2800-ft (853-m) span was longer than the Bronx-Whitestone

Bridge, it was designed for less traffic and was only two lanes wide with a walkway. The plate girder deck was just 8 ft (2.4 m) deep, resulting in a depth-to-span ratio of only 1:350. The bridge was soon nicknamed "Galloping Gertie" because of its motion in relatively light winds. It swayed laterally, but it also developed rippling waves along its length.

On November 7, 1940, a moderate wind of 42 miles per hour (mi/h) [(68 kilometers per hour (kph)] set up severe lateral twisting of the deck as well as longitudinal rippling. The violent motion of the deck soon began to snap the vertical cables, with those remaining quickly becoming overloaded. In a rapid chain reaction, the remaining cables parted and a large portion of the center span crashed into the water below (Brown, 1993) (Figure 10.8).

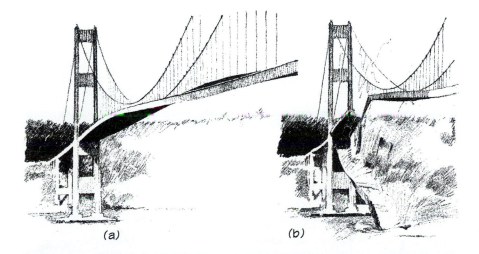

Figure 10.8: Tacoma Narrows Bridge: (a) seconds before the collapse, the deck exhibits the twisting motion which led to (b) the final collapse.

While the bridge had been designed for limited flexibility, what the engineers failed to anticipate was the aerodynamic flutter that finally caused the failure. As the deck deflected sideways, it tended to twist, inclining the roadbed into a winglike slat that would "climb" until the twist reversed and then "dive." Under those particular wind conditions, this oscillating movement became unstable, with the vertical movement (and twisting) progressively increasing. Subsequent wind tunnel testing revealed that the bridge's solid girder configuration was more prone to this aerodynamic effect than compa-

rable open trusses which divided the wind flow into smaller turbulent eddies.

Ever since the Tacoma Narrows collapse, aerodynamic behavior has been a concern for suspension bridge designers throughout the world. Some engineers have tended to depend on open trusses to reduce aerodynamic flutter (Figure 10.9), while others have more recently preferred to intentionally shape the deck as an airfoil designed to induce downward "lift" and reduce large oscillation-producing eddies. The resulting construction is up to 50 percent lighter than comparable American designs (Figure 10.10).

Figure 10.9: Forth Road Bridge [1964, Scotland, spanning 3300 ft (1,006 m)] used open trusses to minimize flutter.

SINGLE-CURVATURE SUSPENSION CASE STUDIES

Burgo Paper Mill

This bridgelike roof structure (1962; Mantua, Italy; PierLuigi Nervi, architect and structural engineer) originally covered an area of 86,000

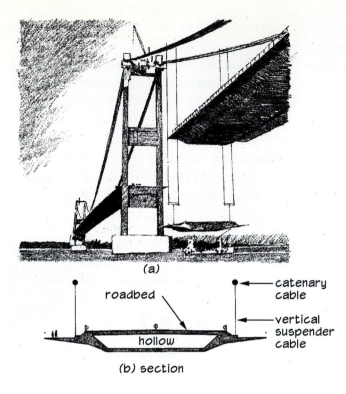

(a)

catenary cable

roadbed

vertical suspender cable

hollow

(b) section

Figure 10.10: Severn River Bridge (1966, England, Freeman, Fox, & Partners, structural engineers) utilizes an airfoil shape to a thin deck to achieve aerodynamic stability. The depth-to-span ratio is 1:324—similar to the failed Tacoma Narrows span (1:350). (a) Construction showing deck section being lifted, and (b) section through the deck which is 10 ft (3 m) deep at the center.

ft² (7992 m²) and was used to house paper manufacturing machinery. The structure spanned in the longer direction (it is typically more economical to span in the shortest direction) in order to allow for future additions for housing new production lines parallel to the original while still maintaining a column-free central area (Nervi, 1963) (Figures 10.11 and 10.12).

The center span of 535 ft (163 m) was achieved by four primary suspension cables, with vertical secondary cables supporting the flat steel roof deck below. Each end cantilevered an additional 140 ft

Figure 10.11: Burgo Paper Mill suspension roof under construction.

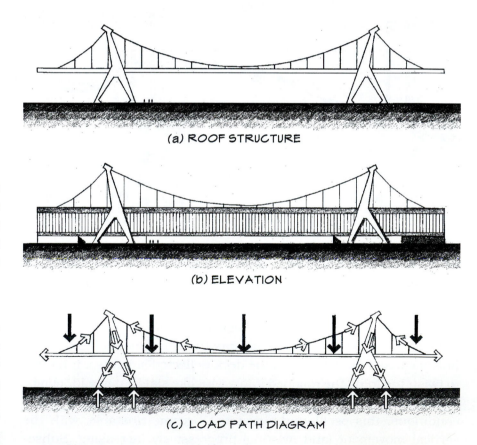

(a) ROOF STRUCTURE

(b) ELEVATION

(c) LOAD PATH DIAGRAM

Figure 10.12: Burgo Paper Mill: (a) section of roof structure, (b) elevation, and (c) load path diagram.

(43 m). The dead weight of the roof deck was used to counteract wind uplift forces. The concrete supports were rigid frames which provided the required lateral stability perpendicular to the span. The entire original structure was supported on four large reinforced concrete piers 164 ft (50 m) tall.

While the cable structure behaved identically to that of suspension bridges, it differed in the way that the horizontal thrust reactions were resolved at each end. Bridge cables are anchored to the ground at each end in massive concrete abutments to resist inward thrust. The paper mill roof cables were not connected to the ground but to the ends of the cantilevering roof deck instead. As a result, the horizontal cable thrust reactions caused substantial compression in the roof deck.

Minneapolis Federal Reserve Bank

A long clear span was achieved in this high-rise building (1973; Minneapolis; G. Birkerts and Associates, architects; Skilling, Helle, Christiansen, Robertson, structural engineers) in order to leave the civic plaza below free of obstructions as well as to eliminate columns which would interfere with the layout of the underground portion of the building below the plaza. The building was designed in two parts: a very large underground secure area (for receiving and processing large amounts of money), and the 10-story office block above [the floor area of each level is 16,800 ft² (1560 m²)], with an open plaza between with only the entry lobby and end supports. As Birkerts explained, "On the one hand it wanted to be opaque and protected and on the other it wanted to be transparent and communicative." (McCoy, 1973) (Figures 10.13 through 10.16).

The building is most notable for its daring and boldly expressed suspension structure of the office block used to span 270 ft (82.3 m) across the plaza. The two end service towers (containing stairs, toilets, service elevators, and mechanical spaces) provide all the vertical support and lateral stability for the office block. Each of these granite-faced end towers have a reinforced-concrete, H-shaped bearing structure that cantilevers vertically from the ground.

The two primary suspension "catenaries" (actually, because they are uniformly loaded horizontally, they are closer to a parabolic shape)

Figure 10.13: Federal Reserve Bank, exterior.

consist of welded steel plate an average of 3 ft (0.91 m) deep and contain 4 in (100 mm)-diameter posttensioning cables. There are eight cables at the top of each catenary, reducing to six, then four, then to two cables at the bottom.

The inward horizontal thrust at the top of the catenaries is resisted by a box truss across the top of the building. This truss is 28 ft (8.5 m) deep, 60 ft (18.3 m) wide, and 270 ft (82.3 m) long. The lines of action of the towers, the truss, and the catenaries cross on a line at each end. The critical connection between these three major elements at the top of each corner of the building is a steel anchor weighing 92 tons (85 metric tons).

The floors above the catenaries are supported by columns (that rest on the top of the catenary). Floors below are suspended from

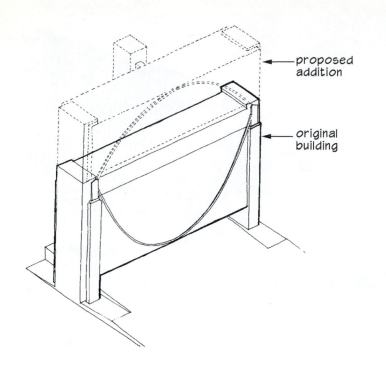

Figure 10.14: Federal Reserve Bank, axonometric detail showing proposed addition (dotted).

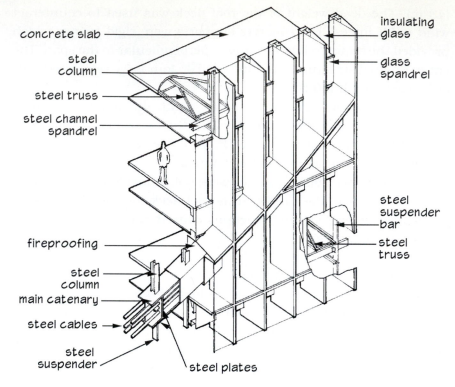

Figure 10.15: Federal Reserve Bank, isometric cutaway detail of office wall.

the catenaries by steel fins. Glass is flush with the surface below the catenary and recessed above, visually emphasizing the different structural behavior.

The floor structure consists of lightweight concrete on steel deck on light steel trusses 10 ft (3 m) on center. These trusses span across the 60-ft (18.3-m) width of the offices leaving the interior column-free. Wind loads are resisted by the diaphragm action of the floors which transfer the loads to the end towers.

Dulles Terminal Building
The Dulles Terminal Building (1962; Washington, DC; Eero Saarinen and Associates, architects; Ammann and Whitney, structural engi-

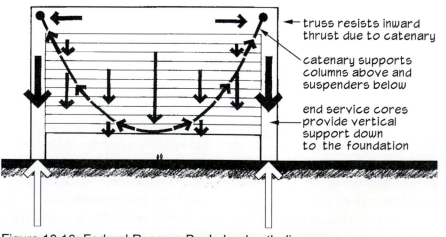

Figure 10.16: Federal Reserve Bank, load path diagram.

neers) is a combination of ingenious planning and expressive architecture. It is notable for its compact plan and short passenger walking distances (an airport amenity made possible by the mobile lounge). It is equally notable for its graceful suspended roof and the colonnades of supporting pylons (Saarinen, 1963; Editor 1960a; 1963a) (Figures 10.17 through 10.19).

The roof is supported by a row of concrete pylons 40 ft (12.2 m) apart on each side. They are 65 ft (19.8 m) tall on the approach side and 40 ft (12.2 m) on the field side. Resembling a huge hammock suspended between concrete trees, it consists of parallel catenary pairs of 1-in (25-mm)-diameter steel cables 10 ft (3 m) apart, with precast concrete panels spanning between them. The outer edge of the roof is poured-in-place concrete forming an edge beam to support the three pairs of cables between the pylons.

During construction, sandbags were temporarily distributed on the precast decking in order to achieve the design curvature of the cables. Once the desired curvature was achieved, concrete was poured around the cables, stiffening them to create inverted arches to resist (along with the dead load of the decking) against wind uplift. The concrete pylons are huge cantilevered columns leaning against the inward thrust of the suspension cables. Each of the 16 taller pylons has 20 tons (18.1 metric tons) of reinforcing steel.

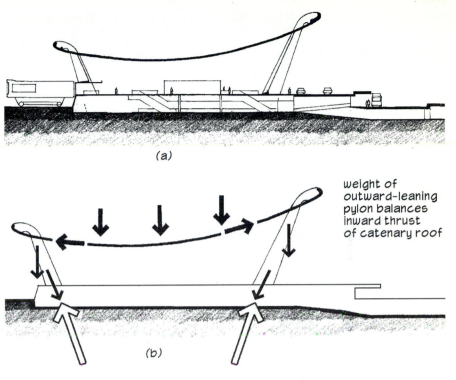

weight of outward-leaning pylon balances inward thrust of catenary roof

Figure 10.18: Dulles Terminal Building: (a) section, and (b) load path diagram.

Figure 10.17: Dulles Terminal Building, exterior.

DOUBLE-CABLE STRUCTURES

Double-cable structures are similar to single-curvature structures with the addition of stabilizing cables below the primary suspension ones to resist wind uplift (Figure 10.20). If the two cables are in the same plane, some additional means of ensuring lateral stability (perpendicular to this plane) must be incorporated (Figure 10.21).

DOUBLE-CABLE SUSPENSION CASE STUDIES

Denver International Airport Terminal
An example of the use of opposing double cables to reinforce fabric roofs, the main terminal Great Hall is the largest tensile roof structure enclosing a single space in the world (1995; Denver, CO; Fentress,

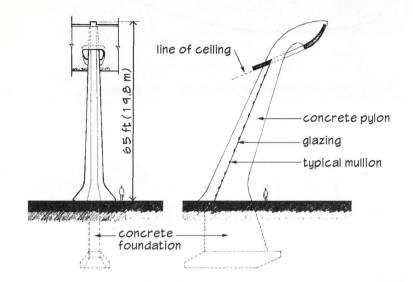

Figure 10.19: Dulles Terminal Building: pylon elevations.

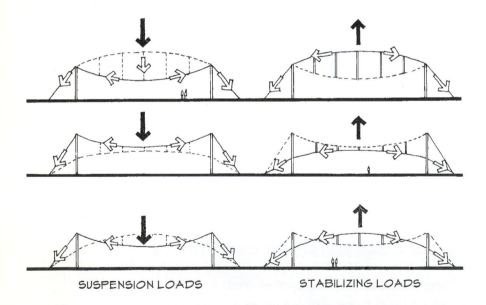

SUSPENSION LOADS   STABILIZING LOADS

Figure 10.20: Three examples of double-cable structures showing paths of loads of the suspension cable (on left) and stabilizing cable (on right).

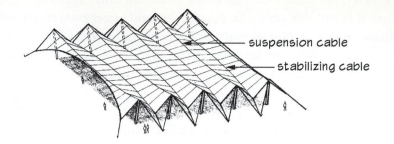

Figure 10.21: Suspension cables and stabilization cables in different planes.

Bradburn, and Associates, architects; Severud Associates, structural engineers). Fabric was chosen for lightness and speed of erection as well as for aesthetic reasons. Alluding to the surrounding snow-capped Rocky Mountains, the peaks are created by 34 steel masts, placed in pairs 150 ft (45 m) apart with 60 ft (18.3 m) between each pair. The fabric sags between the peaks to span 240 ft (63 m) across the Great Hall. The fabric is reinforced by the cables following the ridges and valleys which carry most of the tensile loads. The suspension ridge cables support the gravity loads due to snow and self-weight, while the stabilizing valley cables resist wind lift. A third set of cables connecting the ridge and valley cables at intervals of 40 ft (12.2 m) reinforce the fabric (Landeker, 1994; Stein, 1993; Blake, 1995) (Figures 10.22 through 10.25).

The roof is a double layer of fabric, both made of Teflon-coated fiberglass. The 0.28-in. (7mm)-thick outer layer is the primary structural layer, while the inner one provides an additional acoustical barrier and creates an airspace to reduce heat loss.

A critical detail in this building is the connection between the flexible fabric roof and the rigid walls below. Above the ticketing counters is a triangular clerestory of glass that allows the sky to be seen from the floor of the Great Hall. The upper edge of the clerestory is connected to the fabric. The roof surface moves as much as 3 in (75 mm) with pneumatic tubes expanding and contracting with the movement of the fabric.

The fabric and cables continue past the tubular steel masts to anchor into the conventional building structure at each end. It is these anchors which resist the inward thrust caused by the cat-

Figure 10.22: Denver International Airport Terminal, exterior showing the tent peaks similar to the surrounding snow-capped Rocky Mountains.

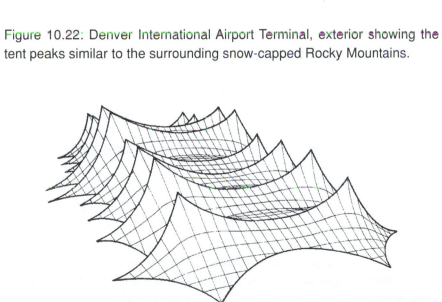

Figure 10.23: Denver International Airport Terminal, geodesic net of fabric roof.

Figure 10.24: Denver International Airport Terminal, interior of the Great Hall.

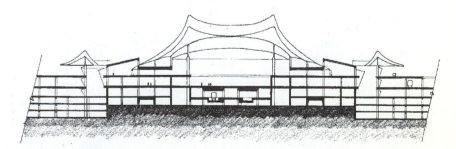

enary fabric roof; the masts contribute only vertical support and behave as though pin-connected at the base.

Figure 10.25: Denver International Airport Terminal, section through the Great Hall; five levels of parking are on each side.

Utica Auditorium

One of the disadvantages in arranging the pairs of cables in a parallel arrangement such as that used in the Denver structure is the necessity of resisting the inward thrust from the suspension cables. In a circular configuration, these thrust forces can be balanced by a compression ring, avoiding the necessity for either guy cables or massive cantilevered pylons (such as those used on the Dulles Terminal Building). One example of such a "bicycle wheel" roof system is the Utica Auditorium (1962; Utica, NY; Lev Letlin Associates, structural engineers) (Figure 10.26). It uses radial suspension cables hung from a 240-ft (63-m)-diameter perimeter concrete compression ring to a center lower tension ring to support the gravity loads. Uplift forces are resisted by a similar pattern of stabilizing cables from the compression ring to upper tension ring. These opposing pairs of cables and the two center tension rings are separated by vertical struts. The compression ring is reinforced concrete and is supported by perimeter columns.

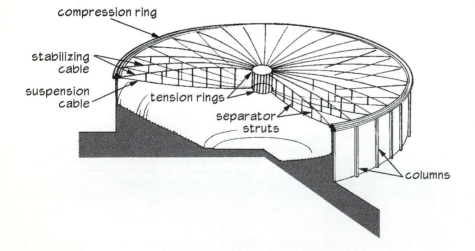

Figure 10.26: Utica Auditorium, cutaway isometric drawing.

DOUBLE-CURVATURE STRUCTURES

Double-curvature structures are *anticlastic* (saddle-shaped, i.e., curvature is positive in one direction and negative in the opposite direction) so that the *suspension* cables in one direction span between supports while the *stabilizing* cables running in a perpendicular direction pull downward to prevent wind uplift (Figure 10.27).

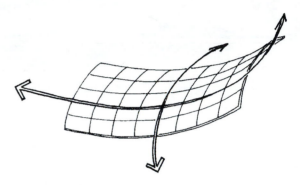

Figure 10.27: An anticlastic shape is typical of double-curvature cable and tent structures and prevents fluttering due to wind uplift.

DOUBLE-CURVATURE SUSPENSION CASE STUDIES

Raleigh Arena

Designed as a livestock-judging pavilion (1952; Raleigh, NC; Deitrick and Nowicki, architects; Severud, Elstad, and Krueger, structural engineers), this early building survives as one of the most expressive examples of a suspension structure. There is a clear distinction between the compressive supporting arch and the tensile supported roof (Editor, 1952) (Figures 10.28 through 10.30).

The saddle-shaped roof responds not only to the structural forces which shaped it but to the spatial needs of enclosed grandstands which seat 5500; unlike the dome, it provides as much space overhead for the topmost spectator as for the lowest. Furthermore, it allows a generous amount of glazing above the seating providing daylighting from all directions (Editor, 1954a).

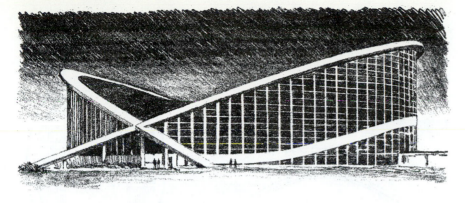

Figure 10.28: Raleigh Arena, exterior.

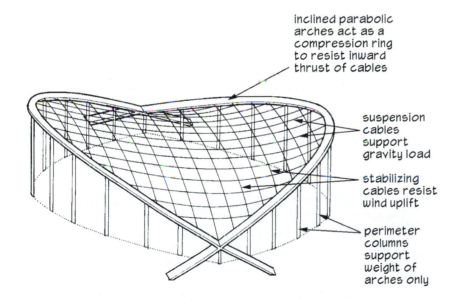

inclined parabolic arches act as a compression ring to resist inward thrust of cables

suspension cables support gravity load

stabilizing cables resist wind uplift

perimeter columns support weight of arches only

Figure 10.29: Raleigh Arena, axonometric drawing of structure.

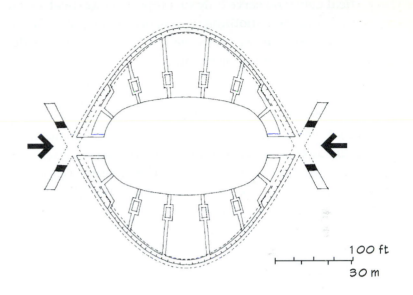

100 ft

30 m

Figure 10.30: Raleigh Arena, plan.

The primary (suspension) cables span 298 ft (90.1 m) between the arches; their diameters range between 0.75 and 1.3 in (18 and 32 mm), and they are spaced at 6-ft (1.8-m) intervals. The secondary (stabilizing) cables span in the opposite direction and are intended primarily to reduce wind uplift. Their diameters range between 0.5 and 0.75 in (12 and 18 mm), and they are also spaced at 6-ft (1.8-m) intervals. The secondary cables are prestressed to prevent slackening in warm weather. The corrugated metal roof deck spans between the primary cables and is covered with 1.5-in (3.7-cm) rigid insulation and built-up roofing (Editor, 1953).

The primary support is provided by two crossed, parabolic, reinforced-concrete compression arches rising to a height of 90 ft (27.4 m). The depth of these arches varies from 15.1 ft (4.6 m) near the crossing to 12 ft (7.6 m) at the top; the thickness is 30 in (76 cm). These are coffered under the bottom to reduce weight and inclined so that the lines of tension in the cables lie in the planes of these arches. Thus the roof load is transmitted through the arches directly to the abutments. While the arches appear continuous through their intersection and on into the ground, they are hinge-jointed at the crossing to prevent introducing large moments in the abutments below. To resist the outward thrust of the abutments, the footings are connected by underground steel cables to resist any possible foundation movement (Voshinin, 1952).

The vertical columns serve only to support the vertical weight of the arches and contribute nothing to supporting the roof. The spacing of these is closer than was necessary structurally; it was determined instead by glazing requirements.

Yale Hockey Rink

Looking like a grounded Viking longboat (1958; New Haven, CT; Eero Saarinen and Associates, architects; Severud-Elstad-Krueger Associates, structural engineers), the form of this building was determined by a combination of functional, aesthetic, and structural considerations (Figures 10.31 through 10.33). Used primarily as a hockey rink, the oval plan permits optimal seating with the majority of the 2900 spectators near the middle. The convex lateral curvature prevents reflected noise from focusing (a problem inherent in domes and other vaulted forms) back at the spectators. Finally, this privileged location in the central campus would not have been accorded the more utilitarian barrel-vaulted structural form commonly used for ice rinks elsewhere; in Saarinen's view, a more dramatic and sculptural form was necessary and justified (McQuade, 1958; Saarinen and Severud, 1958).

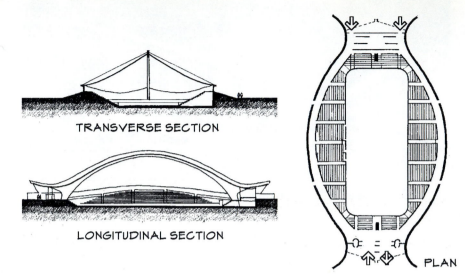

Figure 10.32: Yale Hockey Rink, sections and floor plan.

Figure 10.31: Yale Hockey Rink, exterior.

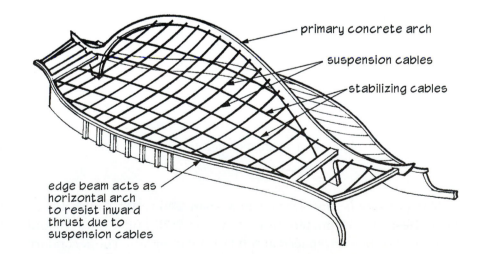

Figure 10.33: Yale Hockey Rink, cutaway perspective.

The primary determinant of the form is the great concrete parabolic arch that spans 240 ft (73 m). At the ends the arch curvature reverses into a 40-ft (12.2-m) cantilever supporting the canopied entrances at each end. Transverse catenary cables are suspended at 6-ft (1.83-m) intervals between the center arch and the curved perimeter walls. In addition to the suspension cables (which are contained within the roof structure), three additional cables on each side were added (as an apparent engineering afterthought) to increase the lateral stability to the concrete arch. The concrete perimeter walls are tilted out and formed at the top into a horizontal arch 7 ft (2.1 m) deep by 18 in (46 cm) wide to resist the inward thrust of the suspension cables.

Two-inch (50-mm)-thick tongue-and-groove wood decking spans in the opposite direction. In addition to resisting bending between the transverse cables, the wood deck acts in tension together with nine longitudinal stabilizing cables on each side to resist wind uplift.

Munich Olympic Stadium
The roof of this stadium (1972; Munich; Behnisch and Partner, architects; Frei Otto, and Leonhardt & Andrae, structural engineers) is a double-curved cable system that is tentlike in behavior and appearance. Designed for the 1972 Olympic Games to accommodate field and track events as well as soccer and equestrian events, it has been used both for competition and leisure activities since then (Figures 10.34 through 10.38).

Actually, the complex designed by Behnisch for the Olympics included the stadium, a sports arena (capacity 14,000, for gymnastics, handball, basketball, and other indoor activities), and a swimming area (capacity 8000, for swimming and diving). All these were depressed into the ground. All utility and support facilities are underground or under the grandstands. The cable roofs were the centerpiece for the games and sheltered vast areas of the designed landscape [800,000 ft² (74,000 m²)] making it the largest tensioned membrane structure in the world at the time it was constructed (Figure 10.35). This roof culminated a long progression of development of tensile structures for Frei Otto that was first documented in his book (Otto, 1954).

Figure 10.34: Munich Olympic Stadium, exterior.

It is a prestressed cable structure with the characteristic double curvature to prevent wind flutter. It consists of steel cables of three different diameters. The wide-mesh roof is composed of 1-in (25-mm) in diameter cables arranged in pairs 2 in (50 mm) apart at 30-in (76-cm) intervals in each direction, with a clamp connection at the intersections. This clamp connection was also used to attach the acrylic panels; a total of 137,000 were required. The edge cables are 3.1 in (80 mm) in diameter. The largest cables are 4.7 in (120 mm) in diameter and are used as guys (connecting the edge cables to the abutment foundations), stays (connecting the peaks to the mast tops), and the dramatic 1440-ft (439-m)-long catenary main cable which supports the front edge. This main cable is subjected to a tension load of up to 5000 tons (4530 metric tons) and consists of a bundle of 10 of these largest cables (Editor, 1971a; 1972).

The primary vertical support is provided by twelve tubular steel masts ranging in height from 165 to 262 ft (50 to 80 m) and up to

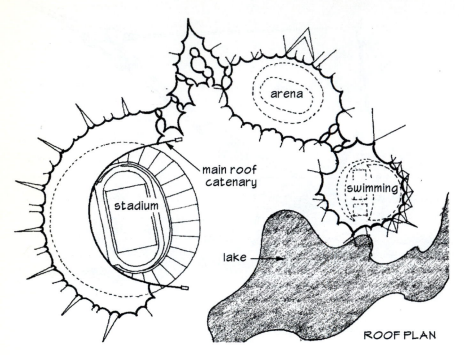

Figure 10.35: Munich Olympic Stadium, roof plan.

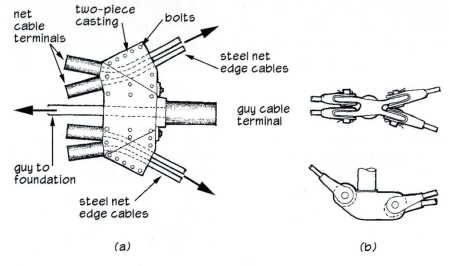

Figure 10.37: Munich Olympic Stadium, details: (a) connection between edge cables and foundation guy, and (b) cast steel terminals supporting a small utility tower under the stadium roof.

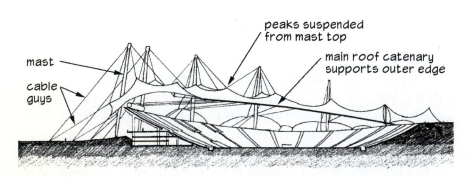

Figure 10.36: Munich Olympic Stadium, section.

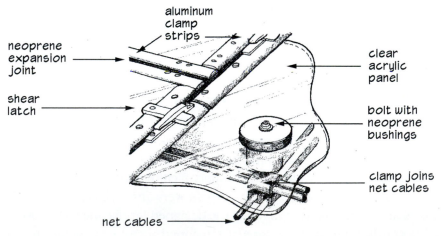

Figure 10.38: Munich Olympic Stadium, detail of connection between mesh cables showing neoprene bushings used to attach acrylic panels. The neoprene joint between the acrylic panels is also shown.

11.5 ft (3.5 m) in diameter with wall thickness up to 3 in (75 mm). These huge masts are located behind the grandstands to prevent an obstruction of the view. Cable stays extend diagonally from the top of each mast to support the peaks of the cable mesh. The cable mesh is pulled from these peaks out over the grandstands by the main catenary cable bundle that is anchored at each end on the opposite side of the stadium. The result of this is a canopy over the grandstands that seems to hover without apparent support. The roof extends over the grandstand in the opposite direction to several more that are closely spaced behind the stands, equalizing the considerable thrust of the primary cable in front.

Two unforeseen problems arose during the planning and design of the roof. The original proposal was for a polyvinylchloride-covered polyester fabric suspended under the cable net (similar to the German pavilion at the Montreal world's fair). However, in order to satisfy the lighting requirements for color television, rigid clear acrylic panels were installed in frames positioned *above* the cable net.

The second problem involved foundations. From the start, the engineers assumed that the structural cables would be held in the ground by prestressed anchors, an accepted practice even for permanent structures. But local building officials required much more expensive and cumbersome dead-weight foundations—gigantic concrete abutments up to 60 ft (18.3 m) deep and 20 ft (6.1 m) wide.

But these difficulties do not detract from the visual excitement and engineering achievement. As one critic concluded, "From afar the Olympic stadium roof is a superb, whale-backed structure, with its huge skin glinting in the sun like an immense sheet of gelatin, and its eight gigantic pylons visibly taking the strain. The best view of all can be had from down on the running track. Seen from here the canopy floats overhead, weightless and transparent like all great pieces of engineering. But will the athletes have time to look?"

Calgary Saddledome

This huge structure (1983; Calgary, Alberta, Canada; G. McCourt, architect; Jan Bobrowski and Partners, structural engineers) is a sports stadium covered with a hyperbolic paraboloid roof consisting of a steel cable net suspended from a concrete perimeter ring. The edge of the saddle surface defines the intersection with the spherical surface of the walls. The network of steel cables carrying precast concrete panels can be compared to a tennis racket twisted out of shape. The pure geometric shapes were selected not for their formal appearance but because of the structural logic and the way they were able to direct the path of the forces down to the foundation (Orton, 1988; Editor, 1983c) (Figures 10.39 through 10.43).

The main structural component of the roof is the concrete compression ring. This is supported vertically at the two low points, and lateral stability is achieved by a series of shear walls (with A-frame bracing at each end of these shear walls). The perimeter columns serve only to support the compression ring. The roof shape is a near-perfect hyperbolic paraboloid so that the suspension (concave up) and stabilizing (concave down) cables have parabolic vertical shapes. The maximum cable span is 443 ft (135 m). Cable paths are arranged in a 20-ft (6-m) grid; doubled suspension cables each having twelve 0.6-in (15-mm) strands and single stabilizing cables of nineteen 0.6-in (15-mm) strands.

Figure 10.39: Calgary Saddledome, exterior from the southeast.

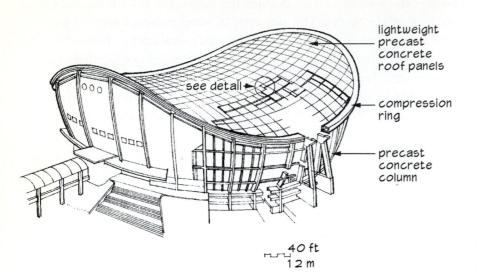

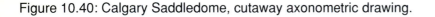

40 ft
12 m

Figure 10.40: Calgary Saddledome, cutaway axonometric drawing.

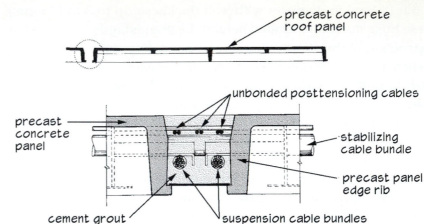

Figure 10.42: Calgary Saddledome, detail section through joint between cast-in-place panels.

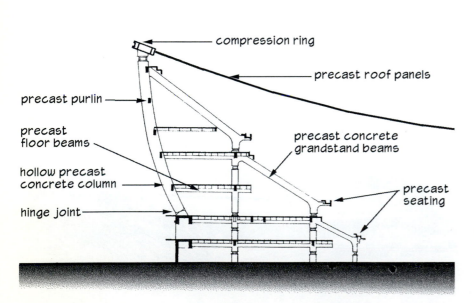

Figure 10.41: Calgary Saddledome, section at roof high point.

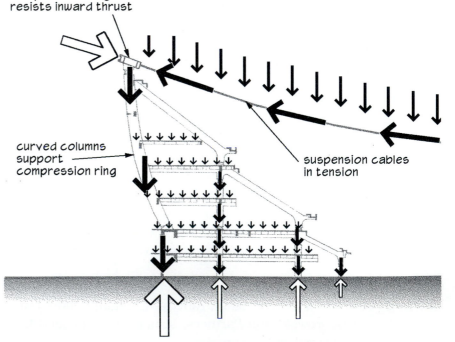

Figure 10.43: Calgary Saddledome, load path diagram.

Lightweight precast concrete panels, 18.6 ft (5.57 m) square by 14 in (350 mm) thick, are supported by three unbonded cables in each direction; these secondary cables were posttensioned after the gap between panels was filled with cast-in-place lightweight concrete. With the completion of this concrete infilling, the roof partially assumed the behavior of a shell. Actually the roof reacts to load in two ways: as a cable net or as a shell.

During construction, the roof was a flexible cable net supported by the compression ring, and thus all the dead load of the structure was supported in this manner. With the roof completed, it reacts to further loading as a rigid shell that is reinforced by the primary cables and posttensioned secondary cables. All live loads are carried by this shell action.

SUMMARY

1. The *parabola* is the funicular shape of a suspension cable loaded uniformly across its horizontal span, ignoring the weight of the cable.

2. The *catenary* is the funicular shape for an unloaded cable and is determined solely by the self-weight of the cable.

3. The term *catenary* is also used more broadly to refer to any curved suspension member which is loaded along its length, regardless of the exact loading distribution. For example, the main cables of a suspension bridge are the catenary cables, even though the curvature more closely approximates a parabola.

4. The *depth* of the sag of a catenary structure determines the horizontal (inward) thrust that is generated; the less the sag, the greater the thrust.

5. Most catenary cables used for building roof structures have sag-to-span ratios of 1:8 to 1:10.

6. Funicular suspension structures may be divided into three categories: *single-curvature*, *double-cable*, and *double-curvature*.

7. *Single-curvature* structures consist of two or more parallel catenary cables spanning between primary supports.

8. *Double-cable* structures are similar to single-curvature structures with the addition of stabilizing cables below the primary suspension cables to resist wind uplift. If the two cables are in the same plane, some additional means of ensuring lateral stability (perpendicular to this plane) must be incorporated.

9. *Double-curvature* structures are *anticlastic* so that the *suspension* cables in one direction span between supports while the *stabilizing* cables run in a perpendicular direction and pull downward to prevent wind uplift.

11

TENTS

Sails and their rigging are tensile structures and nobody understands their nature better than a sailor.

—Horst Berger

A *tent* is a thin, anticlastic tension membrane, supported by a compression arch or mast. It is a variation of a double-curved cable structure where the space between cables is reduced to nothing and the surface becomes a continuous membrane. In a tent, the fabric carries all or part of the tensile forces. Small tents, made entirely of fabric, are typically supported by masts (columns) or arches (Figure 11.1). As the span increases, membrane tension forces increase and the surface area must be subdivided by cables which carry the principal tensile loads with fabric spanning between cables.

If the edge of a tent is flexible (unattached), it is usually shaped into a concave curve to ensure that it remains in tension. Because the edge is a region of high stress, it is usually reinforced with cable which continues to the anchor point. The anchor point may be connected to a guy cable (which transmits tension forces to the foundation), or it may be supported by a mast or compression strut (which transfers compression loads to the ground).

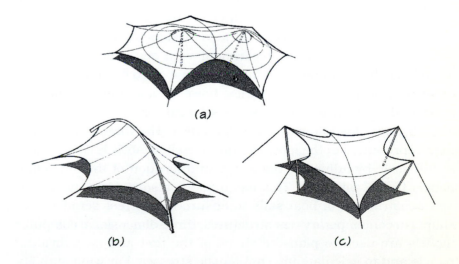

Figure 11.1: Tents with various compressive supports: (a) internal masts, (b) internal arches, and (c) external masts.

DESIGNING TENT STRUCTURES

Horst Berger, an engineer involved with the design of many recent tent structures, writes "While materials and technology have advanced significantly in recent years, there is a general lack of familiarity among most architects with the design and behavior of tents. The temporary nature and vulnerability associated with the words *fabric* and *tent* obscure the fact that these structures are safer and more reliable than many conventional systems—because they are practically weightless and provide a continuous, flexible watertight skin. The complexity of a fabric structure's three-dimensional curvilinear configuration hides the underlying simplicity of its structural behavior—which depends only on tension and curvature for its ability to carry loads. This simplicity makes the visible membrane form a true image of the force-flow itself.

"For fabric structures, architectural form and structural function are one and the same. As a result, engineering and architecture are inseparable, and an understanding of the structure is an essential design tool. Because of the close relationship between visual appearance and structural behavior such an understanding is not difficult to develop. Observing these structures is an excellent way of beginning to be able to design them." (Berger, 1985).

Another way to develop an intuitive understanding of appropriate shapes for tents is to experiment with scale models using a stretchy, lightweight double-knit fabric supported by arches, masts, or strings. At the scale of buildings, however, a minimum of stretch is desired; in fact, tent fabrics are selected for their resistance to stretch under load (among other qualities). The three-dimensional form represented in the model by the stretched fabric is constructed at full scale by adjusting the shape and location of the individual panels before assembly. This technique is also used in the design and construction of boat sails to ensure the correct aerodynamic shape. In contemporary tent structures, three-dimensional computer models are used to plan the shape of the tent and its individual panels and to calculate internal tensile stresses. For wind stability (as well as longevity), it is essential that tents be designed as double-curvature structures (Figure 11.2).

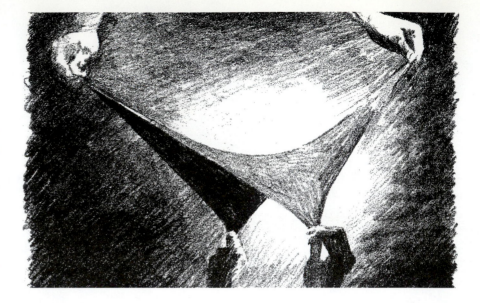

Figure 11.2: The saddle-shape characteristic of most tent structures can be produced and studied by stretching four corners of an elastic material out of its flat plane. Notice that, because the edges naturally assume a concave profile, they remain in tension (straight edges would tend to flutter). In full-scale tents, these edges, which are areas of high stress, are reinforced with steel catenary cables.

SUPPORTS

Tents belong to the same family of center-supported structures as suspension bridges and cable-stayed double cantilevers. They are most easily supported by central masts, but this may be functionally undesirable for nonstructural reasons. Arches or more complex compression structures may be used to provide vertical support (Figure 11.3). Catenary cables can be suspended from side masts to support the membrane peaks at several points (Figure 11.4). Where center supports are used, fabric stress may be reduced by distributing the load over a larger area through the use of a mushroom-shaped mast capital (Figure 11.5).

Figure 11.3: Pavilion, Sea World (1980; San Diego, CA; Horst Berger, structural engineer). Notice that compression struts are used to support the roof peaks thus avoiding the use of central masts. Also, horizontal compression struts below the fabric resolve the thrust forces, eliminating the need for guy cables extending beyond the perimeter of the structure.

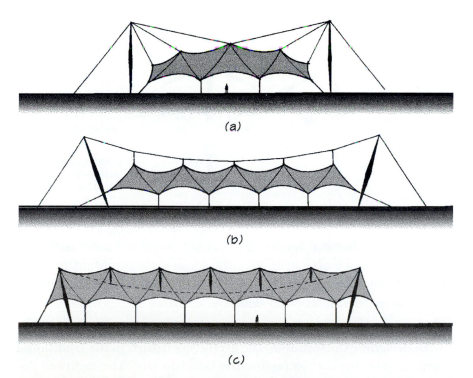

Figure 11.4: Catenary cables suspended from masts may be used to support tent peaks: (a) external masts, (b) external masts with suspension cable, (c) interior masts with suspension cable below fabric-supporting struts.

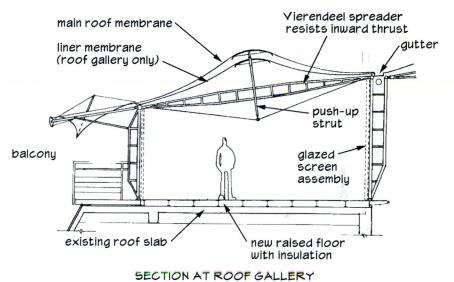

SECTION AT ROOF GALLERY

Figure 11.5: Imagination Building (1994; London; Herron Associates, architects): section through gallery showing mushroom-shaped *push-up* strut used to support the center of the fabric roof.

MATERIALS

Traditionally, tents were considered to be suitable only for temporary structures because of the deterioration of fabrics due to prolonged exposure to sunlight. The development of improved fabrics (notably fiberglass) and coatings which minimize the deterioration due to sunlight (Dupont Teflon, for example) have increased the useful life of tent fabrics to over 20 years, making them suitable for use on permanent structures.

BOUNDARIES

If the boundaries of the tent are flexible, they are typically reinforced with cables. These take on their particular concave shape as a result of the membrane stress patterns and the support system of the structure. Rigid boundaries, such as walls, beams, and arches, can take any shape as long as they create a useful curvature along the edge of the membrane and are capable of resisting the stresses from it.

TENT CASE STUDIES

Haj Terminal, King Abdul Aziz International Airport
The Haj Terminal (1982; Jeddah, Saudi Arabia; Skidmore, Owings, and Merrill, architects; Geiger Berger Associates, structural engineers) was designed to accommodate the 950,000 pilgrims expected to visit Mecca in 1985. The capacity of the terminal at any one time is 50,000 passengers for a period of 18 hours during arrival and 80,000 for periods up to 36 hours during departure (Figures 11.6 through 11.8).

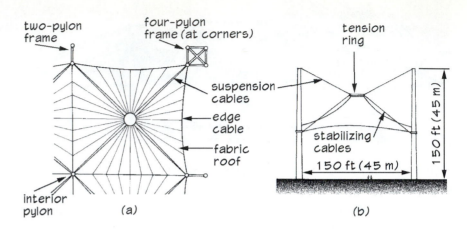

Figure 11.7: Haj Terminal, module (a) plan, and (b) section.

Figure 11.6: Haj Terminal, King Abdul Aziz International Airport, exterior. The tops of the conical tents are suspended on cables from the surrounding four masts.

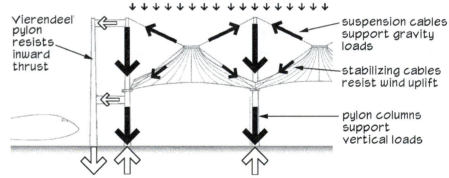

Figure 11.8: Haj Terminal, two-module load path diagram. Four-mast frames at corners and two-mast frames along the edges resist the inward thrusts of the tents. Interior masts are single because the inward thrusts are counterbalanced by tents on all sides.

In designing the terminal, the architects turned to the traditional nomadic structure of the region, the bedouin tent. The terminal design also echoes the temporary tent city constructed for the pilgrimage weeks in the valley of Meena near Mecca. While visiting the area, the designers learned what natives have long known, that being under the shade of an umbrella in the intense desert heat was preferable to being enclosed in a hot building. It also recognized that mechanically air-conditioning and lighting a building of the size needed for the terminal would be extraordinarily expensive, especially considering the short annual period of peak usage. All these considerations led to the choice of a fabric roof which is translucent, transmitting enough diffuse daylight to sufficiently light the terminal. At night, the roof becomes a reflective surface for the pylon-mounted uplights. For cooling, the form and height of the tents utilize natural thermal convection to induce ventilation up and out through the center openings (Editor, 1979).

The tents combine to cover over 4.6 million ft² (430,000 m²), more than any other roof in the world. The basic module is a square conical fabric tent 150 ft (39.4 m) on each side. Twenty-one such modules form a single group, and there are two sets of five groups divided by a landscaped mall (for a total of 210 tent modules). The enclosed and air-conditioned arrival buildings are located under the tents along the outside edge of the terminal units parallel to the aircraft aprons (Editor, 1983b).

Each module consists of a semiconical fabric tent connected at the open center peak to a 13-ft (3.96-m)-diameter steel tension ring and stretched to the perimeter cables which are attached at the four corners to the midheight of the supporting masts. The center tension ring is suspended by paired cables to the top of each of the supporting masts. The Teflon-coated fiberglass fabric is expected to last 20 years. It is reinforced by 32 steel cables that radiate from the tension ring to the perimeter cables; these cables carry the primary tension forces, while the fabric spans between the cables. Once in place and tensioned, the fabric assumes a semiconical saddle shape, the double curvature of which resists wind flutter (Editor, 1980).

The supporting masts (or pylons) are 150-ft (46-m)-tall tubular steel with a 7.4-ft (2.5-m)-diameter at the base tapering to 3.3 ft (1.0 m) at the top. Interior masts support the corners of four adjacent tents; the inward thrusts of these counterbalance each other, and the only lateral load on these cantilevered members is due to wind. At the edges of the group of tents where there is no adjacent tents to counterbalance the inward thrusts due to the tent base (at midheight) and the tension-ring–supporting cables (at the top), the mast is paired and connected with shear panels to create a two-dimensional Vierendeel-type frame to resist the unbalanced lateral loads. At the corners of the group, these thrust loads occur in two directions, and four masts are clustered to form a three-dimensional frame.

Overall, the structure, in the words of the jury for one of the numerous awards the building received, "takes on an aspect of soft monumentality. It is a mirage-like building that floats above the desert floor, matching the experience of flight and reflecting the spiritual quality of the pilgrimage." (Editor, 1983b).

Riyadh Stadium
Horst Berger's involvement in the Haj Terminal (above) contributed to the advancement of fabric structures and led to his engineering role in this more recent Saudi project (1986; Riyadh, Saudi Arabia; Fraser, Roberts, and Partners, architects; Horst Berger Partners, structural engineers). The structure consists of 24 identical tent modules repeated around a circle to form a ring canopy covering the

Figure 11.9: Riyadh stadium, exterior from entry canopy.

Figure 11.10: Riyadh stadium, interior detail showing center ring cables.

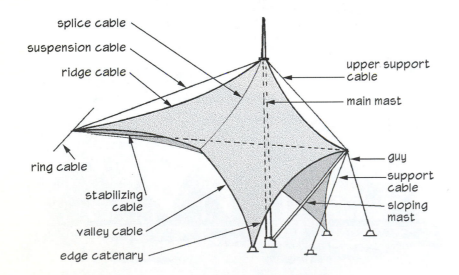

Figure 11.11: Riyadh stadium, single module (one of 24).

grandstands. The open center is over the playing field. Like the Munich Olympic Stadium, the masts are positioned behind the seating to maintain the unobstructed view of the playing field from the grandstands which seat 60,000. The tent covers a total area of 500,000 ft² (46,500 m²) (Figures 11.9 through 11.11).

The fabric membrane is stretched between ridge cables, valley cables, and catenary edge cables. The ridge cables are connected to the main mast and are radial in plan. The valley cables between the ridge cables are connected to the bottom anchor and stabilize the structure against wind uplift; they are also radial in plan. The outer edge of the ridge cables and the outer edge of the catenary edge cables are held at a fixed point created by the sloping mast and the two triangulated cable guys. The inner end of the membrane is attached to a ring cable which counterbalances the outward thrust of the sloping mast and guys. To make the structure erectable and to provide redundancy and additional stiffness, an additional cable system was added. This consists of adding a suspension cable, a stabilizing cable, and an upper support cable all aligned with the ridge cable of each module. These, together with the masts, the rear support cables, and the ring cable form a stable system not requiring the participation of the fabric (Editor, 1985).

The structure includes a roof-washing system designed to maintain the fabric's 8 percent daylight transmittance and 75 percent solar reflectance. The high solar reflectance coupled with the natural convection ventilation induced by the openings at the peak help maintain spectator comfort. Rain drains outward to the lower anchor points to spill into a perimeter drainage basin. The center ring cable supports speaker and field lighting systems; uplights reflect off the underside of the tent at night to provide general illumination of the grandstands.

Mounds Stands, Lord's Cricket Field

When asked to design the new Mounds stands for the Lord's Cricket Field (1987; London; Michael Hopkins and Partners, architects; Ove Arup and Partners, structural engineers), Hopkins used fabric roofs to create an elegant tent, recalling the temporary structures of the seventeenth century erected on the green for a Saturday afternoon's

Figure 11.12: Mounds Stands, Lord's Cricket Field, exterior from the field.

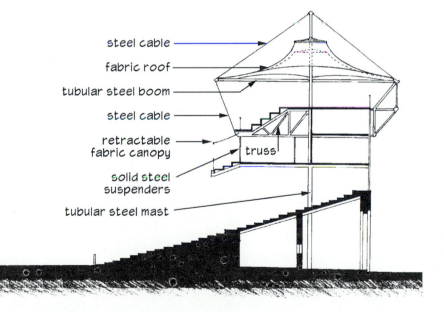

Figure 11.13: Mounds Stands, section.

Figure 11.14: Mounds Stands, interior detail of tent peak showing tension/lifting ring.

tiers of seating, a mezzanine level of services, and the elegant roof which characterizes the structure (Davey, 1987; 1988) (Figures 11.12 through 11.14).

Structurally independent of the existing brick terrace, the tent is supported by six 16-in. (406-mm)-diameter tubular steel columns which also support a spine of steel girders. Cantilevering from the spine are a series of beams which form the floor of the top level and the ceiling above the viewing boxes. At the back of the building, the beams are connected by plate girders that transfer loads to the vertical steel tension rods placed every 59 ft (18 m) between the arches of the colonnade.

The top tier of seating is covered by the fabric tent, stressed by a framework of steel struts and catenary cables. Originally intended to be Teflon-coated fiberglass fabric, PVC-coated polyester was fi-

cricket match. In collaboration with the engineers, Hopkins devised a steel superstructure above the existing stadium to house two new

nally specified due to fire restrictions. The fabric was cut using computer-generated patterns and ultrasonically welded into seven sections that extend between the six masts. Tensioned by steel lifting rings around each mast, the tent rises to a conical peak (Editor, 1987).

SUMMARY

1. A *tent* is a thin, anticlastic tension membrane, supported by a compression arch or mast.

2. If the edge of a tent is flexible (unattached), it is usually shaped into a concave curve to ensure that it remains in tension.

3. For wind stability (as well as longevity), it is essential that tents be designed as double-curvature structures.

4. The development of improved fabrics (notably fiberglass) and coatings which minimize the deterioration due to sunlight (Dupont Teflon, for example) have increased the useful life of tent fabrics to over 20 years.

12

PNEUMATICS

Pneumatic structures distribute loads to supports through air-pressurized membranes. Like cables, they transmit only tensile forces through the plane of their membrane. In addition, because pneumatic structures are shaped in direct response to applied and pressurization loads, they are also funicular.

An understanding of how pressurization forces act on a membrane enclosure is fundamental to the design and analysis of pneumatic structures. The principle is simple: air pressure exerts a uniformly distributed load that is perpendicular everywhere to the membrane surface.

There are two basic types of pneumatic structures: *air-supported* and *air-inflated* (Figure 12.1). Air-supported structures have single roof membranes which are sealed around the perimeter and supported by an internal pressure that is slightly higher than that of the surrounding atmosphere. As a result the entire interior volume of the structure is pressurized.

Air-inflated structures consist of structural elements (such as arches or columns) that are pressurized and thus stiffened into a rigid form which is then used to support an enclosure, the interior of which is not pressurized.

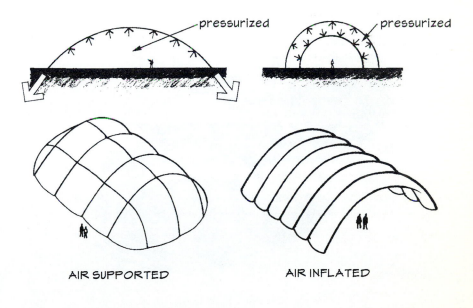

Figure 12.1: Types of pneumatic structures.

AIR-SUPPORTED STRUCTURES

SOAP BUBBLES

A soap bubble is a natural air-supported structure formed by un-equal pressures on either side of a membrane of water. The surface tension of the water acts to limit the expansion of the bubble. When the surface tension reaches the limit of tensile strength of the water (its surface tension), the bubble bursts. Because the internal pressure is acting in all directions equally, the film tends to assume a shape that has a minimum surface area. For a bubble in the air, this shape is a sphere; for a bubble formed on a horizontal surface, the natural shape is hemispherical (Figure 12.2). At all times the pressure forces inside the bubble act perpendicular to the surface. If the base of a bubble on a surface is constrained into a shape other than a circle, the bubble will naturally assume the least-area-surface shape consistent with the perimeter shape and internal pressure (higher pressure results in higher rise for the bubble).

The geometry of adjoining soap bubbles is interesting and relevant to larger pneumatic structures. If two floating bubbles of identical size (identical pressure) come together, they will join and the surface films will meet at a 120° angle to each other and to the dividing partition film (which is planar in the case of equal-size, equal-pressure bubbles). The interior dividing partition is planar because there is equal pressure on each side. If the sizes of the bubbles are different, the interior pressure is different and the dividing partition will bulge into a curve. But the angle between the outer surfaces of the bubbles and the inner partition will always be 120° (Figure 12.3). A mass of any number and size of bubbles will always conform to this 120° geometry (Dent, 1971).

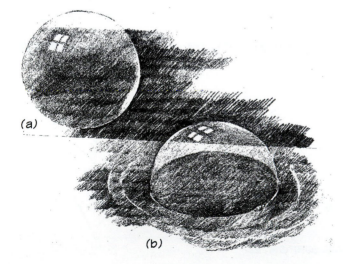

Figure 12.2: Soap bubbles: (a) a sphere floating in air, and (b) a hemisphere on a surface.

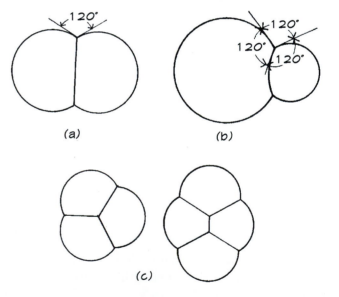

Figure 12.3: One-hundred-and-twenty–degree geometry of adjoining soap bubbles: (a) equal-size bubbles divided by flat partition, (b) unequal-size bubbles (divided by curved partition), and (c) three- and four-bubble masses.

SHAPES

All air-supported structures tend to assume a hemisphere shape. The curvature must be convex in at least one direction (saddle shapes are possible); convex curvature in both directions is more common. In general, most shapes generated by revolving a linear form about an axis can be achieved by an air-supported membrane provided the resulting shape is convex in at least one direction. Angular perimeter shapes result in high stress concentrations at the corners; for this reason, corners are usually rounded in such shapes (Figures 12.4 and 12.5).

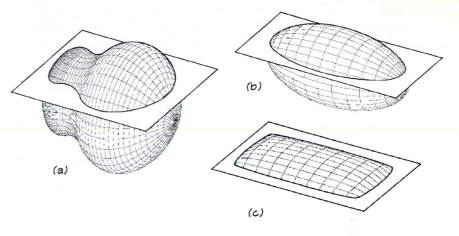

Figure 12.5: Nonspherical air-supported shapes: (a) rotated saddle shape, (b) rotated ellipse, and (c) rectangular perimeter with rounded corners to reduce stress.

LOAD CONDITIONS

Like other structures, air-supported structures are subject to dead loads (membrane self-weight and permanent loads suspended from the membrane) and live loads (snow, rain, wind, and temporarily applied loads). In addition, the structure is subject to pressurization loads which serve to maintain the membrane in tension and thus support the dead and live loads.

Dead loads

For flexible membrane (fabric, for example) air-supported structures, the self-weight load is negligible compared with other loads. Virtually all present and past air-supported structures are of this type; however, if heavier materials are used for future structures (for reasons of insulation or greater permanence, for example), then the self-weight could be considerable.

In general, concentrated dead loads should be avoided due to the large amount of deflection and localized stress that they introduce. Where this is necessary, the load should be distributed over as large an area as possible and the membrane should be appropriately reinforced.

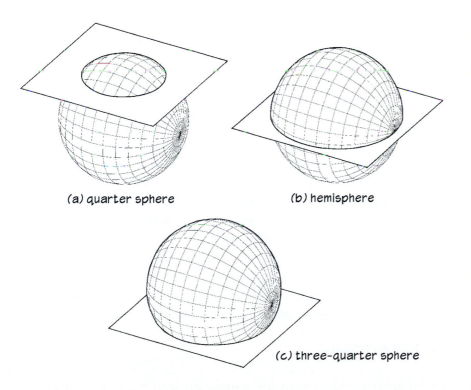

(a) quarter sphere   (b) hemisphere

(c) three-quarter sphere

Figure 12.4: Spherical air-supported structures: (a) quarter sphere, (b) hemisphere, and (c) three-quarter sphere.

Live loads

Snow accumulation is a significant problem for air-supported structures, especially when the rise is relatively small (typical of long spans). In addition to the relatively predictable and uniform loading of snow accumulating, drifting snow tends to accumulate and distort the membrane in a relatively unpredictable manner. As a result, various snow removal strategies have been developed to prevent excessive accumulation.

Wind loading is a significant consideration in air-supported structures. In a steep-rise structure, wind pressure presses against the lower part of the dome on the windward side tending to offset the inward supporting pressure and cause an inward collapse as the pressure is equalized on each side. The internal pressure must be sufficiently great to resist this. In shallow-rise structures, the air accelerates as it passes over the structure and induces aerodynamic lift (similar to that on an airplane wing). The resulting suction above the membrane adds to the supporting pressure below, increasing the tension of the membrane (Figure 12.6).

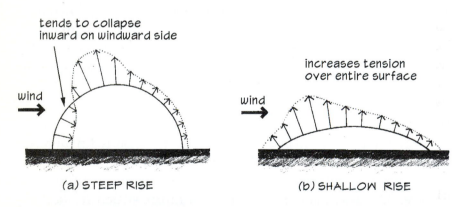

Figure 12.6: Wind loading on (a) steep-rise, and (b) shallow-rise air-supported structures.

Pressurization loads

Pressurization loads act perpendicularly to the membrane and are uniform over the entire structure. For nonsnow conditions, the ac-

tual pressure difference required to support such a lightweight structure is quite small [typically 0.03 lb/in^2 (10.5 N/m^2) or about 1/500th of an atmosphere] (Figure 12.7). This differential is only equivalent to that between the first and sixth floor of a building.

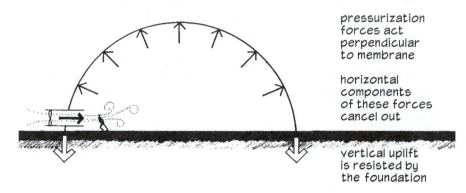

Figure 12.7: Pressurization load path diagram.

Pressurization is typically induced by mechanical fans. The quantity of air required to support the roof is independent of volume and is calculated only to compensate for air leakage. The fan operating costs are approximately equal to air-conditioning costs in a temperate climate (Hamilton et al., 1994). Some experimental structures have used wind for pressurization (Figure 12.8), but the variability of the wind speed makes this method impractical.

Another pressurization strategy utilizes the natural temperature difference between the inside and outside (resulting from passive solar heat gain as well as interior heat sources) which makes the interior air more buoyant. To be effective, however, the temperature difference and the span must both be relatively large.

ACCESS OPENINGS

An inherent problem with air-supported structures is that of providing access to the interior while maintaining pressurization. Conventional hinged doors are not suitable; even under the relatively low pressure difference, they are difficult to open inward and uncontrollable when hinged to swing outward. In addition, under heavy traffic, the doors are open almost constantly and result in large air losses. Air locks (vestibules with two sets of doors) resolve the problem of doors being difficult to open provided traffic is light enough so that only one set of doors is used at a time. This strategy is also widely used with pairs of overhead doors where vehicular access is required.

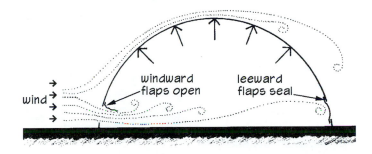

Figure 12.8: Wind-pressurized dome. Openings with interior flaps surround the perimeter. On the windward side, air is admitted; on the leeward side, internal pressure and exterior suction closes the flaps, creating a seal to prevent pressure loss. The system automatically adjusts to changes in wind direction as different door flaps open and close naturally. A 60-ft (18-m)-diameter hemisphere dome of this design was constructed of polyethylene film by University of Oregon architecture students and Professor Donald Peting, and successfully tested at an Oregon beach.

Some structures have utilized "air curtains" where large fans on each side of the hinged doors provide a powerful blast of air to prevent depressurization when doors are opened; however, the resulting turbulence is too great for use in public buildings. Revolving doors provide the necessary air control and are widely used in high-traffic areas of air-supported structures.

DEFLATION CONTROL

Deflation is not, in itself, a failure; the membrane roof is designed to go up and down. It is only a problem when there is damage to the roof or service time is lost. Accidental deflation is typically a result of one of three causes. One is loss of pressure due to a membrane ripping or being cut. Improved structural analysis and fabric strength have minimized large tears. Intentional cuts are seldom large enough to cause depressurization and can be easily repaired.

Another is failure of pressurization equipment either as a result of mechanical malfunction or power failure. This can be prevented by the availability of spare fans and standby electric generators.

The third is collapse due to snow buildup. This has been the cause of several deflations of large air-supported roofs (Minneapolis Metrodome in 1981 and 1982; Dakota Dome in Vermillion, SD, in 1982; and Silverdome in Pontiac, MI, in 1985). In most cases, these resulted from failure or lack of operation of the installed snow removal system. To prevent snow-related collapse, a snow removal system is usually installed to remove the snow either mechanically or by melting. In addition, internal pressure can be increased to compensate for the additional roof load. Finally, in areas prone to heavy snow accumulation, the structure can be designed to intentionally deflate to control severe snow accumulation. The Carrierdome in Syracuse, NY, is so designed and has been deflated intentionally twice (1982 and 1992) with no damage to the roof and was quickly reinflated (Hamilton et al., 1994).

LIFE-CYCLE COSTS

Since the mid-1970s, energy costs related to operating roof pressurization and especially snow melting have risen disproportionately to construction costs. In addition, related operating and maintenance personnel costs have been consistently higher than predicted. As a result of these factors, and the necessary replacement of the roof membrane after its projected life (typically 20 years), the life-cycle cost for large-span, air-supported roofs has generally been higher than originally anticipated (Hamilton et al., 1994).

MATERIALS

While it is useful to use elastic membranes for model studies, virtually all large membrane structures are constructed of materials with a minimum of stretch under load. The final form is determined by shaping the individual fabric panels before fabrication, in much the same manner as tents are shaped. In addition, like tents, since 1974, virtually all large pneumatic structures have been constructed from Teflon-coated glass-fiber fabric. This fabric is resistant to fire as well as solar deterioration and has a life expectancy of over 25 years.

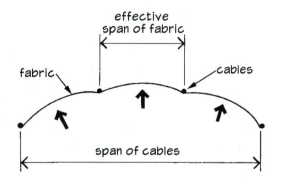

Figure 12.9: Section through large air-supported dome showing the use of cables to relieve membrane stress. The effective span of the membrane is reduced to the spacing of the cables.

Membrane tension increases with the span and decreases with rise. Large-span, shallow-rise structures utilize cables to reduce stress in the membrane; the effective span of the membrane is determined by the cable spacing (Figure 12.9).

ANCHORAGE

Because air-supported membranes transmit only tension forces (in the plane of the membrane), considerable inward thrust is generated and must be resisted. The horizontal thrust is a function of the span and inversely a function of the rise (the smaller the rise the greater the inward thrust). In addition to lateral thrust, all air-sup-

ported structures create an uplift force equal to their ground area times the internal pressure.

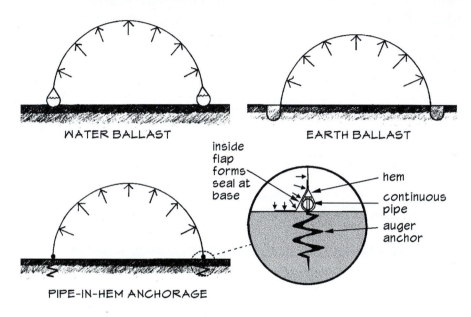

Figure 12.10: Anchorage systems for air-supported structures.

In small structures, it is possible to resist this thrust by anchoring the perimeter to the ground (Figure 12.10). For larger structures, a reinforced-concrete compression ring (acting as a continuous arch) is used to resist inward thrust. For this reason, such structures are typically circular or elliptical in plan. Compression rings which have straight sections in plan are subject to substantial bending stresses and must be designed as beams loaded horizontally.

AIR-SUPPORTED CASE STUDIES

United States Pavilion, Expo 70
This pavilion (1970; Osaka, Japan; Davies, Brody & Associates, architects; Geiger Berger Associates, roof structural engineers) was the first of several long-span, cable-restrained, air-supported struc-

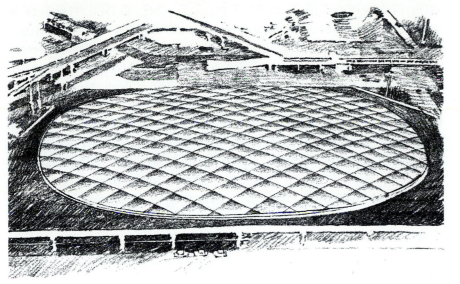

Figure 12.11: United States Pavilion, Expo 70, exterior.

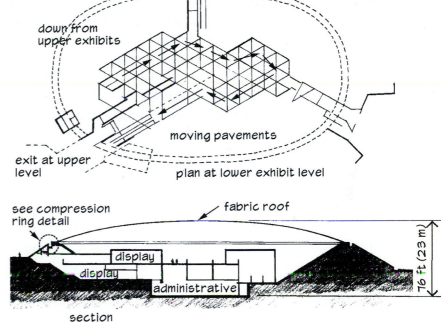

down from
upper exhibits

moving pavements

exit at upper
level

plan at lower exhibit level

see compression
ring detail

fabric roof

display
display
administrative

76 ft (23 m)

section

Figure 12.13: United States Pavilion, Expo 70, floor plan and section.

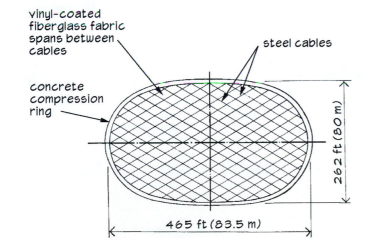

vinyl-coated
fiberglass fabric
spans between
cables

steel cables

concrete
compression
ring

262 ft (80 m)

465 ft (83.5 m)

Figure 12.12: United States Pavilion, Expo 70, roof plan.

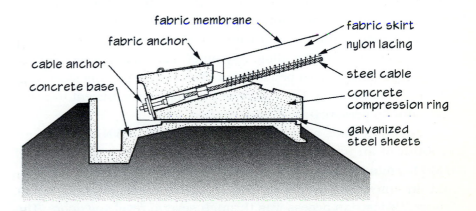

fabric membrane

fabric skirt

fabric anchor

nylon lacing

cable anchor

steel cable

concrete base

concrete
compression
ring

galvanized
steel sheets

Figure 12.14: United States Pavilion, Expo 70, detail section through
reinforced-concrete compression ring.

tures. In plan, the structure was oval-shaped (specifically, a superellipse which is between an ellipse and a rectangle), 465 ft (142 m) long by 265 ft (83.5m) wide with a very shallow rise. This plan shape was determined by a combination of the rectangular site and the need for a continuously curved compression ring to resist the inward thrust. The low profile allowed the structure to resist 125-mi/h (200-km/h) winds and earthquakes (Dent, 1971; Villecco, 1970; Geiger, 1970) (Figures 12.11 through 12.14).

The roof membrane consisted of a vinyl-coated, glass-fiber fabric. It was restrained by steel cables arranged in a diamond pattern, creating a quiltlike appearance. The cables were spaced 20 ft (6 m) apart with diameters ranging from 1.5 in (38 mm) for the shortest to 2.25 in (56 mm) for the longest. The diamond-pattern cable configuration saved materials (25 percent less steel), improved drainage, reduced the number of cable fittings at the ring, and provided a better aerodynamic cross section than alternatives (such as a radial pattern with a center tension ring, or a rectangular pattern similar to a tennis racquet).

The membrane inward thrust was resisted by a reinforced-concrete perimeter compression beam. The cross section of the ring was 4 ft (1.2 m) high and 11.5 ft (3.5 m) wide and rested on a concrete foundation on the top of an earth berm. The ring was designed to slide on the foundation allowing movement due to load variations as well as thermal expansion. Given the pattern of the restraining cables, the shape of the compression ring was funicular for uniform loading (due to pressurization and gravity loads) resulting in compressive stresses only with no bending. Asymmetrical loading (due to wind, for example) introduced bending and was resisted by the steel reinforcement in the ring. The weight of the ring was sufficient to resist uplift due to pressurization and wind.

The interior was pressurized to 0.03 lb/in^2 (10.5 N/m^2, or about 1/500th of an atmosphere) by four fans, each with a capacity of 8000 ft^3/min (3.77 m^3/s). Two similar standby fans were available, and an emergency generator was available in the event of power failure. Pedestrian access was through several revolving doors. The freestanding interior displays were designed to support the roof membrane in the event of accidental deflation.

Silverdome

This covered stadium (1974; Pontiac, MI; O'Dell/Hewlett & Luckenbach, architects; Geiger Berger Associates, roof structural engineers) has many of the features first introduced by David Geiger in the Osaka pavilion: shallow-rise, air-supported roof, with restraining cables in a diamond-shaped pattern, and a perimeter ring. The dimensions of the dome are nearly double those of the original: 722ft (220 m) long by 522 ft (159 m) wide; the roof is 202 ft (61.5 m) above the playing floor at the center (Editor, 1976) (Figures 12.15 and 12.16).

The perimeter ring is an irregular octagon rather than a superellipse. As a result, it is subject to bending forces even under symmetrical (inflation and gravity) loading and behaves as a beam rather than a continuous arch. It is composed of reinforced concrete and built-up steel sections, and is H-shaped in section.

Figure 12.15: Silverdome, exterior.

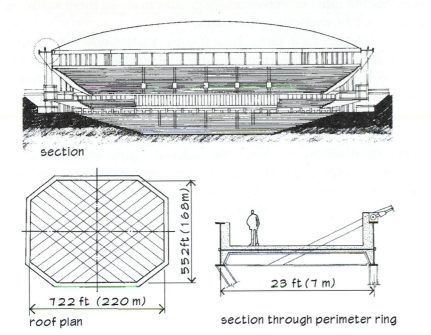

section

roof plan

552 ft (168 m)

722 ft (220 m)

section through perimeter ring

23 ft (7 m)

Figure 12.16: Silverdome: (a) section, (b) roof plan, and (c) section through perimeter ring.

Because the roof had to be elevated to accommodate the required seating, the perimeter ring is supported on steel columns and angled struts (rather than resting continuously on a berm like the United States Pavilion at Osaka). These, along with the footings required to carry the concentrated gravity loads, increased the construction cost considerably.

The roof membrane is Teflon-coated glass-fiber fabric. This was a considerable improvement over the previously available vinyl-coated fabrics. In addition to being more resistant to solar degradation, it is self-cleaning due to the very slick surface which minimizes dirt adhesion. The light transmittance is 8 percent which minimizes the need for electric lighting during daytime events. It consists of 100 panels, formed by the restraining 3 in (75mm)-diameter steel cables which are anchored to the perimeter beam.

AIR-INFLATED STRUCTURES

Unlike air-supported structures which pressurize the entire interior volume, air-inflated structures incorporate inflated structural components (arches, beams, walls, and columns) which are used to form the building enclosure. Only the component is pressurized; the functional interior volume is not.

This has two significant advantages. It eliminates the necessity for air locks which are required for access into air-supported structures. In addition, if one section of an air-inflated component deflates (due to a rupture, for example), adjacent sections are sufficient to prevent total collapse.

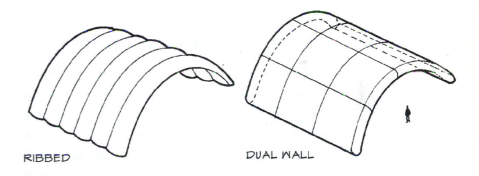

RIBBED   DUAL WALL

Figure 12.17: Air-inflated structures.

There are two primary types of air-inflated structures: *inflated-rib* structures and *dual-wall* structures. Inflated-rib structures are made up of a series of inflated tubes, usually arched, which form a spatial enclosure (vault or dome). Dual-wall structures consist of parallel membranes; the membranes are held together by connecting strings or diaphragms and the space between is pressurized (Figure 12.17).

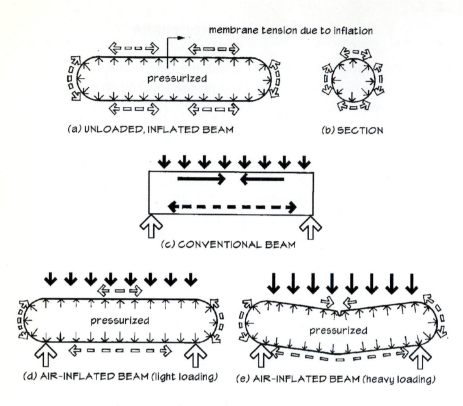

membrane tension due to inflation

pressurized

(a) UNLOADED, INFLATED BEAM   **(b) SECTION**

(c) CONVENTIONAL BEAM

pressurized

pressurized

(d) AIR-INFLATED BEAM (light loading)   **(e) AIR-INFLATED BEAM (heavy loading)**

Figure 12.18: Load-carrying behavior of an air-inflated beam: (a) unloaded, inflated beam in longitudinal tension due to pressure against the ends and in radial tension due to pressure against the sides (b) tends to assume circular cross-section in radial tension. (c) Bending in conventional beam supported at each end causes compression in the top and tension in the bottom. (d) An air-inflated beam, under light loading, has more pressure-induced tension than bending-induced compression and is stable, while (e) an air-inflated beam, under heavy loading, has less pressure-induced tension than bending-induced compression and, therefore, folds and buckles.

STRUCTURAL BEHAVIOR

While air-supported structures require only a slight pressurization to support the roof membrane directly, the pressure in air-inflated components must be considerably greater to make them sufficiently rigid to act as supporting members.

Consider an air-inflated tube (Figure 12.18). When it is inflated (but unloaded), the internal pressure against the ends causes longitudinal tension in the membrane. At the same time, the internal pressure against the side wall tends to press the membrane into a circular shape, creating radial tension in the membrane.

If the tube is supported at each end and loaded uniformly as a beam, the resulting bending action causes compression in the top of the tube and tension in the bottom. If the longitudinal tension in the tube membrane (caused by pressure against the ends) is greater than the bending-induced compression at the top of the tube, then the membrane at the top will remain in tension, and the tube beam will support the load.

If the pressure is decreased so that the longitudinal tension is less than the bending-induced compression at the top of the tube, then the membrane will fold and the beam will buckle and collapse. Increasing the load will cause a similar collapse. Unlike conventional beams, which deflect substantially before total failure, air-supported members collapse suddenly. This is because, once the top of the membrane goes into compression and folds, the effective depth of the member reduces and bending stresses increase, which progressively causes further folding until buckling collapse rapidly occurs. Because all other air-supported members (columns, walls, slabs, and arches) also tend to fail by buckling, their structural behavior is similar to that of air-supported beams.

Effect of depth
Increasing the depth of an air-inflated beam increases its capacity in two ways. Because the area of the end of the beam increases, the pressure-induced longitudinal tension increases. In addition, because the distance between the top and bottom is increased, the bending-induced compression in the top reduces proportionally. Conversely, for similar loading, the internal pressure must be increased if depth is decreased. In general, air-inflated components (beams, arches, etc.) must have larger dimensions than similar conventional components (Figure 12.19).

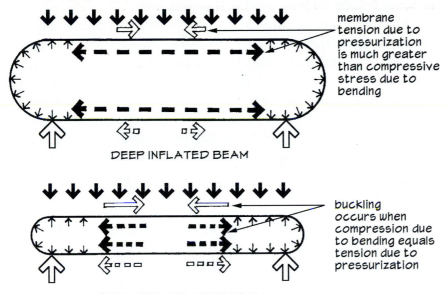

DEEP INFLATED BEAM

membrane
tension due to
pressurization
is much greater
than compressive
stress due to
bending

buckling
occurs when
compression due
to bending equals
tension due to
pressurization

SHALLOW INFLATED BEAM

Figure 12.19: Increasing the depth of an air-inflated beam increases the pressure-induced longitudinal tension while decreasing the bending-induced compression.

Importance of distributing loads

Concentrated loads perpendicular to the membrane cause local deflection, reduce the effective depth, and thus proportionally weaken the air-inflated member. For this reason, concentrated loads and supports must be carefully designed to distribute the force over a large area to minimize localized deflection.

Membrane failure

Membrane failure is also possible in tension (bursting) due to overinflation or to excessive load on walls and columns which are so short that buckling does not first occur. Other factors that can lead to membrane failure are solar deterioration, fatigue due to repeated flexing, abrasion, and punctures.

AIR-INFLATED CASE STUDIES

Several innovative examples were constructed at Expo 70 in Osaka, Japan, but few since.

Fuji Pavilion, Expo 70

This spectacular pneumatic structure (1970; Osaka, Japan; Y. Murata, architect; M. Kawaguchi, structural engineer) was circular in plan [164-ft (50-m) diameter at the base]. From this rose 16 air-inflated arches, each 256 ft (78 m) long and with a 15.2-ft (4-m) diameter. The center arches were semicircular in profile, while at each end the bases of the arches were progressively closer together, pushing the top of the arch higher and causing it to project forward. Membrane walls reinforced with air columns close the ends of the structure (Editor, 1969c; Dent, 1971) (Figures 12.20 through 12.22).

Visitors entered the east end on a ramp to the upper-level exhibition space where photographic images were projected onto a large inflated screen as well as onto the surrounding membrane walls. A restaurant, toilets, and control equipment were housed on a large

Figure 12.20: Fuji Pavilion, exterior.

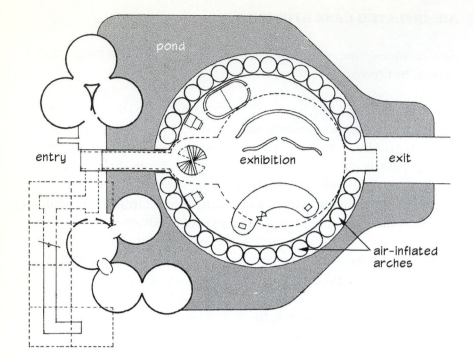

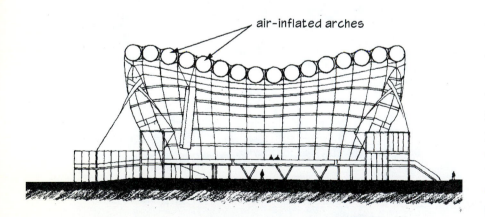

Figure 12.21: Fuji Pavilion, plan.

Figure 12.22: Fuji Pavilion, section.

revolving platform in the center. A moving ramp carried visitors to the lower exhibition level, exiting the west end.

The large-diameter tube arches were fabricated from bright red and yellow polyvinyl fabric with an exterior waterproof coating and an internal coating of PVC to reduce air permeation. The fabric tubes were clamped to steel cylinders anchored to a concrete base. Each tube was pressurized from a peripheral air duct. This pressurization could be varied from 23 to 71 lb/in^2 (8000 to 25,000 N/m^3) as required to meet wind loads; the higher pressure enabled the structure to resist typhoon winds in excess of 125 mi/h (200 km/h).

Floating Theater, Expo 70

The most innovative pneumatic structure (1970; Osaka, Japan; Y. Murata, architect; M. Kawaguchi, structural engineer) of Expo 70 was this remarkable structure which rested on a round steel frame supported by 48 buoyancy bags which floated on a shallow lake. The inflation of each bag was automatically adjusted to respond to changes in the weight distribution caused by audience movement in the theater above. The floating structure rotated slowly across the lake during the 20-minute performance (Editor, 1969d; Dent, 1971) (Figures 12.23 and 12.24).

The theater was enclosed by a roof membrane (PVC-coated polyester fabric) and supported by three large inflated arches which had a profile diameter of 75 ft (23 m) and a cross-sectional diameter of 10 ft (3 m). Like the Fuji Pavilion, the arch tube pressure was varied to respond to wind conditions.

The ceiling membrane was a thin polyester membrane attached to the underside of the arches. The space between the ceiling and roof membranes was maintained under negative pressure to support the ceiling, increase the tension of the roof, and increase the overall stability of the structure. This use of negative pressurization was a major innovation in pneumatic structures and demonstrated that such constructions need not be restricted to simple structural forms. For his pioneering work in pneumatics, Murata received a special medal from the Japanese Ministry of Science and Technology.

Figure 12.23: Floating theater, Expo 70, exterior.

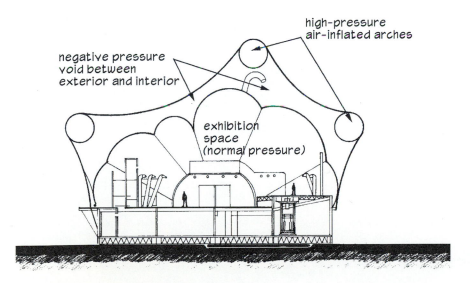

Figure 12.24: Floating theater, Expo 70, section. Note that the space between the ceiling and roof membranes is under negative pressure.

FUTURE OF PNEUMATICS

The future of pneumatic structures is unclear. After the United States Pavilion was constructed at Expo 70, air-supported structures became the roof structure of choice for long-span stadium applications in the 1970s. But following several accidental deflations, public confidence in the reliability of these structures waned and the trend, for more recent stadiums, has been toward tensegrity-type cable roofs (for example, the Georgia Dome and St. Petersburg Suncoast Dome).

Compared with air-supported domes, the spanning capability of air-inflated structures is considerably less, making them less suited for large structures. They are best suited for transportable structures where their advantages of speed of erection, light weight, and compactness after deflation are demanded.

SUMMARY

1. A *pneumatic* structure distributes loads to supports through air-pressurized membranes.

2. Air pressure exerts a uniformly distributed load that is perpendicular everywhere to the membrane surface.

3. *Air-supported* structures have single roof membranes which are sealed around the perimeter and supported by internal pressure slightly higher than that of the surrounding atmosphere.

4. *Air-inflated* structures consist of structural elements (such as arches or columns) that are pressurized and thus stiffened into a rigid form which is then used to support an enclosure, the interior of which is not pressurized.

5. Access to the interior of air-supported structures is accomplished by means of air locks.

6. The pressure in air-inflated components must be great to make them sufficiently rigid to act as supporting members.

13

ARCHES

The arch is, of all constructive forms, the most emo-tional. It is susceptible in possibility and promise to the uttermost degree of fulfillment that the creative imagination can forecast.

—Louis H. Sullivan

An arch is two curves trying to fall.

—Andy Rooney

CORBELING

Corbeling is the intermediate stage between a simple cantilever and a true arch. It consists of successive courses of masonry placed on each side of an opening and extending progressively closer to each other until they meet. The principles were known to the Sumerians and the Egyptians as early as 2700 BC. The true arch form, con-structed of voussoirs (stones cut into wedge shapes and placed in a semicircle) was also known in Egypt and Mesopotamia almost as early as corbeling. To be stable, the corbeling angle must be steeper than 45° (Figure 13.1) (Brown, 1993).

The "beehive" tombs of ancient Greece (circa 1500 BC, Mycenae) are notable examples of corbeling. In the portico of the Tomb of

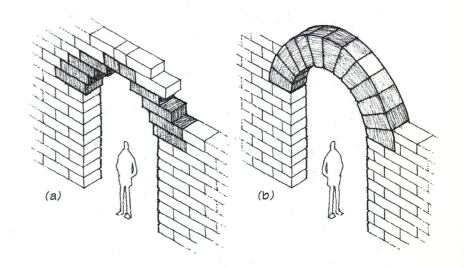

Figure 13.1: Masonry openings: (a) corbeled arch, and (b) voussoir arch.

Clytemnestra (Figure 13.2) corbeling was used to form a two-dimen-sional entrance opening. The same principle was applied three-di-mensionally to form conical beehive "domes" on the interior.

Figure 13.2: Corbeled portico of the Tomb of Clytemnestra.

Figure 13.3: The Packhorse Bridge (Cumbria, England) is a primitive stone arch with characteristic voussoirs radiating from the center.

MASONRY ARCHES

And if you ask brick what it wants, it will say, Well, I like an arch. And then you say, but arches are difficult to make. They cost more money. I think you can use concrete across your opening equally as well. But the brick says, Oh, I know, I know you're right, but if you ask me what I like, I like an arch.

— *Louis I. Kahn*

In Chapter 12, it was shown that for each possible loading condition on a suspended cable, there is a corresponding funicular shape that the cable naturally assumes. A funicular arch is the inverted compressive equivalent of a suspension cable and experiences only axial compression. In other words, for a particular loading condition, an arch that is constructed in the same (but inverted) shape as an equivalent suspension cable will be in compression only and not subject to any bending forces. This is true for both distributed loads as well as for concentrated loads which may vary in magnitude and location (Figure 13.4).

As with a suspension cable, if the loading is distributed uniformly across the horizontal span, the funicular shape is a parabola; if loading is distributed uniformly along the curve of the arch, the funicular shape is a catenary (Figure 13.5). The funicular shape for an arched opening in a masonry wall is between the two. Like the cable, the shallower the arch for a given loading, the greater the lateral thrust generated (Figure 13.6).

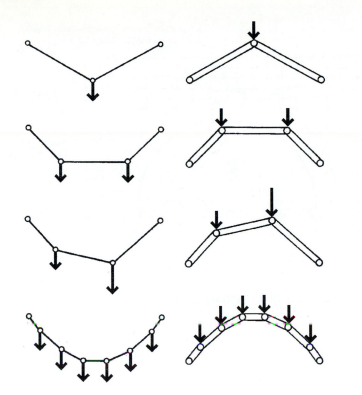

Figure 13.4: Funicular suspension cables and corresponding arches.

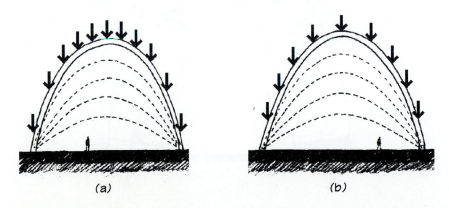

(a)   (b)

Figure 13.5: Funicular arch shapes for distributed loads: (a) catenary for uniform loading along the arch curvature, and (b) parabola for uniform loading across the horizontal span.

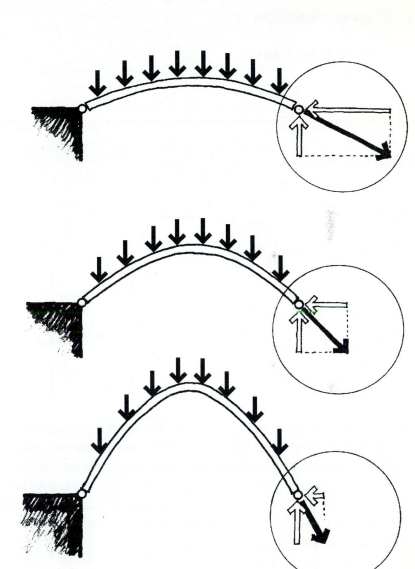

Figure 13.6: Thrust reactions vary inversely with the depth of the arch.

STRUCTURAL BEHAVIOR

The arch never sleeps.

—*Hindu Proverb*

Unlike corbeling which places the cantilevering masonry courses in bending (and thus tension), a true masonry arch depends on wedge-shaped voussoirs to transfer loads laterally entirely by compression (Figures 13.7 and 13.8).

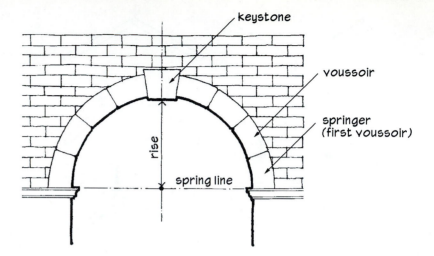

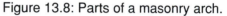

Figure 13.8: Parts of a masonry arch.

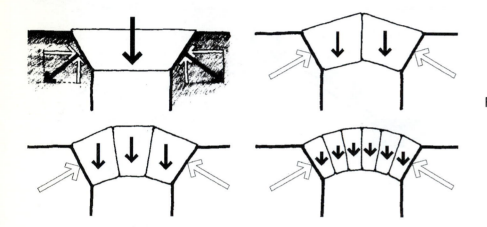

Figure 13.7: Wedge action allows arches to transfer vertical loads to each side using compression only. Notice that as the wedge-shaped voussoir tends to spread supporting surfaces apart as a result of its vertical gravity load. This causes reaction forces on each side perpendicular to the joint (if these reactions were not perpendicular, slippage could occur at the joints). The components of these reactions are vertical load (due to the gravity) and horizontal load (due to thrust).

Line of thrust

The funicular shape of an arch coincides with its *line of thrust* which is the set of resultants of the thrust and weight each part of an arch imposes on the next lower one. For bending to be completely eliminated in an arch, the line of thrust must coincide with the arch axis (Figure 13.9). However, even compressive masonry arches can toler-

Figure 13.9: The line of thrust in an arch is the set of resultants of the thrust and weight each part imposes on the next lower one.

ate a small deviation of the thrust line from the arch axis without developing tension cracks. The middle-third rule states that if the line of thrust stays within the middle third of an arch (or bearing wall or foundation), then only compressive forces will exist and no tension will develop (Figure 13.10).

arch so that its shape is no longer funicular, it will collapse. (The only exception is a triangular arch loaded only at the top, which will remain stable.) To prevent this, the shape of the arch may be constrained so that it does not buckle upward (Figures 13.11 and 13.12).

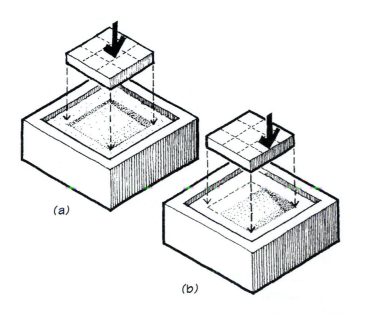

Figure 13.10: Model demonstration of the middle-third rule: (a) force on foundation block is in the center third and results in only compression on the supporting soil, and (b) force is outside the middle third and results in tension (lifting) on portions of the supporting soil. This principle prevents tension from occurring in compressive structures (such as arches) provided the line of thrust is within the center third.

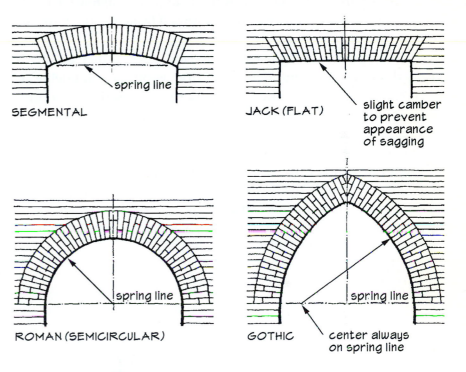

Figure 13.11: Masonry arch types.

Stability

While arches and suspended cables share similar funicular shapes, they are different in their inherent stability under changing loading conditions. If the magnitude or location of loads on a suspended cable changes, the resulting funicular shape of the cable changes and the system remains stable. But if the loading changes on a thin

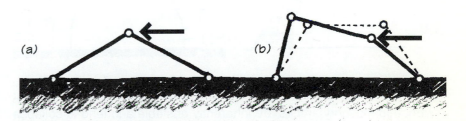

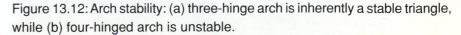

Figure 13.12: Arch stability: (a) three-hinge arch is inherently a stable triangle, while (b) four-hinged arch is unstable.

To see how this works, consider a four-hinged arch (the simplest that is inherently unstable) loaded at the two locations. If the relative loading on the hinge points changes, the funicular balance changes and the hinge with the greater loading will tend to buckle down. But for this to happen the other load point will have to buckle up. If all of the load points can be restrained from buckling upward, then the arch becomes stable.

The same principle applies to curved arches. If they can be restrained so that no point along the curve is allowed to buckle upward, the arch becomes stable. This is the reason that a thin masonry arch (which cannot resist tension or bending) is unstable under changing load conditions. But arches of the same shape which are infilled above with masonry are prevented from buckling upward and are inherently stable. For this reason, nonfunicular arch shapes can be (and, historically, have been) successfully used in masonry structures provided their shape is restrained by surrounding masonry. Examples of nonfunicular shapes are semicircular and pointed arches (Figure 13.13).

Figure 13.13: Masonry arch stability: (a) because masonry cannot resist tension, thin masonry arches are inherently unstable and tend to collapse when there are four or more hinges, and (b) arches surrounded by masonry walls are stable and able to resist varying loads.

MASONRY ARCH CASE STUDIES

Pont du Gard

While the ancient Egyptians and Greeks were familiar with the arch concept, it was the Romans that first developed the arch as an important architectural element. Semicircular arches were used in most of the Roman aqueducts. One remaining example is the Pont du Gard built by the Emperor Agrippa (19 BC; Nimes, France) as part of a 25-mi (40-km) aqueduct. It is one of the most beautiful and impressive examples of ancient stone arch construction (Figure 13.14). The channel at the top is 886 ft (270 m) long; it carried water across the River Gard at a maximum height of 160 ft (49 m)—taller than the nave of any gothic cathedral. There are three tiers of semicircular arches. The lower two consist of broad spans symmetrically arranged one above the other (Brown, 1993).

The longest span (which crosses the river itself) is 80 ft (24.5 m), while the others vary between 51 and 63 ft (15.5 and 19.2 m). On both of the lower tiers, the ends of some of the stones were extended to support construction scaffolding. The water flowed in a cement-lined channel above the third tier, which consists of 35 uniform 11.5-ft (3.5-m) arches. For 20 centuries the aqueduct has stood without benefit of mortar as a testimony to the skill of the masons who cut and shaped its blocks. In 1747 the width of the lowest tier was doubled when a roadway was added beside it with arches that exactly matched the Roman original.

Flying Buttress—the half arch

The arch action of vaulted stone ceilings of medieval churches created large thrust forces that had to be resisted. The earlier Romanesque churches of the period used the weight of massive sidewalls to add a large vertical load component to these horizontal thrust forces; the resultant force of these two components was diagonal. As this line of force progressed further out and down, progressively more vertical load was added (from the accumulated weight of the wall above), and the resultant force increased as the direction became steeper. This allowed the line of force to remain within the critical middle third, keeping the entire wall in compression. But as churches

gardless of how massive the buttress pier above because the horizontal thrust component is still present. But the line of thrust slope is steep enough and the base of the pier wide enough to keep the line of thrust within the middle third of the pier throughout its height (as well as the foundation below grade) (Figure 13.15).

Figure 13.14: Pont du Gard aqueduct (19 BC; Nimes, France) is a beautiful example of an ancient stone masonry arch structure.

became taller and vault spans greater, the thickness of the sidewall necessary for lateral stability became extreme.

Gothic masons developed the flying buttress as a way of bracing the top of the structure against the side forces of the vaulting (and wind loading) while still maintaining a thin sidewall. This allowed the wall to be opened up for large expanses of stained-glass windows which characterized the period. Behaving as a half arch, the line of thrust begins nearly horizontal and becomes increasingly vertical as the weight of the buttress pier accumulates on the way down. Of course, the slope of the line of thrust never reaches vertical re-

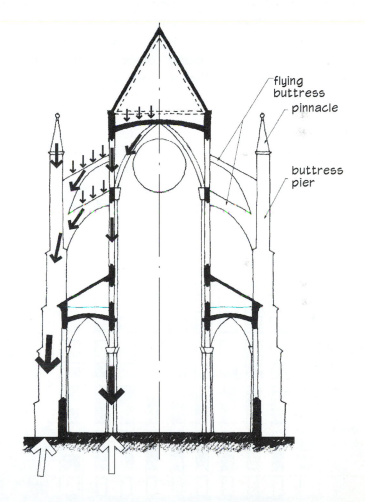

Figure 13.15: Flying buttress (half arch) used to brace the top of gothic church walls against the horizontal thrust resulting from the vaulted stone ceilings. The pointed pinnacles at the top were functional as well as decorative, adding additional weight to the top of the buttress pier.

Phillips Exeter Library

This library (1972; Exeter, NH; LouisI. Kahn, ar chitect) is the most celebrated and powerful contemporary example of the use of the *jack* (flat) arch as a primary design element. The structural system is a brick bearing wall on the perimeter and a concrete frame on the interior. The contemporary brick exterior sits quite comfortably among the surrounding traditional Georgian revival structures of this private school. All four elevations are virtually identical, inviting approach from all directions into the colonnade formed by the jack arch openings on the ground level (Ronner, et al., 1977) (Figures 13.16 and 13.17).

> *It appears simple and graceful, no decorative elements are resorted to, because I did not feel in the air the approval for decorative. I felt the striving not for severity but for the purity that I sense in a Greek temple.*
> —*Louis I. Kahn*

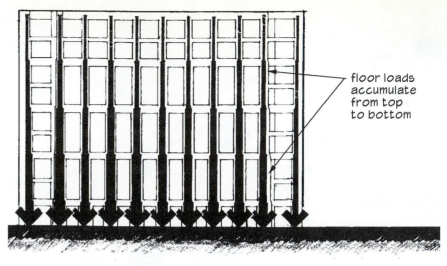

floor loads accumulate from top to bottom

Figure 13.17: Exeter Library, load path diagram.

Each pier of the brick bearing wall narrows as it rises so that the windows are broadest at the top and narrowest near the ground. The thickening of the piers nearer the ground expresses the accumulation of gravity loads collected from the jack arches at each floor. The *intrados* (bottom) of the arches has a slight *camber* (upward bow) to counteract an appearance of sagging that is characteristic of arches which are truly flat.

The concrete floor behind the arches bears on the masonry wall but also acts as a tie to resist the thrust from the arches. Without this tie action, the thrusts from these arches would accumulate across the facade, tending to spread the end piers apart. These would have become buttresses and increased considerably in width in order to resist the horizontal thrust.

Dormitories, Indian Institute of Management

In these dormitories (1974; Ahmedabad, India; LouisI. Kahn, ar chitect), which were a small part of Kahn's design for the entire institute, the rooms are arranged, in groups of 10, around a stairway and tearoom hall. In order to make the rooms contribute to the central idea of anacademic community, corridors were avoided and re-

Figure 13.16: Exeter Library, elevation.

sidual spaces are used for casual and seminar study. The tearoom entrance and location of the stair and washroom serve to protect the rooms from the stair and glare without obstructing cross-ventilation (Ronner, et al., 1977) (Figures 13.18 through 13.22).

Massive brick bearing wall construction pierced with arched openings was used throughout the dormitories and classroom buildings. Kahn used reinforced-concrete ties exposed on the exterior walls to resist the tremendous horizontal thrust generated by the shallow arches. This allowed arched openings to be very close to the end walls where buttressing action was not required.

The thickness of the brick bearing walls varies from 24 in (61 cm) at the ground floor to 12 in (30 cm) at the top floor. The load bearing quality of the brick piers of the west and south facades is further emphasized at the first floor where they dramatically slope outward in the manner of a solid buttress .

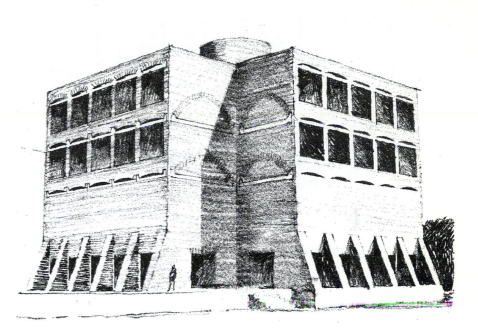

Figure 13.19: Dormitory, Indian Institute of Management, south and east facades showing individual room balconies.

Figure 13.18: Dormitory, Indian Institute of Management, exterior showing northeast facade with shallow arches with concrete ties to relieve lateral thrust.

NONMASONRY ARCHES

Arches are also built of materials which can resist tension (and bending), such as steel, laminated wood, and reinforced concrete. Based on these conditions, there are three configurations that are commonly used in conjunction with these materials, based on end conditions: *rigid* (no hinges), *two-hinged*, and *three-hinged* (Figure 13.23) (as noted above, arches with four or more hinges are unstable). Rigid arches (which include most unreinforced masonry) allow no rotation at the end supports; rigid arches bend as a result of any deflection as well as thermal expansion. Hinges are introduced in arches as a way of controlling bending due to deflection and thermal expansion. Two-hinged arches are hinged at each support; they minimize bending stresses near the supports but bend at midspan. Three-hinged arches reduce bending both at the end supports and also

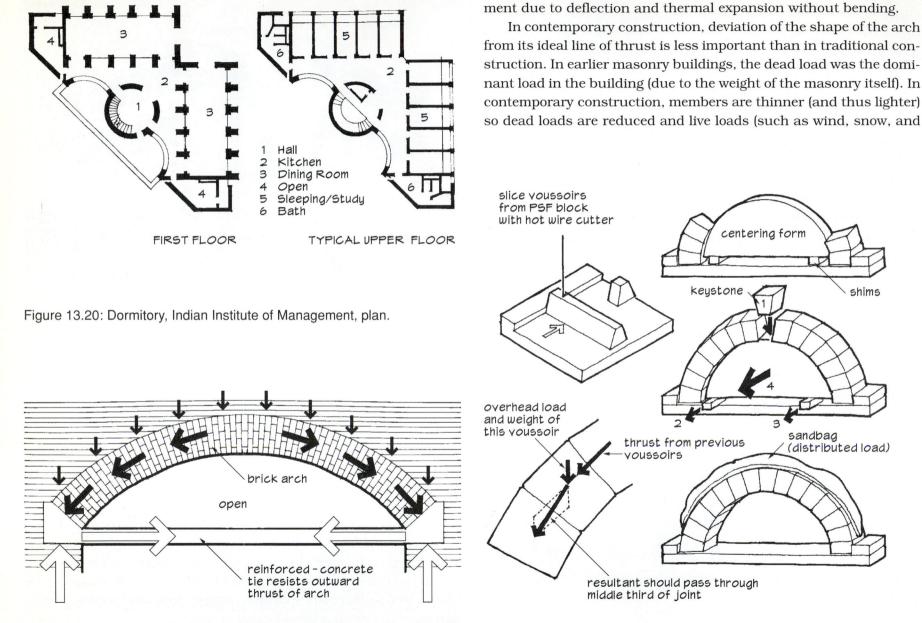

across the entire span due to the middle hinge which allows movement due to deflection and thermal expansion without bending.

In contemporary construction, deviation of the shape of the arch from its ideal line of thrust is less important than in traditional construction. In earlier masonry buildings, the dead load was the dominant load in the building (due to the weight of the masonry itself). In contemporary construction, members are thinner (and thus lighter) so dead loads are reduced and live loads (such as wind, snow, and

1　Hall
2　Kitchen
3　Dining Room
4　Open
5　Sleeping/Study
6　Bath

FIRST FLOOR　　　　TYPICAL UPPER FLOOR

Figure 13.20: Dormitory, Indian Institute of Management, plan.

brick arch

open

reinforced – concrete tie resists outward thrust of arch

Figure 13.21: Dormitory, Indian Institute of Management, arch load path diagram. Like a truss, this arch-tie combination is a thrust-free spanning device.

slice voussoirs from PSF block with hot wire cutter

centering form

keystone　　　　shims

overhead load and weight of this voussoir

thrust from previous voussoirs

sandbag (distributed load)

resultant should pass through middle third of joint

Figure 13.22: Model demonstration of arch construction, showing the necessity of resisting thrust.

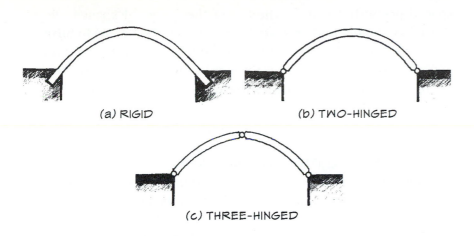

(a) RIGID   (b) TWO-HINGED

(c) THREE-HINGED

Figure 13.23: Arch configurations: (a) rigid; (b) two-hinged reduces bending at ends; and (c) three-hinged, reduces bending (due to deflection and thermal expansion) throughout.

occupants) tend to dominate and vary in magnitude and direction over time. This introduces bending stresses in arches which would have been unacceptable in traditional masonry but is easily accommodated by contemporary materials due to their ability to resist tension and bending.

NONMASONRY ARCH CASE STUDIES

Back Bay Station
This building (1989; Boston; Kallman, McKinnell & Wood, architects) is one of eight that have been constructed along the Orange Line—a recently completed 4.7-mi (7.8-km) railway which extends out from the center of Boston to its suburbs. Three separate railway lines run parallel below street level, defining a narrow site bounded by adjacent buildings and busy streets. It is this configuration of railway tracks which determined the basic plan geometry of the station (Carter, 1989) (Figures 13.24 through 13.26).

The design recalls the spatial generosity and grandeur of the American nineteenth-century railway terminal which focused attention away from the train shed (emphasized in European stations of

Figure 13.24: Back Bay Station, exterior.

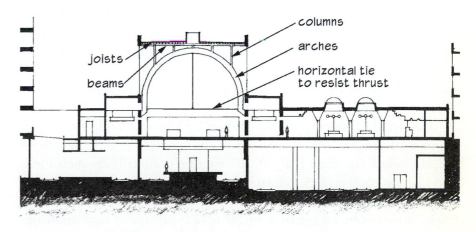

Figure 13.25: Back Bay Station, section.

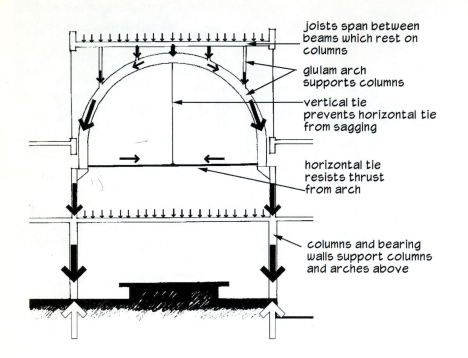

joists span between beams which rest on columns

glulam arch supports columns

vertical tie prevents horizontal tie from sagging

horizontal tie resists thrust from arch

columns and bearing walls support columns and arches above

Figure 13.26: Back Bay Station, load path diagram.

the period) to create vast concourses of civic proportion. This expression of the station as a lofty vestibule to the city has influenced the design of this station. A new station concourse was formed, by increasing the height and width of the central bay. This great hall extends through the site to provide an arcaded link between the adjacent streets.

The architects designed the station hall as an arcade vaulted by a series of arches. While one side of the plan is curved slightly (to accommodate the train tracks), the volume is essentially rectilinear and open at each end. Supported on concrete corbels on brick piers, the laminated timber arches are 32 in (82 cm) deep by 10 in (25 cm) thick, are spaced an average of 20 ft (5.2 m) apart, and span between 50 and 60 ft (15.2 and 18.2 m). The roof structure consists of laminated timber beams above each arch supported by five equally

spaced posts that rest on the top of the arches. Exposed, closely spaced laminated timber joists span between the beams to form the flat roof plane. Lateral thrust is resisted by horizontal bars connecting the base of the arches. A thinner vertical tension rod from the top of the arch supports the horizontal rods at the center to prevent sag.

London Exchange House

This office building (1990; London; Skidmore, Owings, & Merrill, architects and engineers) incorporates bridge technology to span 256 ft (78 m) over a network of railroad tracks below grade. One-story trusses support a plaza over an intermediate floor level between the tracks and office floors. The 10 floors of offices and trading space are supported by four seven-story-tall parabolic steel arches, allowing for column-free floors divided into a central 49-ft (15-m)-wide bay flanked by two 60-ft (18.3m)-wide bays. Floor loads are transferred to the arches by open-web steel trusses that span the bays (Harriman, 1990; Blyth, 1994) (Figures 13.27 through 13.31).

The two perimeter arches (and their connecting columns and beams) are exposed on the exterior and project beyond the wall face to emphasize the form, connections, and function of each structural element. Lateral support is provided to the exterior columns by diagonal struts which tie the exposed frame to the floor edges at each story level (Figure 13.28). The interior arches are exposed only in the two atrium areas.

The arches are segmented parabolas, constructed of straight steel channels that are connected to wide-flange steel columns, which are spaced on 20-ft (6.1-m) centers. Above the arches, the columns act conventionally in compression; below the arch, the "columns" behave as suspenders (in tension), supporting the floor beams. The arches consist of paired channels back to back with an intermediate space, allowing the columns to pass through the center uninterrupted.

Two major diagonal ties at each arch were required to provide lateral stiffness and resistance to buckling in the event of unsymmetrical loading. A horizontal steel tie at the base of each arch resists lateral thrust; intermediate floors also contribute to thrust re-

Figure 13.27: London Exchange House, exterior, showing steel arches used to span 256 ft (78 m). Columns above the arch are in compression; those below are in tension.

sistance. Like the arches, each diagonal is a pair of steel tubes, spaced to allow columns to pass through.

It is worthwhile to compare this building's structural system with the similar (but inverted) concept of the Minneapolis Federal Reserve Bank in Chapter 10.

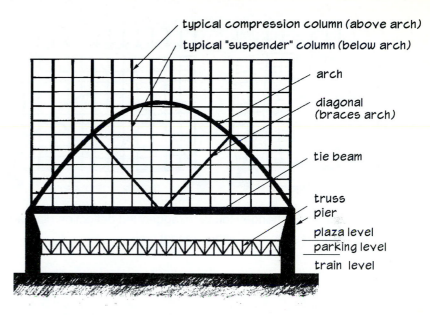

typical compression column (above arch)
typical "suspender" column (below arch)
arch
diagonal (braces arch)
tie beam
truss
pier
plaza level
parking level
train level

Figure 13.28: London Exchange House, primary system components.

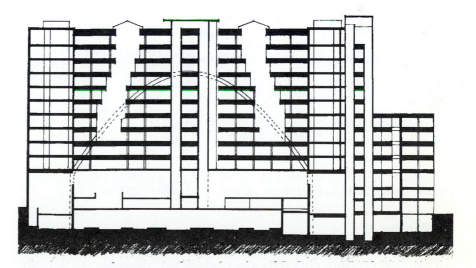

Figure 13.29: London Exchange House, section showing interior arches which are exposed in atrium areas.

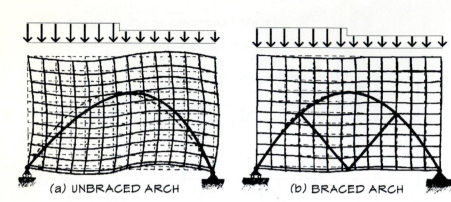

(a) UNBRACED ARCH   (b) BRACED ARCH

Figure 13.30: London Exchange House, exaggerated deflection diagrams: (a) without diagonal ties, and (b) with diagonal ties.

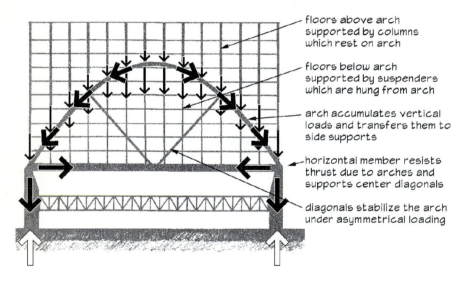

floors above arch supported by columns which rest on arch

floors below arch supported by suspenders which are hung from arch

arch accumulates vertical loads and transfers them to side supports

horizontal member resists thrust due to arches and supports center diagonals

diagonals stabilize the arch under asymmetrical loading

Figure 13.31: London Exchange House, load path diagram.

Maillart bridges

Robert Maillart's bridges, built in the early part of the twentieth century in Switzerland, collectively represent an unsurpassed achievement in arches of lightness and grace. Not only are these concrete structures beautiful, Maillart's designs were usually more economical than those of his rivals (Brown, 1993).

His first bridge to display the lightness and elegance that was to characterize his later work was the Rhine Bridge (1905; Tavanasa, Switzerland). He had been concerned with cracking which appeared in the spandrel walls of an earlier bridge (1901; Zuoz) and in the Rhine Bridge, he omitted the areas that had cracked in the shape of triangular cutouts. This reduced the extremities of the arch to slender fingers of concrete on which the roadbed rested. He also included a hinge at the thinnest section at centerspan to allow for expansion and deflection movement without cracking (Figure 13.32).

Figure 13.32: Rhine Bridge. Note the contrast between the slender refinement of the concrete bridge itself and the massive masonry abutment.

The Salginatobel Bridge (1930; Schiers, Switzerland) is one of Maillart's most famous because of the spectacular grandeur of its site. It spans 295 ft (90 m) over a 250-ft (76-m)-deep precipitous gorge in the Alpine foothills of the Graubüden Canton. The entire

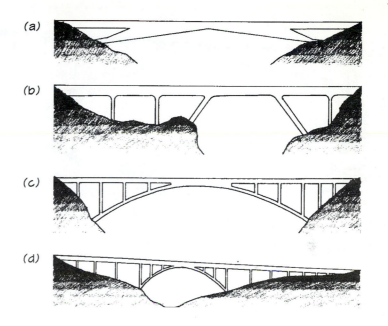

Figure 13.33: Salginatobel Bridge from below.

Figure 13.34: Four other examples of the diversity of Maillart's concrete bridges: (a) Simme Bridge [1940; Garstatt, Switzerland; spanning 105 ft (32 m)], (b) Eau-Noire Aqueduct [1925; Châtelard, Switzerland; spanning 100 ft (30.4 m)], (c) Schwandbach Bridge [1933; Schwandbach, Switzerland; spanning 123 ft (37.4 m)], and (d) Lancy-Genève project [1936; Lancy-Genève, Switzerland; spanning 164 ft (50 m)].

New River Gorge Bridge

This bridge (1978; New River Gorge, WA; Michael Baker, structural engineer) was built to shorten north-south travel in this remote part of West Virginia by some 40 mi (64 km). The arch span is 1700 ft (518 m) and the overall length is 3030 ft (924 m) making it the longest span arch bridge in the world. The steel arch was selected due to a number of site conditions. The 876-ft (267-m) depth of the gorge prevented multispan truss construction. The height necessary for a suspension bridge would have been a hazard for low-flying air traffic in the area. The steel trussed arch design that was built was considered to be the only alternative given the required span, height, and remote location. The Corten steel used for construction weathers without corroding, thus avoiding the need for regular painting (Brown, 1993).

bridge deck slopes upward across its span, supported by an arch that is wider at the abutments—20 ft (6 m)—and narrowing to match the 12-ft (3.5-m)-wide road deck midspan, where it is hinged (Figure 13.33). Other examples of Maillart's diversity are shown in Figure 13.34.

Figure 13.35: New River Gorge Bridge. To appreciate its scale, notice the semitruck whose top is visible at midspan.

SUMMARY

1. *Corbeling* is the intermediate stage between a simple cantilever and a true arch. It consists of successive courses of masonry placed on each side of an opening and extending progressively closer to each other until they meet.

2. A funicular arch is the inverted compressive equivalent of a suspension cable and experiences only axial compression.

3. As with a suspension cable, if the loading is distributed uniformly across the horizontal span of an arch, the funicular shape is a parabola.

4. If loading is distributed uniformly along the curve of the arch, the funicular shape is a catenary. The funicular shape for an arched opening in a masonry wall is between the two.

5. The shallower the arch for a given loading, the greater the lateral thrust generated.

6. A true masonry arch depends on wedge-shaped voussoirs to transfer loads laterally entirely by compression (unlike corbeling which places the cantilevering masonry courses in bending, and thus tension).

7. The funicular shape of an arch coincides with its *line of thrust* which is the set of resultants of the thrust and weight each part of an arch imposes on the next lower one.

8. If the line of thrust stays within the middle third of an arch, then only compressive forces will exist and no tension will develop.

9. If the loading changes on a thin arch so that its shape is no longer funicular, it will collapse; to prevent this, the shape of the arch may be constrained so that it does not buckle upward.

10. Rigid arches allow no rotation at the end supports, which introduces bending as a result of any deflection as well as thermal expansion.

11. Hinges are introduced in arches as a way of controlling bending due to deflection and thermal expansion.

12. Two-hinged arches are hinged at each support; they minimize bending stresses near the supports but bend at midspan.

13. Three-hinged arches are hinged at each end and at midspan; they reduce bending both at the end supports and also across the entire span due to the middle hinge. Three-hinged arches allow movement due to deflection and thermal expansion without bending.

14

VAULTS

A *vault* is a three-dimensional arched structure which transmits forces to supports by compression only. (Vault-shaped roofs, which are designed to resist major tension forces, must be reinforced, appear and structurally behave quite differently, and are considered as *shells* in a later chapter.)

In its simplest terms, a vault is an arch extruded (or rotated) into a third dimension. And like an arch, the vault (traditionally a masonry structure) is purely compressive and unable to resist tension. Because of this, vaults require continuous support along each base. Depending on their shape, compressive vaults fall into two basic types: singly curved *cylindrical vaults* and doubly curved *domed vaults*.

CYLINDRICAL VAULTS

Cylindrical vaults include various sectional shapes including: barrel (semicircular or Roman), catenary (the funicular shape for a vault of uniform thickness), and pointed (Gothic) (Figure 14.1).

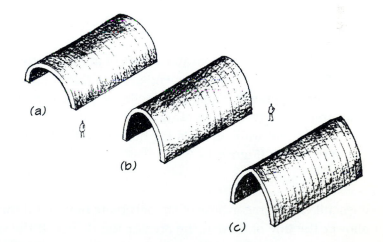

Figure 14.1: Cylindrical vaults: (a) barrel, (b) catenary, and (c) pointed.

STRUCTURAL BEHAVIOR

Load distribution

A vault differs from a comparable series of adjacent arches in its response to a concentrated load. The arches behave independently so that a load applied to one will not be shared by adjacent arches; the total load is directed down the loaded arch only. The shear resistance of the vault allows the load to spread out (at a 45° angle on each side) to adjacent areas (Figure 14.2).

Figure 14.3: Lateral resistance in (a) independent arches and (b) a vault.

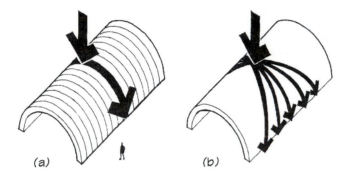

Figure 14.2: Load distribution in (a) independent arches and (b) a vault.

Lateral resistance

A vault also differs from a comparable series of arches in its lateral resistance. The arches behave independently so that a lateral load applied to the end arch will cause all to collapse like a row of dominoes. Again the shear resistance of the lower vault allows it to behave as a pair of shear walls in resisting horizontal loads parallel to the length of the vault (Figure 14.3).

Thrust resistance

Like arches, all vaults (regardless of shape) create horizontal thrust. The shallower the line of thrust, the greater the thrust. If the vault springs directly from the foundation, the friction between the ground and the foundation may suffice to resist spreading.

However, if the vault is elevated to rest on two parallel vertical walls (or on parallel beams on vertical columns), the thrust will cause the tops of the walls to spread apart. One way to contain the thrust is to add horizontal ties between the bases of the vault; this allows the tension of the ties to resist the outward thrust. This is the same principle as the reinforced concrete ties that Kahn used to contain the thrust of arches in the Indian Institute of Management.

The ancient Romans used a different strategy for resisting thrust; they added large amounts of masonry over the lower portion of the vault (*haunch*). In addition to increasing the foundation friction, this *surcharge* redirected the line of thrust to a much steeper angle so that it would lie within the center third of the wall so that it would not overturn. Finally, because the Roman semicircular vault was not funicular (a catenary is the funicular shape for a vault of uniform thickness), the lower portion (below 52°) of the vault tends to buckle upward. The added weight of the surcharge resists this and maintains the entire vault in compression. Later, in the Romanesque period, solid buttresses were added to resist thrust. The flying buttress evolved in the Gothic period to separate thrust resistance from the wall entirely (Figure 14.4).

CYLINDRICAL VAULTING CASE STUDIES

Roman vaulting

The ancient Romans used *groin* (intersecting) vaults to roof spaces with two perpendicular axes. The intersecting vaults of this period had similar dimensions: base height, rise, and width. Because of this similarity, the geometry of the intersection was relatively straightforward and, in the plan, the lines of intersection were straight and at a 45° angle to the vaults (Figure 14.5).

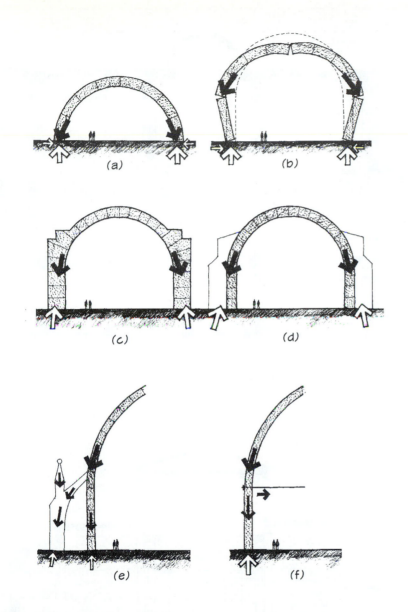

Figure 14.4: Means of resisting lateral thrust in vaults: (a) friction of foundation, (b) tendency of vault resting on vertical walls to spread, (c) Roman semicircular vault with thickened haunch and thick walls, (d) Romanesque solid buttresses, (e) Gothic flying buttresses, and (f) metal ties.

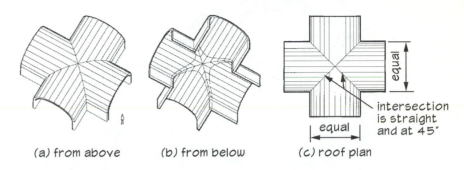

(a) from above   (b) from below   (c) roof plan

Figure 14.5: Roman groin vault: (a) axonometric view from above, (b) axonometric view from below, and (c) roof plan. Notice that because the intersecting vaults are identical, the groin portion is square in plan, and the intersections are both straight and at a 45° angle to the vaults.

The Basilica of Constantine (312 AD; Rome) was begun by Maxentius and completed by Constantine, and was larger in scale than the imperial baths from which its structural form was derived. The central *nave* (main spatial volume) consisted of a center longitudinal vault spanning 83 ft (25 m) intersected by three vaults of identical dimensions, all rising to a center height of 115 ft (35 m) above the floor (Fletcher, 1987) (Figures 14.6 through 14.9).

On each side of the nave were three lower transverse bays separated by massive piers and spanned by barrel vaults. All the vaults were made of unreinforced concrete and were coffered (panels recessed) to reduce weight and to form a decorative pattern. The manner of buttressing used to resist the thrusts of the high vaults is similar to that of later structures (including Hagia Sophia and some Romanesque and most Gothic churches).

Romanesque vaulting

The Romanesque period adopted the semicircular vault of the Roman period. However, Romans intersected only vaults of identical shape and span. Romanesque architects intersected smaller semicircular vaults with larger ones. The resulting intersection was skewed, curving in plan, and created unbalanced thrust forces in

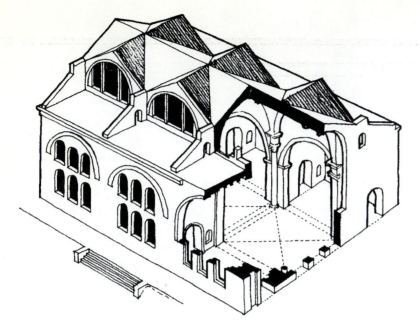

Figure 14.6: Basilica of Constantine, reconstruction.

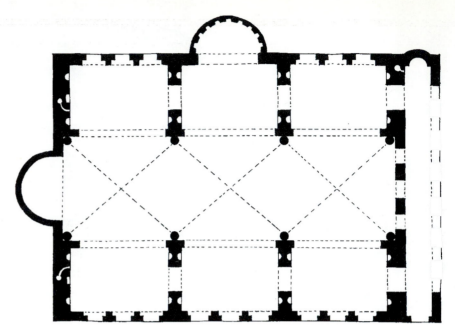

Figure 14.8: Basilica of Constantine, plan.

Figure 14.7: Basilica of Constantine, interior reconstruction.

Figure 14.9: Basilica of Constantine, section.

the groin area. The fact that some of these structures have survived for centuries is attributable to the massive supporting walls and buttresses rather than sound engineering principles (Figure 14.10).

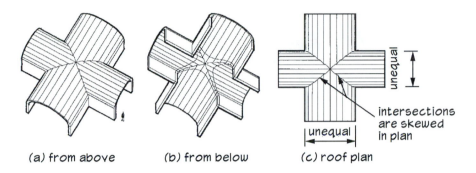

(a) from above   (b) from below   (c) roof plan

Figure 14.10: Romanesque groin vault: (a) axonometric view from above, (b) axonometric view from below, and (c) roof plan. Notice that because the intersecting vaults are of different span, the groin intersections are skewed in plan, resulting in unbalanced thrust forces.

Gothic vaulting

Gothic masons finally resolved the difficulty of intersecting vaults of different spans. The key to the solution was the development of the pointed arch and vault. This geometry allowed vaults over different width bays to have the same height and intersect with the same simplicity and directness that characterized Roman vaulting. In addition, because the pointed vault more closely approximates the ideal funicular catenary, the need for surcharge over the haunches was greatly reduced (Figure 14.11).

> *The flying buttress is something like an organism turned inside out, leaving the skeleton on the outside and any charm of the musculature and the skin on the inside.*
>
> *—Eduardo Torroja*

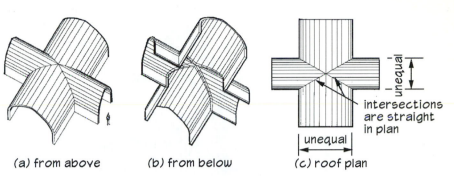

(a) from above   (b) from below   (c) roof plan

Figure 14.11: Gothic groin vault: (a) axonometric view from above, (b) axonometric view from below, and (c) roof plan. Notice that, while the span of the vaults differs and the groin portion is rectangular in plan, the intersections are both straight, like Roman vaulting, and result in balanced thrust forces.

It was the combination of the pointed arch and vault, coupled with the flying buttress, that allowed the structural exuberance that characterized the Gothic period. As the masons' experience and confidence increased, the structures became taller and thinner, while the vaulting geometry became increasingly complex (Figures 14.12 and 14.13).

DOMED VAULTS

A domed vault is an arch of revolution designed (like a masonry arch) to resist compressive forces only. Most domed vaults are circular, although there are elliptical examples. All must be designed to resist lateral thrust; otherwise spreading will occur and perimeter tension will result. This is the principal source of gradual failure of traditional masonry and unreinforced concrete domes, particularly when supported on vertical walls and columns which were inadequate to resist thrust. In addition, if the dome is not a funicular shape, the tendency for it to buckle upward in the haunch area must be resisted, usually by adding a surcharge of additional thickness in this area.

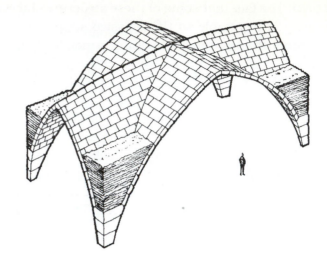

Figure 14.13: Typical gothic vault construction and surcharge.

Figure 14.12: Laon Cathedral (c.1170) isometric section (left section cut through flying buttress; right cut through windows between buttresses).

DOMED VAULT CASE STUDIES

Pantheon

The Pantheon (120 AD; Rome) is the best preserved and one of the most spectacular structures of ancient Rome (Figures 14.14 through 14.17). The entry portico was reconstructed from an earlier temple. The most impressive feature is the great circular rotunda consisting of a coffered hemispherical dome resting on a massive drum. Although 20 ft (6 m) thick, the drum is not solid, consisting instead of

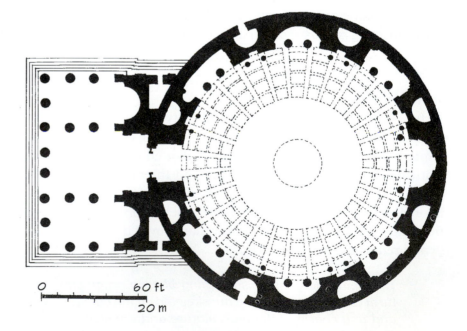

Figure 14.14: Pantheon, plan.

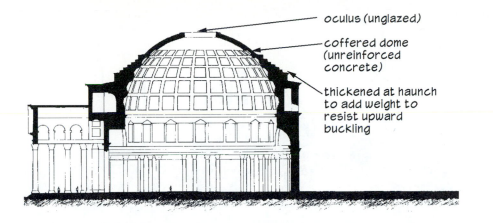

Figure 14.15: Pantheon, section.

oculus (unglazed)

coffered dome
(unreinforced
concrete)

thickened at haunch
to add weight to
resist upward
buckling

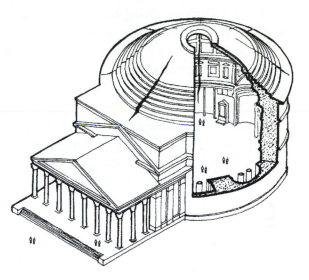

Figure 14.17: Pantheon, axonometric view showing radial tension cracks.

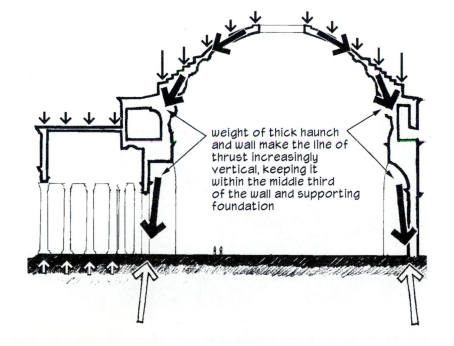

weight of thick haunch
and wall make the line of
thrust increasingly
vertical, keeping it
within the middle third
of the wall and supporting
foundation

Figure 14.16: Pantheon, load path diagram.

eight great piers, supported by relieving arches hidden within the wall. The dome thickness varies from 4.5 ft (1.4 m) near the top to 18 ft (5.5 m) at the haunch and is lightened by recessed coffers (Fletcher, 1987).

The great thickness of the wall coupled with the increased thickness of the haunch near the base of the dome are sufficient to redirect the lateral thrust downward at a sufficiently steep angle to keep the line of thrust within the center third of the base of the wall. The thickened haunch also counteracts the tendency of hemispherical domes to buckle upward in this area. Even with these precautions against thrust, there is evidence of spreading in the base of the dome in the radial tension cracks which have developed in the dome and wall. The cause of these cracks has been recently verified by finite-element computer analysis (Mark, 1993).

Pendentives
The pendentive was developed during the Byzantine period to support masonry domes on arches. The pendentive is developed from a

large hemispherical dome by removing (slicing off) the four sides and top (Figure 14.18). The remaining top opening is covered with a smaller hemispherical dome having a radius equal to that of the opening. Similarly, half domes of the same radius may be abutted to the arched side openings to resist lateral thrust from the top dome and pendentive.

Hagia Sophia, the largest and most inventive Byzantine structure (537; Constantinople; Anthemius and Isidorus, architects) is an excellent example of the use of the pendentive to support a large dome (Figures 14.19 through 14.22). The plan consists of a central space 107 ft (32.6 m) square, with four massive stone piers 25 ft × 60 ft (7.6 m ×16.3 m) tall supporting four semicircular arches form-

Figure 14.19: Hagia Sophia, exterior.

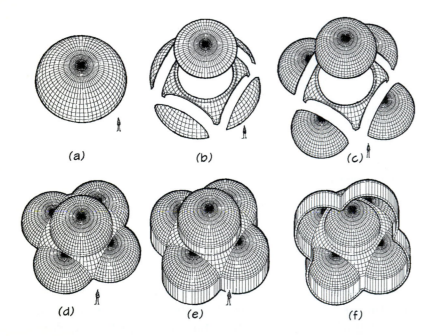

Figure 14.18: Pendentive geometry: (a) large hemispherical dome, (b) with sides and top sliced off, and (c) replaced with smaller-radius hemispherical top dome, and side half domes, which (d) help resist lateral thrust from the top dome and pendentive; with (e) walls and drum under upper dome, from above, and (f) from below.

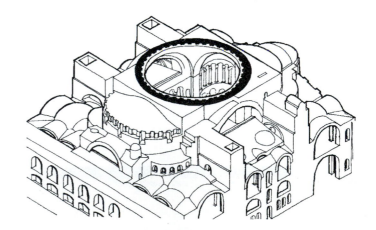

Figure 14.20: Hagia Sophia, isometric view (dome removed to show pendentive).

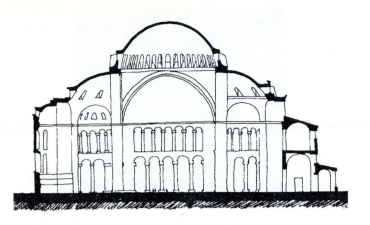

Figure 14.21: Hagia Sophia, section.

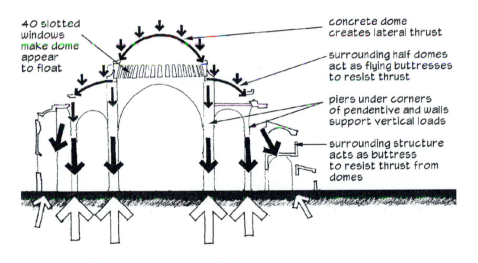

40 slotted windows make dome appear to float

concrete dome creates lateral thrust

surrounding half domes act as flying buttresses to resist thrust

piers under corners of pendentive and walls support vertical loads

surrounding structure acts as buttress to resist thrust from domes

Figure 14.22: Hagia Sophia, load path diagram.

ing the base of the pendentive. The 107-ft (32.6-m)-diameter dome rests on the opening of the pendentive and rises to a height of 180 ft (54.8 m) above the floor. East and west of this central space are great semicircular bays covered with half domes which help resist the thrust of the main dome and pendentive (Fletcher, 1987) (Figure 14.21).

The dome is visually lightened by a ring of 40 arched windows around the base of the dome, producing a ring of diffuse light and creating the illusion that the dome is suspended above the vast interior of the church. In addition, because these windows extend 50° above the horizontal, they may have helped minimize the radial tension cracking present in the Pantheon. Over the centuries, the effects of thrust from the center dome and the pendentive (together with their surcharges) have caused the four main piers to incline outward along the direction of both axes. Still, Hagia Sophia remains the crowning technological achievement of the Byzantine period (Mark, 1993).

Radial tension in Renaissance domes
Radial tension cracking (similar to that noted above in the Pantheon) has been observed in the Florence Cathedral (Figure 14.23). It is an

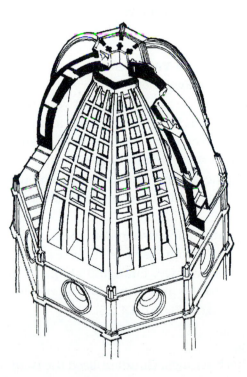

Figure 14.23: Florence Cathedral, dome, cutaway axonometric view showing ribbed interior construction.

octagonal *cloister* dome (generated by the intersection of several pointed vaults) designed by Brunelleschi and completed in 1434. The dome is hollow, consisting of vertical ribs which thicken toward the base (serving to contain the lines of thrust). Spanning 131 ft (40 m), the interior rise above the supporting dome is 113 ft (34.4 m), up to a height of 287 ft (87.5 m) above the floor. Brunelleschi anticipated the radial tension and proposed a set of reinforcing "chains" (some fabricated of stone and iron, and others of wood) to form tension hoops at different heights up the dome. In the end, only one wood chain was installed; the design depended on the pointed gothic profile of the dome and the massive ribs and dome to provide stability. However, cracks were recorded in the dome as early as 1639 and continue to be monitored carefully. To date, no further reinforcement has been added (Mark, 1993). Similar problems developed during the construction of the dome of Michelangelo's St. Peter's Cathedral (Rome); iron chains were added in 1593 and replaced by Giovanni Poleni in 1742.

MODELING FUNICULAR VAULTS

Around the turn of the twentieth century, the Catalan architect Antonio Gaudi used the correspondence between tensile and compressive funicular shapes in his search for the ideal shapes for masonry arches and vaults over complex floor plans (such as the Colonia Guel Chapel). He derived them using corresponding inverted scale models with sagging chains and carefully calculated weights and covered these with canvas to approximate the ideal form for the masonry vaults.

Even today, funicular suspension models are useful to study optimum forms for compressive structures (Figure 14.24). Such models are quite interactive, changing shape in direct response to loading as well as to the amount of sag as determined by member (string or chain) length (Figure 14.25).

Catalan vaulting

In a number of his buildings, Gaudi utilized the traditional Catalonian method of constructing vaults of layers of thin tiles without the use of formwork. To build a dome using the Catalonian method, first a

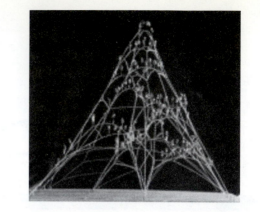

Figure 14.24: Inverted photograph of chain model study of a funicular structure in pure compression (designed and built by architecture students M. Haar, C. Muskopf, B. Kaufmann, and J. Hutchison; S. Sanabria, professor).

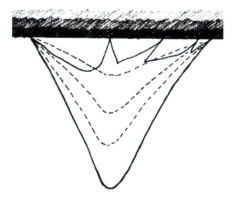

Figure 14.25: Diagram of a family of chain models with identical loading but varying amounts of sag. The least tension (compression if inverted) occurs when the sag is greatest.

perimeter support is constructed. Upon this the first (lowest and outermost) ring of thin [approximately 3/4 in (19 mm)-thick tiles are supported on short, cantilevered wood brackets. On top of this a second layer is added using a rapidly setting mortar; the joints are staggered from the first layer. Once the first layer is completed and the mortar is set—in less than 12 hours—the masons can erect the next ring by standing on the first and adding as many layers of tile as needed by the span of the dome, usually not more than four (Salvadori, 1980) (Figure 14.26). This method was commercialized by the Guastavino Company in the United States during the late nineteenth century and used in the construction of over 2000 buildings (Figure 14.27).

LAMELLA VAULTS

A *lamella* vault consists of intersecting *skew* (diagonal in plan) arches arranged to form a diamond pattern. In the strictest definition, lamella construction consists of short members (*lamellas*) fastened together at an angle forming a basket-weave pattern. Invented in Europe in 1908 by a German building official named Zollinger and introduced to the United States in 1925 (Scofield and O'Brien, 1954), this system is particularly well suited for using members of relatively small size to achieve very large spans of wood, steel, or pre-

cast concrete. The term lamella is also used more loosely to describe similar monolithic structures of cast-in-place reinforced concrete. Lamella vaults may be either cylindrical or domed.

The most popular material for constructing lamella structures is wood. Widely used for vaults and domes during the 1940s and 1950s, it was made practical by the relative low cost of timber and assembly labor. It made efficient use of short timber components in the construction of medium- to large-span buildings. The timber components were prefabricated to a uniform length, beveled and bored at the ends,

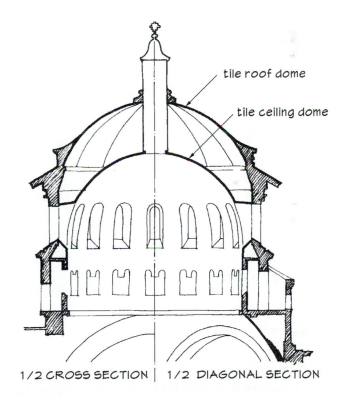

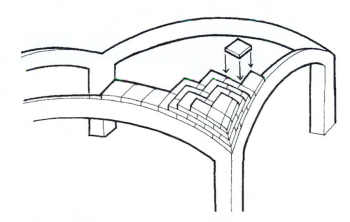

Figure 14.26: Catalan method of constructing a domed vault of thin tiles without formwork. The first row of tiles rests on the perimeter support and temporary cantilever supports; subsequent layers are added after the mortar of the first row is set.

Figure 14.27: Immaculate Conception Convent (circa 1910; Ferdinand, IN; Victor Klutho, architect; Guastavino Company, tile dome contractor), section showing Catalan tile inner and outer domes which were constructed without formwork. The thickness of the multilayer tile dome is approximately 3.5 in (8.75 cm).

and bolted together in the characteristic basket-weave pattern; the exposed lamellas form an attractive ceiling pattern (Figure 14.28).

Steel has also been used for lamella construction. For example, a convention and exhibition hall (1954; Corpus Christi, TX; G. R. Kiewitt, structural engineer) was roofed with a trussed steel lamella vault spanning 224 ft (68 m). In addition, concrete has also been used to construct lamella-type vaults and ribs.

Figure 14.29: Tacoma Dome, under construction.

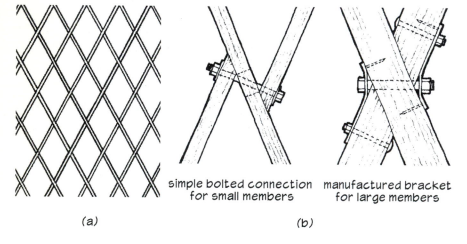

simple bolted connection for small members   manufactured bracket for large members

(a)   (b)

Figure 14.28: Timber lamella construction: (a) basket-weave pattern of lamellas, and (b) connection detail.

LAMELLA CASE STUDIES

Tacoma Dome

At the time of construction, this dome was the largest timber dome in the world (1983; Tacoma, WA; McGranahan Messenger Associates, architects; Western Wood Structures, dome structural engineers). The spherical 530-ft (162-m)-diameter laminated-wood, lamella-type dome rises 110 ft (33.5 m) above its supporting walls and is used for sporting events, exhibitions, and conventions (Eberwein, 1989; Robinson, 1985) (Figures 14.29 through 14.31).

Figure 14.30: Tacoma Dome, interior.

The patented Varax system was used with the beams configured in a triangular pattern. It differs from true lamella construction in that the framing is triangular rather than diamond-shaped due to the very large components involved. However, the archlike behavior and stress distribution is similar due to the patented steel connector that provides a structurally rigid node where the six beams intersect.

The skeleton consists of curved glue-laminated timber (*glulam*) beams and purlins. The beams follow *great circle* paths (that is, they lie on planes passing through the center of the sphere) which results in a single-curvature radius, thus simplifying fabrication. The beams are 30 in (85 cm) deep and 6.75 or 8.75 in (17 or 22 cm) deep; the longest beams are 49 ft (14.9 m) long. The purlins are 5.1 in (13 cm) wide and vary from 9 to 18 in (23 to 46 cm) in depth. The purlins span between the larger beams and support the 1.5-in (37-mm)-tongue-and-groove timber decking.

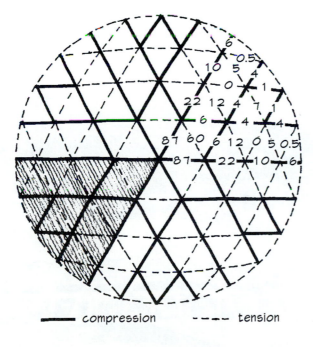

— compression   - - - tension

Figure 14.31: Relative stresses in Varax lamella-type timber dome. Notice that the members most nearly oriented to the arch direction are in compression while others (in the hoop direction) are in tension.

The beams and purlins were preassembled into triangular sections and lifted into place with cranes. Once the dome perimeter framing was installed, the triangular sections became self-supporting and required no scaffolding. This allowed interior trades to work below while dome erection progressed.

The dome is supported by a reinforced-concrete tension ring 3.0 ft × 3.0 ft (91 cm × 91 cm) in cross section and posttensioned to resist outward thrust, and spanning between the 36 concrete columns. The columns and the nonbearing masonry infill walls are 42 ft (12.8 m) high.

This project and other recent timber domes, such as the 533-ft (163-m)-diameter Skydome completed in Flagstaff, AZ, in 1978, and the 502-ft (153-m)-diamter Northern Michigan University Dome completed in Marquette in 1990, have revived interest in lamella timber construction as an attractive and economical alternative to pneumatic, steel, and concrete construction for large-span sports facilities.

Nervi's hangars
In the mid-1930s, the Italian engineer PierLuigi Nervi won a competition to design and build several airplane hangars using concrete lamella-type construction. The designs were economical, intended to be erected quickly, and used concrete ingeniously in a country where steel and wood were traditionally scarce and labor plentiful. He used scale models as well as numerical analysis to analyze the stresses; this is one of the earliest examples of the use of models for quantitative analysis of contemporary, large-span structures (Figure 14.32). Nervi stated, "I designed the structure as a geodetic framework acting together as a whole, as I believed this would give the most economical solution and the one requiring the least steel" (Huxtable, 1960).

The earliest hangars of this series were built with a cast-in-place skeleton and roofed with hollow tiles. Because of the complexity of the formwork, this method proved painfully slow. As Nervi noted, "The actual construction was not easy, and provided yet another illustration of the economic disadvantages of timber formwork whenever reinforced concrete work goes beyond the simplest shapes."

Figure 14.32: Hangar (cast-in-place, lamella-type vault construction), exterior.

The structures typically spanned 330 ft × 135 ft (100 m × 41 m) and were supported on three sides by flying buttresses under the base of each lamella. In order to provide the 165-ft (50-m)-wide opening required to accommodate the airplanes, the front was supported by a concrete space truss spanning over three larger buttresses (Figure 14.33).

To overcome the disadvantages of cast-in-place construction, Nervi redesigned the system to use small precast trusses as the lamella components. Where the lamella ribs crossed, the reinforcing rods were welded and grouted. The design of the supporting system was modified to incorporate a horizontal truss to resist lateral thrust between the more widely spaced A-frame buttresses. The structures proved even stronger than Nervi anticipated. When the Germans retreated from Italy during the last phase of the war, they attempted to destroy the hangars by dynamiting the supporting buttresses. The roofs crashed to the ground below but remained intact, with only a few of the several hundred joints failing (Salvadori, 1980).

Figure 14.33: Hangar, interior.

Palazzetto dello Sport

The Small Sports Palace (1957; Rome; A. Vitelozzi and PierLuigi Nervi, architects; Pier Luigi Nervi, structural engineer; Nervi and Bartoli, general contractors) was one of several structures designed by Nervi and his son Antonio for the 1960 Olympic Games. It was configurable to seat up to 5000 spectators for wrestling, boxing, gymnastics, and volleyball events (Huxtable, 1960; Nervi, 1963) (Figures 14.34 and 14.35).

Figure 14.34: Palazzetto dello Sport, exterior.

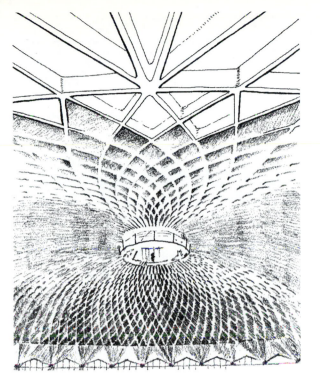

Figure 14.35: Palazzetto dello Sport, interior.

The circular dome has a 197-ft (60-m) diameter and a height of 68 ft (21 m). It incorporates monolithic lamella-type ribs exposed below and spiraling inward toward the center. A compression ring at the center forms a cupola, providing a central source of natural light. The dome is supported around the perimeter on 36 Y-shaped cast-in-place concrete buttresses.

The dome construction method was at least as innovative as the structure itself. It consisted of cast-in-place reinforced concrete formed by 1620 diamond-shaped precast concrete forms which were left in place. The precast forms were cast into the 19 different shapes required from master molds and positioned on scaffolding. The method was economical and resulted in an excellent exposed finish. It was also fast, requiring only 30 days to complete.

Much of the success of this and other Nervi projects is attributable to Nervi's dual role as both contractor and architect-engineer. Many of the projects were successful competition entries, where the design as well as a fixed construction cost was proposed. It is unlikely that Nervi's designs could have been successfully constructed at such low cost using a separate, less innovative contractor.

SUMMARY

1. A *vault* is a three-dimensional arched structure which transmits forces to supports by compression only. It is unable to resist tension. (By contrast, a *shell* is able to resist compression and tension.) Because of this, vaults require continuous support along their base.

2. There are two types of vaults: singly curved *cylindrical vaults* and doubly curved *domed vaults*.

3. Unlike a series of adjacent arches (which act independently), the shear resistance of the vault allows the load to spread out (at a 45° angle on each side) to adjacent areas.

4. Like arches, all vaults (regardless of shape) create horizontal thrust. The shallower the line of thrust, the greater the thrust.

5. *Groin* vaults are intersecting vaults used to roof spaces in two perpendicular axes.

6. Roman groin vaults were semicircular and identical in span resulting in a simple intersection geometry.

7. Romanesque groin vaults were semicircular and different in span (and height) resulting in a complex intersection geometry.

8. This complexity was resolved by the Gothic invention of the pointed vault which allowed the vaults of different spans to be the same height; this simplified the intersection geometry.

9. A domed vault is an arch of revolution designed (like a masonry arch) to resist compressive forces only.

10. All domed vaults create thrust which must be resisted; otherwise spreading will occur and perimeter tension will result.

11. The *Catalonian* method of constructing vaults consists of layers of thin tiles positioned without the use of formwork.

12. A *lamella* vault consists of intersecting *skew* (diagonal in plan) arches arranged to form a diamond pattern.

Part V

SHELL SYSTEMS

15

SHELLS

A *shell* is a thin, curved surface structure that transfers loads to supports by tension, compression, and shear only. Shells are distinguished from traditional vaults by their ability to resist tension. Thus, while the curved shapes of shells may resemble traditional vault forms, their structural behavior and load paths are often significantly different due to this ability to resist tension. Examples of natural shells include eggs, turtle shells, seashells, nutshells, and skulls.

Most architectural shells are constructed of reinforced concrete, although plywood, metal, and glass-reinforced plastics (*GRP*) may be used. These alternative materials are commonly used as shells in boat and automobile construction.

Shells are very efficient in structures (such as roofs) where loading is distributed uniformly and curved shapes are suitable. Because shells are, by definition, very thin, they are unable to resist the local bending induced by significant concentrated loads.

SHELL TYPES

Shells are commonly classified by their shape. *Synclastic* shapes (domes) are doubly curved and have similar curvature in each direction. *Developable* shapes (cones, and cylinders or barrels) are singly curved; they are straight in one direction, curved in the other, and can be formed by bending a flat sheet. *Anticlastic* shapes (saddle shapes including conoids, hyperbolic paraboloids, and hyperboloids) are doubly curved and have opposite curvature in each direction (Figure 15.1). In addition, there are *free-form* shells which are not mathematically derived.

SYNCLASTIC SHELLS

A dome is a major work of art. The perfect blending of sculpture and architecture in displacing space. A dome is the most natural of all forms, a vault of man created in the image of a vault of heaven.

—Michaelangelo

Domes are *surfaces of revolution* created by revolving a curved line about an axis. The most common dome is spherical; its surface is generated by rotating an arc of a circle around a vertical axis (Figure 15.2). The vertical sections around a rotational shell are longitudinal *arch lines* (also known as meridians), and its horizontal sections (all circles) are *hoops* or *parallels*; the largest parallel is the *equator*.

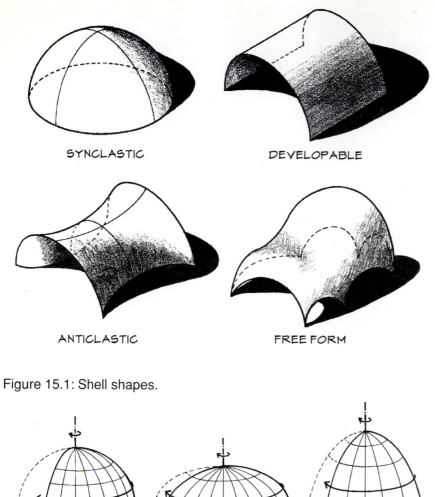

Figure 15.1: Shell shapes.

Figure 15.2: Rotational surfaces.

STRUCTURAL BEHAVIOR

Stresses in a domed shell can be understood as acting in two directions: along *arch* lines and along *hoop* lines. Under uniform loading,

a dome is in compression along arch lines everywhere. In a hemispherical dome, because these arch lines are semicircular, there is a tendency for the dome to be stable on top but to buckle upward in the lower portion (like arches and vaults; Figure 15.3).

In a shell dome (which can resist tension), this upward buckling tendency is resisted by tension along the hoop lines below about 45° above the horizontal. For this reason, shallow spherical domes are in hoop compression only, while deeper spherical domes are in hoop

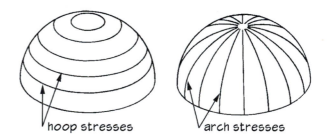

Figure 15.3: Stress directions in a dome.

compression above 45° and in hoop tension below. (This angle of transition varies depending on loading; it is 38° above the horizontal for self-weight loading only; Figure 15.4.) This behavior differs from traditional vaulted domes, which could not resist tension and needed added weight (surcharge) to prevent upward buckling. Furthermore, it allows shell domes to be funicular for any symmetrical loading, unlike vaults and arches which are funicular for only one loading condition (Salvadori and Heller, 1975) (Figures 15.5 and 15.6).

Elliptical domes, being relatively flatter on top than on the bottom, accentuate the upward buckling tendency in the lower region, and thus depend even more on hoop tension for stability. Conversely, parabolic domes, being more sharply curved at the top and less below, are nearly funicular, have less tendency to buckle, and produce less hoop tension.

Resisting thrust

Like arches, all domes develop outward thrust. Although deep domes develop less thrust than shallow ones of comparable spans, even

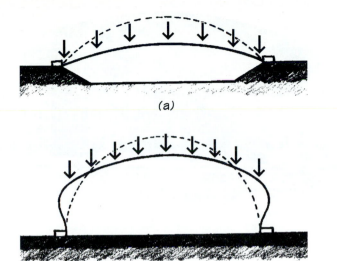

Figure 15.4: Deflection in spherical shells: (a) shallow dome is completely in compression, and (b) lower portion of hemisphere dome tends to buckle upward and is resisted by hoop tension.

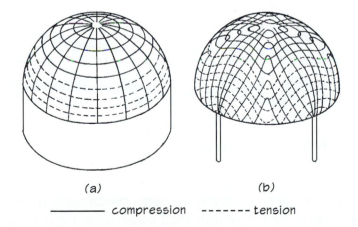

compression ——— tension -------

Figure 15.5: Membrane stresses in hemispherical shells subjected to uniform loading: (a) supported continuously around the base, and (b) supported on four columns.

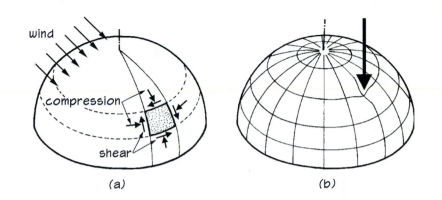

Figure 15.6: Dome: (a) shear resistance to lateral forces such as wind, and (b) local bending stresses due to concentrated loads.

this amount must be resisted. In deep domes, the hoop-tension resistance of the shell itself is usually sufficient. But, in shallow domes, it is common to create a *tension ring* by increasing the thickness of the dome at the base (to accommodate additional tension reinforcement). Since this tension ring resists thrust internally, no additional buttressing is required. This allows the dome to rest on a vertical *drum* wall (or ring of columns) without the need for buttressing. In the case of column support, the tension ring also serves as a ring beam spanning between columns (Figure 15.7).

DOMED SHELL CASE STUDIES

Kresge Auditorium
This dome (1955; Cambridge, MA; Eero Saarinen & Associates, architects; Ammann & Whitney, structural engineers) is a one-eighth sphere, resting at three points. The 27-ft (18.6-m)-high arched openings between the supports are glazed and curved in plan. While the building is a pure and unadorned expression of the structure on the exterior, the dome-shaped interior was recognized as acoustically unsuited for an auditorium function. (Concave reflecting surfaces focus sound resulting in hot spots in areas that receive reflections

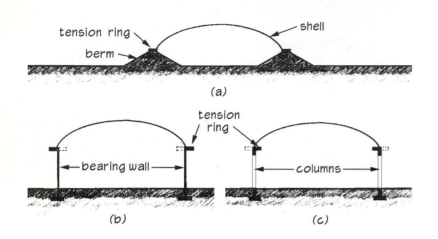

Figure 15.7: Tension ring resists outward thrust at base of dome: (a) continuously supported on ground, (b) continuously supported on drum wall, and (c) supported on columns.

Figure 15.8: Kresge Auditorium, exterior.

from multiple directions.) The areas behind the large window walls act as daylighted public concourses which require light isolation from the performance areas. As a result, the partition and ceiling acoustical enclosures create an "interior" building bearing no visual or functional resemblance to the exterior dome structure (Editor, 1954c) (Figures 15.8 and 15.9).

The radius of the dome is 112 ft (34 m). The typical structural thickness of the reinforced concrete shell is 3.5 in (8.7 cm) thickening to 19.5 in (50 cm) at the three support points to accommodate the concentration of stresses there. The shell edge above the glazed openings is stiffened by a concrete rib which also serves to form a rain gutter. The bearing points are heavily reinforced and behave as pin connections to bending stresses. The bearing points are supported by massive concrete buttress foundations.

The 2-in (50-mm)-thick layer of fiberglass thermal insulation applied over the concrete shell is inadequate by contemporary standards. This is covered by a 2-in (50-mm) thickness of nonstructural

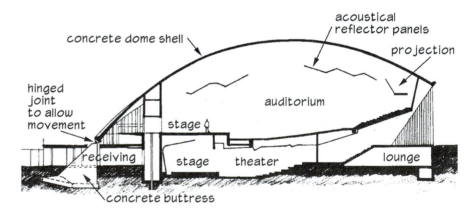

Figure 15.9: Kresge Auditorium, section.

concrete which was necessary for acoustical isolation purposes. Thus the structural efficiency of thin-shell construction was negated by nonstructural considerations. In the end, given the acoustical constraints of the project, the choice of thin-shell construction remains questionable.

Annunciation Greek Orthodox Church

> *It seemed to us three buildings. The first we saw from a distance—a great blue inverted saucer floating above the ground. This was the overwhelming roof of the dome, covered with blue ceramic tile, and 333 feet around. Close up, but still outside, the second building—a series of curves, gently soaring and plunging. And inside, a third, composed of space and color, bright blue, gold, red, somber purple, and the interior of the dome resting on a necklace of light made of glass spheres.*
>
> —*Editor, Milwaukee Journal*

The church (1956, Milwaukee; FrankLloyd W right, architect), one of Wright's last buildings, is large, seating 670 in the main sanctuary. The ground-level sanctuary seating surrounds the altar, like a theater-in-the-round. In the center is a floor opening which looks down into an interior garden below (at the classroom level). Surrounding this is additional balcony seating located in the dome perimeter which cantilevers in all directions (Editor, 1961; Futagawa, 1988) (Figures 15.10 through 15.13).

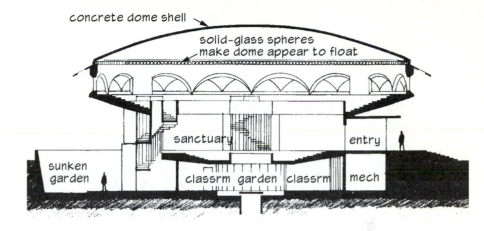

Figure 15.11: Annunciation Greek Orthodox Church, section.

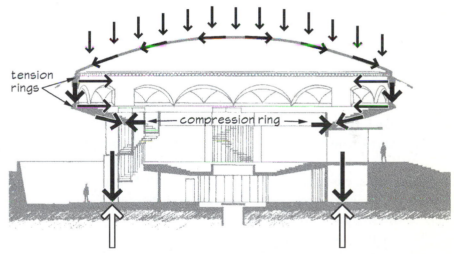

Figure 15.12: Annunciation Greek Orthodox Church, load path diagram.

Figure 15.10: Annunciation Greek Orthodox Church, exterior.

The thin-shell, reinforced-concrete dome has a base diameter of 94-ft (28.6-m) and is quite shallow; its 197-ft (60m)-radius curvature rises only 11 ft (3.3 m) above its base. The structural thickness of 3 in (75 mm) increases to 4 in (100 mm) at the edge which is reinforced to act as a tension ring to resist the considerable outward thrust. It is covered with a 3-in (75-mm) thickness of sprayed-on insulation below and 2-in (50-mm) blue tile roof above.

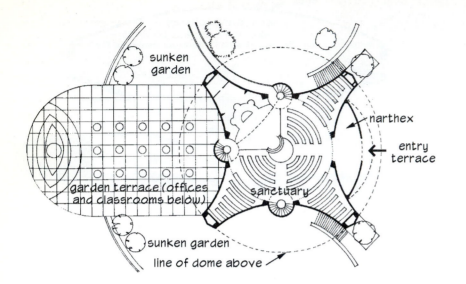

Figure 15.13: Annunciation Greek Orthodox Church, ground level plan.

The shell edge rests on a short vertical drum wall which is pierced by arched windows for daylighting. From the inside, the dome seems to float above the "necklace of light made of glass spheres." This illusion recalls the ring of windows in the Hagia Sophia. The spheres are solid glass, cast into the concrete drum wall; because the spheres nearly touch each other, they contribute substantially to the support of the weight of the dome.

The drum wall is supported on the perimeter of a second, inverted dome which also forms the floor of the balcony. This is reinforced at the perimeter and behaves as a tension ring (again, for the purpose of resisting outward thrust). This inverted dome rests on the four concave-curved bearing walls and pilasters which enclose the ground-level sanctuary and the stairways to the balcony; these extend down to the foundations.

It is remarkable how Wright resolved and expressed this unorthodox structural system into an architectural form that is unified and integrated. The visual and emotional effect of this integration is profound.

Sundome

This recent 270-ft (82.3-m)-diameter stadium dome (1990; Yakima, WA; Loofburrow Architects, architect; J. Christiansen, structural engineer) is notable for its forming method. Divided into 24 pie-shaped segments, each segment is saddle-shaped (concave in the hoop direction, convex in the arch direction), resulting in an umbrella-like ribbed appearance (Randall and Smith, 1991) (Figure 15.14).

The dome rises 40 ft (12.2 m) to a clear height of 80 ft (48.8 m) above the floor. The 24 identical segments arch to a compression ring at the crown of the roof, and their bases are stabilized by a posttensioned concrete ring supported on 24 reinforced-concrete columns. Each shell segment is 4.5 in (11 cm) thick in the lower portion, tapering to 3 in (7.5 cm) near the top. To prevent buckling, 12-in (30-cm)-wide × 30-in (76-cm)-deep ribs were added at the edges of the segments.

Six reusable forms were used to cast the dome. These were built using straight wood joists angled to give the desired saddle shape and sheathed with plywood (see discussion of saddle shells later in this chapter). The shell segments were cast at 60° intervals around the roof to equalize the thrust at the tension and compression rings. The tension ring was cast before the segments, supported by shoring, and posttensioned after the segments were complete.

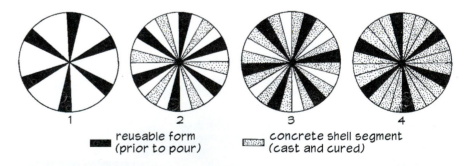

Figure 15.14: Sundome forming sequence.

After casting the first six segments, the forms were lowered, rolled into the new position, and raised into position to cast the next six segments. The process was repeated a total of four times. Christiansen had utilized the same forming method previously in the larger 40-segment Kingdome (1975, Seattle) which spanned 660 ft (201 m).

Air-formed concrete house
This house (1954; Hobe Sound, FL; Elliot Noyes, architect; Wallace Neff, system inventor) was an innovative attempt to reduce the forming costs of small concrete domes in order to make them suitable for residential construction. Planned for one or two bedroom homes, the 30-ft (9.1-m)-diameter prototype dome was 14 ft (4.3 m) high at the center, with segments removed from front and rear to create arched window walls; the interior floor area was 600 ft² (56m²) (Editor, 1954b) (Figure 15.15).

Figure 15.15: Air-formed concrete dome house, exterior.

The "balloon" form was inflated, covered with wire-mesh reinforcement, and sprayed with concrete (this is the Gunnite process which is commonly used for constructing swimming pools).

The construction was layered with an initial (interior) 2-in (50-mm)-thick layer of concrete, followed by vapor barrier and fiberglass insulation, and finally by a 2-in (50-mm)-thick outer layer of concrete. Scaffolding was required only for supporting workers while spraying, which was done in one day. After the concrete cured, the reusable inflatable form was deflated and removed (Figure 15.16). The system has been subsequently used for classrooms and storage facilities.

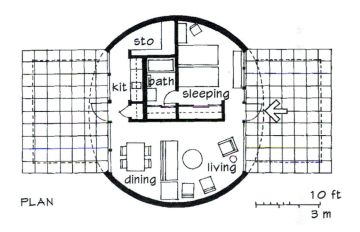

Figure 15.16: Air-formed concrete dome house, one-bedroom plan.

DEVELOPABLE SHELLS

Barrel shells are developable (can be formed by bending a plane), are curved in one direction only, and are formed by extruding a curved line along a straight path. The most commonly used shapes are semicircular and parabolic. They are distinguished from barrel vaults of similar shape by their ability to resist tension. Thus they can be supported at corners (or ends) only, spanning along the longitudinal axis as well as in the direction of curvature. (Recall that because barrel vaults cannot resist tension, they require continuous bearing support along each base.)

STRUCTURAL BEHAVIOR

The structural behavior of barrel shells differs considerably depending on their relative length. *Short* barrel shells have the shorter plan dimension along the longitudinal axis, while *long* barrel shells have the longer plan dimension in that direction.

Short barrel shells
These are also typically supported at the corners and behave in one of two ways (or a combination thereof). The first is for each end to be stiffened into an arch, with the shell acting as slabs which span between the end arches. The second way is for each lower longitudinal edge to be stiffened into a beam, with the thinner shell behaving as a series of adjacent arches spanning between the side beams (Figure 15.17). Because the minimum shell thickness necessary for practical construction (and to meet code requirements) far exceeds that required structurally for short barrel shells under most conditions, they are inefficient and thus seldom used.

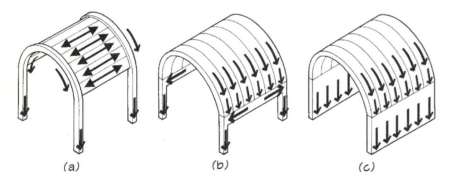

(a)   (b)   (c)

Figure 15.17: Short barrel shell behavior: (a) as slabs spanning between end arches and (b) as a series of adjacent arches spanning between edge beams. Compare this with (c) a barrel vault which must be supported continuously along its base.

Long barrel shells
These are typically supported at the corners and behave as large beams in the longitudinal direction. As a result the stresses in the shell resemble the bending stresses in a beam; the top portion is in compression along the entire length, while the bottom is in tension (Figure 15.18). The diaphragm action of the thin shell provides the necessary resistance to the horizontal and vertical shear inherent in bending behavior (Figure 15.19).

The span-to-depth ratio of long barrels affects both the stresses developed as well as the efficiency in covering a large area. Lower depth-to-span ratios reduce bottom compression and top tension forces, allowing thinner shell thickness. On the other hand, greater depth requires more surface area for a given span. In theory, the optimum depth-to-span ratio is about 2.0, minimizing the total volume of concrete and steel reinforcement required. In practice, ratios between 6 and 10 are common, due to programmatic considerations and the minimum thickness required by code or construction practices.

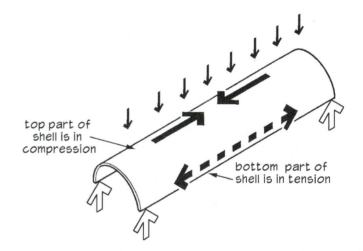

top part of shell is in compression

bottom part of shell is in tension

Figure 15.18: Long barrel shell behaves as a beam spanning between the end supports, developing compression stresses along the top and tension stresses along the bottom.

Edge conditions
In order for a structure to behave as a true shell (in tension and compression only, with no localized bending), it is necessary to maintain the designed shell shape by stiffening both the ends and the longitudinal edges, and by resisting outward thrust.

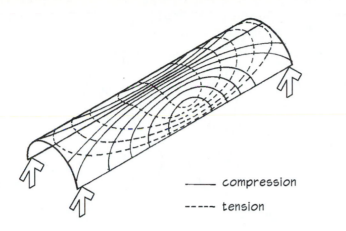

——— compression

- - - - - tension

Figure 15.19: Stress diagram for a long barrel shell subjected to uniformly distributed loading. Notice that tension and compression stresses are always perpendicular to each other. The spacing of the stress contours indicates the concentration of stress in that region (closer spacing means greater stress).

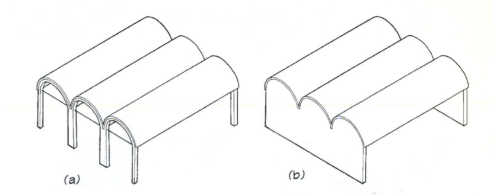

(a)

(b)

Figure 15.20: End supports of multibay long barrel shell: (a) ends stiffened into arches on columns with tie-rods to resist lateral thrust, and (b) end bearing walls which provide vertical support, maintain the shape of the ends of the shell, and behave as shear walls to resist outward thrust.

It is necessary to constrain the ends of the shell in order to maintain its shape under nonfunicular loading conditions. This is typically accomplished by either stiffening the ends by thickening them into arches on supporting columns and adding tie-rods to resist lateral thrust or by using end bearing walls (which provide vertical support, maintain the shape of the ends of the shell, and behave as shear walls to resist outward thrust) (Figure 15.20).

The arch action of the barrel shell occurs along its entire length (not just at the ends). As a result, outward thrust is developed along the entire length also. When the shell is repeated in a multibay configuration, the outward thrusts of adjacent shells balance each other; only the free edges of the first and last shells need to resist thrust. The diaphragm action of the shell acts as a thin beam to transfer the thrust to the end supports; the stiffener acts as a beam flange adding the lateral resistance necessary to prevent the shell edge from buckling. This is commonly done by adding a flange stiffener perpendicular to the shell (Figure 15.21).

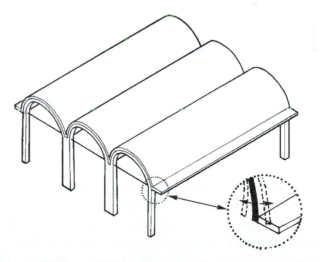

Figure 15.21: Outer shell edges behave as thin beams to transfer thrust to the end supports and should be stiffened to prevent buckling. At the junction of adjacent shells, no flange is needed because the thrusts of each are counterbalanced by the other.

Barrel shapes

Barrel shells can be formed into various cylindrical and conical (curved on one direction only) shapes (Figure 15.22). In addition, groin (intersecting) vaults may be used (Figure 15.23).

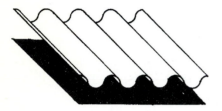

CONTINUOUS

DISCONTINUOUS
(to admit daylight)

TRANSVERSE FOLDING

FREE FORM

Figure 15.22: Barrel shells for covering large areas.

BARREL SHELL CASE STUDIES

Kimball Museum

This museum (1972; Fort Worth, TX; Louis I. Kahn, architect; A. Komendant, structural engineer) integrated the structural use of barrel shells with a quest for diffuse light to create a serene and timeless work of architecture (Figures 15.24 through 15.27).

Like previous Kahn buildings (Trenton Community Center and Boston City Hall, for example), the organization of the Kimball Museum is defined by the *tartan* structural grid consisting of wide bays (containing the "served" galleries) and narrow bays (containing the "servant" circulation and mechanical systems) (Figure 15.25).

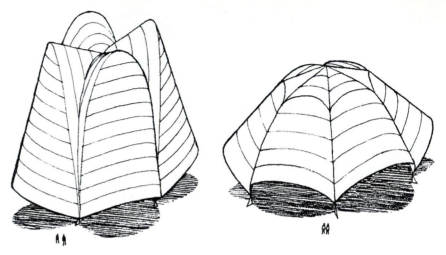

Figure 15.23: Intersecting barrel shells.

The vault is a kind of surface that could receive light. The measure of an interior space is its sense of position to light, and in what way the light confirms the chosen shape of the room. I put glass between the structure members and the members which are not of structure because the joint is the beginning of ornament. And that must be distinguished from decoration which is simply applied. Ornament is the adoration of the joint.

—*Louis I. Kahn*

The roof structure consists of 14 barrel shells spanning bays 100 ft × 23 ft (30.5 m × 7m). Two of these are exterior, forming canopies over walks. The shells are cycloids in section. (Similar in shape to a semiellipse, a cycloid is a curve generated by a point on a circle rolling over a straight line. Like a semiellipse, it is vertical at the spring line.) The shell has a uniform thickness of 4 in (10 cm) necessitated primarily by code restrictions and the space needed for reinforcement. Roof insulation and a lead-coated copper roof are applied above. Support is provided by square concrete columns; walls are nonbearing and surfaced with travertine marble on the exterior and travertine marble and wood on the interior (Ronner, et al., 1977; Editor, 1971) (Figures 15.26 and 15.27).

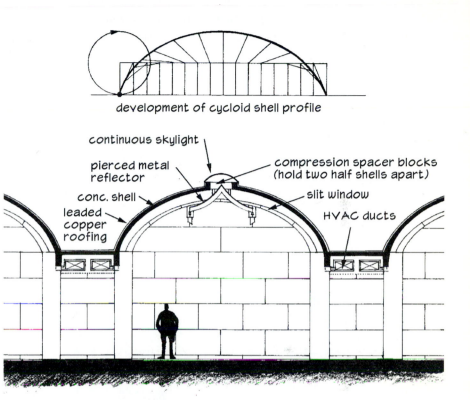

development of cycloid shell profile

Figure 15.26: Kimball Museum, section with diagram showing the development of the cycloid.

Figure 15.24: Kimball Museum, exterior.

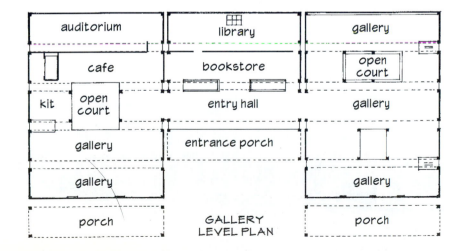

Figure 15.25: Kimball Museum, upper plan.

Most of the shells are pierced with a 3-ft (91-cm)-wide skylight slit down the center. Compressive forces between each side of the shell are transferred across the slit by 11 concrete spacers which serve to hold the two sides apart. The diaphragm action of the upper part of the shell behaves as a horizontal beam to span between the spacers. The shell is thickened around the opening for stability.

The lower edges of the shell are stiffened by a concrete channel shape between adjacent shells. It is a popular misconception that these shells behave as arches spanning only across the 23-ft (7-m) span and resting on the channels which behave as a beam carrying the entire roof load spanning 100 ft (30.5 m). (If this were the case, the required depth of the channel would have been much greater.) Actually, the shells are the primary structure and support the channels which serve only to stiffen the shell edges against buckling (Komendant, 1975).

Figure 15.27: Kimball Museum, interior.

The concrete shells are reinforced by three catenary steel posttensioning cables within each side of the lower portion of the shells in addition to conventional steel reinforcing. At the ends, the shells are thickened to form stiffening arches. A thin glass strip separates these arches from the end walls below, emphasizing that the walls are nonbearing.

Because of the importance of the skylight to the roof structure, it is helpful to appreciate how the skylight admits light. Below each skylight, a curved reflector (fabricated from perforated stainless steel) reflects most of the admitted light up onto the underside of the shell which re-reflects the light downward. The underside of the concrete is unpainted and has a semiglossy finish left by the steel formwork, helping reflect the light admitted to walls and exhibits below. Some of the light from the skylight passes directly through the reflector perforations, but because of the thickness of the reflector, details of the skylight are only visible from directly below; at normal viewing angles, direct skylight is cut off and only reflected light is transmitted giving the underside of the reflector a luminous appearance.

U.S. Plywood office building

While most shells are concrete, sheet plywood can resist tension and compression in its plane and can be bent in a single direction into a barrel shape, making it suitable for fabrication into a shell structure. A row of inverted plywood barrel shells formed a functional and fanciful roof for this small one-story office building (1963; Seattle; G. Kramer, architect; I. Rodney, structural engineer). The client wanted a building that would dramatically advertise the company's products while providing a simple office for an adjoining warehouse (Editor, 1963b) (Figures 15.28 and 15.29).

Figure 15.28: U.S. Plywood office building, exterior.

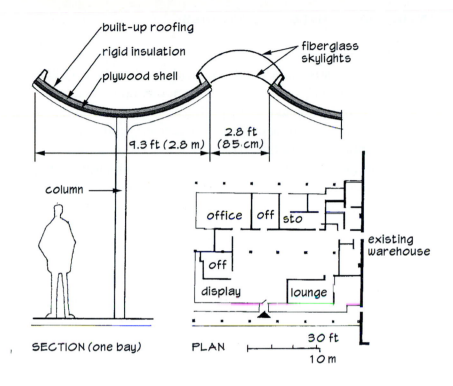

SECTION (one bay)   PLAN

Figure 15.29: U.S. Plywood office building, section and plan.

An experimental roof system was developed for the project, consisting of a 30-ft (9.1-m)-long × 9.2-ft (2.8-m)-wide × 1.25-in (30-mm)-thick shell prefabricated by laminating thin sheets of plywood. Each long edge of the shell was stabilized by a perpendicular stiffener. Each shell was supported at each end by a square tubular steel column. Rigid insulation and roofing membrane were added to the top. Between the inverted barrel shells were sheet-fiberglass skylights bent in the opposite direction and attached to the edge stiffener.

ANTICLASTIC SHELLS

Anticlastic shells are saddle shaped with different curvature in each direction. They include *conoids, hyperbolic paraboloids,* and *hyper-*

boloids. They are also *ruled* shapes because straight lines can be drawn on their surface; conversely, the surface can be generated by a moving straight line. The apparent contradiction of a doubly curved surface generated by straight lines makes anticlastic shells both visually interesting and easy to form.

SURFACE GENERATION

Conoids are generated by sweeping one end of a straight line along a curved path (usually a circular arc or a parabola) and the other end along a straight line (or a more shallow curve; Figure 15.30).

Hyperbolic paraboloids (hypars) are generated by sweeping a convex parabola along a concave parabola of the same curvature. Surprisingly, the same surface can be generated by sweeping a straight line over a straight path at one end and another straight path (skewed relative to the first) (Figure 15.31).

Hyperboloids are generated by rotating a straight line (skewed at an angle) around a vertical axis. A vertical section through this axis is a hyperbola (Figure 15.32).

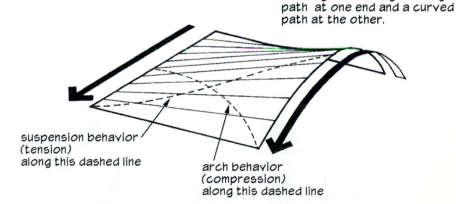

Figure 15.30: Surface generation of a conoid by moving one end of a straight line along a curved path and the other end along a straight line. Notice that sections cut diagonally to the straight-line generators (dotted) are curved creating a shallow saddle shape.

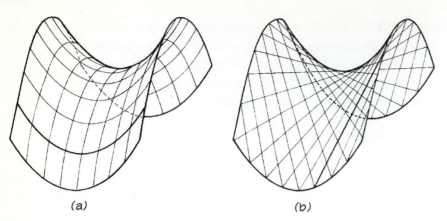

(a)   (b)

Figure 15.31: Two methods for generating a hyperbolic paraboloid: (a) by sweeping a convex parabola moving along a concave parabola, and (b) by sweeping a straight line over a straight path at one end and another non-parallel straight path.

STRUCTURAL BEHAVIOR

In general, stresses in saddle shells relate to the direction of curvature. For shell roofs, compression stresses follow the convex curvature (arch action), while tension stresses follow the concave curvature (suspension action) (Figure 15.33).

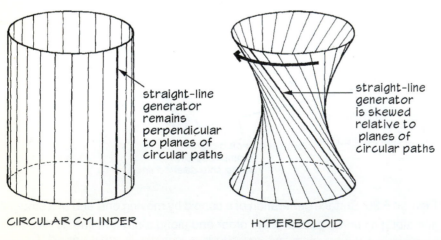

CIRCULAR CYLINDER   HYPERBOLOID

Figure 15.32: Surface generation of a circular cylinder and a hyperboloid.

ANTICLASTIC SHELL CASE STUDIES

Zarzuela Hippodrome

This early shell structure (1935; Madrid; E. Torroja, architect and structural engineer) was one of most famous and graceful examples of the use of hyperboloid umbrella shells. The cantilevered configuration allowed positioning of the main support columns behind the spectators allowing an unobstructed view of the racecourse. A total of 30 shells, arranged in three groups (12, 6, 12) sheltered the grandstands. A slender vertical member in the rear of each umbrella provided the tension necessary to prevent the shell from tipping toward the front (Torroja, 1958) (Figures 15.34 through 15.38).

The shell bays were 16.5 ft × 65 ft (5 m × 19.8 m), cantilevering 42 ft (12.8 m) over the grandstands and 23 ft (7 m) over the top promenade behind. The thickness of the shell varied from 2 in (50 mm) at the free edges to 5.5 in (137 mm) at the crown of the vaults over the main supports.

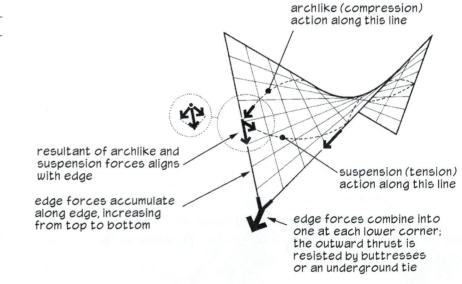

archlike (compression) action along this line

resultant of archlike and suspension forces aligns with edge

edge forces accumulate along edge, increasing from top to bottom

suspension (tension) action along this line

edge forces combine into one at each lower corner; the outward thrust is resisted by buttresses or an underground tie

Figure 15.33: Tension and compression stresses in a straight-edged hypar. Lateral stability is provided by vertical ties to the top corners to prevent tipping.

Figure 15.34: Zarzuela Hippodrome, center grandstand.

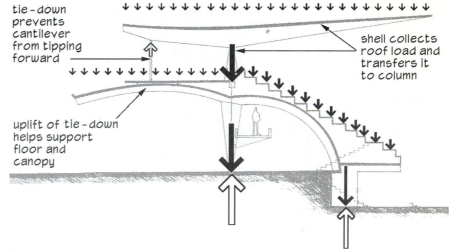

tie-down
prevents
cantilever
from tipping
forward

shell collects
roof load and
transfers it
to column

uplift of tie-down
helps support
floor and
canopy

Figure 15.36: Zarzuela Hippodrome, load path diagram.

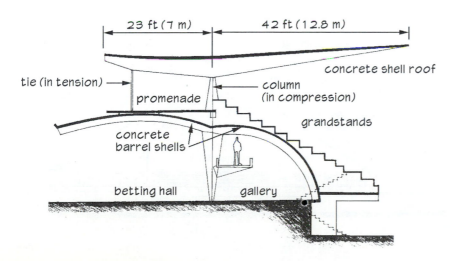

23 ft (7 m)

42 ft (12.8 m)

concrete shell roof

tie (in tension)

promenade

column
(in compression)

grandstands

concrete
barrel shells

betting hall

gallery

Figure 15.35: Zarzuela Hippodrome, section.

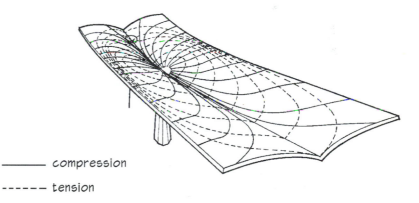

——— compression

- - - - - tension

Figure 15.37: Zarzuela Hippodrome, shell canopy stress contours.

The shell theory in the 1930s was insufficient to analyze this structure. As a result, a full-scale prototype was constructed and tested until it failed. It proved to be three times stronger than required to meet normal loading conditions. It is a tribute to the

planetarium dome is a lobby used for exhibitions and general circulation. A stair spirals around the dome up to the rooftop observation platform on which telescopes are mounted for night use. The top edge of the shell extends to above eye level to shield observers from surrounding city lights. Additional exhibition space as well as offices and support facilities are located in the basement (Figures 15.39 and 15.40).

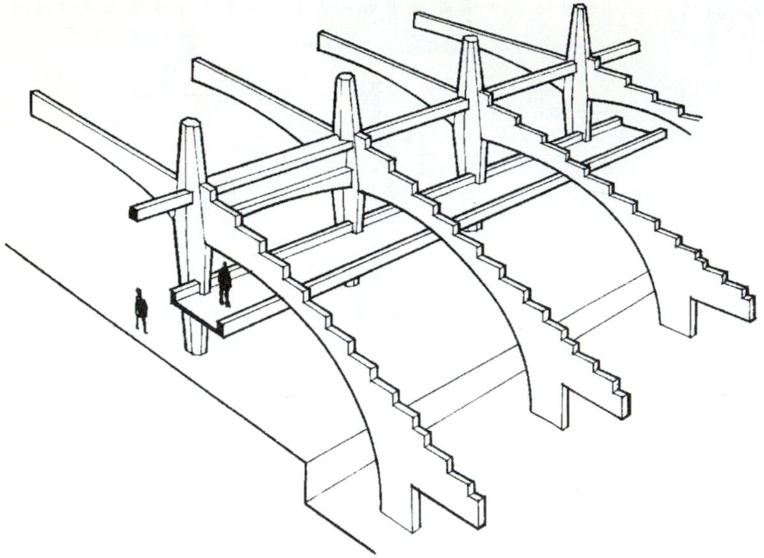

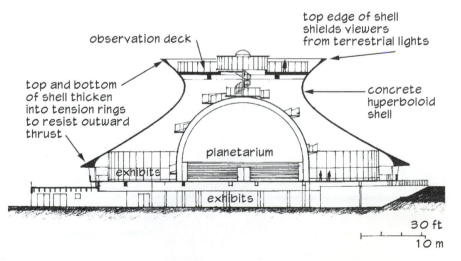

Figure 15.38: Zarzuela Hippodrome, grandstand structure showing beams used for lateral stability (floor slabs, ceiling, and roof shells are omitted).

design that the structure withstood several bombardments (1936) during the Spanish Civil War and was perforated 26 times and extensively cracked by the vibrations of nearby explosions. It remained structurally sound and required only minor grouting to repair the damage.

The columns were tapered (thin at top and bottom) to permit movement due to thermal expansion of the shells. In order to provide lateral stability, massive beams connected the columns at midheight (the floor of the promenade level).

McDonnell Planetarium

This building (1963; St. Louis, MO; Hellmuth, Obata & Kassabaum, architects; A. Alper, structural engineer) is enclosed by a 160-ft (49-m)-diameter reinforced-concrete hyperboloid shell, a saddle shape commonly used for the large cooling towers for nuclear plants. Its shape is unrelated to the 60-ft (18.3-m)-diameter hemisphere dome inside used to enclose the planetarium. The space surrounding the

Figure 15.39: McDonnell Planetarium, exterior.

Figure 15.40: McDonnell Planetarium, section.

The average shell thickness is 3 in (75 mm) thickening into tension rings at the top and bottom to resist the outward thrust at both locations. The lower ring is reinforced with 36 posttensioned tendons and also serves as a ring beam spanning between the 12 columns which support the entire shell perimeter. The exterior surface is waterproofed with a synthetic rubber compound, while the interior is insulated and plastered.

Warm Mineral Springs Inn
This small motel (1958; Venice, FL; V. Lundy, architect; D. Sawyer, structural engineer) used a forest of hypar umbrella shells for the roof structure. Seventy-five small shells are arranged in a checkerboard pattern so that the height of adjacent shells are staggered 2 ft (60 cm) to provide a perimeter clerestory. As a result, the umbrellas appear to float as freestanding forms (Editor, 1958c) (Figures 15.41 through 15.43).

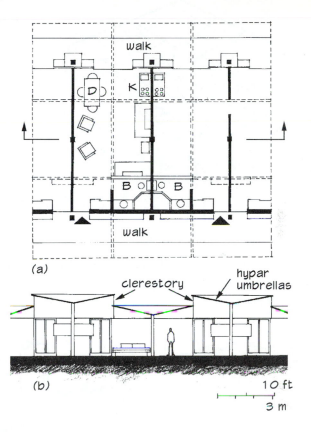

Figure 15.42: Warm Mineral Springs Inn, typical motel unit: (a) plan and (b) section.

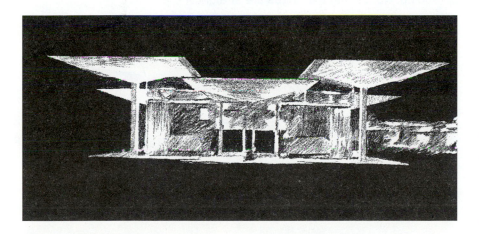

Figure 15.41: Warm Mineral Springs Inn, office exterior.

Each 14.4-ft (4.4-m)-square, 2-in (50-mm)-thick shell was site cast and consists of four adjacent hypars. They are supported only in the center by a square precast column, using a welded connection. The column rests on a subsurface footing and is laterally supported by the floor slab. The roof drains through column drains.

This hypar umbrella configuration was new in the United States but had been widely utilized by Felix Candela (thin-shell construction's most prolific advocate) earlier in the decade in Mexico (Figure 15.44). Candela's projects were often industrial constructions where the system was an economical choice due to relatively lower labor costs (and relatively higher costs of alternative steel construction). Candela also often utilized a different arrangement of four hypars to create a square "dome" supported on four corners. This configuration required a perimeter tie to resist thrust (Faber, 1963) (Figure 15.45).

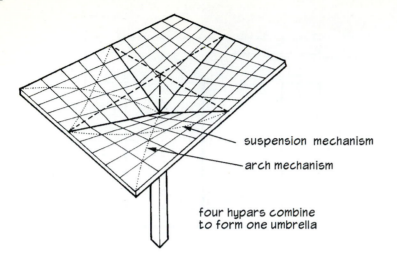

Figure 15.43: Typical umbrella geometry consisting of four hypars with a center column. Notice that the square (or rectangular) perimeter edge consists of straight lines.

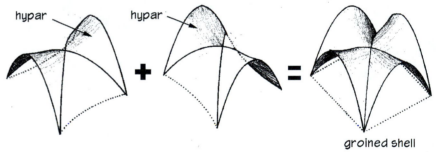

Figure 15.45: Hypar "dome" requires perimeter tie to resist thrust-induced spreading. Notice that the ridges are straight.

Figure 15.44: Coyoacan (Mexico) Market (1955; Felix Candela, architect and engineer) utilized hypar umbrellas as the roof structure.

Figure 15.46: Forming a groined shell from two hypars.

Los Manantiales Restaurant

Like vaults, shells can be intersected to form groined shapes. This restaurant (1958; Xochimilco, Mexico; J. and F. Ordonez, architects; F. Candela, structural engineer) is perhaps Candela's greatest achievement in shell design. The octagonal groined vault consists of four intersecting hypars. The lotus form spreads over a diameter of 150 ft (46 m). As the thin, outward-tilting shell edges approach the ground, the curve reverses sharply before retracing its upward sweep.

The height is 19 ft (5.8 m) at the center and 33 ft (9.9 m) at the top of the outer edge (Faber, 1963) (Figures 15.46 through 15.48).

The structure behaves by arch-action compressive forces following the convex curvature and accumulating in the groins (valleys) where they are transferred by arch action to the supports. The outward thrust at the base created by this arch action is resisted by underground steel ties; as a result, the foundations support only vertical loads. The overhangs are supported by a combination of the convex arch action and the concave suspension action along the ridges.

The shell is extraordinarily thin, varying in thickness from 0.6 in to 1.2 in (17 mm to 34 mm). It is reinforced with 0.3-in (8-mm)-diameter steel mesh throughout plus two additional 0.63-in (15-mm)-diameter steel bars around the perimeter. The underground ties consisted of five 1-in (25-mm)-diameter steel bars.

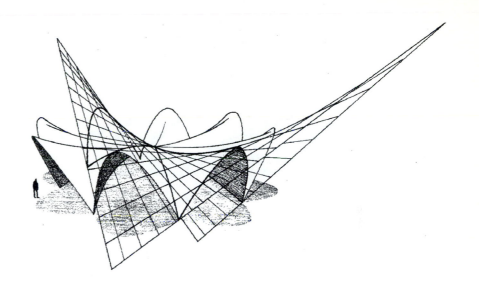

Figure 15.48: Los Manantiales Restaurant, development of the shell from four hypars.

CONOIDS

Like hypars, conoids are saddle shaped. However, the membrane stresses cannot be calculated as simply as for a hypar, and they are considerably more difficult to form.

Lecheria Ceimsa loading dock

This loading dock (1952; Tlalnepantla, Mexico; C. Recamier, architect; F. Candela, structural engineer) is one of the few built examples of conoid shells. The roof is a combination of cantilevering conoids (forming a canopy over the trucks being loaded) and barrel vaults (over the center bay). The conoid, because of its tapering profile, is particularly well suited for cantilever applications. *Tympans* (stiffeners) run above these shells, containing the thrusts and reducing stress concentration above the columns, while leaving the visible underside undisturbed (Faber, 1963) (Figure 15.49).

The steepness of the conoids required a complicated formwork due to the fact that the surface is ruled in only one direction. Can-

Figure 15.47: Los Manantiales Restaurant, exterior.

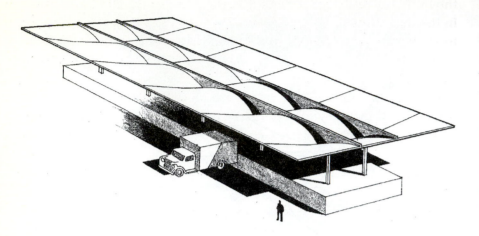

Figure 15.49: Lecheria Ceimsa loading dock roof consists of cantilevering conoids and barrel shells.

dela tried bending the boards in the direction of the curves, but the boards warped out of shape. New forms were constructed with transverse supporting arches and straight boards, slightly tapered, and laid in the direction of the generators. This method worked but was very tedious to construct.

Because of these difficulties, once he developed a simple method for analyzing hypars, Candela built no more conoids (except for a small overhang on the Lederle Laboratories cafeteria). Other examples of conoid roofs are rare.

IRREGULAR SHELLS

Traditional vaults, which support loads by compression stresses only, are restricted to funicular forms which directly respond to the loading conditions. The ability of shells to resist tensions allows much greater freedom of form. While most shells are variations of the mathematically generated surfaces described above, irregular (free-form) shells can be designed to respond to aesthetic and functional considerations and still be structurally satisfactory. In general, such forms are shaped, understood, and analyzed in terms of similar regular shell forms.

IRREGULAR SHELL CASE STUDIES

TWA Terminal

Located at Kennedy International Airport, the Trans World Airlines Terminal (1962; New York, NY; Eero Saarinen and Associates, architects; Ammann and Whitney, structural engineers) was designed, in Saarinen's words, "To catch the excitement of the trip" (Editor, 1962a). Kennedy (formerly Idlewild) was the first airport (and maybe the last) to have separate terminals built to the specifications of individual carriers. The result is an "architectural free-for-all" of competing styles and design. A comparatively small structure in the midst of this collage, the TWA terminal is easily the most visually exciting (Editor, 1958b; 1962b) (Figures 15.50 through 15.52).

Looking like a giant bird poised for flight, the main building consists of four concrete shells resting on four Y-shaped columns. Each shell is separated from the others by a skylight band. The two larger shell vaults soar up from the supporting members; the adjacent smaller ones are subordinated to the sweep of the larger ones. Altogether, they are the graceful integration of 700 tons (635 metric tons) of steel and 4000 yd³ (3058 m³) of lightweight concrete. The roof thickens from 7 in (225 mm) next to the edge beams to 11 in (28 cm) along the crown to 40 in (1.0 m) at the juncture of the four wings of

Figure 15.50: Trans World Airlines Terminal, exterior.

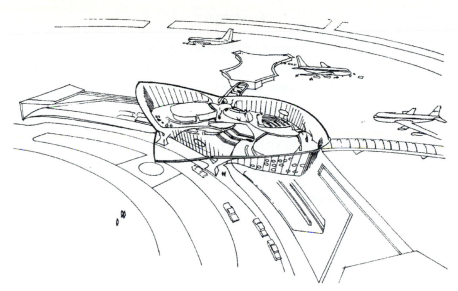

Figure 15.51: Trans World Airlines Terminal, cutaway perspective.

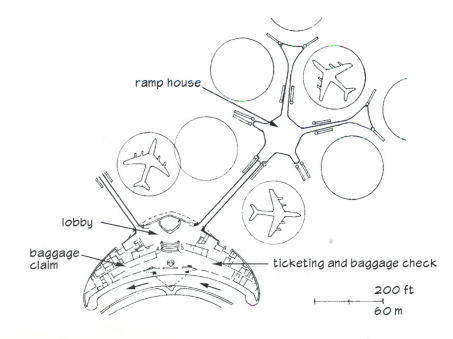

Figure 15.52: Trans World Airlines Terminal, plan.

the building. At the buttresses the roof is about 3 ft (914 cm) thick. In the four transition areas, where the steel reinforcing is sufficient to transfer the roof's 6000-ton (5,442-metric-ton) dead load down into the buttresses, the steel rods from the roof are so closely placed that a specific order of insertion had to be followed to crowd the rods together in the 35-in (89-cm)-wide sections. It should be noted that this design was determined primarily by aesthetic, rather than structural, considerations. Because of this, the thickness of the shells and the depth of the edge beams are relatively large compared with those of other shell structures (such as those by Candela, for example).

This simple and graceful sculptural form belies the unprecedented complexity of the formwork necessary to create it. Designed originally in model form, the architect's construction drawings were derived from the models. The contractor then translated these into additional drawings necessary for the construction of the formwork. A special scaffolding system was developed to allow the compound-curved surfaces toformed to a tolerance of less than 0.25 in (6 mm) from the architect's drawings (Editor, 1960b; 1960c).

If a similar project were built today, the construction drawings would be derived directly from a three-dimensional computer model. But the complex and labor-intensive formwork would remain. This is what has discouraged the design and construction of similar structures and the reason that shell structures with the drama and grace of the TWA terminal are virtually unknown in recent years.

Heinz Isler

In the forefront of recent shell-form development is the Swiss engineer Heinz Isler. His method of design utilizes a funicular model consisting of a suspended membrane which is then stiffened and inverted to determine the optimum shape for a thin-shell dome. Isler's earliest experiments (in 1955) involved hanging wet fabrics in catenary shapes outside in the winter, allowing it to freeze, then inverting it and studying the resulting shape. More recent studies involve using flexible *isotropic* (i.e., having the same strength and stiffness properties in all directions) membranes and stiffening them with resins.

While this principle has long been understood (and used around the turn of the century by Antonio Gaudi to determine the shape of the Colonia Guel Chapel), Isler's more precise techniques have led to a greater understanding of edge conditions and the ideal shapes for resolving them (Figure 15.53). Thus, while the edges of Isler's shells depart from simple geometric shapes, they are entirely consistent with the stresses present in shell edges. As a result, his extremely thin shells remain in pure compression under most loading conditions, developing none of the tension cracks found in most shells. As a result, these beautiful roof shells require no waterproofing, with some 30-year-old examples remaining free of leaks (Isler, 1994; Ramm and Schunck, 1986) (Figure 15.54).

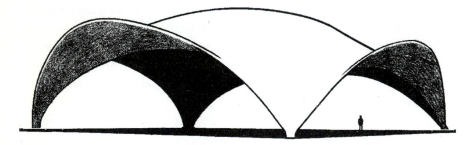

Figure 15.53: Wyss Garden Center (1961; Solo Thurn, Switzerland; Heinz Isler, structural engineer).

Figure 15.54: Sicily Company Building (1969; Geneva, Switzerland; Heinz Isler, structural engineer).

SUMMARY

1. A *shell* is a thin, curved surface structure that transfers loads to supports by tension, compression, and shear only. Shells are distinguished from traditional vaults by their ability to resist tension.

2. *Synclastic* surfaces are doubly-curved and have similar curvature in each direction.

3. *Developable* surfaces are singly curved; they are straight in one direction, curved in the other, and can be formed by bending a flat sheet. Cones and cylinders (or barrels) are developable.

4. *Anticlastic* surfaces are doubly curved and have opposite curvature in each direction. Saddle shapes (including conoids, hyperbolic paraboloids, and hyperboloids) are anticlastic.

5. *Free-form* surfaces are those which are not mathematically derived.

6. Domes are *surfaces of revolution* created by revolving a curved line about an axis.

7. *Arch lines* (also known as meridians) are the vertical (longitudinal) sections around a dome. Under uniform loading, a dome is in compression along arch lines everywhere. In a hemispherical dome, because these arch lines are semicircular, there is a tendency for the dome to be stable on top but to buckle upward in the lower portion.

8. *Hoops* (or *parallels*) are the horizontal sections (all circles) of a dome; the largest parallel is the *equator*. In a shell dome (which can resist tension), this upward buckling tendency is resisted by tension along the hoop lines below about 45° above the horizontal. For this reason, shallow spherical domes are in hoop compression only, while deeper spherical domes are in hoop compression above 45° and hoop tension below.

9.   Like arches, all domes develop outward thrust. A perimeter *tension ring* may be used to resist thrust in shallow dome shells.

10.   *Short* barrel shells have the shorter plan dimension along the longitudinal axis. These are typically supported at the corners and behave in one of two ways (or a combination thereof). The first is for each end to be stiffened into an arch, with the shell acting as slabs which span between the end arches. The second way is for each lower longitudinal edge to be stiffened into a beam, with the thinner shell behaving as a series of adjacent arches spanning between the side beams.

11.   *Long* barrel shells have the longer plan dimension in that direction. These are typically supported at the corners and behave as large beams in the longitudinal direction. As a result the stresses in the shell resemble the bending stresses in a beam: the top portion is in compression along the entire length, while the bottom is in tension.

12.   *Conoids* are generated by sweeping one end of a straight line along a curved path (usually a circular arc or a parabola) and the other end along a straight line (or a more shallow curve).

13.   *Hyperbolic paraboloids* (hypars) are generated by sweeping a convex parabola along a concave parabola of the same curvature. The same surface can be generated by sweeping a straight line over a straight path at one end and another straight path (skewed relative to the first).

14.   Stresses in hypars relate to the direction of curvature. Compression stresses follow the convex curvature (arch action), while tension stresses follow the concave curvature (suspension action).

15.   *Isotropic* materials have the same strength and stiffness properties in all directions.

16

FOLDED PLATES

The load-carrying capacity for a flat, thin surface structure is limited to small-scale applications. Its strength and stiffness can be dramatically increased by folding which, in turn, increases its effective depth and thus its bending resistance (Figure 16.1).

A *folded plate* is a folded planar surface structure that transfers loads to supports primarily by tension, compression, and shear, with bending occurring only between folds in the surface of the plane. Because the spacing between folds is small compared with the span, bending forces in the slab are small compared with the tension and compression forces.

Folded plates are efficient in structures (such as roofs) where loading is distributed uniformly and uneven shapes are suitable. Most are constructed of reinforced concrete, although plywood, metal, and glass-reinforced plastics may be used where large spans are not required.

The efficiency of folded plates approaches that of curved shells, and folded plates have the advantage of planar construction. Like curved shells, they are particularly suited to roof structures. Theoretically, they need to be thicker than comparable shells because of the need to resist the local bending between folds. In practice, the minimum thickness is most often determined by the thickness required to place reinforcing and meet code requirements.

STRUCTURAL BEHAVIOR

In most aspects the structural behavior of folded plates is similar to barrel shells and differs considerably depending on their relative length. *Short* folded plates have the shorter plan dimension along the longitudinal axis, while *long* ones have the longer plan dimension in that direction.

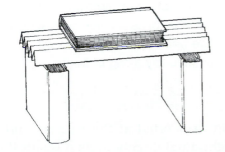

Figure 16.1: Folding greatly increases the depth (and thus the bending resistance) of thin materials.

Short folded plates

These are also typically supported at the corners and behave in one of two ways (or a combination thereof). The first is for each end to be stiffened into a three-hinged frame, with the plate acting as slabs which span between the end frames. The second way is for each lower longitudinal edge to be stiffened into a beam, with the thinner folded plate behaving as a series of adjacent three-hinged frames spanning between the side beams (Figure 16.2). Because the minimum thickness necessary for practical construction (and to meet code requirements) far exceeds that required structurally for short folded plates under most conditions, they are inefficient and thus seldom used.

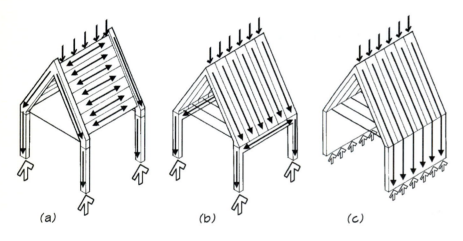

(a)   (b)   (c)

Figure 16.2: Short-folded-plate behavior: (a) as slabs spanning between three-hinged end frames and (b) as a series of adjacent three-hinged frames spanning between edge beams. Compare this with (c) a gable roof which must be supported continuously along its base.

Long folded plates

These are typically supported at the corners and behave as large beams in the longitudinal direction. As a result the stresses in the folded plate resemble the bending stresses in a beam; the top portion is in compression along the entire length, while the bottom is in tension (Figure 16.3). The diaphragm action of the thin plate provides the necessary resistance to the horizontal and vertical shear inherent in bending behavior (Figure 16.4).

The span-to-depth ratio of long folded plates affects both the stresses developed as well as the efficiency in covering a large area. Lower depth-to-span ratios reduce bottom compression and top tension forces, permitting a thinner shell thickness. On the other hand, greater depth requires more surface area for a given span. In theory, the optimum depth-to-span ratio is about 2.0, minimizing the total volume of concrete and steel reinforcement required. In practice, ratios between 6 and 10 are common due to programmatic considerations and the minimum thickness required by code or construction practices.

Edge conditions

In order to control buckling, it is necessary to maintain the designed cross-sectional shape by stiffening both the ends and the outermost longitudinal edges, and by resisting outward thrust. It is necessary to constrain the ends of the folded plate in order to maintain its shape under various loading conditions. This is typically accomplished either by stiffening the ends by thickening them into three-

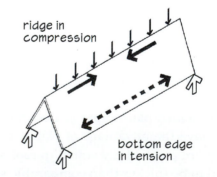

ridge in compression

bottom edge in tension

Figure 16.3: Long folded plate behaves as a beam spanning between the end supports and develops compression stresses along the top and tension stresses along the bottom.

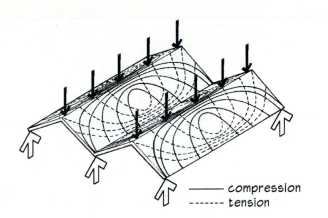

——— compression
------- tension

Figure 16.4: Stress diagram for a long folded plate. Notice that tension and compression stresses are always perpendicular to each other. The spacing of the stress contours indicates the concentration of stress in that region (closer spacing means greater stress).

hinged frames on supporting columns and adding tie-rods to resist lateral thrust or by using end bearing walls (which provide vertical support, maintain the shape of the ends of the shell, and behave as shear walls to resist outward thrust) (Figure 16.5).

Outward thrust is developed along the entire length, not just at the ends. When the plate is folded in a multibay configuration, the outward thrusts of adjacent bays balance each other; only the free edges of first and last plates need to resist thrust. The diaphragm action of the plate acts as a thin beam to transfer the thrust to the end supports; the stiffener acts as a beam flange adding the lateral resistance necessary to prevent the plate edge from buckling. This is commonly done by adding a flange stiffener perpendicular to the plate (Figure 16.6).

Optimal profile shape
The greater the depth of a folded plate, the greater its bending resistance over a given span. Thus, steep plates can be thinner because of reduced tension and compression forces in the edges. But this results in increased folded plate surface area for a given area cov-

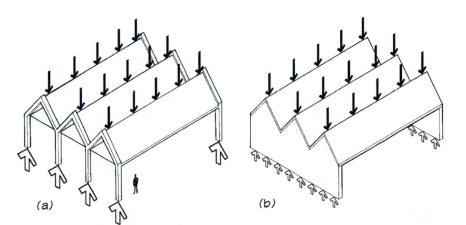

(a)   (b)

Figure 16.5: End supports for multibay long folded plates: (a) ends stiffened into three-hinged frames on columns with tie-rods to resist lateral thrust and (b) end bearing walls which provide vertical support, maintain the shape of the ends of the shell, and behave as shear walls to resist outward thrust.

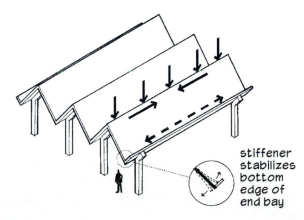

stiffener stabilizes bottom edge of end bay

Figure 16.6: Outer shell edges behave as thin beams to transfer thrust to the end supports and should be stiffened to prevent buckling. At the junction of adjacent shells, no flange is needed because the thrusts of each are counterbalanced by the other.

ered. Conversely, shallow sloped folds are more efficient in coverage but result in higher stresses. A slope of 45° theoretically minimizes the total material required; this may be modified by nonstructural considerations (Figure 16.7).

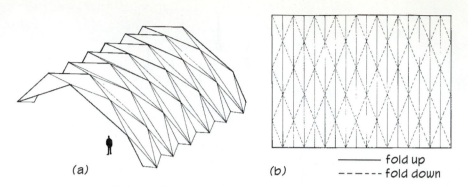

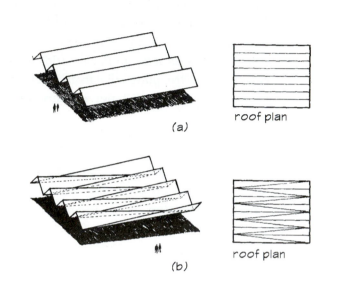

Figure 16.7: Folded-plate panel shapes: (a) parallel, and (b) tapered.

The spacing between folds is usually determined by a combination of the possible span given the minimum thickness practical due to construction and code restraints. For example, if the minimum practical thickness of a reinforced concrete folded plate is found to be 3.0 in (75 mm) and a slab of this thickness will safely span 7 ft (2.1 m), then this slab width should be used (any less would not fully utilize the capacity of the slab; any more would fail in bending) (Figure 16.8).

Another consideration in determining the folded-plate profile in concrete construction is the economy of forming. If plywood is used as a forming material, its available size must be a consideration (Figure 16.9).

Figure 16.8: Paper folded-plate "barrel vault" exercise: (a) exterior, and (b) folding pattern. Renzo Piano designed a mobile structure using this configuration for sheltering sulfur-mining equipment.

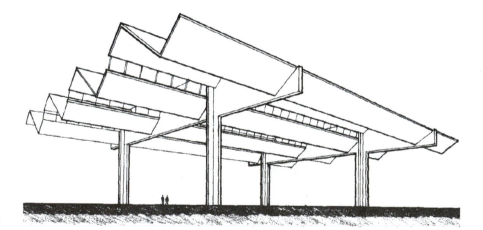

Figure 16.9: Design for a zee-section folded-plate roof with clerestories, project (1947, F. Candela, structural engineer).

Materials

Most folded-plate roofs are constructed of reinforced concrete. However, fabrication and structural analysis methods for plywood folded plates are available (Carney, 1971), and considerable research has been done on the use of plastic-coated cardboard for temporary folded-plate structures (Sedlak, 1973).

FOLDED PLATE CASE STUDIES

American Concrete Institute headquarters building
One of the requests made of the architect was to "use concrete imaginatively" in the design of the institute's new headquarters building (1957; Detroit; Yamasaki, Lewinweber and Associates, architects). The dominant visual feature of the building is the reinforced-concrete, folded-plate roof which is supported solely by the interior corridor bearing walls. The roof extends beyond the nonbearing curtain walls to provide shade. The mullions act as tie-downs to stabilize the roof against uplift. The interior hall is illuminated by skylights between the tapered roof panels where they join in the center of the building (Editor, 1956; 1958c) (Figures 16.10 through 16.13).

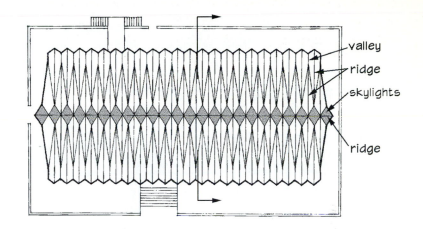

Figure 16.11: American Concrete Institute headquarters building, plan.

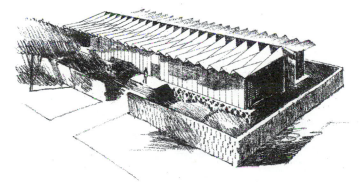

Figure 16.10: American Concrete Institute headquarters building, exterior.

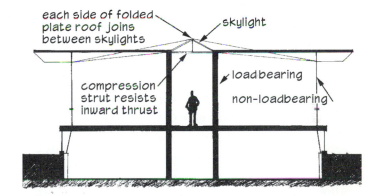

Figure 16.12: American Concrete Institute headquarters building, section.

Illini Hall
From the outside this folded-plate dome seems to hover above the ground (1963; Champaign, IL; Harrison & Abromivitz, architects; Ammann & Whitney, structural engineers). The hall was conceived as a huge bowl sunk into the ground permitting easy access to the perimeter exhibition lobby as well as the midheight of the seating. The multipurpose arena seats up to 16,000 for sporting events (Figures 16.14 through 16.16).

The 400-ft (122-m)-diameter dome is folded to prevent buckling in the reinforced-concrete shell which averages 3.5 in (8.7 cm) in thickness. The dome is supported at the perimeter on a tension ring which contains the outward thrust. This is, in turn, supported by a similarly shaped bowl (also with a folded surface) which supports the seating and is the ceiling of the perimeter lobby. The outward thrust created by the supporting bowl at the top is also contained by the perimeter tension ring. The bowl rests on a supporting founda-

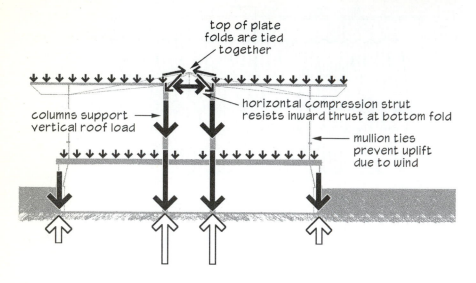

Figure 16.13: American Concrete Institute headquarters building, load path diagram.

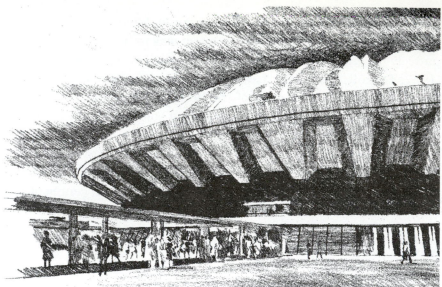

Figure 16.14: Illini Hall, exterior showing folded-plate dome roof, tension ring, and supporting folded-plate bowl.

tion which is a circular compression ring to withstand the inward thrust at the bottom. The underside of the dome is sprayed with 2 in (50 mm) of acoustical insulation to minimize sound reflection; the exterior is coated with a waterproofing material.

Avocado School

This elementary school (1963; Homestead, FL; Robert Browne, architect; WalterC. Harry & Associates, structural engineers) is a typical example of the widespread use of folded-plate roofs on public school buildings in the United States during the late 1950s and 1960s. It houses 600 students and contains 22 classrooms, a cafetorium, a library, and administrative spaces. The roof system was selected for its economy of construction and attractive appearance. The top panels of the roof are pierced with skylights for daylighting, which is diffused and reflected by the adjacent sloped panels. The roof cantilevers beyond the columns and wall line to shelter the exterior circulation walk in this warm climate (Editor, 1963f) (Figure 16.17).

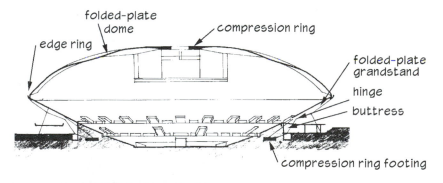

Figure 16.15: Illini Hall, section.

Ninety plates were used to cover the roof of the school. Each measures 9 ft (2.7 m) wide, 70 ft (21.3 m) long, and 3 in (75 mm) thick. Forming costs were reduced through the use of reusable ply-

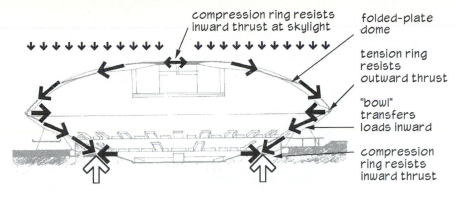

Figure 16.16: Illini Hall, load path diagram.

Figure 16.17: Avocado School, exterior showing 3-in (75-mm)-thick, reinforced-concrete, folded-plate roof.

wood panels. Spaces between folded plates have interconnected steel reinforcing dowels which were grouted to provide a continuous rigid connection. The top of the roof was waterproofed with liquid-applied roofing; the underside was painted with added acoustical absorption panels. The nonbearing exterior walls are stucco over concrete block masonry.

UNESCO Conference Building

This building is part of the headquarters for the United Nations Educational, Scientific, and Cultural Organization (UNESCO) (1958; Paris; Breuer & Zehrfuss, architects; PierLuigi Nervi, structural engineer). The adjacent larger Y-shaped building houses the offices of the organization, while this smaller building houses auditoria and meeting rooms. The building is trapezoidal in plan, 415 ft (44.2 m) long, and utilizes folded plates for the roof and for the end bearing walls, the tallest being 103 ft (31.4 m) high (Kato, 1981; Nervi, 1963; Editor, 1955) (Figures 16.18 through 16.21).

The roof is unique in the use of a curved horizontal slab that intersects the conventional plate folds. Over the larger 220-ft (67-m) span, this slab curves up at midspan to increase the bending resistance of the folded plate without further increasing the overall depth. Even with enhancement, the folded plate is 17.3 ft (5.3 m) deep.

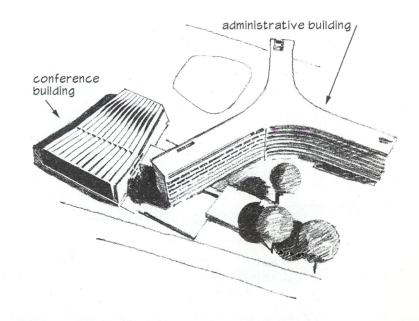

Figure 16.18: UNESCO Conference Building, exterior (shown adjacent to the larger Y-shaped office building).

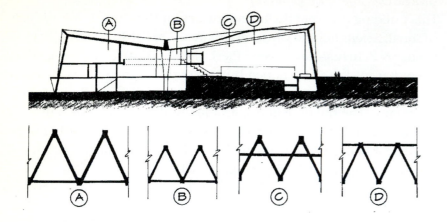

Figure 16.19: UNESCO Conference Building, building section with typical folded-plate roof sections.

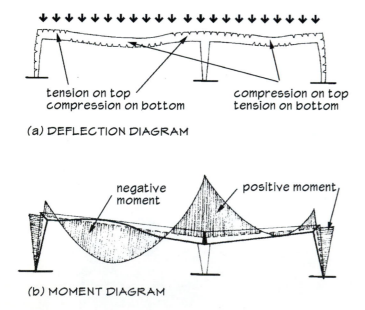

(a) DEFLECTION DIAGRAM

tension on top
compression on bottom

compression on top
tension on bottom

negative moment

positive moment

(b) MOMENT DIAGRAM

Figure 16.20: UNESCO Conference Building, folded-plate roof: (a) deflection diagram, and (b) moment diagram showing how the moment distribution determined the location of the curved reinforcing slab.

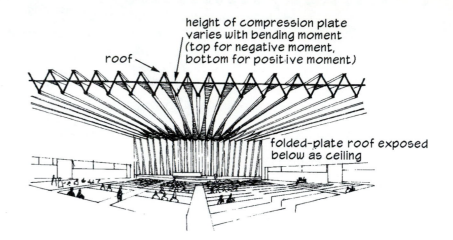

roof

height of compression plate varies with bending moment (top for negative moment, bottom for positive moment)

folded-plate roof exposed below as ceiling

Figure 16.21: UNESCO Conference Building, interior section perspective.

At each end, the folded roof changes direction to become a vertical bearing wall. The folded-plate wall is deepest at the roof intersection, tapering to a thin section at the base. This results in a rigid connection at the roof (like a table), contributing to the bending resistance of the roof by reducing the effective span. The folded roof is exposed on the interior as a corrugated ceiling that is both visually interesting as well as acoustically efficient, reflecting and diffusing sound from the faceted surface.

SUMMARY

1. A *folded plate* is a folded planar surface structure that transfers loads to supports primarily by tension, compression, and shear, with bending occurring only between folds in the surface of the plane.

2. The stiffness of folded plates is generated by their folded geometry and the depth of the folds.

3. The efficiency of folded plates approaches that of curved shells, and they have the advantage of planar construction.

4. *Short folded plates* have the shorter plan dimension along the longitudinal axis. They are typically supported at the corners and behave in one of two ways. The first is for each end to be stiffened into a three-hinged frame, with the plate acting as slabs which span between the end frames. The second way is for each lower longitudinal edge to be stiffened into a beam, with the thinner folded plate behaving as a series of adjacent three-hinged frames spanning between the side beams.

5. *Long folded plates* are typically supported at the corners and behave as large beams in the longitudinal direction. As a result the stresses in the folded plate resemble the bending stresses in a beam: the top portion is in compression along the entire length, while the bottom is in tension.

6. Folded-plate *depth-to-span ratios* between 6 and 10 are common due to programmatic considerations and the minimum thickness required by code or construction practices.

7. In order to control *buckling* in a folded plate, it is necessary to maintain the designed cross-sectional shape by stiffening both the ends and the outermost longitudinal edges and by resisting outward thrust. Openings should be avoided on or near the folds.

Part VI

SYSTEM SYNTHESIS

17

STRUCTURAL MATERIALS

Every master knows that the material teaches the artist.

—Ilya Ehrenburg

The principal structural materials are timber, steel, concrete, and masonry.

TIMBER

Like all materials delivered by the forces of Life, wood is rather more adaptable and less rigid and schematic than other materials.

—Eduardo Torroja

Wood is the structural material most familiar to us. It is popular for several reasons. It is the only major material that is organic in origin. It is a renewable material, and it can be assembled into buildings with a few, relatively simple hand and portable power tools. Because of this, it is commonly used for single-family residential construction in areas of the world (especially North America) where it is abundant.

Because of its organic origin, wood is not an isotropic material; all its physical properties depend on whether they are measured parallel or perpendicular to the grain. Wood has relatively equal compression and tension strength properties parallel to the grain. In this direction, compression strength is roughly comparable to weak concrete (but is only about one-sixth as strong perpendicular to the grain).

Virtually all structural woods are softwoods (the architectural use of hardwoods is for interior and exterior trim); pine, spruce, and fir are the most important species for structural use. *Allowable stresses* (structural stresses which include an allowance for safety) for each species vary considerably. For example, allowable compressive stresses parallel to the grain vary from 325 to 1850 lb/in^2 (2.24 to 12.76 MPa) for commercially available grades and species of framing lumber (Allen, 1985).

The most traditional forms of timber construction, the log cabin and heavy timber frame are rarely used today, due primarily to the high material cost of large timber members, the inefficient structural use of the material, and its poor thermal insulating qualities. The development of the mass-produced wire nail and the commercial availability of dimension lumber led to the development of, first, the balloon frame and, subsequently, the platform frame that is in common use today. Recent developments have overcome many of the limitations of traditional lumber.

FRAMING LUMBER

Framing lumber is sawn directly from logs and consists of *timbers*, *dimension lumber*, and *boards*. Timbers are 5 in (127 mm) or more in the least dimension. They are used for beams and lintels (typically three to four times as deep as they are wide), and columns and posts (typically square in cross section) (Figure 17.1).

Dimension lumber is 2 to 4 in (50 to 100 mm) thick and 2 in or more wide and is most commonly used in lengths from 8 to 16 ft (2.4 to 4.8 m). It is used for joists, columns, studs, and decking. Boards are less than 2 in (25 mm) thick and 2 in or more wide. Traditionally, they were used for roof decking, wall sheathing, or subfloors.

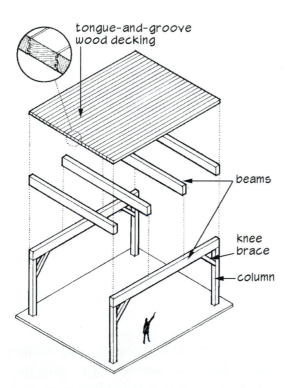

tongue-and-groove
wood decking

beams

knee
brace

column

Figure 17.1: Post-and-beam construction using heavy-timber columns and beams.

Today, manufactured panels (such as plywood) are used for these applications; boards are seldom used anymore for structural applications.

WOOD PANELS

Structural wood panel products were developed to replace boards for decking, subfloors, and wall sheathing. They are more nearly equal in strength in their two principle directions than solid-wood products. Shrinking, swelling and splitting are greatly reduced. The standard size is 4 ft × 8 ft (120 cm × 240 cm) although larger sizes are manufactured for special applications. They fall into three categories: *plywood*, *nonveneered panels*, and *composite panels*.

Plywood
Plywood consists of an odd number of wood veneers glued together to form a large panel. The grain in outer veneers runs in the same direction, usually parallel to the length of the panel. Inner veneers alternate in perpendicular directions. Thicknesses range from 0.25 to 0.75 in (6 to 18 mm).

Nonveneered panels
Nonveneered panels are made of reconstituted wood fibers bonded together to a panel. *Oriented-strand board* (OSB) is made of long strandlike wood particles compressed and glued into three to five layers; the strands are oriented in perpendicular directions in each layer (much like plywood). *Waferboard* consists of large flakes of wood compressed or bonded into a single layer. *Particleboard* consists of small particles compressed and bonded into a single layer; it is available in a variety of densities. Of the three, OSB is generally strongest and stiffest; it is rapidly replacing plywood for most structural applications.

Composite panels
These consist of a nonveneered core bonded between surface veneers. They are primarily used for furniture and interior applications but seldom for structural applications.

LAMINATED TIMBER

Today, large structural wood members are usually produced by gluing many layers of thinner wood together under pressure to produce *glue-laminated timber (glulam)*. Any size member can be laminated; this is limited only by handling and transportation requirements. Large depths are achieved by laminating 1.5-in (37-mm) thicknesses; long members are created using long tapered *scarf* or *finger* joints.

Wood can be laminated into a variety of shapes including curves, branching forms, angles, and varying cross sections (Figure 17.2). In general, glulams are stronger than comparable conventional lumber members due to the ability to cut out defects prior to lamination and the ability to properly orient the grain direction in curved members. While glulams cost more per unit size, this is often offset by their greater strength which allows a smaller size to be used. In many cases, solid members are unavailable in the size, shape, or quality required.

MANUFACTURED WOOD COMPONENTS

Trussed rafters are lightweight trusses assembled from 2×4 and 2×6 (37 mm × 87 mm and 37 mm × 137 mm) dimension lumber using toothed plate connectors (Figure 17.3). They are most commonly used for light-frame residential roof construction and are usually spaced at 24-in (61-cm) intervals, which is determined by the maximum allowable span of 0.5-in (50mm)-thick plywood or OSB roof decking.

Plywood *I-beams* and *box beams* (Figure 17.4) are usually shop-fabricated from a combination of dimension lumber and plywood for long-span applications; they can also be field-fabricated. The principal tension and compression stresses are carried by the dimension lumber in the top and bottom chords; the web member is plywood. The components are assembled using glue and nails (which serve only to hold the components together under pressure until the glue cures).

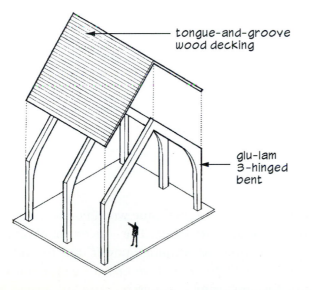

Figure 17.2: Laminated timber three-hinged bent (frame).

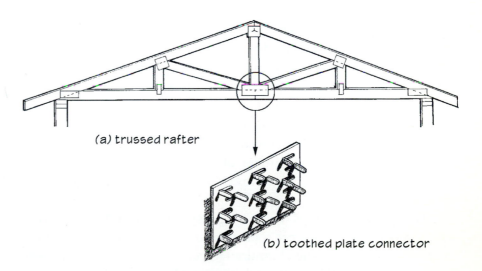

Figure 17.3: (a) Trussed rafters in light-frame wood construction, and (b) toothed plate used for their manufacture.

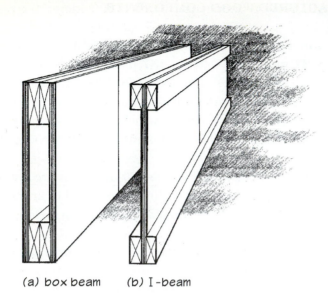

(a) box beam   (b) I-beam

Figure 17.4: Plywood beams: (a) box beam, and (b) I-beam.

Laminated veneer lumber (LVL) consists of wood veneers oriented vertically, with the grain in each oriented lengthwise (Figure 17.5a). *Parallel-strand lumber* (PSL) consists of long strandlike wood particles oriented lengthwise and compressed and glued together (Figure 17.5b). LVL is used for beams and lintels; depths range from 5.5 to 18 in (14 to 46 cm); lengths to 30 ft (12.2 m). PSL is used for these and for columns; depths range from 9.25 to 18 in (23 to 46 cm), lengths to 30 ft (12.2 m). These are factory produced in continuous lengths and cut to project specifications. Both are substantially stronger and stiffer than solid lumber of comparable dimensions. They are accepted alternatives to plywood and steel beams in light-frame construction.

I-beam joists are used where longer spans exceed the capacity of solid lumber joists. They are a proprietary product consisting of top and bottom chords made of laminated veneers, with the center web made of either OSB or plywood (Figure 17.5c). These are factory produced in continuous lengths and cut to project specifications. While the cost is greater than for solid lumber of comparable capac-

ity, the required depths are usually less or intermediate supports may be eliminated, helping to offset the added material cost. Depths range from 9.25 to 24 in (24 to 61 cm), and lengths to 40 ft (12.2 m).

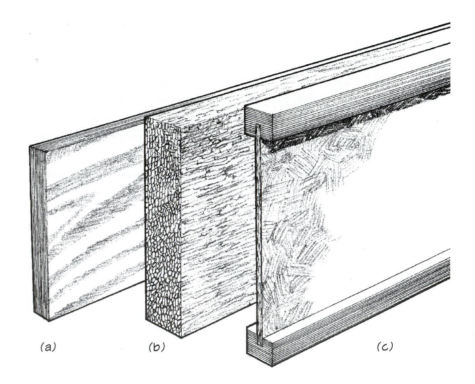

(a)   (b)   (c)

Figure 17.5: Manufactured lumber: (a) laminated veneer lumber, (b) parallel-strand lumber, and (c) I-beam joists.

CONNECTORS

One of the advantages of light-frame wood construction is the ease with which connections are made. The conventional nail is the most commonly used connector (although power nailers and staplers are frequently used for highly repetitive operations), followed by bolts, anchor bolts (for anchoring to concrete), and lag screws (heavy hex-headed screws).

In addition to the toothed plate used for trussed rafter fabrication (Figure 17.3b), hundreds of standard proprietary sheet-metal connectors are available for strengthening timber construction. The most common are the joist hanger, truss anchors, and cross-bridging (Figure 17.6).

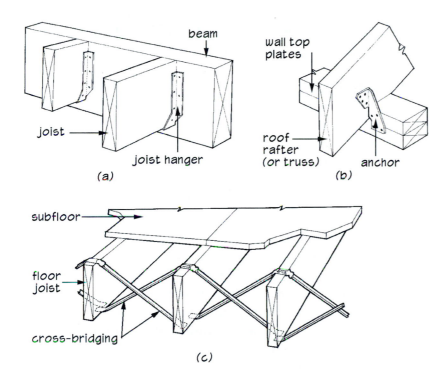

Figure 17.6: Light-frame timber connectors: (a) joist hangers, (b) truss anchors, and (c) cross-bridging.

FIRE PROTECTION

Heavy timbers [members which are at least 5 in (127 mm) in the least dimension] tend to char under fire conditions forming an outer layer of ash which insulates the inner layer from the heat of the fire.

As a result, heavy timber construction is considered fire resistant by most building codes. Thinner wood components burn more easily, are considered combustible if exposed, and may require protective covering (gypsum, for example).

Wood may be treated to resist fire by impregnating it with certain chemicals that greatly reduce its flammability. Its primary application is for nonstructural partitions and other components in buildings of fire-resistive construction. The cost of fire-retardant treatment is so great that it is seldom used in single-family residential construction.

DECAY AND INSECT PROTECTION

Wood can also be treated to resist decay and insects. Creosote (which is widely used for engineering structures such as bridges) is an oily derivative of coal and is seldom used for architectural applications due to its odor, toxicity, and unpaintability. Pentachlorophenol is an oily preservative that is also toxic and unpaintable. The most widely used architectural treatment is waterborne salts; most are based on copper salts. While temporary protection can be achieved by brushing or spraying, the most long-lasting protection requires pressure impregnation.

Most wood-attacking organisms and insects need both air and moisture to survive. Most can be kept out of wood by designing and building a structure so that all wood components are kept dry at all times. This requires keeping all wood clear of soil and concrete and properly ventilating attic and crawl spaces (Allen, 1985).

STEEL

In steel, tenacity and resistance predominate, its edges and the contours of the assembly are impressive; its potent lightness is overwhelming.
—Eduardo Torroja

Steel is an alloy of iron and carbon. Additional additives can contribute special qualities. The addition of nickel, for example, can be added to make stainless steel. Modern steels have a carbon content of about

0.2 percent. If the carbon content exceeds 1.7 percent, cast iron results. Cast iron is hard and brittle and has a lower modulus of elasticity than steel. Very low carbon content (less than 0.1 percent) produces wrought iron, which is comparatively soft and malleable.

MANUFACTURING

Molten steel is cast into large ingots which are then shaped by a series of rollers into either *hot-rolled* shapes (such as H-shaped *wide-flanges, channels, tees, angles, bars,* and *plates*) or into thin-sheet rolls which are subsequently shaped into lighter-weight *cold-rolled* profiles. Most structural steel is hot-rolled; the primary structural applications for cold-rolled steel are corrugated steel decking and light-framing members.

DESIGNATIONS

Wide-flange sections are used for beams and columns and are designated by their depth by weight per lineal foot; for example, *W12 × 106* designates that the member is a wide-flange shape, 12 in (30 cm) deep and weighs 106 lb/ft (158kg/m). Angle sections are designated by *L* followed by the nominal lengths and thickness of the two legs. Channel sections are designated as *C* followed by depth (in inches) and the weight in pounds per linear foot.

CORROSION RESISTANCE

Most steels rust when exposed to air and moisture and thus require protection in the form of painting or other coating. Stainless steel is inherently corrosion resistant, but is too expensive for most building structural applications.

Certain steel alloys develop an initial layer of rust which then stabilizes and does not progress further. Most such weathering steels are proprietary (Corten, for example) and develop an attractive dark brown patina. However, when used for exposed applications, care must be taken to prevent waterborne staining of adjacent materials such as concrete.

FIRE PROTECTION

Steel remains the structural material with the greatest strength, which is approximately equal in tension and compression. However, while steel will not burn, in the presence of fire its strength is reduced dramatically. Because of this, exposed steel members must be protected by insulating them with fire-resistant insulation (such as gypsum) or coating them with thick layers of special intumescent paint (which expands greatly under charring conditions producing the required insulation thickness).

STEEL CONNECTIONS

Connection methods
Structural steel members are connected using *rivets, bolts,* or *welds.* A rivet is a cylindrical steel pin with a formed head. It is installed by heating it white hot and inserting it into holes in the materials to be joined. Its head is held in place by a heavy hand hammer and the other end is bradded with a pneumatic hammer, to form a second head. When the rivet cools, it shrinks, drawing the members tightly together. In building construction, riveting has been almost entirely replaced by bolting and welding which are less labor intensive.

There are two types of structural bolted connections: *shear* and *friction.* Both types incorporate bolts inserted in holes slightly larger than the shank of the bolt, and a threaded nut that is tightened (usually by means of a pneumatic impact wrench). Shear connections depend only on the shear resistance of the bolt, and the tension developed by tightening is not critical. Friction connections require that the bolt be tensioned reliably to 70 percent of its ultimate tensile strength to produce the tight clamping forces necessary to allow the surfaces of the two members to transfer the load between them by friction alone. Special heat-treated, high-strength bolts are used for friction connections.

Electric arc welding allows unification of the entire structure into a single, monolithic whole. Properly designed and installed, welded connections can be stronger than the members they join in resisting both shear and moment forces. Quality control is more critical than in riveting or shear bolting, requiring that welders be specially trained and tested periodically. Special radiographic testing can be used to ensure the quality of critical welds. Bolts are commonly used in welded connections to temporarily align members prior to welding.

Shear and moment connections

Framing connections between steel beams and columns are classified by the degree to which they are designed to restrict rotation between the two members (Figure 17.7). A *shear* (or *framed*) connection is designed to transmit forces by means of shear only. Typically, it connects the beam web to the column. Because it does not connect the beam flanges to the column, it contributes little to the transferring of bending moments from one member to the other. As a result, it is considered to behave like a pinned connection and cannot be counted on to contribute to the lateral stability of the building frame.

A *moment* connection is designed to be completely rigid and transmit all bending moments between the beam and column. As such it requires that the beam flanges be rigidly connected to the column and that the strength of the connection at the flanges be at least equal to the flanges themselves. Often a shear tab is shop-welded to the face of the column and field-bolted to the beam. It supports the beam until it is welded and permanently contributes to the shear resistance. Because it is usually difficult to achieve adequate moment transfer using bolted connections alone, they are seldom used for flange moment connections (Allen, 1985).

COMPONENTS

Open-web steel joists

Open-web steel joists (also known as *bar joists*) are lightweight, mass-produced trusses. They are typically used for roof and floor structures and are closely spaced—usually 4 to 8 ft (1.2 to 2.4 m) on center—resting on steel beams or masonry bearing walls (Figure 17.8). They are usually covered with steel or precast concrete decking. They are typically fabricated using pairs of angles as the top and bottom chords and round steel bar as diagonal web members arranged in a triangular pattern. While standard depths range from 8 to 72 in (20 to 183 cm) and spans to 144 ft (44 m) are possible, most applica-

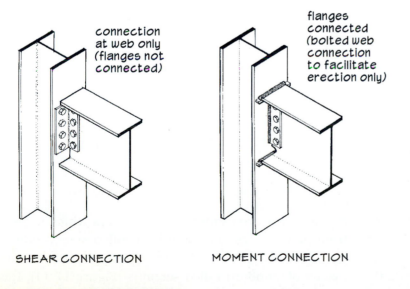

SHEAR CONNECTION — connection at web only (flanges not connected)

MOMENT CONNECTION — flanges connected (bolted web connection to facilitate erection only)

Figure 17.7: Framing connections.

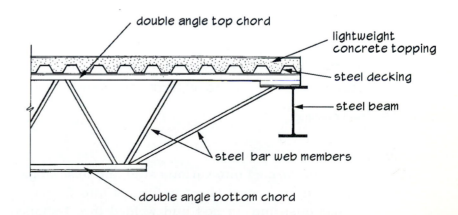

double angle top chord

lightweight concrete topping

steel decking

steel beam

steel bar web members

double angle bottom chord

Figure 17.8: Open-web steel joist.

tions use joists less than 24 in (60 cm) deep to span up to 40 ft (13 m) (Allen, 1985). Joist girders are similar but are heavier and used as primary framing members, replacing *wide-flange* beams where depth is not a limiting consideration.

Decking
Metal decking is used in roof and floor structures to span between beams or open-web joists. It is a sheet of steel that has been cold-formed into a corrugated shape. The stiffness (and span) of the decking is determined by the *gauge* (thickness) of the sheet and the depth of corrugations. There are four types of steel decking. *Form decking* is a simple corrugated shape designed for use as a permanent form for structural concrete without contributing to its strength. *Roof decking* is designed for use with rigid insulation but no concrete topping. *Composite decking* is designed to work with concrete topping by acting as tensile reinforcement. *Cellular decking* is manufactured by welding a corrugated steel sheet over a flat one; this creates a rigid deck while providing voids that can be used for electrical wiring (Figure 17.9).

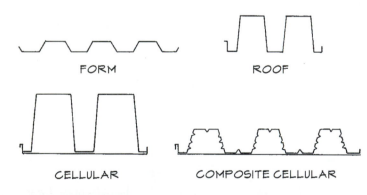

Figure 17.9: Steel decking.

Light-framing members
Steel can also be cold-formed into various stud and joist shapes suitable for light framing. Steel sheet is formed into C-shaped and Z-shaped sections, and formed and welded into I-shaped sections (Figure 17.10). Cold forming increases the strength of

the steel as a result of the realignment of its crystalline structure. Present equipment is only capable of cold forming relatively thin materials.

The cost of steel light-framing members is less than for comparable wood lumber. It is widely used for commercial construction but has not been accepted to the same degree for residential construction, primarily due to the specialized equipment required and the reluctance of carpenters to work with steel materials.

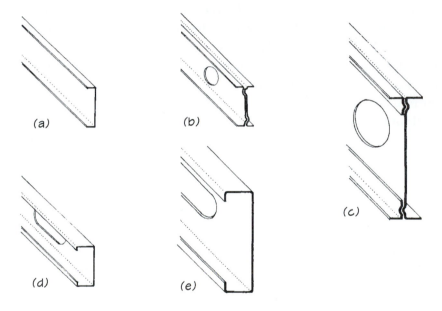

Figure 17.10: Cold-formed light-framing members: (a) channel stud, (b) double stud, (c) double joist (d) cee stud, and (e) cee joist.

Built-up sections
Plate girders and bents are examples of members which are shop-fabricated from plates, bars, and standard rolled steel sections. A *plate girder* is a very heavy and deep beam for applications that exceed the capacity of standard rolled sections (Figure 17.11). Heavy columns are fabricated in the same way.

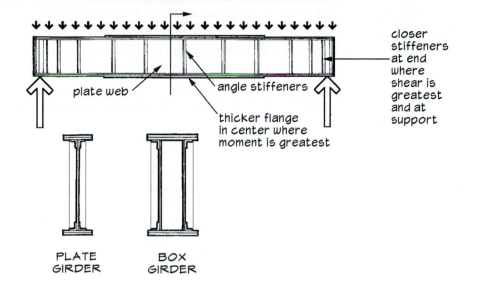

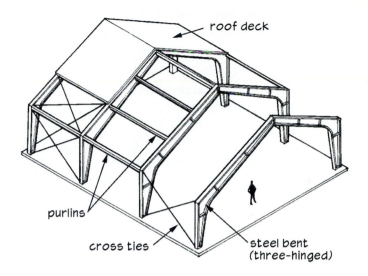

Figure 17.11: A plate girder is built up from plate and bar steel and standard rolled sections. Notice that the flange thickness increases near the center of the span where tension and compression forces are greatest; vertical stiffeners are more closely spaced at the ends where vertical shear is greatest.

A *bent* (also known as an arch) is a frame thickened at the haunch to resist bending there; it is most commonly hinged at each base and at the peak (Figure 17.12).

CONCRETE

> *We are all victims of the rectangle and the slab. We go on living in boxes of stone and brick while the modern world is dying to be born in the discovery that concrete and steel can sleep together.*
> —*Frank Lloyd Wright*

Concrete was invented by the ancient Romans and improved by Joseph Aspdin who developed and patented portland cement (named for the English limestone that it resembled) in 1824 (Allen, 1985).

Figure 17.12: Three-hinged steel bent.

Concrete is produced by combining portland cement, coarse and fine *aggregates* (gravel and sand), and water and allowing the mixture to harden. Curing (hardening) occurs when the cement combines chemically with water to form strong crystals that bind the aggregate together into a monolithic mass. Considerable heat (known as the *heat of hydration*) is given off during this chemical reaction. Some shrinkage usually occurs as excess water dries after curing.

REINFORCING

> *In reinforced concrete, steel gives tenacity to stone and concrete gives mass to steel.*
> —*Eduardo Torroja*

> *Reinforcing rods are the play of a marvelous secret worker that makes this so-called molten stone appear wonderfully capable—a product of the mind.*
> —*Louis I. Kahn*

Reinforced concrete was developed in the 1850s simultaneously by several people. Prior to this, the use of concrete was limited to structures which behaved in compression only, because unreinforced concrete has virtually no strength in tension. It was this development that contributed tension resistance to concrete that allowed its use for bending- and buckling-resistant members such as beams (Figure 17.13), slabs, and columns (Figure 17.14).

concrete to resist compression. Steel is also used to control cracking that would result from thermal contraction and curing shrinkage. To enhance the bond and to prevent slippage, the surface of steel-reinforcing bars are deformed during the hot-roll manufacturing process.

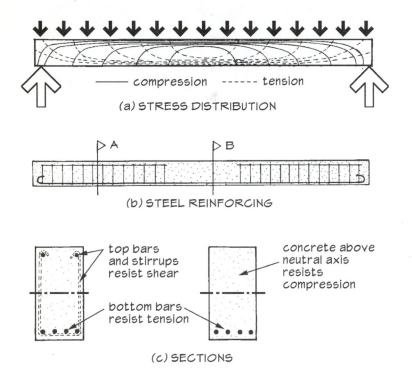

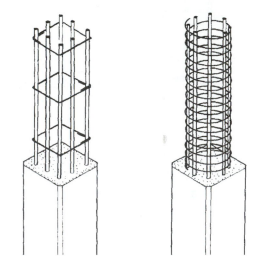

Figure 17.14: Reinforcing in concrete columns.

Figure 17.13: The location of reinforcing in a concrete beam is determined by the presence of tension: (a) stress distribution, (b) steel reinforcing, and (c) sections. The vertical bars (stirrups) are used to resist shear that develops near the ends as tension forces move diagonally upward.

The basic theory of reinforcing concrete is simple: place the steel where tension occurs in a structural member and allow the

FORMWORK

Site-cast concrete is shaped by formwork which acts as a mold until curing is complete. Formwork is usually constructed of wood (especially plywood), steel, or fiberglass. The formwork must be strong enough to support the weight of reinforcing and concrete as well as resist the hydrostatic pressure of the concrete in liquid form. As a result, some formworks are major structures themselves requiring specialized engineering on larger projects. The cost of formwork is considerable, making it desirable to reuse forms whenever possible.

PRECASTING

The high cost of forming site-cast concrete led to the development and current popularity of precast-concrete technology. Precast concrete is manufactured using permanent, reusable forms at an industrial plant. The cast units may be cured using steam to accelerate the process. After curing, the members are transported to the site by truck and erected using a crane (Figure 17.15). Field connections between members are made by welding steel inserts cast into the members at the time of manufacture.

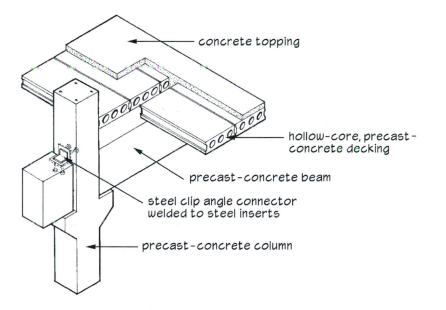

Figure 17.15: Precast-concrete column, beams, and decking.

When a moment connection is required between members, the ends of reinforcing rods are left exposed so that they overlap at the joint. The space around the exposed reinforcing is grouted with a special nonshrinking concrete. After curing, the joint is rigid and as strong as if the entire structure had been site cast.

PRESTRESSING

Beam and column precast members are often prestressed. This is done by utilizing special steel cable for reinforcing which is pulled under considerable tension prior to the concrete curing. After curing, when the ends of the steel cables are cut, these tension forces are transferred to the concrete, drawing it into compression. In the case of beams and planks, where the prestressed reinforcing is located on the bottom only, the internal stress causes the beam to bow upward slightly, producing camber. Once the beam is installed and subjected to the designed dead load, deflection offsets this camber and results in a straight member. Precasting is most economical when there is a large number of identical members required and the number of variations which require form modifications are minimized.

MASONRY

Masonry is one of the oldest structural materials, dating back to the fourth millennium BC with the construction of palaces and temples of sun-dried brick. Over the centuries, the process of masonry construction has remained essentially the same, stacking small modular units to make large walls and arches. Because the units are so small, the final product can be of almost any form ranging from a planar surface to an undulating serpentine wall.

Mortar is the glue that holds the individual units together. Modern mortar consists of portland cement, sand, and water; lime is usually added to increase workability.

BRICK

Brick is the smallest masonry unit, sized to fit the mason's hand. The earliest bricks were made by the *soft mud* process, whereby wet clay was pressed into molds and allowed to dry.

> *Architecture starts when you carefully put two bricks together. There it begins.*
> —*Ludwig Mies van der Rohe*

Today most bricks are mass-produced using the *stiff mud* process in which low-moisture clay is extruded through a rectangular die and sliced using wire cutters. After molding, bricks are dried for 1 or 2 days, and then fired in a kiln to a temperature of 2400° F (1300°C) at which the clay vitrifies into a ceramic material. The color of the brick depends on the composition of the clay and the temperature of the kiln.

While there is not a standard brick size, the most common size in the United States is the modular brick which is designed to construct walls in modules of 4 in (100 mm) horizontally, and 8 in (200 mm) vertically in three *courses*, allowing 3/8 in (9 mm) for mortar thickness.

Bonds

Bonds are the patterns in which bricks are laid (Figure 17.16). They include *running* (or header) *bond, common bond, Flemish bond,* and *stack bond.* Bricks may be designated by their orientation within the wall (Figure 17.17).

Reinforcing

Like concrete, brick has negligible tension resistance. The same deformed steel bars may be used to reinforce where tension occurs.

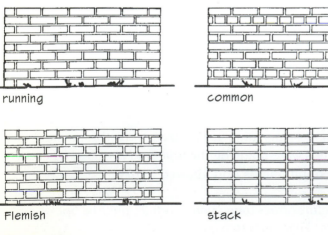
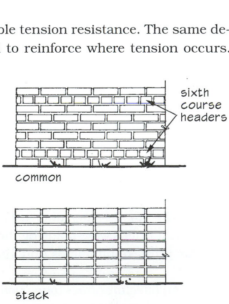

Figure 17.16: Brick bonds.

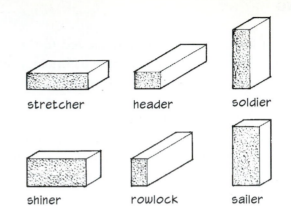

Figure 17.17: Brick orientations.

One method is to add vertical and horizontal rods in the center void between two *wythes* (widths) of brick and then fill the void with grout. Another method is to use manufactured reinforcing (fabricated of heavy-gauge wire welded in a truss pattern), which is laid flat in every ninth *bed* (horizontal) joint. Reinforced brick columns are built by laying a hollow brick tube, inserting vertical and tie reinforcing rods, and filling the center with concrete.

STONE

Stone masonry is the oldest type. It consists of arranging pieces of rock in the desired shape, with or without mortar. Rock is classified as *igneous* (deposited in a molten state; includes granite), *sedimentary* (deposited by the action of water; includes limestone and sandstone), and *metamorphic* (igneous or sedimentary rock transformed by heat and pressure; includes slate and marble).

While some fieldstone intended for rubble masonry may be simply collected from surface and ground deposits, most building stone is cut from quarries in large blocks and then cut in a plant to the desired size for masonry use. Stone may be reinforced in a manner similar to brick. Stone masonry patterns are classified by the shape of the stones (irregular *rubble* or rectangular *ashlar*) and bonds (based on brick bonds) (Figure 17.18).

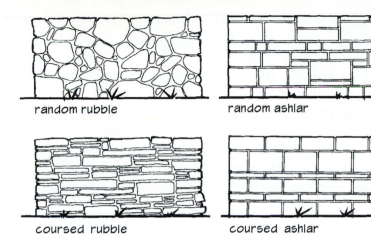

Figure 17.18: Stone masonry patterns.

random rubble   *random ashlar*

coursed rubble   *coursed ashlar*

OTHER STRUCTURAL MATERIALS

FABRICS

Structural fabrics define lightweight tensile structures such as tents and pneumatics. As a primary structural element, it must span between supporting elements, withstand wind and snow loads, and be safe to walk on. As the envelope, it must be airtight, waterproof, fire resistant, and (in most cases) translucent.

Structural fabrics consist of the structural base material (fiberglass or polyester cloth) which is covered with a surface coating (such as polyvinyl chloride, Teflon, or silicone). Teflon-coated fiberglass has been used for most of the tent and pneumatic roof structures built since 1975.

PLASTICS

Most architectural plastics are nonstructural. Even *glass-reinforced plastic* (fiberglass), which is used structurally for boats and motor vehicles, is seldom used for structural purposes in buildings (although it is becoming widely used for ornamental purposes). The reason is principally economic; fiberglass is not cost effective for large structures where its moldability is not an advantage. However, complex repetitive forms for site-cast concrete structures (such as waffle slabs) may economically be made of fiberglass.

ALUMINUM

Aluminum is often used instead of steel in structures where weight is a primary consideration. It is available in alloys having strength similar to steel, is extrudable, weighs one-third that of steel, and does not corrode. Recent developments that have lowered the cost of aluminum production and welding now make it attractive for many applications, especially for exterior exposed components. Additional corrosion resistance can be achieved by anodizing the surface, an electrolytic process that may be used to add color as well as protect.

SUMMARY

1. Wood is not an isotropic material; all its physical properties depend on whether they are measured parallel or perpendicular to the grain.

2. Virtually all structural woods are softwoods; pine, spruce, and fir are the most important species for structural use.

3. *Allowable stresses* are permissible structural stresses which include an allowance for safety.

4. *Framing lumber* is sawn directly from logs and consists of *timbers, dimension lumber,* and *boards.*

5. *Timbers* are 5 in (127 mm) or more in the least dimension.

6. *Dimension lumber* is 2 to 4 in (50 to 100 mm) thick and 2 in or more wide.

7. *Boards* are less than 2 in (25 mm) thick and 2 in or more wide. Today, they are seldom used for structural applications, having been replaced by manufactured panels (such as plywood).

8. *Plywood* consists of an odd number of wood veneers glued together to form a large panel.

9. *Oriented-strand board* (OSB) is made of long strandlike wood particles compressed and glued into three to five layers; the strands are oriented in perpendicular directions in each layer (much like plywood). It is the strongest and stiffest manufactured wood panel product.

10. *Waferboard* consists of large flakes of wood compressed or bonded into a single layer.

11. *Particleboard* consists of small particles compressed and bonded into a single layer.

12. *Composite panels* consist of a nonveneer core bonded between surface veneers.

13. *Glue-laminated timbers (glulams)* are large structural wood members produced by gluing many layers of thinner wood together under pressure.

14. Manufactured wood components include trussed rafters and plywood I-beams and box beams.

15. *Laminated veneered lumber* (LVL) consists of wood veneers oriented vertically, with the grain in each oriented lengthwise.

16. *Parallel-strand lumber* (PSL) consists of long strandlike wood particles oriented lengthwise and compressed and glued.

17. *I-beam joists* consist of top and bottom chords made of laminated veneers and a center web made of either OSB or plywood.

18. *Steel* is an alloy of iron and carbon. It is formed into *hot-rolled* shapes (such as H-shaped *wide-flanges*, *channels*, *tees*, *angles*, *bars*, and *plates*) or into thin-sheet rolls which are subsequently shaped into lighter-weight *cold-rolled* profiles.

19. Most steels rust when exposed to air and moisture and thus require protection in the form of painting or other coating.

20. Exposed steel members must be protected from the high temperatures caused by fire by insulating them with fire-resistant insulation or coating them with thick layers of special intumescent paint.

21. Structural steel members are connected using *rivets*, *bolts*, or *welds*.

22. Framing connections between beams and columns are classified by the degree to which they are designed to restrict rotation between the two members. A *shear* (or *framed*) connection is designed to transmit forces by means of shear only. A *moment* connection is designed to be completely rigid and transmit all bending moments between the beam and column.

23. *Open-web steel joists* (also known as *bar joists*) are lightweight, mass-produced trusses.

24. *Steel decking* is a sheet of steel that has been cold-formed into a corrugated shape. It is used in roof and floor structures to span between beams or open-web joists.

25. Light-framing steel members are cold-formed into various stud and joist shapes.

26. *Concrete* is produced by combining portland cement, coarse and fine *aggregates* (gravel and sand), and water and allowing the mixture to harden. *Curing* (hardening) occurs when the cement combines chemically with water to form strong crystals that bind the aggregate together into a monolithic mass.

27. *Steel reinforcing* adds tension resistance to concrete, allowing its use for bending- and buckling-resistant members such as beams, slabs, and columns.

28. *Formwork,* which acts as a mold for concrete until curing is complete, is usually constructed of wood (especially plywood), steel, or fiberglass.

29. *Precast* concrete is manufactured using permanent, reusable forms at an industrial plant. The cast units may be cured using steam to accelerate the process; after curing, the members are transported to the site by truck and erected using a crane.

30. *Prestressed* concrete utilizes special steel cable for reinforcing which is pulled under considerable tension prior to the concrete curing. After curing, when the ends of the steel cables are cut, these tension forces are transferred to the concrete, drawing it into compression.

31. Most bricks are mass-produced using the *dry-press* process in which low-moisture clay is extruded through a rectangular die and sliced using wire cutters. After molding, bricks are dried for 1 or 2 days and then fired in a kiln until vitrification occurs.

32. Masonry *mortar* consists of portland cement, sand, and water; lime is usually added to increase workability.

33. *Bonds* are the patterns in which the bricks or stones are laid; they include *running* (or header) *bond, common bond, Flemish bond,* and *stack bond.*

34. *Stone* masonry patterns are classified by the shape of the stones (irregular *rubble* or rectangular *ashlar*) and bonds (based on brick bonds).

35. *Teflon-coated fiberglass* is the fabric used for most of the tent and pneumatic roof structures.

36. *Aluminum* is often used instead of steel in structures where weight is a primary consideration; it is available in alloys having a strength similar to steel, is extrudable, weighs one-third that of steel, and does not corrode.

18

STRUCTURAL LAYOUT

*If your structure does nothing more than support the
building, it is being underutilized.*
—Edward Allen

Before beginning to lay out the structural system, the design-related characteristics of the components should be considered.

PRELIMINARY CONSIDERATIONS

BEARING WALLS

Bearing walls are best used to support loads uniformly distributed along their length, including slabs and closely spaced joists. Because beams and girders introduce concentrated loads, they are seldom supported by bearing walls; columns are commonly used instead. Where concentrated loads must be supported by a bearing wall, the wall should be strengthened in that location by adding reinforcement or by thickening the wall into a pilaster.

The placement of bearing walls in plan is dictated by their role as supporting elements. Because of this, it is essential to plan the spacing and placement of the walls in careful coordination with the building's functions. Because economic considerations require that the arrangement of bearing walls be as uniform as possible, this makes bearing walls more attractive for building types such as schools, apartments, and motels.

Regularly spaced bearing walls may act as shear walls to contribute lateral stability. They may be used alone if they are arranged in both directions. If they are oriented in one direction only, other members (such as bracing or rigid column connections) can be used to provide lateral stability. Shear walls should be well distributed in plan and placed as symmetrically as possible, especially in taller buildings.

Openings can be made in bearing walls by installing headers (beams) over the opening. For greater plan flexibility, beams and columns can be used in combination with bearing walls (Figure 18.1).

As a general rule, in multistory buildings, the walls should align above one another. However, it may be possible to open up the ground-floor plan (for a lobby, for example) by designing the wall on the second floor as a deep beam to transfer loads to perimeter columns on the first floor (Figure 18.2).

COLUMNS

Columns may be used to support either beams (and trusses) or slabs (including decking and joists). Because columns do not tend to enclose space, they have less impact than bearing walls on the

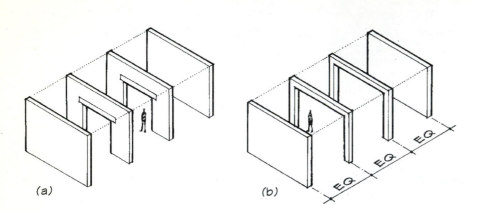

Figure 18.1: Opening up bearing-wall plans: (a) openings can be created in walls using headers, and (b) beams and columns can be combined with bearing walls.

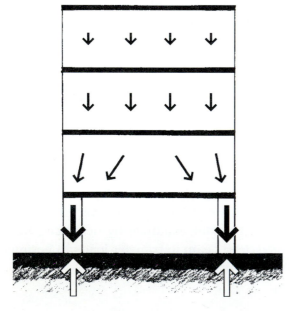

Figure 18.2: Bearing walls may act as deep beams to span across an opening below.

planning of building spaces. This makes columns a good choice where the interior spaces of the building do not follow a repetitive structural module or where rooms are irregular in shape or size. Columns provide the maximum openness in the plan and allow the interior space configuration to be changed by moving nonstructural partitions. When used with beams, columns are practical over a greater range of spans and bay proportions.

Steel and site-cast column-and-beam systems can provide lateral support by behaving as a rigid frame. This requires that joints be rigid. (It is difficult to achieve rigid joints in precast concrete and timber framing, and other means of lateral support must be used.) Rigid frames are desirable because they cause little interference with the plan and services of a building. However, rigid frames are most efficient with regular bay spacing. Generally, rigid frames necessitate deeper beams and heavier columns than would be required with a comparable braced frame or shear walls. Rigid frames are not well suited for tall spaces or very long spans.

When used with beams, columns must be located on the centerline of the beams. Column spacing can vary up to the spanning capacity of the beam, although it is most economical to utilize a regular grid spacing.

BEAMS

Beams may be laid out in one or both directions with joists, slab, or decking spanning between them (Figure 18.3). For rectangular structural grids where joists and beams are used, it is usually more economical for beams to span in the shorter direction and joists in the longer. Where slabs and beams are used, the slabs usually span in the shorter direction and beams in the longer (Figure 18.4).

FLAT PLATES

Flat plates are two-way slabs that are supported by columns only without the use of beams. (The term *flat plate,* as it is being broadly used here for preliminary design purposes, includes all flat, two-way structures such as waffle slabs and space frames, as well as the flat concrete plate.) The absence of beams permits greater plan flexibility, allowing columns to be placed in irregular patterns. It also

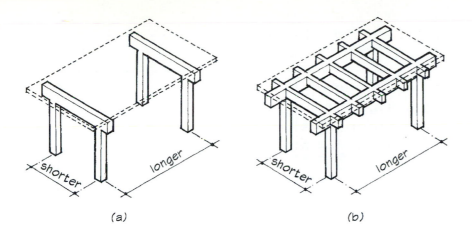

Figure 18.3: Beam layouts: (a) one-way beam and slab, and (b) two-way girder and beam.

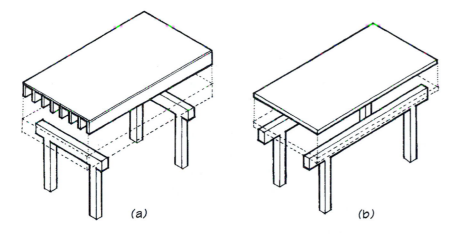

Figure 18.4: Efficient span directions for (a) joists and beams, and (b) slab and beams.

reduces the total structural depth required while simplifying construction techniques.

The rigid connection between the plate and supporting columns can provide the required lateral resistance. This may require increased plate depth as well as heavier columns. Alternatively, shear walls or frame braces may be used to increase lateral resistance.

The most economical column arrangement for flat plates is a square grid. However, much greater flexibility is possible in a column arrangement with only moderate cost increases, making this combination particularly suited for irregular and free-form plans. However, with the exception of space frames, the shallow depth of the plate limits the system to relatively short spans (Figure 18.5).

SYSTEM SELECTION

The first step is to select one or more alternative framing systems based on the project design criteria. This should be done very early in the schematic design phase, recognizing that the decision might change later. Figure 18.6 shows various design criteria and the structural types most suitable for them.

Structural design should be a two-way street, giving and taking with form and space until an optimum synthesis is achieved.

—Edward Allen

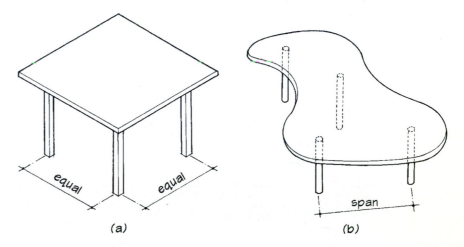

Figure 18.5: Flat plates (a) are most economical using square column bays and (b) are well suited for irregular shapes and column spacing.

DESIGN CRITERIA	Light-frame timber	Heavy-frame timber	Masonry bearing wall	Steel frame (hinge connections)	Steel frame (rigid connections)	Steel open-web joists	Steel space frame	Steel decking	Site-cast concrete: one-way slab	Site-cast concrete: two-way plate	Site-cast concrete: two-way slab	Site-cast concrete: one-way joists	Site-cast concrete: waffle slab	Precast concrete: solid slab	Precast concrete: hollow-core slab	Precast concrete: single tee	Precast concrete: double tee	RATIONALE
Exposed, fire-resistant construction		■	■						■	■	■	■	■	■	■	■	■	Inherently fire-resistive construction
Irregular building form	■		■						■									Simple, site-fabricated systems
Irregular column placement										■	■		■					Systems without beams in roof or floors
Minimize floor thickness										■				■				Precast-concrete systems without ribs
Allow for future renovations	■	■	■	■	■	■			■			■						Short-span, one-way, easily modified
Permit construction in poor weather	■	■	■	■	■	■	■	■						■	■	■	■	Quickly erected; avoid site-cast concrete
Minimize off-site fabrication time	■		■						■	■	■							Easily formed or built on site
Minimize on-site erection time		■		■	■	■	■							■	■	■	■	Highly prefabricated; modular components
Minimize low-rise construction time	■	■		■	■	■	■											Lightweight, easily formed or prefabricated
Minimize medium-rise construction time				■	■				■					■	■			Precast, site-cast concrete; steel frames
Minimize high-rise construction time				■	■													Strong; prefabricated; lightweight
Minimize shear walls or diagonal bracing			■		■				■	■	■							Capable of forming rigid joints
Minimize dead load on foundations	■	■				■												Lightweight, short-span systems
Minimize damage due to foundation settlement	■	■		■											■	■		Systems without rigid joints
Minimize the number of separate trades on job	■		■															Multipurpose components
Provide concealed space for mech. services	■					■										■		Systems that inherently provide voids
Minimize the number of supports							■						■					Two-way, long-span systems
Long spans																	■	Long-span systems

Figure 18.6: Framing system selection chart.

EVOLUTION OF THE FRAMING PLAN

If the building structure is to be fully integrated with the architectural design, the two must evolve simultaneously, beginning with the earliest preliminary sketches. The following design procedure will ensure that integration. It is an evolutionary and reiterative process that begins with a plan bubble diagram and progresses through a series of overlays to a framing plan that shows the preliminary layout and sizing of the main structural members (Figure 18.7). For simplicity, the process is shown here as linear; in practice, any design process is more cyclic, with many sequential steps repeated several times. But each cycle (even those that might seem unproductive) is informative and contributes understanding to the steps that follow.

This is not *the* process; it is *a* process, and most readers will choose to modify this to be compatible with their own design methods (Figures 18.8 through 18.15). As you proceed, remember that the structure should do more than simply support the building. It can create exciting visual rhythms, patterns, and textures. It can create sculptural form. It can direct the flow and division of space. It can define scale. It can modulate light.

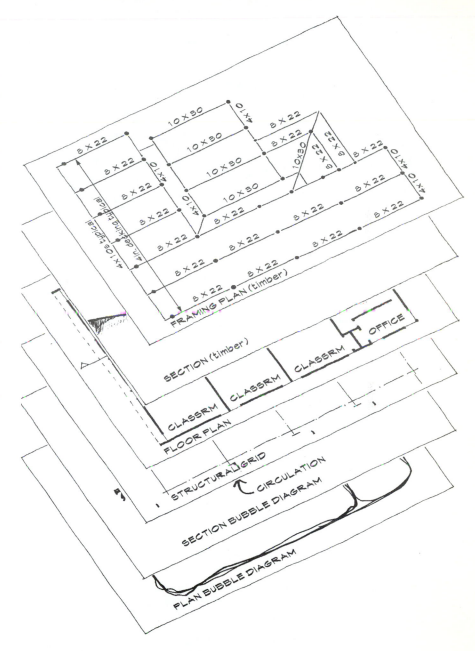

Figure 18.7: Sequence of tracing overlays leading to a framing plan for a small church.

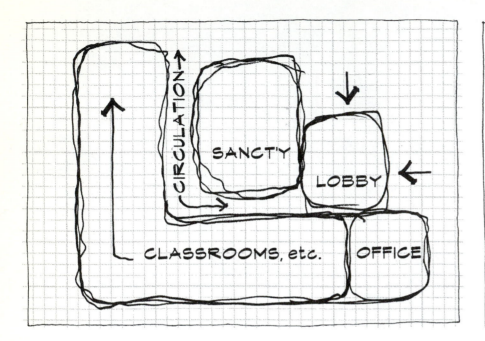

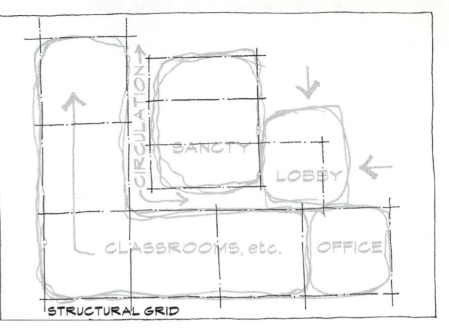

Figure 18.8: Begin with a plan bubble diagram. Even during this diagrammatic stage of plan development, freehand sketches should be drawn to scale on tracing paper. A graph paper underlay is helpful.

Figure 18.9: The freehand floor plan should be immediately followed up with a tracing overlay sketch showing the structural grid, a set of lines which determine the width of the structural bays (spans of beams and slabs), and the location of column rows and bearing walls. Remember that this grid will have a profound effect not only on the structural system but on nonstructural design issues such as the space and form of the building, the flow and division of space, circulation, and daylighting. At this stage, it is unlikely that the grid will fit the rough plan, but do not try to revise it or the floor plan yet.

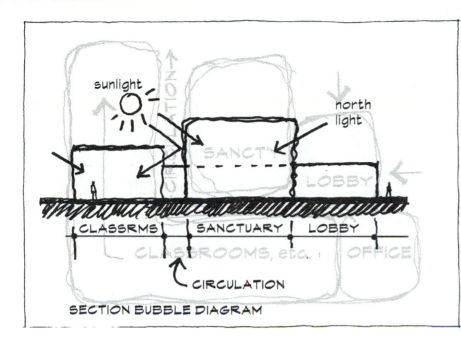

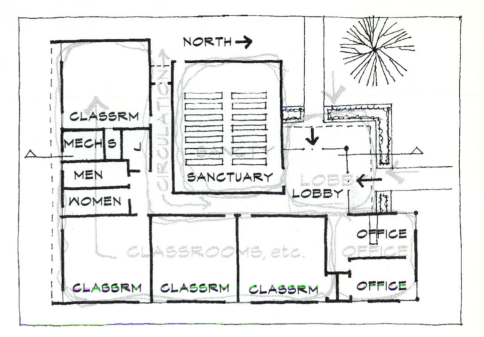

Figure 18.10: Instead of revising the floor plan (or the grid), make a diagrammatic cross-sectional overlay over that plan to study roof forms and interior volumetric relationships. As this cross section evolves, it should suggest how the spatial organization in section will affect the framing layout, and vice versa. It will also provide insight to natural lighting opportunities in the form of clerestories, windows, skylights, and roof monitors (Moore, 1985).

Figure 18.11: Next, refine the plan bubble diagram into a floor plan overlay that works with the structural concept. This step usually requires several iterations. Follow up with a new structural grid overlay.

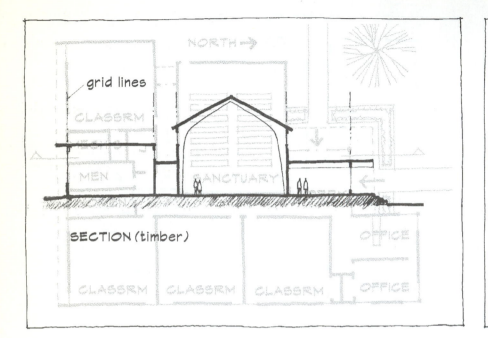

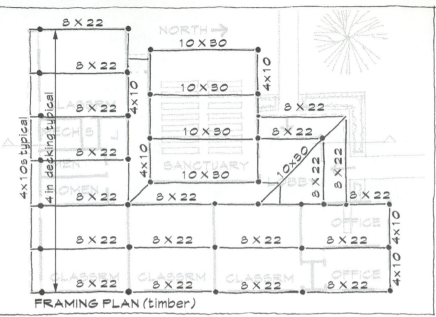

Figure 18.12: Select a structural system from Figure 18.6 (laminated timber, in this example) and draw a new section overlay (over the plan) incorporating this system.

Figure 18.13: Next, draw a freehand framing plan overlay. Over the structural grid, begin by drawing the bearing lines over some of the grid lines. These represent the location of continuous support members—either beams (or trusses) or bearing walls. Most of these bearing lines will be in a single direction. Decking, joists, or a slab will span between these bearing lines in the opposite direction. Decide whether bearing walls or columns (or a combination) will be used for vertical support. If columns are to be used, space them out along the bearing line. The spacing should not exceed the span limit of the beam; but since that is unknown, assume column spacing roughly equal to the distance between bearing lines. If practical, columns should fall on the grid-line intersections. Beams will usually be required around floor openings such as stairs, with columns at each corner. At this point, go to the preliminary sizing charts in Appendix A and size the components of the structural system selected earlier. The charts may suggest that the spans you have selected for beams and decking are too long (or too short) to be efficient. Revise the layout as necessary. Finally, indicate the preliminary member sizes on the plan.

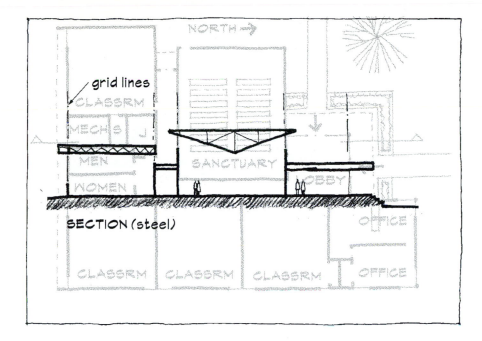

Figure 18.14: To try an alternative structural system (steel open-web joists and trusses in this example), repeat the step in Figure 18.12, beginning with another section overlay. Specifically, try running the trusses (or beams or bearing walls) in the opposite direction along the grid lines. This is a good exercise to gain a fresh insight into a familiar problem.

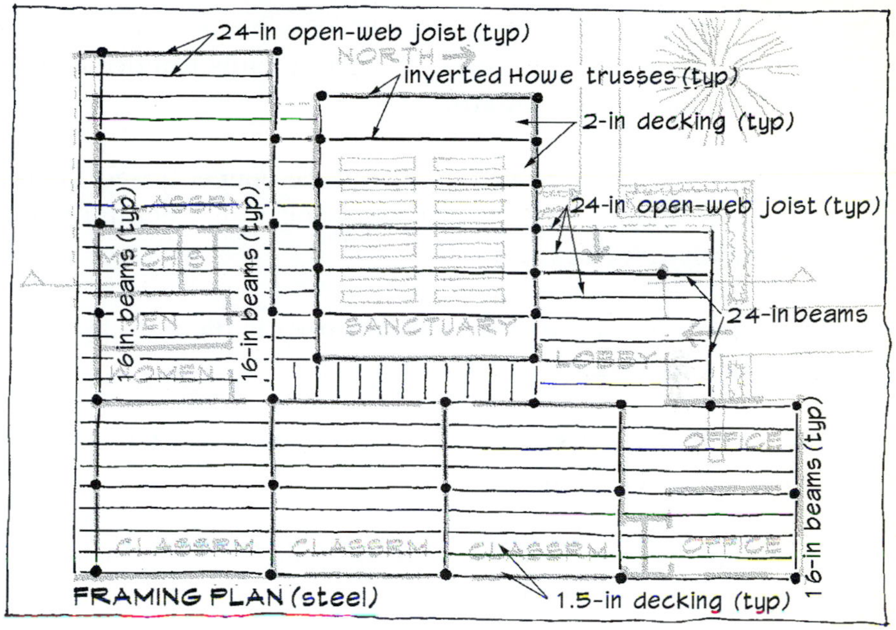

Figure 18.15: The alternative framing plan for this structural system (with preliminary sizing) is overlaid on the section.

SUMMARY

1. Bearing walls are best used to support loads uniformly distributed along their length.

2. Because beams and girders introduce concentrated loads, they are seldom supported by bearing walls; columns are commonly used instead.

3. The placement of bearing walls in plan is dictated by their role as supporting elements.

4. Regularly spaced bearing walls may act as shear walls to contribute lateral stability.

5. Openings can be made in bearing walls by installing headers (beams) over the opening.

6. In multistory buildings, the walls should align above one another.

7. Columns may be used to support either beams (and trusses), or slabs (including decking and joists).

8. Steel and site-cast column-and-beam systems can provide lateral support by behaving as rigid frames.

9. Beams may be laid out in one or both directions with joists, slab, or decking spanning between.

10. Integrate the building structure with the architectural design by developing both simultaneously using a sequence of tracing overlays. It should begin with a plan bubble diagram and progress through a series of overlays to a framing plan that shows the preliminary layout and sizing of the main structural members.

Appendix A

PRELIMINARY DESIGN CHARTS

The architectural designer is aware that the thickness, depth, or height of any structural system is closely related to the span of the system and to such variables as the spacing of structural elements, loads and loading conditions, continuity of system, cantilevering, etc. The designer is also aware that the structure should be considered at an early stage in the design synthesis because of the influence it will have upon the design. These charts (Figures A.1 through A.7) have been developed to provide the architectural designer with a quick and easy method of obtaining this basic structural information without the necessity of detailed mathematical analysis of the many possible structural solutions that might logically be integrated with the preliminary design.

Each chart indicates the range of thickness, depth, or height relative to the span normally required for each of the systems indicated. This normal range is a composite of analytical solutions, structural design tables, and many constructed architectural examples. The few structures that may exceed the range of these charts are generally composed of double systems or the combination of two or more integrated systems. Sometimes one system may be an exten-

sion of another system, and in these cases the span and height should be considered for only the primary system. These charts then consider only the normal use of a single system and do not consider the extreme possibilities for either depth or span.

To use the charts effectively, a designer must determine the approximate span required for the design, then choose a system appropriate to the design requirements and read vertically from the appropriate span to the center of the range, then horizontally to the left of the chart to determine the normal thickness, depth or height. If, however, greater-than-normal loads are anticipated or a wider than normal spacing of members is desirable, the upper portion of the range should then be used. If light loads, or closer-than-normal spacing of members are anticipated, the lower portion of the range should then be used.

Structures such as frames, arches or suspension systems can be used to cover or enclose both rectangular or circular spaces. In these cases, the upper portion of the range is more appropriate for rectangular or vaulted areas, the lower portion for circular or denied areas.

Thicknesses or depths, where indicated across the top of these charts, reflect the averages for the spans indicated. These figures may, however, need some adjustment. For example, domed areas would require somewhat less thickness or depth of material than vaulted areas, or the thickness indicated for folded plates should be increased somewhat if the lower portion of the range is used, and decreased if the upper portion is used.

The use of cantilevers extended from normal spans or a continuous beam system would generally result in less thickness or depth of a system for a given span, and would indicate the use of the lower portion of the range, or even below in some cases. For cantilevers, multiply the span by a factor of two or three to determine the equivalent simply supported span and use this to determine thickness or depth.

The masonry vault and dome charts below have been included for comparative use only. However, if their use is anticipated with contemporary materials and methods of construction, the lower portion of the range should be used.

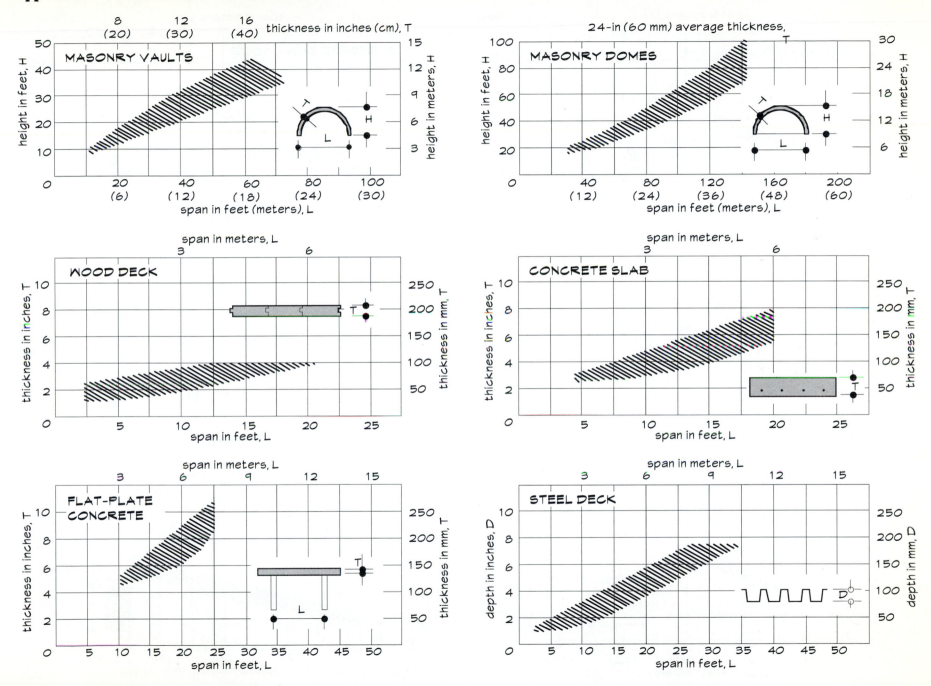

Figure A.1: Preliminary design charts.

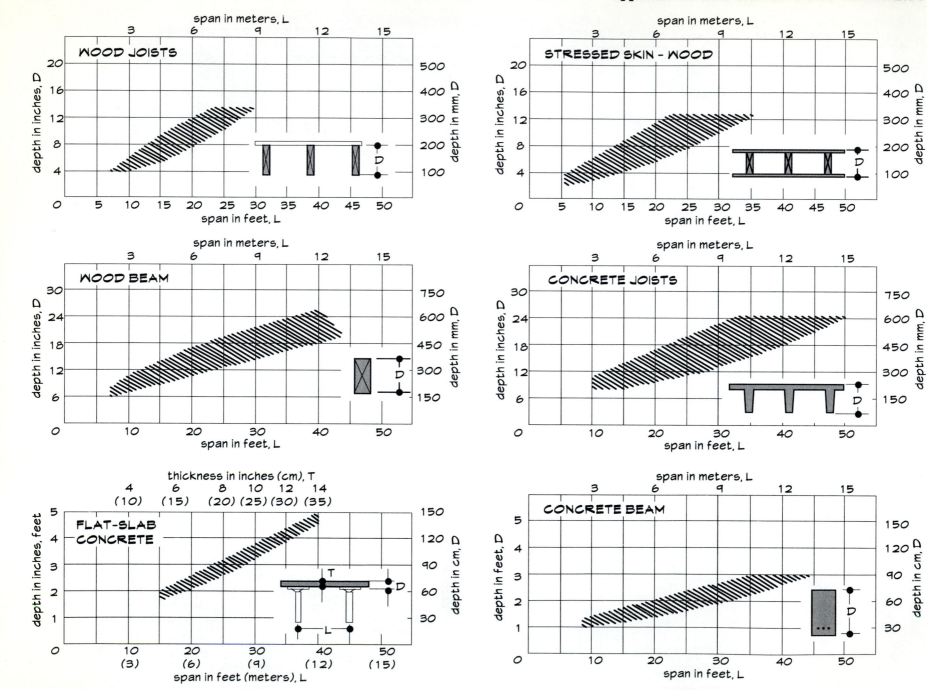

Figure A.2: Preliminary design charts (continued).

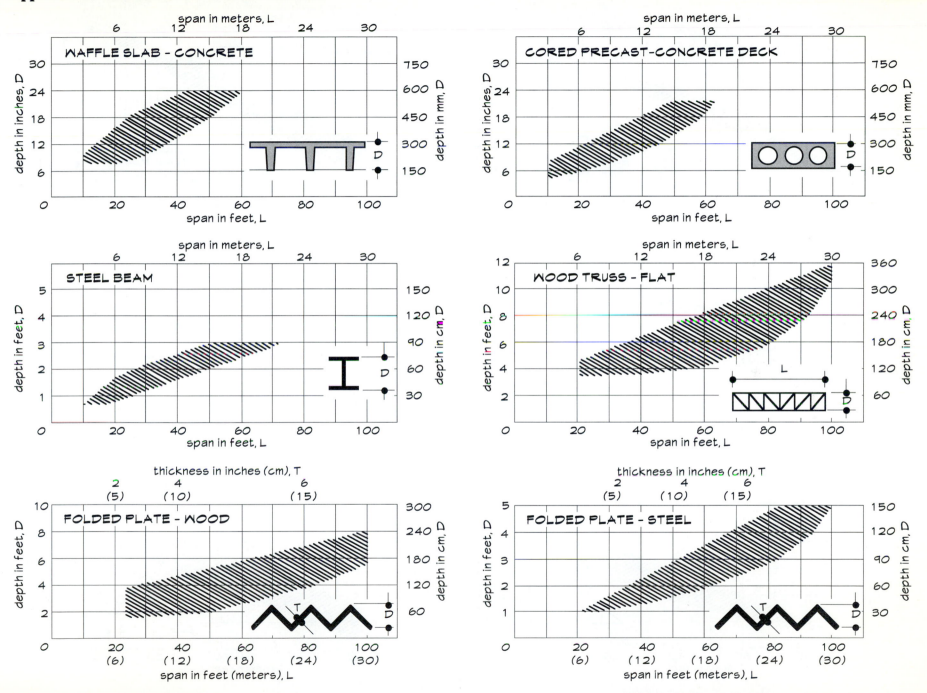

Figure A.3: Preliminary design charts (continued).

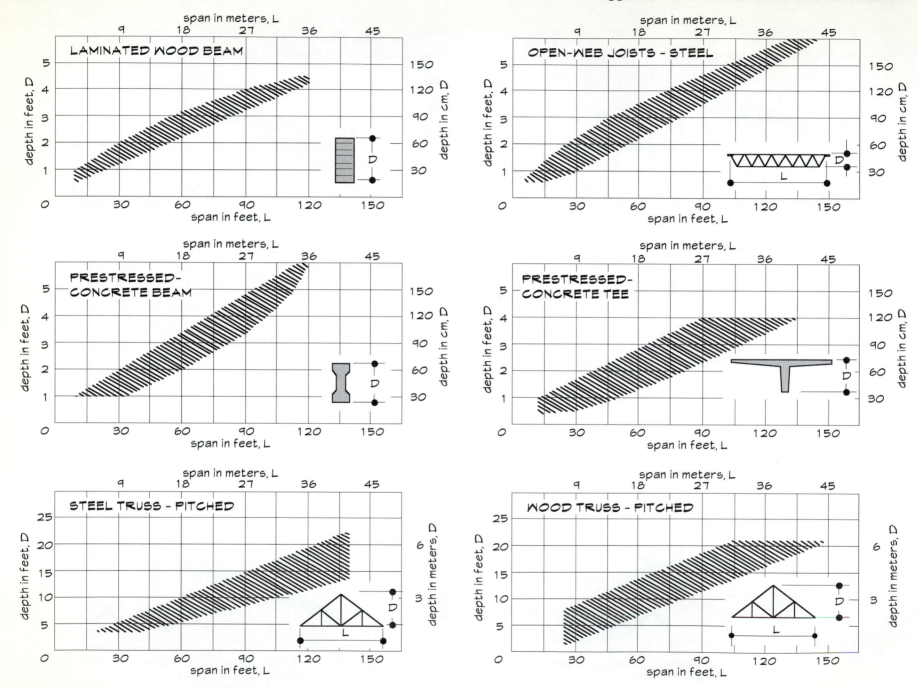

Figure A.4: Preliminary design charts (continued).

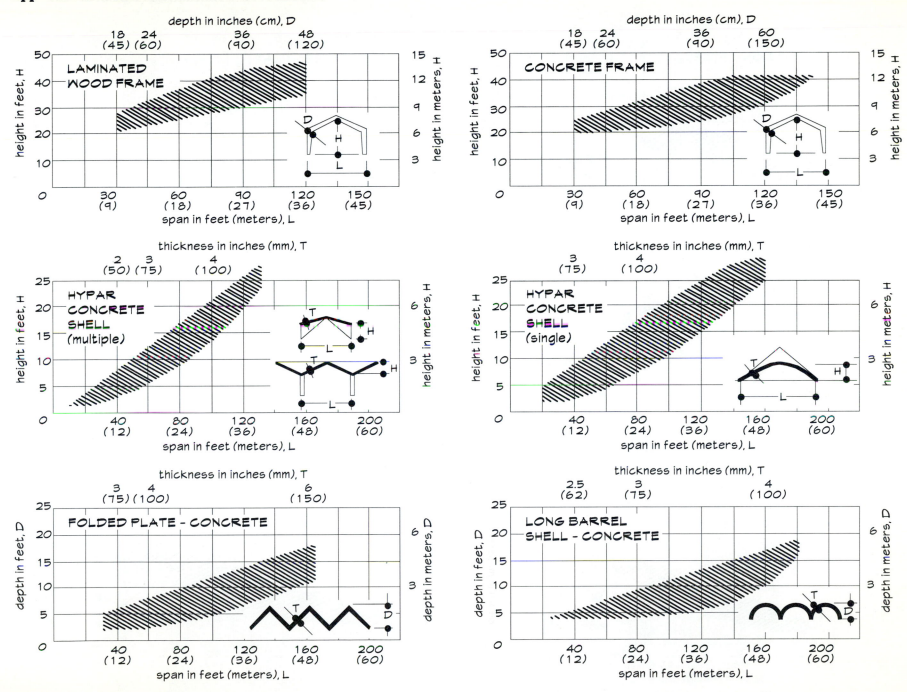

Figure A.5: Preliminary design charts (continued).

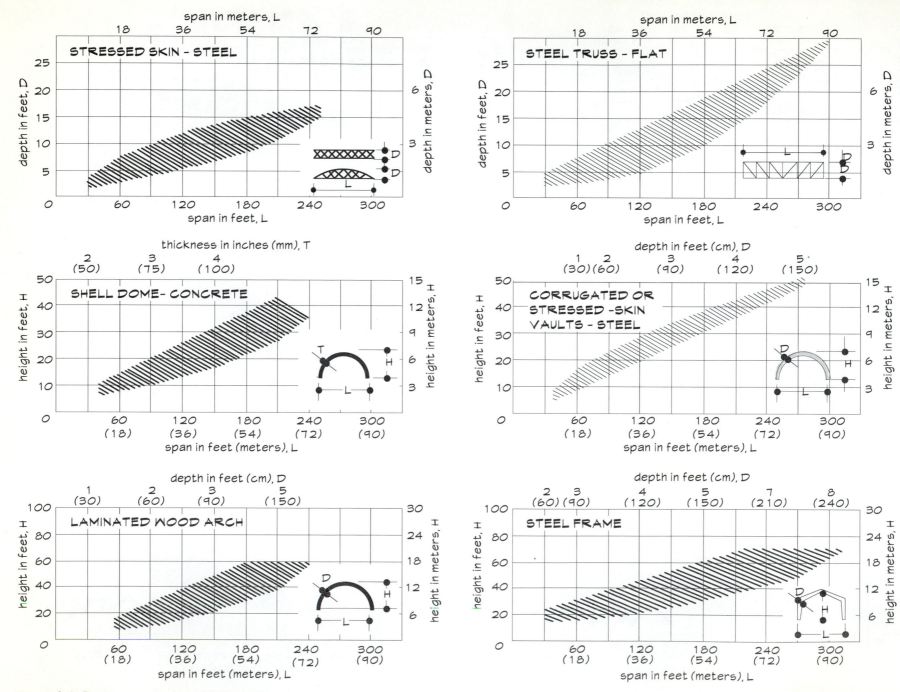

Figure A.6: Preliminary design charts (continued).

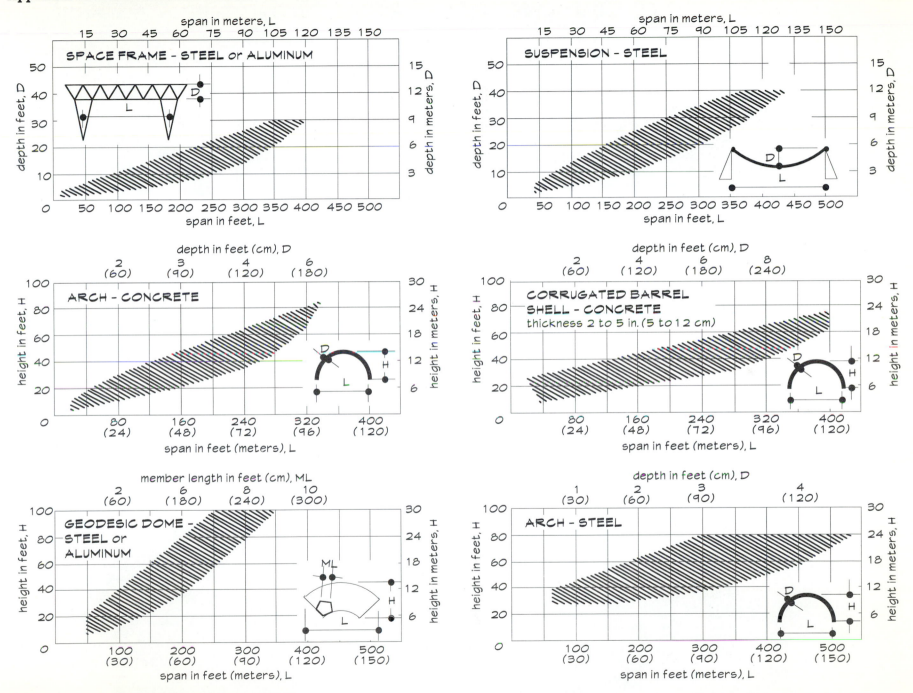

Figure A.7: Preliminary design charts (continued).

ILLUSTRATION CREDITS

With the exception of Figures 5.17 and 8.26, all drawings and photographs are by the author. The following sources (see Bibliography for complete citations) were used as the basis for individual figures.

1.14	Kellogg, 1994	4.7	Schodek, 1992	5.24	Levy, 1991
1.19	Salvadori and Heller, 1975	4.10	Salvadori and Heller, 1975	5.25	Levy, 1991
1.20	Kellogg, 1994	4.11	Orton, 1988		
1.24	Salvadori and Heller, 1975	4.12	Orton, 1988	6.2	Van Loon, 1994
1.25	Salvadori and Heller, 1975	4.14	Taylor and Andrews, 1982	6.3	Van Loon, 1994
1.26	Kellogg, 1994	4.17	Orton, 1988	6.4	Van Loon, 1994
1.27	Salvadori and Heller, 1975	4.18	Orton, 1988	6.5	Haeckel, 1887
		4.20	Orton, 1988	6.6	Salvadori and Heller, 1975
2.2	Gordon, 1973	4.21	Berger, 1996 (after Graef)	6.7	Corkill, et al., 1993
2.4	Salvadori and Heller, 1975	4.23	Brookes and Grech, 1992	6.8	Pearce, 1978
2.7	Salvadori and Heller, 1975	4.24	Brookes and Grech, 1992	6.9	Pearce, 1978
2.8	Gordon, 1973			6.12	Freeman, 1989
2.11	Kellogg, 1994	5.2	Corkill, et al., 1993	6.13	Freeman, 1989
2.12	Kellogg, 1994	5.4	Gugliotta, 1980	6.14	Editor, 1967
2.13	Kellogg, 1994	5.5	Gugliotta, 1980		
2.16	Gordon, 1973	5.6	Editor, 1970	7.1	Kellogg, 1994
		5.7	Editor, 1970	7.2	Kellogg, 1994
3.2	Brookes and Grech, 1990	5.9	Editor, 1980	7.5	Engel, 1964
3.3	Brookes and Grech, 1990	5.10	Editor, 1980	7.6	Kellogg, 1994
3.4	Brookes and Grech, 1990	5.11	Editor, 1988	7.11	Weese and Assoc., 1978
3.7	Brookes and Grech, 1990	5.12	Editor, 1988	7.13	Kellogg, 1994
3.8	Brookes and Grech, 1990	5.13	Editor, 1988	7.15	Ching, 1997
3.9	Brookes and Grech, 1990	5.16a	Fuller, 1964	7.16	Fitch and Branch, 1960
3.10	Frampton, et al., 1993	5.17	Fuller, 1964	7.20	Ronner, et al., 1977
3.11	Frampton, et al., 1993	5.18	Rastorfer, 1988	7.22	Safdie, 1974
		5.19	Rastorfer, 1988		
4.2	Schodek, 1992	5.20	Rastorfer, 1988	8.2	Kellogg, 1994
4.4	Thompson, 1917	5.22	Robison, 1989	8.4	Allen, 1980

8.6	Schodek, 1992	10.19	Editor, 1963a	14.7	Fletcher, 1987
8.7	Schodek, 1992	10.20	Engel, 1968	14.8	Fletcher, 1987
8.8	Kellogg, 1994	10.23	Berger, 1996	14.9	Fletcher, 1987
8.9	Kellogg, 1994	10.25	Blake, 1995	14.12	Clark and Mark, 1984
8.10	Kellogg, 1994	10.26	Berger, 1996	14.13	Mark, 1993
8.11	Torroja, 1967	10.29	Berger, 1996	14.14	Fletcher, 1987
8.12	Kellogg, 1994	10.30	Editor, 1952	14.15	Fletcher, 1987
8.13a	Torroja, 1967	10.32	McQuade, 1958	14.17	Mark, 1993
8.14	Elliott, 1992	10.33	Sandaker and Eggen, 1992	14.20	Fletcher, 1987
8.20	Kellogg, 1994	10.35	Thiem, 1972	14.21	Fletcher, 1987
8.22	Coulton, 1977	10.36	Thiem, 1972	14.23	Kostof, 1985
8.24	Ronner, et al., 1977	10.37	Thiem, 1972	14.27	Guastavino Co., date unknown
8.25	Ronner, et al., 1977	10.40	Orton, 1988	14.30	Robinson, 1985
8.26	Galileo, 1638	10.41	Orton, 1988	14.31	Melaragno, 1991
8.31	Kostof, 1985	10.42	Orton, 1988		
8.32	Brown, 1993			15.5	Salvadori and Heller, 1975
8.33	Brooks and Grech, 1992	11.1	Engel, 1968	15.6	Salvadori and Heller, 1975
8.34	Brooks and Grech, 1992	11.2	Berger, 1996	15.9	Editor, 1954c
8.36	Brooks and Grech, 1992	11.4	Engel, 1968	15.11	Futagawa, 1988
8.38	Wright, 1957	11.5	Blyth, 1994	15.13	Editor, 1961b
8.40	Orton, 1988	11.7	Editor, 1982	15.14	Randall and Smith, 1991
8.45	Cowan, 1971	11.11	Berger, 1996	15.16	Editor, 1954b
8.47	Salvadori, 1980	11.13	Editor, 1987	15.22	Engel, 1968
8.48	Futagawa, 1972	11.14	Editor, 1987	15.23	Engel, 1968
8.52	Sandaker and Eggen, 1992			15.25	Ronner, et al., 1977
8.55	Macdonald, 1994	12.3	Dent, 1971	15.26	Ronner, et al., 1977
8.56	Huxtable, 1960	12.6	Dent, 1971	15.30	Engel, 1968
		12.12	Geiger, 1970	15.31	Engel, 1968
9.3	Engel, 1964	12.13	Dent, 1971	15.33	Engel, 1968
9.6	Thonton, et al., 1993	12.14	Villecco, 1970	15.35	Torroja, 1958
9.13	Siegel, 1975	12.16	Editor, 1976	15.37	Torroja, 1958
9.16	Kellogg, 1994	12.17	Schodek, 1992	15.38	Torroja, 1958
9.18	Kellogg, 1994	12.21	Dent, 1971	15.40	Editor, 1963c
9.19	Kellogg, 1994	12.22	Dent, 1971	15.43	Faber, 1963
9.24	Arnell and Bickford, 1984	12.24	Dent, 1971	15.45	Faber, 1963
9.26	Orton, 1988			15.48	Faber, 1963
9.28	Orton, 1988	13.1	Brown, 1993	15.49	Faber, 1963
9.30	Orton, 1988	13.2	Brown, 1993	15.51	Editor, 1958b
9.31	Orton, 1988	13.3	Brown, 1993	15.52	Editor, 1962b
9.32	Orton, 1988	13.10	Kellogg, 1994		
9.33	Orton, 1988	13.14	Brown, 1993	16.7	Engel, 1968
9.34	Editor, 1969b	13.15	Fletcher, 1987	16.8	Editor, 1989
		13.16	Ronner, et al., 1977	16.9	Faber, 1963
10.5	Brown, 1993	13.20	Ronner, et al., 1977	16.11	Editor, 1958c
10.7	Brown, 1993	13.22	Kellogg, 1994	16.12	Editor, 1958c
10.9	Brown, 1993	13.25	Carter, 1989	16.15	Editor, 1963d
10.10	Brown, 1993	13.28	Harriman, 1990	16.18	Editor, 1955
10.11	Nervi, 1963	13.29	Harriman, 1990	16.19	Kato, 1981
10.12	Nervi, 1963	13.30	Harriman, 1990	16.20	Kato, 1981
10.14	Futagawa, 1974	13.34	Brown, 1993	16.21	Kato, 1981
10.15	Futagawa, 1974				
10.18a	Editor, 1960a	14.6	Gardner, 1980	17.6	Simpson Co., 1996

17.7   Allen, 1985
17.10   Allen, 1985
17.13   Allen, 1985
17.14   Allen, 1985
17.15   Allen, 1985
17.16   Packard, 1981
17.17   Packard, 1981
17.18   Packard, 1981

18.6   Allen, 1985

A.1   Corkill, et al., 1993

BIBLIOGRAPHY

Allen, E., 1980, *How Buildings Work.* New York: Oxford University Press.

———, 1985, *Fundamentals of Buildings Construction.* New York: John Wiley and Sons.

———, and Iano, J., 1995, *The Architect's Studio Companion.* New York: John Wiley and Sons.

Andrews, W., 1968, *Architecture in Chicago and Mid-America.* New York: Atheneum.

Arnell, P., and Bickford, T., 1984, *Charles Gwathmey and Robert Siegel: Buildings and Projects 1964-1984.* New York: Harper and Row.

Berger, H., 1985, "The evolving design vocabulary of fabric structures," *Architectural Record,* March, pp.152-156.

———, 1996, *Light Structures—Structures of Light.* Basel, Switzerland: Berkhäuser.

Birdair, Inc., 1995, *Tensioned Membrane Structures.* Amherst, NY: Birdair, Inc., 65 Lawrence Bell Drive.

Blake, E., 1995, "Peak condition," *Architectural Review,* February, pp.60-63.

Blaser, W., ed., 1990, *Santiago Calatrava: Engineering Architecture.* Boston: Birkhauser Verlag.

Blyth, A., ed., 1994, *Architects' Working Details 2.* London: Emat Architecture.

Borrego, J., 1968, *Space Grid Structures.* Cambridge, MA: M.I.T. Press.

Brookes, A., and Grech, C., 1990, *The Building Envelope.* London: Butterworth Architecture.

———, 1992, *Connections: Studies in Building Assembly.* New York: Whitney Library of Design.

Brown, D., 1993, *Bridges.* New York: Macmillan.

Carney, J., 1971, *Plywood Folded Plates: Design and Details.* Research report #121. Tacoma, WA: American Plywood Association.

Carter, B., 1989, "Back Bay arches," *Architecture,* December, pp.65-69.

Ching, F., 1979, *Architecture: Form, Space & Order.* New York: Van Nostrand Reinhold.

———, 1997, *A Visual Dictionary of Architecture.* New York: Van Nostrand Reinhold.

Clark, W., and Mark, R., 1984, "The first flying buttresses: a reconstruction of the nave of Notre-Dame de Paris," *Art Bulletin,* March, pp.47–65.

Corkill, P., Puderbaugh, H., and Sawyers, H., 1993, *Structure and Architectural Design.* Davenport, IA: Market Publishing.

Coulton, J., 1977, *Greek Architects at Work: Problems with Structure and Design.* London: Elek.

Cowan, H., 1971, *Architectural Structures.* New York: Elsevier.

———, and Wilson, F., 1981, *Structural Systems.* New York: Van Nostrand Reinhold.

Davey, P, 1987, "An elegant tent provides a festive setting for cricket," *Architectural Review,* September, pp.40–45.

———, 1988, "An elegant tent provides a festive setting for cricket," *Architecture,* September, pp.70–71.

Dent, R., 1971, *Principles of Pneumatic Architecture.* London: Architectural Press.

Eberwein, B., 1989, "World's largest wood dome," *Classic Wood Structures.* New York: American Society of Civil Engineers, pp. 123–132.

Editor, 1952, "Parabolic pavilion," *Architectural Forum,* October, pp.134–137.

———, 1953, "Parabolic cable roof," *Architectural Forum,* June, pp.170–171.

———, 1954a, "The great livestock pavilion complete," *Architectural Forum,* March, pp.131–137.

———, 1954b, "Air–formed concrete domes," *Architectural Forum,* June, pp.116–118.

———, 1954c, "Long-span concrete dome on three pendentives," *Progressive Architecture,* June, pp.120–124.

———, 1954d, "St. Louis Planetarium: Design Award Citation," *Progressive Architecture,* June, pp.134–135.

———, 1955, "UNESCO headquarters design modified for building," *Architectural Record,* August, pp.10–11.

———, 1956, "Concrete Institute plans a new headquarters building," *Architectural Record,* August, pp.10–11.

———, 1958a, "The dome goes commercial," *Architectural Forum,* March, pp.121–125.

———, 1958b, "TWA's graceful new terminal," *Architectural Forum,* January, pp.78–85.

———, 1958c, "Siege de l'institut Américain du ciment, Détroit, Michigan," *L'Architecture D'Aujourd'hui,* April, pp.31–32.

———, 1960a, "A new airport for jets," *Architectural Record,* March, pp.175–181.

———, 1960b, "Shaping a two-acre sculpture," *Architectural Forum,* August, pp.119–123.

———, 1960c, "The concrete bird stands free," *Architectural Forum,* August, pp.119–23.

———, 1961a, "Saarinen," *Architectural Forum*, September, pp.112– 113.

———, 1961b, "Spirit of Byzantium: FLLW's last church," *Architectural Forum*, December, pp.83–87.

———, 1961c, "The Climatron," *AIA Journal*, May, pp.27-32.

———, 1962a, "I want to catch the excitement of the trip," *Architectural Forum*, July, pp.72–76.

———, 1962b, "Saarinen's TWA Flight Center," *Architectural Record*, July, pp.129–134.

———, 1963a, "Dulles International Airport," *Progressive Architecture*, pp.90–100.

———, 1963b, "Experimental plywood roof in Seattle," *Architectural Forum*, April, p. 122.

———, 1963c, "Spool-shaped planetarium for St. Louis," *Architectural Forum*, August, pp. 92–94.

———, 1963d, "Giant Illinois dome nears completion," *Architectural Forum*, March, p. 117.

———, 1963e, "University of Illinois spectacular," *Architectural Record*, July, pp. 111–116.

———, 1963f, "Budget school offers pleasant environment," *Architectural Record*, October, pp. 218–219.

———, 1966, "Bucky's biggest bubble," *Architectural Forum*, June, pp.74–79.

———, 1967, "The U.S. pavillion," *Japan Architect*, August, pp.38–45.

———, 1969a, "The space frame roof and the Festival Plaza," *Japan Architect*, April, 54–59.

———, 1969b, "Boston City Hall," *Architectural Record*, February, pp.140–144.

———, 1969c, "The Fuji Group Pavilion," *Japan Architect*, April, pp. 60–62.

———, 1969d, "Floating Theater," *Japan Architect*, April, pp.63–65.

———, 1970, "Festival Plaza: joints are key to world's largest space frame," *Progressive Architecture*, April, p. 62.

———, 1971a, "Munich's Olympic games site topped by cable-suspended roof," *Engineering News Record*, September 23, pp.18–19 .

———, 1971b, "Post-tensioned shells from museum roof," *Engineering News Record*, November 11, pp.24–25.

———, 1972, "Munich Olympics," *Design*, September, pp.30–35.

———, 1976, "A profile of the two largest air-supported roofs," *Architectural Record*, January, pp.141–143.

———, 1979, "Tent structures designed to endure," *Architectural Record*, mid-August, pp.85–93.

———, 1980, "A vast space frame wraps New York's convention center like a taut fabric," *Architectural Record*, Mid-August, pp.47–56.

———, 1982, "Invitation to the Haj," *Progressive Architecture*, February, pp.116–122.

———, 1983a, "A field of tents in the sky," *Architectural Record*, September, pp.84–85.

———, 1983b, "Huge, soaring tents on the desert," *AIA Journal*, May, pp.276–279.

———, 1983c, "Calgary 'saddles up' arena," *Engineering News Record*, December 22, pp.50–51.

———, 1985, "Riyadh stadium roof spans 485 ft," *Engineering News Record*, July 25, pp. 29–31.

———, 1986, "Space frame odyssey," *Architectural Record*, September, pp.106–117.

———, 1987, "Marlebone Cricket Club Mound Stand," *Architecture*, September, pp.151–156.

———, 1988, "Grand Louvre: le cristal qui songe," *Techniques and Architecture*, September, pp.128–132.

———, 1989, "Mobile structure for sulfur extraction," *Architecture and Urbanism*, March, pp. 170–173.

Elliott, C., 1992, *Technics and Architecture*. Cambridge, MA: MIT Press.

Ellis, C., 1989, "Pei in Paris: the pyramid in place," *Architecture*, January, pp.43–46.

Engel, H., 1964, *The Japanese House: A Tradition for Contemporary Architecture*. Rutland, VT: Charles E. Tuttle.

———, 1968, *Structural Systems*. New York: Praeger.

Faber, C., 1963, *Candela / the Shell Builder.* New York: Reinhold.

Fitch, J., and Branch, D., 1960, "Primative architecture and climate," *Scientific American,* vol. 203, pp.134–145.

Fleig, K., 1978, *Alvar Aalto*. Zurich: Verlag fur Architektur Artemis.

Fletcher, B., 1987, *A History of Architecture*. 18th ed., London: Butterworth.

Fox, H., 1981, "Kenneth Snelson: portrait of an atomist," in Snelson, K., 1981, *Kenneth Snelson* (exhibition catalog). Buffalo, NY: Buffalo Fine Arts Academy.

Frampton, K., Webster, A., and Tischhauser, A., 1993, *Calatrava Bridges.* Zurich: Artems.

Freeman, A., 1989, "Reglazing a celebrated dome greenhouse," Architecture, March, pp. 88-89.

Fuller, R. B., 1964, *Aspension Structure.* U.S. Patent 3,139,957, Washington, DC: U.S. Patent Office.

Futagawa, Y., ed., 1971a, *Eero Saarinen: John Deere Building.* Tokyo: Global Architecture.

———, ed., 1971b, *Louis I. Kahn: Richards Medical Research Building and Salk Institute for Biological Studies.* Tokyo: Global Architecture.

———, ed., 1972, *Mies van der Rohe: The New National Gallery.* Tokyo: Global Architecture.

———, ed., 1973a, *Gunnar Birkerts and Associates.* Tokyo: Global Architecture.

———, ed., 1973b, *Eero Saarinen: Dulles International Airport.* Tokyo: Global Architecture.

———, ed., 1974, *Le Corbusier: Sarabhai House and Shodhan House.* Tokyo: Global Architecture.

——, ed., 1988, *Frank Lloyd Wright Monograph 1951–1959.* Tokyo: A.D.A. Edita.

Galileo, G., 1638, *Discoursi e dimonstrazioni matematiche.* Trans. Crew, H., and de Salvio, A., 1914, New York: Macmillan.

Gardner, H., 1980, *Art through the Ages.* New York: Harcourt Brace Jovanovich.

Geiger, D., 1970, "U.S. pavilion at Expo 70 features air-supported cable roof," Civil Engineering, March, pp.48-49.

Gfeller-Corthesy, R., ed., 1986, *Atelier 5.* Zurich: Ammann Verlag.

Glancy, J., 1989, *New British Architecture.* London: Thames and Hudson.

Gordon, J., 1973, *Structures: or, Why Things Don't Fall Down.* New York: Da Capo Press.

Guastavino Company, date unknown, product literature.

Gugliotta, P., 1980, "Architects' (and engineers') guide to space frame design," *Architectural Record,* mid-August, pp.58-62.

Guinness, D., and Sadler, J., 1973, *Mr. Jefferson, Architect.* New York: Viking.

Haeckel, E., 1887, *Report of the Scientific Results of the Voyage of HMS Challenger,* Vol. 18, Part XL—Radiolaria. Edengurgh 1880–1895. Reprinted, 1966, New York: Johnson Reprint Corp.

Hamilton, K., Cambell, D., and Gossen, P., 1994, "Current state of development and future trends in employment of air-supported roofs in long-span applications," *Spatial, Lattice, and Tension Structures. Proceedings of the IASS-ASCE International Symposium, Atlanta.* New York: American Society of Civil Engineers, pp.612–621.

Harriman, M., 1990, "London bridge," *Architecture,* September, pp.109–112.

Huxtable, A. L., 1960. *Pier Luigi Nervi.* New York: Braziller.

Isler, H., 1994, "Concrete shells today," *Spatial, Lattice and Tension Structures: Proceedings of the IASS-ASCE International Symposium, Atlanta.* New York: American Society of Civil Engineers, pp. 820–835.

Jahn, G., 1991, "Stretched muscles," *Architectural Record,* June, pp.75-82.

Kallmann, G., and McKinnell, M., 1975, "Movement systems as a generator of built form," *Architectural Record,* vol. 158, no. 7, November, pp.105–116.

Kappraff, J., 1991, *Connections: The Geometric Bridge Between Art and Science.* New York: McGraw-Hill.

Kato, A., ed., 1981, *Pier Luigi Nervi and Contemporary Architecture. Process Architecture,* April, no. 23.

Kellogg, R., 1994, *Demonstrating Structural Behavior with Simple Models.* Fayetteville, AR: School of Architecture, University of Arkansas (photocopy).

Kenzo Tange Associates, ed., 1987, "Master plan for Expo 70 and master design of trunk facilities," *Kenzo Tange Associates: Process Architecture,* no. 73, pp.102–103.

Kimball, R., 1989, "The riddle of the pyramid," *Architectural Record,* January, pp. 58–61.

Komendant, A., 1975, *18 Years with Architect Louis I. Kahn.* Englewood, NJ: Aloray.

Kostof, S., 1985, *A History of Architecture: Settings and Rituals.* New York: Oxford University Press.

Krieger, A., 1988, *The Architecture of Kallmann McKinnell & Wood.* New York: Rizzoli.

Landeker, H., 1994, "Peak performance: the Denver International Airport Terminal," *Architecture,* August, pp.45– 52.

Ledger, B., 1994, "The biosphere reborn," *Canadian Architect,* September, pp.25–28.

Levy, M., 1991, "Floating fabric over Georgia Dome," Civil Engineering, November, pp.34–37.

———, Castro, G., and Jing, T., 1994, "Hypar-tensegrity dome, optimal configurations," *Spatial, Lattice and Tension Structures. Proceedings of the IASS-ASCE International Symposium, Atlanta.* New York: American Society of Civil Engineers, pp.125–128.

———, and Salvadori, M., 1992, *Why Buildings Fall Down.* New York: Norton.

Lin, T., and Stotesbury, S., 1988, *Structural Concepts and Systems for Architects and Engineers.* New York: Van Nostrand Reinhold.

Macdonald, A., 1994, *Structure and Architecture.* Oxford: Butterworth Architecture.

Mahler, V., 1972, "Olympiastadion," *Architectural Forum,* October, pp.26–32.

Mark, R., ed., 1993, *Architectural Technology Up to the Scientific Revolution.* Cambridge, MA: MIT Press.

Marks, R. W., 1960, *The Dymaxion World of Buckminster Fuller.* New York: Reinhold.

McCoy, E., 1973, "Federal Reserve Bank of Minneapolis and IBM Information Systems Center," in Futagawa, Y., ed., *Gunnar Birkerts and Associates.* Tokyo: Global Architecture.

McQuade, W., 1958, "Yale's Viking vessel," *Architectural Forum,* December, pp.106–110.

Mero Structures Inc., P.O. Box 610, Germantown, WI 53022 (product literature, 1994).

Melaragno, M., 1991, *An Introduction to Shell Structures.* New York: Van Nostrand Reinhold.

Moore, F., 1985, *Concepts and Practice of Architectural Daylighting.* New York: Van Nostrand Reinhold.

Nakamura, T., 1984, *Eero Saarinen.* Tokyo: Eando Yu.

Nervi, P. L., 1963, *Pier Luigi Nervi: Buildings, Projects, Structures 1953–1963.* New York: Praeger.

Orton, A., 1988, *The Way We Build Now.* London: E & FN Spon.

Otto, F., 1954, *The Hung Roof.* Berlin: Bauwelt.

Packard, R., 1981, *Architectural Graphic Standards.* New York: John Wiley and Sons.

Pearce, P., 1978, *Structure in Nature is a Strategy for Design.* Cambridge, MA: M.I.T. Press.

Prenis, J., ed., 1973, *The Dome Builder's Handbook.* Philadelphia: Running Press.

Pugh, A., 1976, *An Introduction to Tensegrity.* Berkeley, CA: University of California Press.

Ramm, E., and Schunck, E., 1986, *Heinz Isler.* Stuttgart: Krämer Verlag.

Randall, F., and Smith, A., 1991, "Thin-shell concrete dome built economically with rotating forming and shoring system," *Concrete Construction,* June, pp.490–492.

Rastorfer, D., 1988, "Structural Gymnastics for the Olympics," *Architectural Record,* September, pp.128–135.

Robinson, K, 1985, *The Tacoma Dome Book.* Tacoma, WA: Robinson Publishing.

Robison, R., 1989, "Fabric meets cable," *Civil Engineering,* February, pp.56–59.

Ronner, H., Jhaveri, S., and Vasella, A., 1977, *Louis I. Kahn: Complete Works.* Boulder, CO: Westview.

Rosenbaum, D., 1989, "A dream of a dome in St. Pete," *Engineering News Record,* August 10, pp.37–40.

Rosenthal, H. W., 1962, *Structural Decisions.* London: Chapman and Hall.

Saarinen, E., 1962, *Eero Saarinen on his work.* New Haven: Yale University Press.

———, 1963, "Dulles International Airport," *Architectural Record,* July, pp.101–110.

———, and Severud, F., 1958, "The David S. Ingalls Rink," *Architectural Record,* October, pp 154–160.

Safdie, M., 1974, *For Everyone a Garden.* Cambridge, MA: MIT Press.

Salvadori, M., 1980, *Why Buildings Stand Up.* New York: Norton.

———, 1990, *The Art of Construction.* Chicago: Chicago Review Press.

Salvadori, M., and Heller, R., 1975, *Structure in Architecture.* New York: Prentice Hall.

Sandaker, B., and Eggen, A., 1992, *The Structural Basis of Architecture.* New York: Whitney Library of Design.

Schodek, D., 1992, *Structures.* Englewood Cliffs, NJ: Prentice Hall.

Schueller, W., 1977, *High-Rise Building Structures.* New York: Wiley Interscience.

———, 1996, *The Design of Building Structures.* Upper Saddle River, NJ: Prentice Hall.

Scofield, W., and O'Brien, W., 1954, *Modern Timber Engineering.* 4th ed., New Orleans: Southern Pine Association.

Sedlak, V., 1973, "Paper shelters," *Architectural Design,* December, pp. 756–763.

Siegel, C., 1975, *Structure and Form in Modern Architecture.* Huntington, NY: Robert E. Krieger.

Simpson Company, 1996, *Wood Construction Connectors,* catalog C-96, Pleasantton, CA: Simpson Strong-Tie Company.

Snelson, K., 1981, *Kenneth Snelson* (exhibition catalog). Buffalo, NY: Buffalo Fine Arts Academy.

———, 1989, *The Nature of Structure.* New York: The New York Academy of Sciences.

Stein, K., 1993, "Snow-capped symbol," *Architectural Record,* June, pp.105–106.

Sudjic, D., 1986, *Norman Foster, Richard Rogers, James Stirling.* London: Thames and Hudson.

Tange, K., 1969, "The Expo 70 master plan and master design," *Japan Architect,* April, pp.16–20.

Taylor, J., and Andrews, J., 1982, *John Andrews: Architecture a Performing Art.* New York: Oxford University Press.

Taylor, R., 1975, *Architectural Structures Exclusive of Mathematics.* Muncie: Ball State University Press.

Thiem, W., 1972, "Olympic site designed for the future," *Progressive Architecture,* August, pp.58–65.

Thompson, D., 1917, *On Growth and Form.* Cambridge, UK: Cambridge University Press.

Thornton, C., Tomasetti, R., Tuchman, J., and Joseph, L., 1993, *Exposed Structure in Building Design.* New York: McGraw-Hill.

Torroja, E., 1958, *The Structures of Edurardo Torroja.* New York: F.W. Dodge.

———, 1967, *Philosophy of Structures.* Berkeley: University of California Press.

Van Loon, B., 1994, *Geodesic Domes.* Norfolk, UK: Tarquin.

Villecco, M., 1970, "The infinitely expandable future of air structures," *Architectural Forum,* September, pp.40–43.

Voshinin, I., 1952, "Roof structure in tension," *Architectural Forum,* October, p. 162.

Weese, H. and Associates, 1978, *Four Landmark Buildings in Chicago's Loop.* Washington, DC: U.S. Government Printing Office.

Wilson, F., 1987, "Of space frames, time, and architecture," *Architecture,* August, pp.80–87.

Wright, F. L., 1957, *A Testament.* London: Architectural Press.

Yarnall, M., 1978, *Dome Builder's Handbook No. 2.* Philadelphia: Running Press.

Zalewski, W., and Allen, E., 1997, *Shaping Structures.* New York: John Wiley and Sons.

INDEX